A. Mitchell Palmer:
POLITICIAN

A Da Capo Press Reprint Series

CIVIL LIBERTIES IN AMERICAN HISTORY

GENERAL EDITOR: LEONARD W. LEVY
Claremont Graduate School

A. Mitchell Palmer:
POLITICIAN

BY STANLEY COBEN

DA CAPO PRESS • NEW YORK • 1972

Library of Congress Cataloging in Publication Data

Coben, Stanley.
   A. Mitchell Palmer: politician.
   (Civil liberties in American history)
   Bibliography: p.
   1. Palmer, Alexander Mitchell, 1872-1936.
  I. Series.
  E748.P24C6 1972   973.91'3'0924 [B]   79-180787
  ISBN 0-306-70208-8

This Da Capo Press edition of *A. Mitchell Palmer: Politician* is an
unabridged republication of the first edition published in New
York and London in 1963. It is reprinted by special arrangement
with the author.

Copyright © 1963 Columbia University Press

Published by Da Capo Press, Inc.
A Subsidiary of Plenum Publishing Corporation
227 W. 17th St., New York, New York 10011

Manufactured in the United States of America

E
748
·P24
c6
1972

A. Mitchell Palmer:

POLITICIAN

A. MITCHELL PALMER IN 1924

A. Mitchell Palmer:

POLITICIAN

BY STANLEY COBEN

COLUMBIA UNIVERSITY PRESS
New York and London 1963

This study, prepared under the Graduate Faculties of Columbia University, was selected by a committee of those Faculties to receive one of the Clarke F. Ansley awards given annually by Columbia University Press.

To Beth and Celia

PREFACE

The enigma of A. Mitchell Palmer is an arresting one. How can we reconcile the progressive reformer of pre-World War I years —the champion of the underprivileged—with the militant Attorney-General who violated civil liberties to an extent unprecedented in American history? Referring to the Palmer Raids of 1919–20, a leading authority on constitutional law asserts: "The Attorney-General carried through the greatest executive restriction of personal liberty in the history of this country." A historian agrees: "Perhaps at no time in our history had there been such a wholesale violation of our civil liberties." A political scientist who examined the period charged that Palmer's "Gestapo" had "torn up the Bill of Rights at the first flash of red in the western sky." * Labor leaders denounced him for a series of injunctions against striking workers, and for his sensational accusations that major postwar strikes were part of a world-wide Communist conspiracy. Furthermore, Palmer advocated and almost obtained a drastic peacetime sedition law, which union officials and liberals feared would end free discussion of controversial issues.

Yet, as a congressman before World War I, Palmer vigorously supported advanced progressive legislation. He was eager to go further than Woodrow Wilson and Democratic congressional leaders in the direction of child-labor legislation, the protection of workers, and women's rights. Despite threats of

* Readers are referred to the following books: Zechariah Chafee, Jr., *Free Speech in the United States* (Cambridge, 1941), p. 214; William R. Leuchtenburg, *The Perils of Prosperity, 1914–1932* (Chicago, 1958), p. 78; Karl Schriftgiesser, *This Was Normalcy* (Boston, 1948), p. 61.

retaliation from industrial interests in his district, he played a key role in sharply lowering protective tariffs.

After serving as Wilson's floor leader in the 1912 Democratic national convention, Palmer frequently acted as the President's spokesman in Congress during debate on the New Freedom legislation. Labor leaders and social reformers thought of him as one of their most valuable friends in the House of Representatives, and union officials gave valuable support to his election campaigns. Even after he became Attorney-General in 1919, Palmer's first policies aimed at a cautious return to the administration's prewar liberalism. He refused to intervene in strikes and he recommended pardons for most of the political prisoners arrested during the war.

Also puzzling, in the light of his repressive policies as Attorney-General, are Palmer's religious beliefs. A devout Quaker, he refused the War Department portfolio in 1913, declaring that the work would conflict with his religious tenets. Until the United States entered World War I, he risked public displeasure by expressing outright pacifism.

Palmer was a paradox: a "liberal demagogue." His career is evidence that these are not necessarily contradictory terms. One object of this study is to explain the enigma, with some hope that the explanation will add to the understanding of the progressive reform movement in general and of the Wilson administration in particular.

Another object of this work is to portray an unusually successful twentieth-century politician. Palmer had a meteoric political career. Only three years after the young small-town lawyer defied a local Democratic machine and won a congressional primary race in 1908, he was one of the most influential managers of the House of Representatives. By that time, too, he acted as undisputed head of the Democratic Party in Pennsylvania, the nation's second most populous state. Two years later, after refusing a place in Wilson's Cabinet, he became chairman of the executive committee of the Democratic national committee, recognized as one of the leaders of his party. By 1920, after a breathtaking career as Attorney-General—rounding up Reds, demanding injunctions against labor unions, fixing prices—Palmer was the favorite Presidential candidate of Democratic politicians. Yet he fell from power as swiftly as he had attained it. Only a little over twelve years after he first ran for office, Palmer announced his retirement from politics. The final object of this study is to account for both the extraordinary rise and the rapid downfall.

New York   STANLEY COBEN
February 1963

ACKNOWLEDGMENTS

A. Mitchell Palmer declared on several occasions his willingness to have "history" render final judgment on his actions as a public official. Even before he left office, however, Palmer took steps to make it difficult for historians to reach a verdict. He removed most of his important records from the Alien Property Custodian's office and from the Justice Department files, and these, as well as almost all his other papers subsequently disappeared.

It would have been almost impossible to unravel the story of Palmer's career, even to the extent that I have, without an extraordinary amount of assistance. In tracking down letters to and from Palmer I frequently received aid beyond the call of duty, especially from the staffs of the manuscript and newspaper divisions of the Library of Congress, the Historical Society of Pennsylvania, the New York Public Library, the Free Library of Philadelphia, the Franklin D. Roosevelt Library, the Easton Public Library, the Monroe County Historical Society, and the Yale, Princeton, and Columbia University Libraries. Archivists in the Justice Department and Labor Department divisions of the National Archives helped me find important documents including reports on investigations of Palmer's activities. Several scholars, among them Donald Johnson, Father John Smith, Clarke Wilhelm, and Kurt Wimer shared with me the fruits of their own research; and most helpfully they allowed me to use their copies of correspondence to which I did not have access. Many of Palmer's friends, relatives, and associates supplied me with information which I could not otherwise have obtained; these interviews and letters are listed in the footnotes. Frederick B. Tolles went far out of his way to discover material about Palmer's ancestors and early life. Mrs. A. Mitchell Palmer, one of the most gracious hostesses in the hospitable city of Washington, regaled me on many occasions with stories about her husband. An almost uncanny analysis of Palmer's handwriting by graphologist Thea Stein Lewinson helped sharpen my impression of Palmer's many-faceted personality.

William E. Leuchtenberg read this manuscript and its predecessors more times than either he or I care to remember. From start to finish I have had the benefit of his encouragement and advice; every page that follows has been improved by his suggestions. Searching questions by Robert D. Cross obliged me to reexamine my interpretations of Palmer's behavior at several points, saving me from numerous errors. John A. Garraty, Walter Gelhorn, and David B. Truman read the entire manuscript and offered many valuable criticisms. The comments of my friends Richard M. Abrams, David Burner, Clyde Griffen, Doris A. Platzker, James D. Shenton and Kurt Wimer were invariably useful. The colossal patience of my family and friends sustained me throughout my long preoccupation with Palmer.

I am grateful to the Ansley Award Committee of Columbia University for the prize which made publication of this book possible.

A large part of Chapter 3 appeared first in the *Pennsylvania Journal of History and Biography*. I wish to thank the editors of that journal for permission to reprint this material.

CONTENTS

CHAPTER I

A PENNSYLVANIA POOR BOY'S PROGRESS

In 1813, Obadiah Palmer came across the Delaware Water Gap, the magnificent, deep gorge separating Pennsylvania and New Jersey about eighty miles north of Philadelphia. Obadiah, on his way from his home in Clintondale, New York, to a Quaker meeting in Fishing Creek, Pennsylvania, decided to take advantage of the well-known hospitality of Daniel Stroud, also a Quaker, who owned 4,000 acres just beyond the Gap. It is Palmer family legend that during the evening Obadiah spent with the Strouds he fell in love with another overnight visitor, a lovely kinswoman of the family, Sarah Van Vleit. The next morning, Stroud mentioned that he would build a grist mill on his plantation if he could find a miller. Obadiah looked again at Sarah and, recalling that he had once worked in a mill for a day or two, announced that he was indeed a miller. According to A. Mitchell Palmer, Obadiah "got the job, married the girl, and here we Palmers have been ever since." [1]

Stroud began to sell lots on his plantation, and a small town grew up. By 1835, Stroudsburg was large enough to be named seat of sparsely settled Monroe County, and Obadiah had persuaded other members of his family to move from New York. With his brother, John, who had been a butcher in Dutchess County, he started to raise cattle and distribute beef—handling meat, as Mitchell later put it, "from the meadow to the consumer." [2] John and Obadiah also became pillars of the local Society of Friends. In 1827 the brothers led a group which split from the orthodox body and formed a Hicksite Society. One hundred years afterward, A. Mitchell Palmer served as a trustee of this society.[3]

The meat business stayed in the family for three generations, but not on Mitchell's side. His grandfather, Obadiah's son Charles Stroud Palmer, left the firm in 1850. Charles, who died when Mitchell was fourteen, was in many ways typical of the male Palmers: genial, exceptionally charming, active in the local Democratic Party, a leader of the Stroudsburg Masonic Lodge. A friend recalled: "He had a cordial grasp of the hand of everyone he met, was ever ready to do a man a favor." At the same time, he was an aggressive, ambitious entrepreneur, who moved from place to place, always fairly successful, though never as successful as he wanted to be, and always hoping that the next move would make his fortune.[4]

In several of his enterprises, Charles had the assistance of his eldest son, Samuel Bernard Palmer. Samuel too was affable and a good story teller with a relish for local politics, but he was neither as aggressive nor as self-confident as his father. In 1864, Samuel moved from Stroudsburg to join Charles, who, after trying several other businesses, had bought a lumber yard in nearby Moosehead, Luzerne County. About a year later, he married a Luzerne County girl, nineteen-year-old Caroline Albert. They were still living in Moosehead when their third child, their second boy, was born in 1872. They named him Alexander Mitchell, after the president of Lehigh Valley Railroad, which the Palmers occasionally served as bridge builders and repairers. Three more children were born into the family after Mitchell.

The Palmer family fortunes were at a high point when Mitchell arrived. A large deposit of ochre had been found on the lumber company's grounds, and the firm had used it to expand into the paint business. By this time, however, the Palmers were using their lumber to build bridges. In 1878, Charles designed a popular wood-and-iron-combination bridge and decided that his fortune lay in bridge building. He sold his share of the lumber firm, returned to Stroudsburg, and started a construction business. He became active in local politics again, and served for several years as justice of the peace for the borough of Stroudsburg.[5]

When Charles Palmer returned to Stroudsburg, Samuel tried to strike out for himself in western Pennsylvania; but within two years he was obliged to rejoin his father in business. The construction firm of Charles S. Palmer and Son fared poorly, especially after the senior member died in 1886; Samuel earned barely enough to support his large family.[6]

Nevertheless, it soon became clear that sacrifices would have to be made to send Mitchell, the most gifted of the six children, to college. Mrs. Palmer had a passion for learning, and Mitchell, according to a friend of the family, "inherited his love for books and knowledge" from her.[7] He demonstrated a rare ability to learn quickly and to use his learning skillfully in speech and writing. One month after his fourteenth birthday, he graduated first in his class from Stroudsburg High School. Then he was sent to the Moravian Parochial School in Bethlehem for a year to prepare further for college. Although he passed the entrance examinations for Lehigh University, his family decided that he must enter a Quaker school, and he enrolled at Swarthmore College, near Philadelphia, at the age of fifteen. To make this possible, the Palmers borrowed money from Dr. Joseph H. Shull, who was the family physician, and from other friends.[8]

Freshman class photographs show young Palmer as a tall, husky, handsome boy with a mischievous grin and serious eyes. For a class portrait, he stood on one edge of the group, then dashed around to the other, so that his face appears on both sides of the picture. His boulder of a chin and heavy, straight nose gave him a rugged appearance despite a delicate mouth and smooth, fair skin.[9]

A fellow student remembered him as "a very young and very boyish looking lad, who came down to Swarthmore from the hills of Monroe County on a September day in 1887." But even then, his friend recalled, he "had his future mapped out. . . . The vision of the Hon. Alexander Mitchell Palmer, a lawyer and statesman, was . . . clearly outlined before that youngster's gaze." [10] His Swarthmore classmates were aware of Palmer's ambitions and talents, but they pegged him a lazy man. The class prophet, a close friend of Mitchell, delivered her prophesies in the form of a dream, in which she sat by the seashore while the waves brought in bottles containing messages about the postgraduate careers of her classmates. Palmer's bottle was the last to arrive: "I grew almost desperate at the thought of awaiting it, for I well remembered the indifference of the individual at college." Finally the bottle was seen, "making its way languidly towards me. . . . That bottle was characteristic of its sender—it would not hurry." [11]

Palmer's roommate, William C. Sproul, later Republican Governor of Pennsylvania, made the class presentations just before graduation. "Mitch," he declared when he came to Palmer's name, "you are a worthy gentleman—young and handsome, and well endowed with talent. You can orate, elocute, write for print, sing, and, on rare occasions, you have been known to study, but no one ever knew you to run any danger of over-exertion. You love a good time, Mitch, but of all the various pleasures of your life I do not believe there is anything so enjoyable to you as a good rest." [12]

Palmer, it is true, loved luxury and ease; he developed a taste for fine art, good music, and well-prepared food. But he seldom allowed such passive desires to interfere with his strong need for power and prestige. There is no reason to believe that he did so in college, the judgments of his classmates notwithstanding. The role Palmer adopted as a relaxed, congenial fellow, one of the boys, came easily to him; but he used it to cover an insistent drive to excel his fellows. The "lazy" young student ranked first in his class at graduation. In his senior year he was elected president of an unusually large and active class and was selected for Phi Beta Kappa.[13]

Above all his other college accomplishments, Palmer excelled as an orator. An observer at the junior class oratorical contest in April, 1890 (won by Palmer, then not quite eighteen), commented on "the graceful manner and gestures of this speaker and his clear enunciation. He had complete command of his voice and his delivery at all times was forceful, but it was generally observed that the speaker had much power in reserve that would have strengthened the oration in parts." When he learned to control this power, Palmer was able to address large gatherings, even outdoors, without the aid of a microphone. His winning oration was compared to that of his leading competitor, Sproul, who showed "nervousness" and "experienced difficulty in bringing out the full force of his argument." [14]

Palmer's college speeches were filled with trite phrases and extravagant figures of speech; but they abounded, nevertheless, with unusual life and strength. He could already manipulate words and ideas, as well as people. His prize-winning oration began:

The present generation is confronted with an evil which is fast sucking the life blood from our nation. The rocks upon which are built all democratic institutions are being assailed, and every year the cloud of distress is growing thicker and lowering its dark shadows about us. . . . O, for the days of Washington, Hamilton, and Jefferson, when impurity in elections was unknown! Is it possible that the halcyon days of this greatest of republics are come and gone, and, like Rome of old, she is to grovel in the dust, dashed down by the corruption of her own sons? [15]

To call for reform in the name of traditional values was typical of the well-educated young men of Palmer's generation who eventually assumed leadership of the progressive movement. This oration was but one expression of the devotion to established institutions which underlay Palmer's reform sentiments. His first article for the Swarthmore newspaper extolled the lifelong loyalty of students to their alma mater. In his address as senior class president on Class Day, Palmer proclaimed: "Next to the sacred relation between parent and child, that of professor to student is the most important to youth." The solution he advocated, in his prize-winning speech, for the corruption "sucking the life blood from our nation," was adoption of the Australian or secret ballot. "With a free and unpolluted ballot, there will follow many other needed changes, which, once attained, will render our government the best yet conceived by man." [16] Among those who shared these attitudes with Palmer was the young Princeton professor Woodrow Wilson, who also found in ballot reform and in spiritual uplift the cure for what was ailing American democracy.[17]

For Palmer, a commitment to political reform did not preclude an aspiring lawyer's sympathy with the problems of the businessman. In his commencement address, a plea for legal reform, Palmer asserted:

It is an insult to the litigants in our civil courts to assert that the average men who sit in the jury box are their equals. Totally ignorant of the technicalities of business which are every day called in question, not sufficiently interested in the triumph of justice to care whether the right or wrong side wins, wholly devoid of knowledge of the principles of law, our juries are but little fit to decide the questions of almost vital importance which are brought before them.[18]

His commencement oration offered evidence that Palmer had learned something about law and courts even before he began his formal training. Clearly he had also learned a great deal about politics by the time he graduated. Twenty years later, a friend remembered that as an undergraduate Palmer was

a politician, astute and successful. . . . As political manipulator, he and his roommate, "Bill" Sproul, trained together, and their success in college politics and diplomacy are still a Swarthmore tradition. They belonged to that class of '91, which, entering college as the largest bunch of Freshmen in numbers and pounds that Swarthmore had ever seen, took everything in sight and quickly arrogated to itself a leadership in all that was going on. Mitchell and his partner were chiefs among them and between these two they captured everything worth while in the way of college honors.[19]

When he left Swarthmore, Palmer had close friends from influential families in Philadelphia and other large Pennsylvania cities. Nevertheless, he made the crucial decision to return to Stroudsburg. He was moved, in part, by loyalty to his parents. Equally important, he belonged to a well-known family, long active in local Democratic politics, and could be certain of the assistance that a boy of modest means required to get started in a profession and in politics. Once Palmer returned, his family's associations and the district's party structure determined his political affiliation. Thereafter he would be a Democrat in a solidly Republican state.

He came home to a small town. The population, about 1,800 when he was born, was now about 2,500—but Stroudsburg was still the county seat and the largest town in Monroe County. There were slate quarries in Monroe, and a few small factories, but the region remained largely agricultural and relatively poor compared to the flatter, more fertile country to the southwest.[20]

When Palmer was born, Monroe's population was homogeneous, old-American stock, descended from the early English, Scotch-Irish, Dutch, and German settlers of the region. No more than a handful of the German and Irish immigrants who had recently poured into Pennsylvania settled in Monroe. As Palmer grew up, it remained an area of native-born white families, most of whom had lived in the region for generations. The Eastern and Central European immigration to Pennsylvania in the last years of the nineteenth century also missed Monroe. In 1900, less than four percent of the population was foreign-born, a lower percentage than that of 1870. In contrast, the number of foreign-born in the North Atlantic States as a whole increased about thirty-eight percent between 1890 and 1900.[21] The population of Monroe became somewhat ingrown, wary of strangers and new ideas. Palmer's lifelong distrust of the "new immigrants" and his failure to understand their ideas and ambitions, derived in large part from attitudes he imbibed in Monroe County.

Slavic, Irish, Welsh, and German immigrants settled in neighboring Carbon County to work in the coal mines and clay pits. Important industries arose in Northampton County, south of Monroe, especially around Bethlehem, where the Bethlehem Steel Company mushroomed after Charles M. Schwab took it over in 1903. Schwab preferred to hire low-cost immigrant labor; consequently, eastern European immigrants flocked to Bethlehem and overflowed into nearby Easton, a flourishing industrial and commercial center with two canals and two railroad lines running into the city. Other recent immigrants went to work in Northampton's large cement industry. Most of Northampton and Carbon counties, however, like Monroe and sparsely settled Pike County to the north of Monroe, was rough, hilly agricultural land.[22] The immigrants who manned the factories and mines were a minority of the population, and they were viewed with suspicion by the long-settled old-American majority.

Monroe, Carbon, Northampton, and Pike counties constituted the twenty-sixth election district. A Democratic district, it had not joined the rapidly growing industrial and the prosperous farm areas of Pennsylvania that switched their allegiance to the high-tariff Republican Party in 1860.[23] Underpaid and mostly unorganized mine, quarry, and factory workers held many grievances that a Democrat could promise to alleviate; but candidates in the district could not be elected without support from the conservative majority. Palmer adopted an attitude ideal for his district and well suited to his temperament. He would stand between the opposing economic interests—or, as he more likely thought of it, above them—doing justice to all.

Palmer's first problem after graduation was to find a way of earning a living while he studied law. Judge Samuel S. Dreher, whose family had long been friendly with Palmer's, promised to appoint the young man court stenographer for the Forty-Third Judicial District if he learned shorthand. Since the nearest business school was in Scranton, about forty miles away, Palmer spent four months during the fall and early winter of 1891 there. He lived in a local boardinghouse, attended Wood's Business School mornings, and sat in the local courthouse afternoons, observing courtroom procedures.[24]

When he became court stenographer, Palmer began to study law as a clerk in the office of John B. Storm, a former congressman and the foremost attorney in the district. Although some of the most promising young lawyer–politicians in the area had studied under Storm, including J. Davis Brodhead, who would precede Palmer as congressman, and Harvey Huffman, Democratic county chairman when Palmer first ran for office, Storm chose Palmer as his junior partner when the young man was admitted to the bar in 1893.

Storm's large and lucrative practice included duties as local counsel for the Lehigh Valley and the Delaware, Lackawanna and Western railroads. Shortly after taking Palmer into his office, Storm fell ill, and the junior partner took over most of the practice. When Judge Dreher died and Storm succeeded to his place on the bench, Palmer took over the law office completely. Storm died in Stroudsburg, August 13, 1901.[25]

Palmer thus became one of Monroe County's leading attorneys before he was thirty. His activities, however, were those of a man with higher political and financial ambitions. In addition to managing his practice, Palmer devoted time to the state bar association, the Knights of Pythias, and the Knights of Malta, and served as Exalted Ruler of the local lodge of Elks. In 1900, he was elected president of the Stroudsburg Democratic Club and member of the county's Democratic executive committee.

Any excuse was enough to elicit a speech from him. He lectured the literary department of the Epworth League on Alexander Hamilton, and delivered a Fourth of July oration to the assembled citizens of Stroudsburg. After McKinley's assassination, Palmer delivered a eulogy in the local Episcopal church. When the Grand Commander of the State Knights of Malta visited Stroudsburg, Palmer greeted the dignitary with a speech. He traveled through the district in the fall of 1900 speaking for the Democratic national ticket, and took two weeks off from his practice in 1902 to stump eastern Pennsylvania with the Democratic nominee for governor.[26]

Palmer began to invest in such important Stroudsburg business corporations as the local water and street railway companies. From his investments he obtained not only direct income, but also appointments as counsel for these concerns. He liked to tell of how he went over the list of stockholders of the Stroudsburg National Bank, with the idea of buying one of them out so that he could become solicitor for the firm. He chose an old farmer named Levi Drake and spent a good part of one hot summer afternoon walking next to Drake as he plowed, persuading him to sell. A few years later, Palmer became a director, and eventually won operating control of the bank. He joined a local golf club and although he played badly and invariably paid more attention to discussions of politics and business than he did to his game, he was elected president of the club. By the time he went to Congress in 1909 he served on the board of directors of at least half a dozen corporations.[27]

Probably the most important investment Palmer made in these early years was in the Times Publishing Company, which put out the largest of the city's two daily newspapers. By 1898 he was vice-president and a director of the firm and in January, 1901, at the age of twenty-eight, he led a group which bought complete control. Palmer made the *Times* his official organ; it mirrored his political ideas, reported his speeches, and chastised his enemies, sometimes in phrases only Palmer could have written. In 1907, the *Times* purchased its only competitors, the Stroudsburg *Daily Democrat* and the Monroe *Democrat,* a weekly. When Palmer bucked the regular Democratic machine to run for Congress in 1908, his opponents, without a journal of their own, were forced to buy advertising space in Palmer's papers.[28]

On November 23, 1898, Palmer married Roberta Bartlett Dixon, of Baltimore and Easton, Maryland. Although they attended Swarthmore together—Roberta was two classes behind Palmer—their romance began after both had graduated. A pretty girl, taller than most, Roberta was quiet, even retiring, and her clothes were simple, occasionally austere. The Dixon family ranked among the wealthiest in Easton, Maryland. Roberta's father, Robert B. Dixon, was president of the Easton National Bank and leading stockholder in the local water, ice, and gas and electric companies, as well as a building and loan association. He also owned a lumber business, an insurance agency and the largest coal company in the area. He had important holdings in Baltimore, including a shoe manufacturing plant and a bank. Relatives owned a large Baltimore paper-bag company, another important bank, and one of the largest insurance companies in the country. Active politically, Robert Dixon had recently been elected Republican state senator. At Palmer's wedding, three congressmen and a United States senator attended, along with such minor notables as Pennsylvania state senator-elect William C. Sproul.[29]

In spite of all his efforts, Palmer still found his progress in politics blocked at the lowest local level. In Monroe County, a small clique controlled nominations and appointments, and although Palmer became friendly with these men, he never was admitted to the inner circle. The most influential of the group, Dr. Joseph Shull, had been Palmer's benefactor when he needed funds for college tuition. Shull, a graduate of Bellevue Hospital Medical School, also had a law degree and boasted a sizable legal practice. Harvey Huffman, who lived a few doors from Shull, and often ate dinner with him, Huffman's law partner W. B. Eilenberger, B. F. Morey, and R. F. Schwarz were the important members of the Shull faction. These five men controlled the county Democratic executive committee and succeeded one another as chairman.[30]

They viewed Palmer as an upstart, a young man who presumed too much. Faced with such formidable opposition, Palmer realized that tact, friendliness, and talent were not enough for rapid political advancement—he became more openly aggressive. A feud between Shull and Howard Mutchler, head of the Northampton County Democratic organization, inadvertently furthered Palmer's career. Shull wrested the Democratic nomination for Congress from Mutchler in 1902 and the Northampton boss retaliated in 1904 by opposing Shull's renomination. Instead, Mutchler backed J. Davis Brodhead, son of former United States Senator Richard Brodhead. Brodhead won the primary election, but Shull's adherents, charging fraud, prepared to run their man on a third-party ticket. Palmer announced that he and his newspaper would back the regular party candidate, but the Monroe County Democratic executive committee, after hearing Palmer's arguments for party loyalty, voted him down by 20–1 and endorsed Shull. Palmer then charged in the *Times* that "the efforts of County Chairman Schwarz to have his committee throw away their allegiance to party and follow the personal fortunes of Mr. Shull brand him as a traitor to the party." Shull drew enough votes in the November election to throw the election to the Republican congressional candidate Gustav Schneebeli.[31]

During the next few years Palmer completed his break with the county organization. The conflict approached a climax in 1907, when Palmer helped prosecute party leaders Schwarz and Morey, accused of selling supplies to the State Normal School in East Stroudsburg, of which they were trustees. Palmer's enemies charged that he participated in the case only to obtain revenge. Morey, as county chairman, had allegedly rebuffed Palmer's request in 1897 that he be given the Democratic nomination for state senator. Palmer was twenty-five years old, and Morey told him he was too young. Schwarz successfully opposed Palmer's election as chairman of the district's delegation to the state democratic convention in 1902, and afterward Schwarz joked with his friends about Palmer's threat to ruin him.[32] Whether their stories were true or not, the two men certainly blocked Palmer's path, and so did Shull.

As a result of the Republican victory over the divided Democrats in the 1904 congressional election, Democratic leaders in the four counties reached an agreement designed to eliminate such conflicts. The nomination for Congress was to be rotated: in 1906 to Northampton, in 1908 to Monroe, in 1910 to Pike, and in 1912 to Carbon. A county "trial primary" would decide the district nominee. When the agreement was made public, it was acclaimed by the district's Democrats. In 1906, J. Davis Brodhead was chosen as the Democratic candidate in a "trial primary" in Northampton County. Unopposed in the regular primary, which was required by state law, Brodhead easily triumphed in November.[33]

Monroe's turn came next, and it seemed a foregone conclusion in 1908 that the county organization would arrange Shull's nomination. Mutchler, however, would not forget the past. He visited Stroudsburg and made it known that he wanted to honor the rotation agreement, but that he refused to support Shull. Nevertheless, the county organization again endorsed its chief. The situation was made to order for Palmer. He asserted later that Mutchler had approached him first; but in any case, when the Monroe "trial primary" was held, Palmer, sure of the Northampton leader's support, campaigned to keep voters away from the polls. The rotation system, he argued, was designed to keep the "bosses" in power; his slogan was "Rotation is rot." Palmer's opponents found it difficult to get their case before the public. They were obliged to buy advertising space in the *Times* until a few weeks before the election when they started their own weekly newspaper. Only 634 voters turned out for the "trial primary" and 633 of them voted for Shull.[34]

When Palmer filed his name for the regular primary, Shull and his supporters complained bitterly that he was violating a published agreement which he had not criticized before. Mutchler's two Easton newspapers replied that, since Pike County never ratified the rotation agreement, it had never gone into effect. Palmer, who played no role in drawing up the compact, called it part of a plot to keep good men out of office. When Mutchler asked him for a pledge that he would not run for renomination in 1910, Palmer refused; but by that time Mutchler was trapped—it was either Palmer or Shull.[35]

Congressman Brodhead backed his old friend, telling a joint meeting of the Democratic clubs of South Bethlehem, "I would have come ten times the distance from Washington to South Bethlehem to speak in behalf of the one man in Monroe County who had the nerve and sound party interest to stand out for me when Shull made his bolt in 1904." Then Mutchler threw his whole political machine behind Palmer; his lieutenants organized large meetings which Palmer addressed and his newspapers attacked Shull with a vengeance. On the other hand, the largest and one of the most progressive Democratic papers in the area, the Easton *Argus,* condemned Palmer as "the tool of Boss Mutchler," and warned that "a vote for Palmer is a vote for Mutchler." [36]

Palmer campaigned with the knowledge that his following

in Monroe rivaled that of the county machine. A large proportion of Monroe's citizens were acquainted with the congenial Palmer family; many had known three generations of Palmers. Mitchell, well-known in his own right through myriad social, political, and religious associations, had traveled around the district many times, speaking for the party. His friends formed a large and enthusiastic group of campaign workers; the young men who used to gather with Palmer in Albert Eckert's barber shop to swap stories and arrange weekend parties now put up posters and helped out at rallies.[37]

Palmer's appearance and manner were tremendous assets. In a white jacket, his habitual costume, he always appeared impeccably dressed. He was a tall, heavy-set man with prematurely gray hair, handsome and self-confident; his large jaw gave him a look of determination. Palmer used to walk slowly from his home to his law office or his bank, stopping every few steps to greet a friend, shake a hand, tip his hat to a lady. When he stopped for a moment to chat he skillfully put friends and acquaintances at ease.[38]

Shortly before the election, Shull's faction became desperate. Believing that they were faced with a ruthless opponent who was out to destroy them politically, the county leaders dug up everything in Palmer's past which could be unfavorably interpreted. They publicized the alleged "betrayal" of Schwarz and Morey, along with the story of Shull's loan to the Palmer family, and they mentioned other loans from Shull to the Palmers, alleging that the loans had never been repaid despite the family's promises and Mitchell's flourishing legal practice.[39]

Palmer won all four counties in the primary election. The county organization managed to make the contest close in Monroe, but Palmer's majority in the district as a whole ran about two to one. After the excitement of the election died down, Palmer arranged a party and sent invitations to every Democrat in Stroudsburg.[40] With hospitality, graciousness, and the promise of patronage to come, he charmed the party rank and file; thereafter, he won huge majorities in Stroudsburg and in Monroe County. The defeated leaders, however, never forgave him and waited for a chance to turn the tables.

In the general election Palmer was opposed by former Republican Congressman Schneebeli. The chief issues raised by Palmer and his supporters were Schneebeli's record in Congress, and "Cannonism," the autocratic power of the conservative Republican Speaker of the House, Joe Cannon. Palmer avoided the tariff question, which might cost him votes in industrial areas long indoctrinated by protectionist arguments. At a giant Easton rally, Palmer accused Schneebeli of missing 101 of 134 roll calls while in Congress and of making only one speech during his term, a short typewritten message sent to the House clerk to read. Congressman (later Governor) William Sulzer of New York also turned the normal difficulties of a first term against Schneebeli by declaring that although he served in Congress with Schneebeli, he had neither seen nor heard the Republican candidate. Sulzer went on to declare that Palmer would make "Uncle Joe" Cannon recognize him, or "something will be heard to drop." Palmer challenged his opponent to a debate on "the issues," but Schneebeli, a German-born lace manufacturer who still spoke with a pronounced accent, refused. Palmer won the election by 3,742 votes, the largest majority the district ever had given a congressional candidate.[41]

CHAPTER II

THE WORKINGMAN'S FRIEND

A veteran Republican congressman, one of the managers of the House during Palmer's first term, remarked, "A district that sends a man to Congress only one or even two terms had just about as well not send him at all. The leaders well know what districts in the country are in the habit of sending a man for such short periods, and when such a man comes, he is not placed on any committee of any importance because it is recognized that he cannot climb to the top." [1] Palmer went to Congress in 1909 as representative from a district which had elected ten different congressmen in eighteen years. The district was further stigmatized among Democrats by talk that it had become the pocket borough of Charles M. Schwab, president of the Bethlehem Steel Company. Palmer's committee assignments in the Sixty-first Congress reflected not only the low status common to freshman members, but also congressional leaders' opinions about his district and his chances of reelection: he was appointed to two committees, neither of which had met during the Sixtieth Congress.[2] Forced to start from the very bottom, Palmer advanced without benefit of the prerogatives and opportunities accorded members of important committees.

First scheduled business of the Republican-controlled House, which convened March 15, 1909, was consideration of the bill that became the Payne-Aldrich Tariff. Public feeling against high protection was strong at the time—the tariff was popularly regarded as one of the primary causes of rising prices and as the "mother of all trusts"—and in 1908 both Presidential candidates promised to lower tariffs. Although the House version actually reduced many important schedules, the Democratic strategists found it politically expedient to oppose the measure as an ultraprotectionist betrayal of Republican promises. Palmer had avoided the issue in his election campaign, but he had assimilated the current arguments in favor of low rates. Knowing he must depend upon his speaking ability to bring him recognition in the House, he mastered the intricacies of several important schedules; then, perfectly prepared, he requested an opportunity to speak.

In Palmer's state the tariff was always a live issue. Most Pennsylvanians were for it, and the higher the rates the better. Democratic House leaders, in apportioning the limited time allocated to them, may have felt that a Pennsylvanian's plea for party unity might succeed with those Democrats who feared to antagonize powerful manufacturing interests in their districts; on March 31, 1909, only sixteen days after he was sworn in, they granted Palmer time to speak against the Payne bill.

Palmer first apologized elaborately for his presumption in addressing his more experienced colleagues so soon. He was, however, "fresh from the country," and could "speak from the viewpoint of the great body of the people outside this House." Then, in a deep, resonant voice, that could be heard clearly in the most distant gallery seat, Palmer bitterly attacked the tariff, exhorting his fellow Democrats not to support the measure. He demonstrated not only his remarkable speaking ability but an imposing fund of knowledge about various tariff schedules and the related industries. The speech drew attention to the new congressman and may have earned him an assignment to the Ways and Means Committee he received in the next Congress; it foreshadowed the important role he would play in writing the Democratic tariff bills of 1912, which never became law, and the Underwood tariff of 1913, which did.[3]

He proclaimed that, "so far as my observation goes,"

no tariff bill that was ever framed has trampled so ruthlessly upon the rights of the ultimate taxpayer as does the present measure. Never before has even the Republican party been so regardless of the cost which the practice of the protection theory brings home to the poor people. Never before have so many of the necessities of life been taxed so heavily for the encouragement and assistance of the great industrial concerns which control the manufacture and production of those necessities.

Pleading for a united opposition, Palmer addressed himself especially to Democrats from industrial districts who were under pressure to vote for the bill. After pointing out that the 1908 Democratic platform declared unequivocally for tariff reduction, he declared:

If you will pardon a personal reference, I might say that I represent in this House a district in the great industrial state of Pennsylvania which has within it large protective interests which in their magnitude compare very favorably with those of any other district represented in this House. Within the four counties of my district is the great Pennsylvania slate belt, where 85 per cent of the slate used in America is mined, manufactured and produced. We have enormous interests in the manufacture and production of cement. We have one mill alone which is large enough to have recently taken a single order for a million barrels of that product, and within my district also are the works of the great Bethlehem Steel Company with 10,000 voting employees, even in these Republican times.

The prosperity of these concerns was of great importance to his constituents, Palmer pointed out, but when the voters of his district had had a chance to choose between him and a Republican candidate who stood for a high protective tariff, they rejected the high tariff nominee by a large majority. "Therefore . . . I say that I should not only be unfaithful to my party, but untrue to my constituents if I refused in this House to follow the Democratic lead for a reduction in the tariff taxes in the interests of the great consuming masses as against the interest of the great producing classes." Palmer was implying, of course, that all Democratic congressmen, having run on the same tariff plank, were similarly obligated. He went on to assert: "I, for one, am perfectly ready to support an inheritance tax, and I should be ready, in addition, to support a graduated income tax."

Although it was late at night when the new congressman's time expired and he expressed a willingness to yield the floor, his Democratic colleagues demanded that he receive additional time and that the clock be turned back if necessary. The chairman pro tem granted the time and Palmer went on to criticize the tariff schedules on glass and lumber. Many of the nation's largest glass-producing firms were located in Pennsylvania. By a careful and detailed comparison of European and American costs of production and prices, Palmer showed that "if the rates on glass proposed in the Payne bill are cut to one-third, the American manufacturer will still have considerable leeway."

He proceeded to criticize the lumber tariff, climaxing his speech with a denunciation of Gifford Pinchot, head of the government Forestry Bureau, who had recently opposed cutting lumber rates. Although Palmer disclaimed any intention of "reflecting upon the integrity and ability of the distinguished head of the Forestry Bureau," he read a letter from "a skilled forestry engineer," Thomas P. Ivy of New Hampshire, which clearly assigned base motives to Pinchot's high tariff views. Ivy observed that Pinchot had accepted $150,000 from a group of lumbermen to start a Chair of Lumbering at the Yale School of Forestry, one of Pinchot's pet projects; he suggested that the lumber barons must have expected something in return. Furthermore, in 1906, both houses of Congress had passed a resolution ordering an investigation of the "lumber trust." No report was ever made. According to Ivy, "The investigation was a farce" and "was virtually suppressed by some strong power within the late [Roosevelt] administration." Pinchot, a "strong power" within the Roosevelt administration, had acted as Roosevelt's adviser on conservation policies. The letter continued:

Thirdly, it has been openly stated in the public press that Mr. Pinchot, in conjunction with leading lumbermen like Blodgett, Long and Weyerhaeuser, was forming a lumber corporation of $300,000,000 capital stock to take over a very large portion of the timber land of the country. This statement was never denied.

Gifford Pinchot, a public servant of inestimable value, was a man quick to take offense. Frequently, he considered personal opponents to be enemies of the American people. Although Palmer took his assault on Pinchot as a matter of course

—one more attack on a high Republican official, one more attempt to show that the Payne–Aldrich tariff was written for the benefit of monopolistic capitalists—Pinchot probably took another view of the matter. After the attack he became one of Palmer's most implacable enemies.

Palmer's speech did not have its intended effect on party discipline. Thirty-seven Democrats ignored their congressional leaders and their national platform and voted against a reduction in the lumber tariff. The speech may not have helped Palmer at home, either. The day after he addressed the House, steel companies throughout Pennsylvania, including Bethlehem Steel, cut wages by ten percent. The reductions, the firms announced, were "on account of the depression in business due to the fear of a reduction in the tariff." As soon as the Payne–Aldrich bill passed, wages were raised, and Judge Elbert Gary, chairman of United States Steel, asserted, "Business will improve rapidly from now on." [4]

It was several months before the new congressman again took a prominent part in debate. Then, once more, he greatly impressed his colleagues with his oratorical ability, appearance, and poise. Although they were unaware of the fact, congressmen also witnessed an example of Palmer's talent for obscuring his personal objectives with skillful rhetoric and powerful appeal to party feeling.

On July 20, 1909, Representative Walter I. Smith of Iowa introduced a resolution designed to protect government employees from being overcharged by bonding companies for the fidelity bonds required of all civil servants. The amendment forbade government acceptance of fidelity bonds with premium rates higher than those of 1903, which Smith considered fair. [5]

Palmer vigorously protested the resolution, which he described as "a long step in the advance toward the obnoxious regulation of private affairs of individuals and corporations." He also tried to label the bill an example of "Cannonism," complaining that it had been introduced in a manner not prescribed by House rules. The Republican leaders, he argued, were trying to "force the Members of this House to support a

piece of new legislation without ample opportunity for its consideration." This was "only another link in the chain of evidence which has convinced the people of this country beyond a
doubt that the House of Representatives is not controlled by
its membership . . . but that it is absolutely and entirely dominated by the sweet will of the majority of the Committee on
Rules." Nothing was wrong with the House rules as written in
the rules book, Palmer declared, but the real rules of the
House were not in the book. Members found out what the
rules were only by listening "with bated breath" to Representatives Dalzell and Smith, who brought in the reports of the
Committee on Rules.[6]

When Palmer finished, Representative Eugene F. Kinkaid
of New Jersey took the floor and congratulated him "on what
I consider the best explanation and best defense of the Democratic attitude on the question of rules now existing in the
House." Kinkaid, however, refused to vote with Palmer in defense of the bonding companies, which he said had tried to
"hold up" the government.[7] Only four representatives joined
Palmer in voting against Smith's resolution.[8]

Two years later, Representative Smith introduced another
bill to protect government employees against avaricious bonding companies, and Palmer again charged the Republicans with
trying to "steam-roller" the bill through Congress. The House
passed the bill, but it was killed in the Senate.[9]

Most of Smith's evidence for the need of bonding legislation
came from hearings before the House Appropriations Committee in 1909. The most important testimony was given by J.
Kemp Bartlett, head of the U. S. Fidelity and Guaranty Company of Baltimore, one of the largest bonding firms. Bartlett
represented twelve large companies at the hearing.[10] In the
course of debate on the House floor, Palmer stated, "I have no
interest, direct or indirect, in any bonding company doing business in the United States or anywhere else." J. Kemp Bartlett,
however, was Mrs. Palmer's cousin, and Robert B. Dixon,
Palmer's father-in-law, was one of Fidelity's directors. When
Palmer referred in debate to his personal knowledge of a Balti-

more company whose profits on fidelity bonds made them willing to take large losses on government contract bonds, his information undoubtedly came from his relatives.[11]

Whatever his motivation for opposing punitive legislation aimed at bonding companies, Palmer did not take advantage of other opportunities to protect his relatives' financial interests. He once told of arguing about the tariff with a Baltimore friend who was in the shoe business. "Of course he is a protectionist. I think that if I had been a shoe manufacturer in recent years, I might have been a protectionist myself." The Baltimore shoe manufacturer was probably either Palmer's father-in-law or his brother-in-law, William Dixon, chief executives of the Dixon-Bartlett Shoe Company, but Palmer remained a firm advocate of lower tariff rates on boots and shoes.[12]

Palmer made only one more lengthy speech during his first term in Congress. On March 22, 1910, he addressed the House for an hour, charging President Taft and the Republican Congress with failure to keep their campaign promises—especially Taft's promise of tariff reduction—and with abrogation of Theodore Roosevelt's conservation policies. Taft he chided as a "rather pliant executive" who had sent nine conservation bills to Congress.

They were met with open arms by the distinguished and disinterested conservationist who presides over the destinies and sits on the lid and keeps the key to the padlock of the Committee on the Public Lands. Oh yes, he said, he would introduce them if the President would kindly put his name on the back and say "Please Mr. Chairman:" he would carry out the President's policies, and it looks as if he had carried them out into the bonfire behind the Public Land Committee's back yard.

In the coming (1910) campaign, Palmer concluded, "we shall not talk about anything else except the broken promises, the unkept pledges, the unfilled obligations of the Republican Party." Palmer was frequently interrupted by laughter and applause from the Democratic side of the House.[13] Back home, his easy humor and partisan invective were enthusiastically received even by the newspaper that most strongly opposed his renomination.[14] It must have occurred to congressional leaders that at last the twenty-sixth Pennsylvania district had a representative who was not going to be "rotated."

Democratic House leaders evidently decided that if Palmer returned they would elevate him a few notches in the congressional hierarchy and give him a place among the policy makers. Before Congress adjourned, he was appointed vice-chairman of the Democratic congressional campaign committee, an unusual responsibility for a freshman member, and he was invited to address the annual Democratic get-together and fund-raiser, the Jefferson Day dinner in Washington, April, 1910.[15]

Palmer's fast rise was due not only to the ability he showed on the House floor, but perhaps equally to the friendships he quickly cultivated with such veteran Democratic leaders as Oscar Underwood, Champ Clark and John Sharp Williams. He was a pleasant companion and a superb raconteur. On the House floor, he followed the directions of party leaders; loyalty, a frank manner, and his emphatic speaking style won him a reputation for integrity. Williams, minority leader in the Sixty-first House, recalled that when "Mitchell Palmer first came to the House as an untried Representative . . . I happened to be . . . in a position where it was part of my duty to learn about men, to know whether they were trustworthy or not. . . . I heard all sorts of things about all sorts of men coming in, but I never heard one line of adverse conversation about Mitchell Palmer even from the Republicans." [16]

Palmer's quick success proved a valuable campaign asset in 1910. He told one audience that while he hesitated, out of modesty, to refer to his record, it was nevertheless true that he had been recognized on the floor of the House more often than any other representative of the district since John Storm. He boasted that he had secured the passage of more pension bills than any other congressman from the area since the Spanish-American War. He was introduced to local crowds as vice-chairman of his party's congressional campaign committee—a small honor in Washington perhaps, but an impressive distinction in a district accustomed to being represented by obscure, rotated congressmen. His campaign for reelection was strongly endorsed by Champ Clark, slated to be Speaker of the House if the Democrats won the election.[17]

Despite his exertions on behalf of constituents and party, Palmer faced dangerous opposition to his renomination. Early in 1910, he knew that Mutchler was against him and that Brodhead would seek another term. Palmer was forced to appeal directly to the workingmen of Northampton County, especially to the thousands of politically aroused workers on strike against the Bethlehem Steel Company.

Palmer wrote an address strongly supporting the establishment of a Bureau of Mines and inserted it in the *Congressional Record* for distribution to the many coal miners of Carbon and Northampton counties.[18] He took great pains to give as much assistance as possible to the Bethlehem strikers, but continued to profess neutrality so as not to antagonize his middle-class and farm supporters.

Most of the steel workers struck on February 4, 1910. The dismissal of several men who refused to work on Sunday provided the immediate issue; but the extremely low wages paid unskilled and semiskilled workers and the poor working conditions were actually the chief complaints. Palmer first became openly involved when he received a telegram from David Williams, chairman of the strikers' executive committee, asking for a government investigation of conditions at the Bethlehem plant. Palmer was prepared for the telegram, if indeed he did not suggest it. He immediately made an appointment with President Taft, and three hours later met with him to discuss the strikers' request. The President, persuaded that an investigation was needed, sent Palmer to see Secretary of Commerce and Labor Charles Nagel to make the necessary arrangements. Eight hours after Palmer received Williams' telegram an investigation was ordered.[19]

Early in March, the strikers' executive committee passed a resolution calling upon the government to cancel its contracts with Bethlehem Steel because inexperienced strikebreakers were producing inferior goods. Faced with the possibility that the plant, which depended heavily upon government orders for armor plate and cannon, might be closed, local businessmen called a meeting to oppose the strikers' resolution. They telephoned Palmer on March 30 and asked him to attend, but he refused, reaffirming his neutrality. The businessmen then sent a committee to Washington to convince their congressman that the strikers' resolution could cause the disruption of the Lehigh Valley's economy. The delegation arrived on the night of March 30.

Palmer had contacted the strike leaders, who also sent a committee. Both groups spent the entire day of March 31 in Palmer's office, trying to win his support. Palmer finally told the business group flatly that he would not oppose the workers' demands for the cancellation of Bethlehem's contracts. But he put off the strike leaders, protesting that it would be improper for him to support their resolution actively until he knew the results of the investigation he had inspired. He agreed, however, to endorse publicly the workers' demand for federal legislation limiting the working day to eight hours.[20]

Charles Schwab, enraged at the outcome of the conference, warned Bethlehem and South Bethlehem businessmen that unless he received additional local support he would close his plant without further ado. The frightened businessmen called a meeting and, after hearing addresses by Schwab and Brodhead, resolved to condemn the strikers' actions. Their resolutions were brought to Washington on April 5 by a committee of fifty-five. Palmer introduced the group to Taft, who assured them that labor disputes did not warrant abrogation of government contracts. The following day, a strikers' committee led by Williams and J. Tazelaar, an AF of L organizer assigned to the strike, went with Palmer to see the President, who listened patiently to their grievances.[21]

Three weeks later, the government's report on conditions at Bethlehem Steel was submitted to the Senate. It verified almost all the strikers' complaints about wages and working conditions: 2,322 Bethlehem employees worked twelve hours daily, seven days a week; and 61 percent of the company's workers earned eighteen cents an hour or less. Palmer hailed the report as "the best thing for organized labor that has happened in the last ten years. It shows what wrongs unorganized labor suffers." [22] Publication of the report failed to prevent the strikers from being starved into submission, but it succeeded in strengthening Palmer's claims for renomination.

Mutchler and Brodhead did not give up without a fight. At first the Northampton boss hesitated to antagonize Palmer. His newspaper opened the campaign with an editorial asserting that both candidates were "capable, honest and efficient men." Each had "served the district in Congress and made records the people who elected them can well feel proud of." But, the editorial continued, Northampton County, whose wealth and population were much larger than Monroe's, ought to be represented by one of her own. Besides, the district had given Palmer his chance, and according to the local tradition he ought to be willing to step down, as Brodhead had done two years before. This argument was reiterated by campaign orators in the early stages of the race.[23]

Palmer also opened his campaign on a moderate note. He spent his time almost exclusively in Northampton, explaining, "The reason why I am in Northampton County and expect to stay, is that Monroe, Pike and Carbon counties are tied to the mast for Palmer and are absolutely secure and need no more attention." He ran again as the defender of the people's interests against the bosses. His supporters asked the voters whether they would again allow Boss Mutchler to choose a candidate for them, or would rebel and show they could select better men by themselves. When the campaign got rougher, Palmer told an audience that Mutchler was opposing him because he had always refused to "turn in the alley off Northampton Street and, going down on Bank Street, in a little office over a saloon beg for a nomination of a boss." [24]

Palmer, who had once ridiculed Shull for "making a great howl" about being denied a second term in Congress,[25] now argued that it was unwise for the district to elect a man for a single term only:

I have been to Washington and I have learned what every man who has served a single term . . . has learned—that a single term is almost useless alike to the member and the people. Washington is a big

city. The House of Representatives is a big body, numbering 391
of the ablest men in the nation. A fellow who goes down there from
the country with no experience in the parliamentary game don't
know what he can get and it takes two years to learn how to play
the game.

Brodhead, Palmer acknowledged, had also served one term,
"but conditions are continually changing and the man who
misses a term . . . returns practically as a stranger. In Congress
everything goes to seniority. . . . If the present representative is
returned he will be able to be close to the speaker, [and will]
get good committee assignments—assignments that are worth-
while." [26] Palmer refuted criticism that he was breaking the rotation agreement by reminding his audiences that 1910 was
Pike County's year for the nomination, and that he already had
been endorsed by the Pike County Democratic committee.[27]

By mid-May, Brodhead knew he was beaten. Palmer told a
large audience that an emissary from Mutchler suggested that
his candidate might withdraw if an acceptable peace could be
arranged. Charles Schwab, however, would not give up so easily. He made the trip down to Bank Street and, in the office
over the saloon, held a two-hour conference with Mutchler and
Brodhead. The next day, Brodhead intensified his campaign.
Speakers attacked Palmer's character and revived the stories
about his past that had circulated in 1908. Businessmen throughout the district received letters from Schwab announcing his
preference for Brodhead. Palmer retaliated by accusing Mutchler of offering substantial bribes in exchange for blocs of
votes.[28]

Schwab, attempting a master stroke, allowed Brodhead to
"settle" the fourteen-week-old strike. Previously, Schwab had
refused to discuss the strike with anyone; he even informed a
delegation of local businessmen that his labor relations were
none of their business. When Brodhead called him, however,
he listened, and he agreed to consider the strikers' terms of
capitulation—if Brodhead would present them. The strikers,
near collapse, grasped at the opportunity; as a result of Brodhead's mediation they were rehired, although without recognition of their union.[29]

Brodhead gained little labor support by "settling" the strike. Palmer asked audiences why his opponent waited until two weeks before the election to call his friend Schwab, and why the Bethlehem president supported a man who claimed to be labor's friend.[30]

The Brodhead camp made a final attempt to prevent the influential Central Labor Union of Easton from officially endorsing Palmer's candidacy. But when representatives of the seventy-five unions which constituted the Central Union met to discuss the campaign, they were overwhelmed by pressure from Palmer and his well-organized supporters. The president of the Central Labor Union of South Bethlehem, A. J. Ferguson, was on hand to back Palmer's cause with the assertion that "it is an open secret that he [Brodhead] is not a friend of the workingman." [31] David Williams, leader of the Bethlehem strike, called Brodhead's part in the settlement "a damnable treachery" to the strikers. Williams' statement was seconded by J. Tazelaar, the AF of L national organizer who had helped manage the strike, and by James Lucas, Craneman's union representative, who told the Central Union that it was "worth a Bethlehem Steel worker's job to open his mouth against Brodhead" in South Bethlehem. Palmer spoke for over an hour, recalling his services in the cause of labor. After his speech, the union voted to endorse him.[32]

Palmer was renominated by a vote of 10,051 to 6,044. Mutchler's newspaper complained that although Brodhead had ended the strike, "the Monroe man's majority was swelled by the support given him by union labor." [33] In the fall, Palmer devoted himself to aiding the Democratic state ticket. With a minimum of further campaigning on his own behalf, he was reelected in November by almost 8,000 votes, a two-to-one majority, twice the size of his record victory in 1908.

Meanwhile, the Democratic state ticket suffered a crushing defeat. The day after the election, Palmer announced that although his sole political desire was to be of service to his home district, he was prepared to help revitalize and bring new leadership to the state party.[34]

CHAPTER III

THE PRACTICAL REFORMER

Pennsylvania's version of the two-party system was described in the New York *Times* early in 1911: "There have always been two Republican parties there, one called 'Republican' and the other called 'Democratic.' The leaders of the two parties were in partnership, the 'Republican' leaders being the senior partners and the 'Democratic' leaders combining something of the qualities of junior partners with something of the qualities of clerks." [1]

The Republican "senior partners" took the political plums. They controlled the legislature and most of the congressional districts. Since the Civil War, they had elected every United States senator and, with the exception of one man, every governor. Republicans ran all the state boards and commissions, appointed the judges, usually got the federal patronage, and generally controlled Pennsylvania's major cities.

Some tasty crumbs remained for the loyal opposition, however. Many state commissions, by law, had to have minority party representation. Only half of the state's real-estate assessors, for example, could be members of the majority party. A certain number of magistrates and registrars had to be Democrats. Each county board of commissioners was required to have a Democratic representative. [2] The Republican governors who appointed these men made their selections after consulting Republican state and city bosses, who in turn received recommendations of deserving Democrats from cooperative Democratic chieftains. Joe Guffey, who was close to the party leadership for more than forty years, later wrote: "As long as the Democratic Party was in the minority, there were always Democratic leaders more interested in picking up patronage crumbs from the Republican table than they were in winning elections." [3] Especially deserving, from the Republican point of view, were Democrats who saw to it that their party nominated weak candidates for important elections and helped collect Democratic votes for Republican primaries if the machine was challenged.

From 1897 to 1911, the Democratic state boss was Colonel James Guffey, who also served during part of this time as Pennsylvania's national committeeman. Guffey rose to power as one of the leaders of the Bryan, free-silver wing of the state party.[4] Once on top, however, he showed what one Democrat politician called "tendencies to deal with the enemy" within the state and with the most conservative state bosses in national politics.[5] Only one Democrat was elected to an important state office while Guffey ran the party. It took a series of major scandals and a flood of muckraking stories to elect Democrat William H. Berry state treasurer for one term in 1905. Local reform movements had to operate without much backing from the state party. When Democrat George W. Guthrie wrested the Pittsburgh mayor's chair from the Republican machine in 1905, he had to fight the regular organization in Colonel Guffey's home town.[6] The Bryan Democratic League was forced to overcome "the bitterest possible antagonism" from Guffey and his associates in order to elect a majority of the Pennsylvania delegates to the Democratic national convention of 1908.[7] Appropriately, Guffey's last official act as national committeeman was to join with other conservative state bosses and vote for Alton B. Parker instead of Bryan for temporary chairman of the 1912 convention.[8]

By 1910, revolts simmered throughout the nation against conservative Democratic state regimes. Groups of young, progressive Democrats helped Woodrow Wilson topple the Smith machine in New Jersey, removed the California party machinery from the hands of Hearst and the Southern Pacific, and began to undermine Joe Bailey's political rule in Texas, and Guffey's in Pennsylvania.[9] Many more progressive Democrats might have come to power if the Wilson administration had not been obliged in 1913 to bolster shaky conservative machines with federal patronage in order to pass its legislative program.[10]

In Pennsylvania, the machine received sufficient warning of rising opposition. The Bryan League organized a statewide campaign in the spring of 1908 and captured fifty-two of the sixty-four delegates to the Democratic national convention. A group of political novices led by Roland S. Morris, a Princeton graduate and successful lawyer from Philadelphia, managed this coup. Morris' lieutenants included attorney Francis Fisher Kane, another Princeton graduate and Philadelphian; Warren Worth Bailey, editor of the *Johnstown Democrat;* and Jere S. Black of York, another former Princeton man.[11]

Equally dangerous opposition arose among dissatisfied local politicians, who scented victory in the nationwide dissatisfaction with Taft's administration and in Pennsylvanians' discontent with their corrupt state government. Many Democratic politicians preferred the fruits of victory to the leftovers handed down by Republicans to state and big-city Democratic leaders.

Guffey and his associates in the state party leadership, State Committee Chairman Arthur G. Dewalt, State Senator James Hall, and Charles Donnelly and Thomas J. Ryan, who controlled the party machinery in Philadelphia, attempted to stave off trouble with a plea for unity against the common enemy. The state central committee met in Allentown on April 7, 1910, to plan for the coming gubernatorial campaign; leaders of the Bryan League, as well as other influential Democrats, were invited to attend.[12]

The meeting appeared to be a success. Chairman Dewalt spoke of the need for united action if the party was to take advantage of its golden opportunity to conquer the Republicans in November. Congressman William B. Wilson, former secretary-treasurer of the United Mine Workers, and a man whose influence was appreciated and feared by the Guffey faction,[13] seconded Dewalt's call for unity. A letter from Congressman A. Mitchell Palmer, then busy introducing a delegation of striking steel workers to President Taft, was read, and it too counseled harmony. So pervasive was the tone of conciliation that the old guard agreed, after moderate protestations, to Carbon delegate James I. Blakeslee's motion that a committee of five under the chairmanship of Vance B. McCormick be authorized to raise $20,000 for the state party organization. Regular leaders feared that if an independent group collected party funds it might become the nucleus of a rival organization.[14] Later, these fears were proved entirely justified.

A large majority of the state committeemen agreed that C. Larue Munson, who had startled Pennsylvania politicians by nearly winning a contest for State Supreme Court justice in 1909, would be the best candidate for governor. Munson, considered a progressive Democrat, had the almost unanimous backing of reform groups within the party.[15] Just before the state Democratic convention met in mid-June, Munson's backers heard rumors that Democratic leaders, in an Atlantic City meeting with prominent Republicans, had arranged to prevent the nomination of their candidate. It was reported that Philander C. Knox, Taft's Secretary of State, wanted the Republican nomination, but that Boies Penrose, who dominated the Republican state party, preferred someone of more malleable character in the state house. With a weak Democratic candidate, Penrose could sidetrack Knox.[16]

Some substance was given to the rumors when the Republicans departed from their custom of holding conventions prior to the Democrats'. Munson's supporters, however, thought they knew their man, and they felt sure that they had the votes to nominate him. At midnight, on the night before the Democratic convention opened, Munson announced his withdrawal from the race for reasons of health. The next day, the regular organization leaders declared that they backed State Senator Webster Grim for the nomination.[17]

Progressive Democrats raised such an uproar that Charles Donnelly called Palmer to a three-hour private meeting, during which he offered to drop Grim in favor of the thirty-eight-year-old Stroudsburg congressman.[18] If there was an agreement between the Democratic leaders and Penrose, Palmer's nomination probably would not have violated it: a first-term congressman from the northeastern corner of the state, he had never held public office before 1908. Palmer certainly would have been acceptable to the reformers; he already had earned a reputation in Congress as one of the most progressive young Democrats, and he was known in his district as a prolabor representative.[19] Party regulars, on the other hand, believed that Palmer would support them if he won. In fact, Guffey's first lieutenant, James Hall, had taken the precaution of sending Palmer a check for $500 to help his campaign for renomination, or "to aid you in any manner you deem best," and Palmer never returned the money.[20]

Nevertheless, Palmer refused the nomination. He thought he saw a clear road upward in the House, and he chose sure reelection to the uncertainties of a statewide campaign. Palmer later claimed that he urged Donnelly to accept former state treasurer William Berry, whom the reformers had hastily agreed to support. But all the delegates from Palmer's district voted for Grim, and Blakeslee, a county chairman in Palmer's district, was nominated for state secretary of internal affairs, indicating that Palmer was keeping a foot in both camps. The convention chose Grim over Berry, whose nomination would have been just as offensive to Penrose as that of Munson.[21] A few days later, the Republicans held a one-hour convention, agreeing on a platform and choosing a state ticket headed by John K. Tener, a former big-league baseball pitcher who had been elected to Congress in 1908.[22]

Disgruntled Democrats, led by Bailey, McCormick, Guthrie, and labor leader John J. Casey, joined independent Republicans in forming a third party, which nominated Berry. Palmer chose a different role for himself: "a regular of the regulars," acceptable to the reformers and professionals alike. Grim, he knew, would be beaten badly, and the Democratic leadership could then be overthrown. To take control and win elections once they were in power, the progressives would need the cooperation of regular party workers, especially the county chairmen. Palmer, experienced and astute enough to know what professional politicians thought of bolters, refused to desert the party organization and campaigned actively for Grim.[23]

Palmer was a farsighted and clever man, a superb manipulator of both his opponents and his associates. Later he was to ruin his career with a wrong guess about the future, but this time he guessed right. In the November election, Palmer's district was one of the few that gave Grim a plurality. The state-wide race between Tener and Berry was remarkably close; Tener received 415,614 votes, Berry 382,127, and Grim only 129,395.[24] In contrast to Grim's overwhelming defeat, Democrats swept the 1910 elections in most states, gaining control of Congress, even winning the governorship in Maine.

Palmer, reelected to Congress by a two-to-one majority, wasted no time in starting the movement toward party reorganization. "While I have no desire to mix into state politics," he announced a day after the election, "I shall not run away from this problem." [25] Two months later, he met with Vance McCormick in Baltimore and "sat up all night long," Palmer later recalled, "planning how we could get a spontaneous, extemporaneous movement going." [26] Palmer had already discussed the matter with other Pennsylvania Democrats in Congress. In accordance with a plan drawn up with McCormick, Palmer arranged a meeting of the five Pennsylvania Democrats in the Sixty-first Congress and the four elected to the Sixty-second Congress. He persuaded all nine to sign a letter to McCormick's committee requesting a meeting of the state central committee to discuss party reorganization. A similar letter to McCormick's group was sent by a majority of the Democrats in the state legislature.[27]

Meanwhile, McCormick's committee followed through with its part of the plan. The committee issued a report stating that it had been unable to raise funds because Pennsylvania Democrats believed that money donated to their party was turned over to Republicans. The report concluded that only new party leaders could regain the voters' trust. Following the report, McCormick's committee issued a letter urging an immediate meeting of the state central committee; a telegram was dispatched to State Chairman Dewalt with the same request. Dewalt, of course, refused. Pressure on the state chairman mounted, however, as a large majority of the county chairmen and most of the state's Democratic newspapers declared in favor of a meeting. Guffey, recently bankrupted, was too busy with his tangled financial affairs to deal with an incipient revolt within the party. Hall and Donnelly persuaded Dewalt to call a meeting while they still had a chance to retain power. Five days after refusing to act, Dewalt summoned the central committee to meet on March 2, 1911, at Harrisburg.[28]

A week before the central committee met, the reorganizers rallied their forces at a meeting in the Bellevue-Stratford Hotel in Philadelphia. The occasion was the anniversary dinner of the Democratic Club of Philadelphia, an organization controlled by the progressive wing of the city party. Speakers included Guthrie, Palmer, Senator Thomas P. Gore of Oklahoma, and the newly elected governor of New Jersey, Woodrow Wilson.

Palmer's speech differed considerably from those delivered by his fellow reformers. Neither angry, triumphant, nor inspirational, his tone was that of a shrewd politician seeking the votes of other politicians. Aiming beyond a large part of his audience, Palmer directed his speech especially at the wavering Democratic state committeemen. He promised party unity and victory, rather than revolt and reform.

I speak as a regular of the regulars. I have followed the organization in this state in good times and bad, although always to defeat and never to victory. I supported with my voice, and my vote, the nominee [Grim] of the Allentown convention. . . . I speak for a body of Democratic voters who have grown sick and tired of always following their leaders to defeat in the state.

There is no necessity for any man's head to drop into the basket. It is not a case which calls for an operation. It demands treatment. Those of us who have loyally followed the organization in the past have a right to demand that the unswerving confidence which we have reposed for years in those who have held official places in the party's organization shall now be justified.

Party leadership, declared Palmer, should be turned over to the reorganizers, because they could win.[29]

The day before the central committee convened, Palmer was asked what would happen if the committee rejected demands for a reorganization. "Well, it probably means a third party, that's all," he replied, again raising before the professionals the spectre of certain defeat in coming elections.[30] When the meeting began, Blakeslee immediately offered a resolution giving Democratic congressmen present the privilege of the floor but not the right to vote. After some wrangling, the resolution passed—the Guffey-Hall-Donnelly group did not wish to antagonize the seven congressmen present; but as a consequence, Palmer obtained a chance to speak.[31]

McCormick's committee made its final report, recommending that a committee of seven be appointed to name a new state committee chairman and a new national committeeman. Three of the seven would be appointed by the present chairman, Dewalt, three by the McCormick committee, and one by the Democratic congressmen. A group appointed in that manner, of course, would split four to three in favor of reorganizer candidates. Members of the old guard thereupon launched a bitter attack on McCormick and his associates, charging them with trying to take over the party and having attempted to wreck it in 1910; the McCormick group, they continued, had contributed next to nothing to the party and was too inexperienced to manage it.

Few state committeemen dared defend McCormick and his plan openly. A neutral newspaper reported: "The regulars were confident and hilarious and took advantage of every opportunity to jeer the apparently small delegation which surrounded McCormick and Palmer." [32] When Palmer finally addressed the meeting, he spoke in the conciliatory vein he had used at the Bellevue-Stratford. "My position," he said, "is a little different from that of the vast majority of the men who are calling for a new deal. I have stood for party regularity. I have followed the party in good and bad. I have no fight or quarrel with the Chairman of this State Committee and with the members of the

Democratic National Committee, but I have my ear to the ground." The Democrats, he asserted, could win Pennsylvania if they adopted the report of the McCormick committee. "We are now on the verge of a great Democratic victory," Palmer proclaimed, and he urged the committeemen not to throw it away.

He assured his listeners that no ulterior motives lay behind his support of the reorganizers. People who said otherwise were guilty of "a base and outlandish slander and falsehood. In the first place, they say that Palmer wants something, to be leader, Chairman, or God knows what else. I can't find words strong enough to characterize its falsehood. I am not a candidate." [33] When he finished, "The ovation accorded Palmer was a surprise to the regulars, who had thus far commanded all the applause." [34]

The state committee was tense and quiet during the vote on the McCormick committee's plan. According to Palmer, just as voting began a delegate from Pike County arrived at the hall, walked down the aisle, and slipped into a vacant seat. He had heard neither the resolution nor the debate. "How shall I vote?" he asked the man in the next seat. "Aye," advised his neighbor. He voted "Aye," and the resolution carried by one vote. Two years later, Palmer obtained a postmastership for the tardy Pike County delegate.[35]

When the seven-man committee assembled under the chairmanship of Congressman William B. Wilson on March 14, it quickly chose Guthrie to replace Dewalt as state chairman and Palmer to succeed Guffey as national committeeman. The meeting then degenerated into five and one-half hours of what a reporter called "washing of the dirtiest kind of political linen." Charles Donnelly, leader of the old-guard representatives present, reminded the other committeemen that only two weeks before they had all heard Palmer disclaim any desire for party office; now he was to be made national committeeman. He then accused Palmer of having solicited votes for Congress in the recent primary election on the grounds that his opponent, J. Davis Brodhead, was a Catholic. A reorganizer member of the committee, Joseph O'Brien, district attorney of Lackawanna County, jumped to his feet to deny the story, his face "purple with rage." One of Donnelly's two old guard colleagues on the committee disassociated himself from the accusation. Chairman Wilson said he did not believe a word of Donnelly's tale, but if it were true, he declared, he would repudiate his friendship with Palmer and reverse his vote. Pressed to reveal his source, Donnelly named Howard Mutchler.[36]

Palmer was a hard and often ruthless campaigner, but he was too clever to raise such an explosive issue in a campaign he was almost certain to win (and did win), easily. Nor was he likely to have brought up the question out of strong personal feeling. He and Brodhead had been friends for years, both had studied law in John Storm's office,[37] and Brodhead later served under Palmer in the Alien Property Custodian's office.[38] Mutchler's accusation largely reflected the animosity he felt toward Palmer as a result of the bitter primary campaign of 1910. However, the religious issue had long been a divisive one in Pennsylvania Democratic politics,[39] and it was fortunate for Palmer and the reorganizers that it blew over quickly.

Guffey and his associates refused to accept the Wilson committee report as binding. One of Guffey's associates approached William Berry with a proposal that Dewalt would resign in favor of Guthrie, if Guffey were allowed to serve out his term as national committeeman. When that offer brought no response, Donnelly suggested that both Palmer and Guffey surrender their claims to the post of national committeeman and that Judge James B. Gordon be named as a compromise choice.[40] Most of the reorganizers considered Gordon a member of the old machine and saw no need to compromise.

During an interview in Stroudsburg, Palmer tried to explain how a man without ambitions had come to such a position of power.

I desire to say that any man who asserts that my course in endeavoring to effect a reorganization of the party in this state has been actuated by a desire for personal advancement . . . is a willful and malicious liar. Every man of intelligence in the state who reads the daily newspapers knows that I am not a candidate for National Committeeman; that I earnestly besought the Committee of Seven not to name me for that position and it was only after Democrats all over the state insisted that I should take it . . . that I finally decided to accept the place temporarily.[41]

Once he accepted the place "temporarily," Palmer kept it and ran the Pennsylvania party with a iron hand until 1921, when he decided he had had enough of politics and stepped down.

To settle the dispute over the Wilson committee report, another meeting of the state central committee was called for July. By this time, the committeemen realized which way the political winds were blowing. Palmer predicted the reorganizers would have a majority of fifteen to eighteen votes, and he probably underestimated the margin.[42] When the committee convened, however, it quickly divided into two meetings, with the old guard withdrawing to another location. Forty-seven of the eighty-three committee members stayed with the reorganizers. By electing substitutes for all absentees, and counting some with doubtful credentials, the rump-meeting participants, led by Dewalt, numbered thirty-eight. The old guard elected its own state chairman to replace Dewalt, but when Guthrie's administration started functioning, no one questioned its authority.[43]

The fight against Palmer, on the other hand, was carried into the national committee. There, William Jennings Bryan of Nebraska and Josephus Daniels of North Carolina led the fight to seat Palmer, while conservative bosses Tom Taggart of Indiana and Roger Sullivan of Illinois supported Guffey's right to retain his seat. Taggart made the telling point that state committees had the right to fill vacancies on the national committee, but not the right to create them, as the Pennsylvania committee was trying to do. Homer Cummings recalled that he and several other committeemen whose sympathies were with Palmer voted for Guffey because according to national committee rules the Colonel's term ran until the next national convention. After Daniels' motion to seat Palmer was defeated, 30 to 18, Bryan warned Guffey that he and his supporters meant "to

see to it that there is another national committee chosen which
will not have any Guffeys on it." Woodrow Wilson wrote
Palmer that he thought the decision of the national committee
"in the long run will do not harm, but good." by arousing additional reform sentiment in the country.[44]

Guffey retained the formal trappings of power on borrowed
time. Palmer took no chances in 1912. Before the state convention, which would elect delegates-at-large to the national convention and recommend a candidate for national committeeman, Palmer called Guthrie, McCormick, Blakeslee, and
Bailey to a conference in Washington.[45] He feared that, through
trickery, the old guard might win part of the delegation to the
Baltimore convention and force the election of a compromise
candidate for national committeeman. Of 183 delegates to the
state convention, 112 were claimed by the Guffey faction.[46] It
seemed possible that the old guard might divide the reorganizers' coalition. Their plan, apparently, was to draw off the
professionals who were trying to follow a likely winner, first by
spreading doubts that the reorganizers actually had a majority,
then by proposing a variety of their own candidates. Judge
Gordon, one of the most respected Democratic politicians in
the state before the Guffey regime took over,[47] was already
being widely discussed as a compromise choice for national
committeeman. Gordon himself was seeking Bryan's invaluable
support.[48]

The day before the state convention, the reorganizers cau-
cused until midnight. Palmer, a skillful manager of such meetings,[49] acted as chairman.[50] Some reorganizers protested that
forcing delegates to follow decisions of a caucus majority recalled old-guard methods; even Vance McCormick's newspaper
called the well-organized caucus an "unprecedented method of
procedure in the recent history of the Pennsylvania Democracy." [51]

Nevertheless, the caucus decisions stuck. Reorganizer delegates reassembled in a theater at ten the next morning. After
another pep talk, they marched to the convention hall, accompanied by a loud brass band. Ushers, on hand in large num-

bers, refused to allow anyone into the delegates' section who could not show one of the carefully distributed delegates' tickets, and well before the convention opened the galleries were thoroughly packed with reorganizer supporters. As a result of this thorough marshalling of superior forces, the reorganizers triumphed completely. In a final effort to divide their opponents the old guard nominated Judge Gordon for presiding officer; but Gordon, although still personally popular with some reorganizer delegates, lost by thirty-seven votes to the caucus choice Joseph O'Brien. Then Palmer read the platform he had prepared as chairman of the resolutions committee and debated its provisions with Gordon.[52] "His voice was husky from much speaking both on the floor and in the committee, but he was heard all over the hall," a reported noted.[53] All the reorganizers' candidates were elected by large majorities, and the platform was adopted without modification.

The reorganizer's complete victory testifies not to the inevitable triumph of innocent idealism, but to the necessity of practical politics for the success of a reform movement. Palmer's indispensible role in this success was to bridge the gap between reformers and professional politicians. He was progressive enough to satisfy the reformers, yet shrewd and strong enough to control the county chairmen and their organizations.

Palmer returned to Congress in April, 1911, as head of the Democratic Party in Pennsylvania. His new eminence in national politics gave him powerful leverage in Congress. Pennsylvania would have more votes in the 1912 national convention than any state but New York, and the two Democratic House chieftains, Majority Leader Underwood and Speaker Clark, hoped for the presidential nomination. Palmer's astonishingly rapid ascent into the small coterie—comprised mostly of southerners—which managed the House was due as much to his position in Pennsylvania as to the ability he had shown and the friends he had made during his first term.

Palmer was elevated to the Ways and Means Committee, the most potent group in the House. That committee wielded authority over committee assignments, a prerogative stripped from Speaker Cannon in 1910 because he used it frequently to intimidate congressmen of both parties. The Ways and Means Committee also bore responsibility for originating tariff legislation, and the Democrats had swept the 1910 elections partly because they pledged a lower tariff. Palmer ranked next to last on the committee in seniority; but before the Sixty-second Congress ended Chairman Underwood acknowledged that Palmer was his "right arm." [54]

The first to formally recognize Palmer's high position in the new House were Pennsylvania's nine other Democratic congressmen. They gathered in the Ways and Means Committee room early in June, 1911, to thank the state party leader for their excellent committee assignments. The nine together offered Palmer an appropriate gift; they pooled their patronage allotments and gave him the right to select one of his constituents for a lucrative job in the House sergeant-at-arms office.[55]

This new concentration of power infuriated "Uncle Joe" Cannon, who had been subjected to merciless criticism from politicians, newspapers, and magazines of all political persuasions because of his autocratic use of the Speaker's privileges. Early in 1912 he arose in Congress and reminded his fellow representatives of the bitter protests which had come from every side when the appointment power was concentrated in his hands. Now, charged Cannon, the same power rested in the hands of two Democrats. Was that better? "Czar Cannon!" he roared indignantly, "yet Czar Underwood and my friend, in whose eye I look, Czar Palmer, made the organization . . . [of the Sixty-second Congress]." [56]

The overwhelming Democratic triumph in the 1910 congressional elections was the party's first national victory since the election of 1892. Yet, as *The Nation* observed just before the Sixty-second House met in April, 1911, the Democrats "are as far as possible from having had from the country a vote of confidence. All that has been given is a vote of want of confidence in the Republicans. The Democrats have merely an opportunity." [57]

Even the most sympathetic political observers doubted the

Democratic Party's ability to pass a constructive legislative program. The party had long appeared hopelessly split between populists and bourbons, between urban reformers and the big city machines. Southern members with long tenure traditionally dominated the party in Congress, and their record had enabled Republican Speaker Thomas B. Reed to assert: "The Democratic party wants no legislation. . . . All the Southern men who control the party ask for is to be left alone." The *North American Review* in August, 1892, described the party as "a hopeless assortment of discordant differences, as incapable of positive action as it is capable of infinite clamor." [58] In 1910, Herbert Croly, a shrewd analyst of the progressive movement was equally certain that the Democrats were incapable of governing the nation. All their leaders were over-fearful of a strong federal government, Croly averred, and solutions to the most serious national problems could not be found within their states'-rights philosophy. Two weeks after the 1910 election, *The Nation,* which had high hopes for the new Democratic House, reported: "The Republicans are already prophesying . . . that the Democrats will make such a mess of things in the next House that the country will disgustedly and gladly fly back to the arms of the Republican party." [59] A nationally prominent Democrat visited his party's congressional leaders early in 1911 and then confided to a reporter:

I am loath to say it, but I find the Democratic leaders of the House children in statesmanship, unequal to the constructive work which they must undertake. The tariff problems are beyond them; their differences of opinion as to schedules appear irreconcilable; the party lacks cohesion and unity, and I can only see trouble ahead.[60]

Democratic House leaders, especially Palmer and Underwood, were fully aware that many Americans who had turned against the Republicans in 1910 nevertheless doubted that the Democrats could govern. The House chieftains believed that Americans had voted for a program as well as for a party. Democrats had long been advocates of tariff reform and economy in government; these were Cleveland's policies, and they could be traced back to Jackson's administration. Democratic leaders agreed, early in 1911, to make these reforms their first objectives. Only if legislation embodying them were passed could their party's critics be refuted; and unless they were refuted the Democratic Presidential candidate would have little chance in 1912.

House Democrats met in caucus on April 1, just before the Sixty-second Congress convened, to agree on a program for the session. The atmosphere was one of uneasiness and distrust. Party caucuses had been discontinued during the sixteen years of Democratic minorities, and members disagreed about procedures for making and enforcing caucus decisions. Many of the new congressmen were northern progressives sensitive because of warnings that they would be pushed around by more experienced southerners. The only newspaper reporter at the gathering observed that the group was tense—obviously unsure of itself and of its leaders.

Palmer struck the reporter as a "young man and a hard, earnest worker . . . who made a deep impression on the membership." Soon after the meeting opened, Palmer presented the recommendations of a subcommittee which had been studying means of reducing the expense of Congress. "Myself and two others," Palmer began, "were selected as the most cold-blooded of the [Ways and Means] Committee, to seek out and abolish the useless offices!" His words and manner, the reporter noted, provoked a burst of laughter which "finally broke the high tension that had gripped all present." [61] Palmer continued in a vein calculated to disperse the tension permanently. "During the Spanish-American War," he declared, "somebody's friend told somebody's cousin that somebody's aunt had heard someone say that a plot was on foot to dynamite the Capital. Thirty-eight extra policemen were added. They have remained ever since." He suggested removing them from the payroll, along with employees and officials of the clerk's document room (abolished in 1895), and scores of other apparently unneeded House employees. The caucus accepted his recommendations almost unanimously. [62]

Palmer's proposals were sent to committees and introduced

as individual measures starting early in the session. The first
to appear on the House floor was a resolution, introduced by
Representative James L. Lloyd of Missouri, to abolish the jobs
of sixty-five House clerks, messengers, assistant doorkeepers,
and janitors. By this time, many Democratic congressmen had
had second thoughts about their economy drive. The jobs to be
abolished were usually given to political appointees, and Democratic congressmen had not been able to offer such rewards to
needy friends, relatives, or constituents for many years. A Democratic newspaper observed on April 3 that "Persons have come
to Washington from all over the whole blessed country fondly
anticipating jobs under the incoming Democratic Congress."
Lloyd, however, pointed out that "We are acting in response to
a caucus resolution." Palmer supported the measure by quoting
Jefferson, Cleveland, and past Democratic platforms to the effect that the Democrats had always been the party of economy
in government. He also reminded his fellow party members of
their obligation to vote in accordance with caucus decisions.
Lloyd's resolution was adopted, although many Democrats must
have been wistful as they watched these cherished spoils being
destroyed by their own votes.[63]

Another of Palmer's economy measures reached the floor in
July, when Representative John J. Fitzgerald of New York
moved that the House omit the customary bonus of a month's
pay heretofore given congressional employees as compensation
for the time Congress was not in session. Palmer again reminded
Democrats of the resolution passed by the April 1 caucus,
"with practical unanimity, deciding that hereafter this extrava-
gance should be lopped off." When Representative Frank Clark
of Florida declared that he could not remember any discussion
of that particular economy in caucus, Palmer's reply was immediately forthcoming: "The gentleman is mistaken. I drafted
the resolution myself. I offered it in the caucus. I explained it
in the caucus and it was adopted almost unanimously." The
House passed Fitzgerald's motion by a large margin.[64]

In December, Palmer carried the idea of economy in government too far, even for his fellow Democrats. He introduced

a resolution reducing travel allowances for congressmen from twenty cents a mile to ten cents. The old rate, Palmer argued, had been set at a time when travel was much more expensive and time consuming; ten cents a mile was more than enough now. He sarcastically apologized for introducing his measure so close to Christmas, "when the shops in Washington are filled with articles of beauty and great expense, appealing to Members of the House to be purchased for Christmas presents for their families and others." Before Palmer finished, a reporter noted, there was a "buzz of indignant dissent from members on both sides of the House." No one denied Palmer's facts, but several congressmen furiously questioned his motives. Republican Representative William E. Humphrey of Washington suggested that Palmer was willing to take a lower allowance because the amount he received was trivial, since he lived so close to Washington. How about members who lived farther away and had to transport their families? Was Palmer trying to separate southern and western representatives from their wives and children? He suggested that Palmer introduce an amendment "to reduce our salary so that he will suffer along with the rest of the Members."

Representative James R. Mann of Illinois, Minority Leader and one of the most effective needlers in Washington, gibed: "I have often noticed that most of us desire to cut off something of very little concern to us, but of great use to somebody else. Most of us desire to economize at the expense of our neighbor." Palmer, he pointed out, was able to maintain his lucrative law practice by making frequent trips home, while congressmen from more remote districts had had to give up their businesses.

The debate became steadily more acrimonious. Humphrey, whom Palmer accused of attempting to gain a salary increase by subterfuge, was probably the angriest participant. Fitzgerald finally called for a truce: "Mr. Chairman, it ought to be possible to discuss this question of mileage without leading to bloodshed on the floor of the House." Before hostilities could resume, a vote was called for, and the House rejected Palmer's resolution 139 to 55.[65]

"Uncle Joe" Cannon, who seems to have genuinely liked and admired Palmer, gave the younger man some friendly advice: "For this Congress coming in as it does with a Democratic majority for the first time in almost sixteen years in this House, there is plenty of work and great work for it to do. And let me say to the gentleman from Pennsylvania [Mr. Palmer] with the greatest courtesy and the highest respect, that I believe the country will not approve of the waste of time over the saving of cents here and there, when the great affairs touching expenditures that aggregate nearly a thousand million dollars are neglected. . . ." [66]

As Palmer was entrusted with increasing responsibilities by House leaders, he inevitably came into conflict with veteran congressmen. Experienced members resented his sudden rise and the peremptory tone he sometimes adopted. Even representatives who respected the Pennsylvanian's abilities were antagonized when he began assigning committee rooms. Actually, anyone who took on that perplexing task would have been the victim of considerable hostility; but Palmer, grasping for power in the House, went ahead despite obvious warning signs. A new House office building had been opened three years before, and rights to certain committee rooms were still disputed. Some of the new Democratic chairmen aggravated the situation by insisting that since their committees were going to handle much more work than they had under Republican leadership they needed more space. When these delicate problems were brought to Underwood, he asked Palmer to find solutions. Before long, all those with complaints came directly to Palmer, who apparently was glad to take on the thankless job.

Early in the special session, Palmer introduced a resolution assigning new office space to a dozen House committees. Representative Charles C. Carlin of Virginia (who later helped manage Palmer's 1920 campaign for the Presidential nomination), objected, claiming that his committee had not received

fair treatment, and questioning Palmer's authority to appor-
tion rooms. Robert L. Henry, chairman of the Rules Committee, defended Palmer:

Mr. Henry: We found out that somebody had to take hold of
the matter and work out a solution of the conflicts between gentlemen and committees. Accordingly we called upon the gentleman
from Pennsylvania [Mr. Palmer] and the gentleman from Alabama
[Mr. Underwood] and asked them if they could help us out.[67]
Mr. Carlin: It seems to me it is becoming the habit of Members
to call on them for everything that is done around here.
Mr. Henry: They have been doing so well what they have done
and what has been intrusted to them to do that I think we do well
in going to them.[68]

Palmer continued to assign rooms until early in the next
Congress. Then criticism of his decisions became so bitter that
he announced to the House that he was relinquishing the task.
"I do not want this authority which gentlemen think I have
assumed of seeing various people in the House and thrashing
out this question . . . and I shall not, therefore, introduce any
more of these resolutions." Minority Leader Mann mocked
Palmer: "In a moment of childishness, he said . . . 'I will not
play in your backyard if I can not have my way.'" [69]
After the Democrats, pushed by Palmer, had dealt with the
problems of economy and simplicity in government, they moved
on to the major part of their program: tariff reform. Democratic leaders decided to take up the iron and steel schedule
first; it was the most controversial and would draw public attention to their work. Palmer was asked to head a subcommittee appointed to draw up the new schedule. Probably it
would have been more expedient to have avoided the assignment—Pennsylvania manufacturers and workers had long been
obsessed with the necessity for high metal duties, and the last
Pennsylvania Democrat to enjoy a long and influential career
in Congress, Samuel J. Randall, was a rabid protectionist.
Nevertheless, in the interests of his party, and perhaps of his
own national reputation, Palmer took on another politically
dangerous task.
When Palmer's bill was published, late in January, 1911,

Republican Senator George T. Oliver of Pennsylvania protested that it represented the "most radical departure in the direction of free trade that has been proposed by any party during the last 70 years." [70] The bill reduced duties on many iron and steel products 50 percent or more and proposed a long free list. Palmer opened debate on his handiwork before a crowded House on January 26. In an hour-and-a-half-long speech, he devoted himself largely to debunking an idea that was dogma in Pennsylvania—that a high tariff ensured the prosperity of both industry and workers. This belief was only half accurate, Palmer asserted. The tariff increased manufacturers' profits, he acknowledged; but provided no benefit for workers. He used the Bethlehem Steel Company as an illustration:

Mr. Schwab, the President of that company, says that a tariff is absolutely necessary in order to keep his men employed and in order to make a fair return upon his capital. In all these years that he has been keeping his men employed in Bethlehem, as the reports of the Department of Commerce and Labor show, they have been getting wages, 61 per cent of them, as low as 18 cents an hour and less, some down to as low as 4 cents an hour. During all that time, Mr. Schwab's company was able to build its capital stock out of profits from $300,000 to $15,000,000, and last year this company declared a dividend of . . . $1,500,000 in one year upon an original investment of $300,000. I tell you I listen with little patience to these great capitalists who say, "Give us this tariff in order to enable us to get an honest return upon our capital and an honest wage for our laboring men." . . . We are writing a tariff law which may result in such competition that the American consumer will get his article at a lower price than he gets it now; and perhaps my distinguished constituent, Mr. Schwab, will be compelled to be satisfied with something less than the exorbitant profits which he has been able to earn upon his investment.[71]

The next day, Palmer charged that his speech and his role in drafting the steel schedule had led to threats of political reprisal: "I have received my notice from the Bethlehem Steel Company—though indirectly—that because of this so-called act of treachery to them . . . and to Mr. Schwab—I am marked again for slaughter at their hands." [72]

Republican Congressman Edward Moore of Pennsylvania,

a vociferous defender of protection, chided Palmer for taking a position contrary to that of his constituents. "The gentleman has come to be a leader of his party; he is the modern Democratic Henry of Navarre of the Keystone State!" Palmer had been elected with labor support, Moore declared, yet he was pressing for a tariff which would hurt the very workingmen who had put him in power.[73] In reply, Palmer admitted again that tariff reduction would lower profits—manufacturers would have to cut their prices in order to meet foreign competition—but he denied that employment or wages would be affected. He answered Moore in words which must have warmed the hearts of American labor leaders. "The American manufacturer will be compelled to employ all the labor which he now employs and he will pay the labor just what he must, no more and no less. He will pay the labor just as much as labor can compel him to pay, just as he does today." [74] Only a few hours after Palmer completed his address, the Democrats forced a vote on the metal bill. According to the Philadelphia *Record:* "The Democratic steam roller, manipulated by leader Oscar Underwood and continuously oiled and greased by A. Mitchell Palmer of Pennsylvania, crushed Republican opposition." [75]

In February, 1912, a month after the new metal schedules passed the House, Boies Penrose, who helped squash the bill in the Senate, gave a preview of the campaign line he would use in 1914 when Palmer threatened his Senate seat: "If the metal bill which has been passed by the Democratic House should become a law, two results would inevitably follow. . . . Wages would be reduced and production curtailed; or else establishments would be closed altogether and metal employees thrown on the general labor market to bring down still further the wages of labor." [76]

On one point, however, Palmer deviated significantly from his low-tariff principles, indicating that there still were limits to the political sacrifices he would make for his party. The hills and valleys of Palmer's district were not especially good for farming, but they were ideal grazing land, as Obadiah Palmer had discovered a century before. Steel workers might not be harmed by lower tariffs, but sheep raisers felt certain they would be ruined by cheap imports of wool. Palmer's neighbors appealed to him, and he and Underwood, who also had wool producers in his district, saw to it that a moderate tax on wool was retained in the wool and woolens tariff bill passed by the House.[77]

Palmer's last important action in the Sixty-second Congress was his battle for legislation to protect quarry workers through government inspection of working conditions. His efforts illustrated an important change that was taking place in the party of Cleveland and Bryan. Palmer was one of many young northern Democrats, most of them from urban areas, elected with important and even decisive support from labor. These men, caught up in the great reform wave sweeping the nation, cherished objectives far beyond the traditional party goals for social welfare legislation.

In his long speech supporting the quarry inspection bill, Palmer noted that 85 percent of the slate produced in the United States was mined in his district. Incomplete coroners' records, he declared, showed 323 deaths from quarry accidents for the preceding ten years, in Northampton County alone, as well as an enormous number of injuries. When pressed by Cannon to explain why, if quarry inspection was so necessary, Pennsylvania did not require it, Palmer replied:

I, myself, drafted a quarry inspection bill, which I have twice presented to the Pennsylvania legislature and which I have argued before their committees time and time again, but for some reason, generally suspected to be the close affiliation between certain of the operators of these quarries and the Republican organization which has been all-powerful in that legislature [I have been unsuccessful.][78]

House passage of the quarry inspection bill added yet another achievement to the impressive record of the Sixty-second Congress. The Democrats had demonstrated that if raised to power they would use the federal government to realize the political and economic reforms demanded by millions of Americans. A politically neutral observer commented: "The Democrats have not made a mess of things in the House. Responsibility has given them wisdom. They have used their power sanely." [79]

After an advance to leadership almost unprecedented in congressional history, Palmer emerged from his second term as one of the most influential men in his party, with every indication that his amazing rise was not yet over. In battles for what he believed to be the ideals of his party he had made enemies; but he had also won respect. When Oscar Underwood visited Palmer's district in October, 1912, he told an enthusiastic crowd:

I know of no man in all the time that I have served in Congress who, in so short a time, has obtained the high position in the House of Representatives, commanded the following, and achieved the leadership your Congressman has. He has reached the point where the door is open to . . . almost any high honor he desires to reach out for.[80]

CHAPTER IV

MAKING WILSON PRESIDENT

A. Mitchell Palmer was not responsible for the fact that by mid-1911 the effort to reorganize the Democratic Party in Pennsylvania had also become a movement to nominate Woodrow Wilson for the Presidency. The nucleus of the movement was a group of influential Princeton alumni with strong personal ties to Wilson. Roland Morris, who became Pennsylvania Democratic state chairman in 1913, was a student at Lawrenceville when he first met Wilson in 1890. After several meetings with the inspiring Princeton teacher, Morris changed plans, enrolled at Princeton instead of Yale, and in the following four years took every course Wilson offered.[1] Joe Guffey, Palmer's most reliable political lieutenant, came to Princeton a year before Morris, met Wilson a few weeks after he entered, and talked with him frequently thereafter. Even after Wilson became President of the United States Guffey continued to address him as "professor." [2]

Morris, Guffey, and Francis Fisher Kane had helped lead Wilson's alumni supporters in his squabbles with the Princeton administration when Wilson was university president. "I cannot tell you how often I look back with interest and gratitude to that little conference at Mr. Kane's house," Wilson wrote Morris in June, 1910, "and to all the intimations I have had of your own influence. I am very hopeful that the future will bring us still closer together." [3] Guffey arranged a dinner in 1908 so that Wilson could meet Pittsburgh alumni sympathetic to his Princeton reforms. Two other reorganizers among the Princeton alumni, Jere S. Black and William W. Roper, also took Wilson's side in the intra-university struggles.[4]

Former Princeton men were not the only members of the reorganization movement to favor an early commitment of the state party to Wilson's candidacy. Wilson was a natural leader for the college-educated business and professional men like McCormick, Guthrie, and Berry, who headed the Pennsylvania reform movement. As governor of New Jersey, he seemed to be providing the kind of progressive government that many Democrats in neighboring Pennsylvania longed for in their own state.

Starting when he was president of Princeton, Wilson made many speeches in Pennsylvania; his ideas, talents, and commanding personality were widely known in the state. He won considerable attention in April, 1908, when he declared before a Pittsburgh audience that individuals responsible for the sins of corporations should be punished, just as individual wrongdoers were. Two years later, he returned to Pittsburgh and vehemently attacked the "money power" before local Princeton alumni. In November, 1910, he called for ballot reform before the City Club of Philadelphia.[5] After Wilson was elected governor, Vance McCormick recalled, "we took him in a special car through one of our Congressional districts on a speechmaking tour." [6] Wilson took sides in the fight for control of the Pennsylvania party in a speech at the important reorganizer rally held in Philadelphia on February 21, 1911. Four months later at Harrisburg he addressed the Pennsylvania Federation of Democratic Clubs, controlled by the reorganizers.[7]

In March, 1911, Warren Worth Bailey was able to tell Wilson accurately that he commanded the support of the Pennsylvania reformers.[8] As late as July, however, the Stroudsburg *Times,* reported that Palmer opposed an immediate declaration by the state party in support of Wilson's candidacy. Palmer, the account stated, admired Wilson but was politically indebted to the Governor's chief opponent, Speaker Clark, and dependent upon Clark for future advancement in Congress.[9]

Palmer probably had some hope of keeping Pennsylvania neutral in the early maneuvering for the Democratic presidential nomination. Obligated to Clark, he owed an even heavier debt to Oscar Underwood, also a candidate for the nomination. Palmer was not one to forget his friends when they needed help; equally important, he did not want a reputation for ingratitude. Furthermore, if he came to the convention as leader of a large uncommitted delegation, Palmer would enjoy enormous bargaining power, and it must have occurred to him that in such a position he might even be regarded as a "dark horse."

The pressure which finally forced Palmer to take sides came not from his fellow reorganizers, but from the old guard. In an attempt to ride the reform wave which was engulfing them, the deposed party leaders declared themselves for Wilson ahead of the reform wing; as early as mid-1911 Charles Donnelly demanded that the party immediately endorse Wilson.[10] To prevent the old guard from returning to power with the assistance of a popular Presidential candidate, Palmer felt obliged to champion Wilson in Pennsylvania. He assumed his new role enthusiastically, effectively disguising the fact that he had been pushed into the Wilson camp.

In July, 1911, a rump meeting of the old-guard members of the state committee voted to endorse Wilson for the 1912 presidential nomination. Palmer, having no alternative, obtained a similar endorsement from the regular meeting, controlled by the reorganizers.[11] After the meeting, Palmer cabled Wilson a detailed report that made clear which faction within the state organization comprised his true and most valuable supporters. Wilson replied that he was "deeply gratified" to have the support of the Pennsylvania party.[12]

By mid-April, 1912, the national movement to nominate Wilson was beginning to lag. On April 9, when Speaker Clark overwhelmed him in the Illinois primary, Wilson admitted: "I fully expected to carry the state." Clark won the entire Illinois delegation.[13] Two days later, New York delegates agreed to place themselves under the unit rule, synonomous with Boss Charles Murphy's rule; and Murphy, it was known, opposed Wilson's nomination.[14]

Two days before the Pennsylvania primary election a shaken Wilson went to Pittsburgh in an effort to keep his bandwagon

moving in Pennsylvania, at least. The next day, he wrote
Palmer that he had received a "very gratifying reception" and
was cheered by what friends there told him of the situation.
He looked forward with "a certain degree of confidence" to
the results.[15]

The Pennsylvania primary resulted in a great victory for
Wilson—a boost to the morale of the entire Wilson movement.
At least forty of the sixty-four delegates elected were Wilson
men; only three avowed anti-Wilson men were elected.[16] With
twelve more Pennsylvania delegates to be chosen by the reor-
ganizer-controlled state convention, an impressive group of
at least fifty-two convention votes was assured. A few weeks
later, Wilson picked up forty votes in Texas; these, along with
twenty-four from New Jersey, constituted a nucleus of 116 certain votes enabling Wilson's managers to begin negotiations
for the nomination.

Despite his commitment, Palmer prudently invited both
Clark and Wilson to address the opening of the Democratic
state convention in Harrisburg on May 6. Palmer introduced
the two candidates by waving his arm toward them, crying,
"Two tall pieces of Presidential timber!" [17] When the convention opened its deliberations the following day, the reorganizers' caucus had already decided all issues, and Palmer was obviously in control. Twelve Wilson delegates-at-large were
elected, all of whom, Palmer felt certain, were dependable.[18]

If Palmer was not by this time completely and permanently
tied to Wilson's candidacy, a controversy which arose in the
resolutions committee of the state convention solidified his
commitment. Palmer introduced a resolution instructing the
delegates-at-large to vote for Wilson's nomination. Judge Gordon, leader of the old-guard forces still trying to capture the
Wilson movement within the state, attempted to impugn
Palmer's sincerity. Palmer reported indignantly to Wilson that
Gordon

suggested an amendment which should bind the delegates to vote
for you 'until his name shall be withdrawn from the convention.'
I objected to this language being inserted in the resolution because

of the fear that it would go out to the country that we anticipate that your name might be withdrawn from the Convention. . . . The Resolutions Committee took my view and it was so reported to the Convention.[19]

By defeating Gordon's amendment, however, Palmer so thoroughly committed himself to Wilson that he found it impossible to back out at a later date.

A few days after the state convention, Representative Richmond P. Hobson, one of the leaders of the Democratic Party in Alabama, visited Stroudsburg. He publicly stated that Palmer would make an excellent President and suggested a Palmer-Underwood ticket should the convention become deadlocked. Hobson would not have made such a suggestion without the concurrence of the Alabama party leader, Oscar Underwood, himself a Presidential candidate with supporters in almost every southern delegation. A week later, Fred B. Lynch, Democratic national committeeman from Minnesota, declared that Palmer would be his state's choice as a compromise candidate if it became clear that neither Wilson nor Clark could win; and Lynch said that he expected a stalemate.[20] Already Pennsylvania's seventy-six convention votes were acting as a powerful magnet.

Palmer was quickly inducted into the inner circle of Wilson's preconvention advisers. He arranged for the entire Pennsylvania delegation to meet with Wilson at Princeton, and he held a private conference with the Governor in Trenton.[21] Early in June, eight or ten high-level Wilson advisors, including Palmer, met with the candidate in Philadelphia's Bellevue-Stratford Hotel. At this top-level strategy meeting it was decided that Palmer, a quick, sure parliamentarian and an excellent speaker, would be floor leader of Wilson's forces at the national convention; Representative Albert S. Burleson of Texas would take charge of lining up delegates; and William F. McCombs, Wilson's campaign manager, would assume general control.[22]

When the convention opened on June 24, some political observers still doubted Palmer's ability to control his delegation.

On June 21, William J. Brennen, delegate from Pittsburgh, announced: "I do not intend to vote for Governor Wilson at Baltimore and I think I can name seven or eight others who will not." The New York *World* quoted Attorney James A. Wakefield of Pittsburgh as saying: "Champ Clark will have twenty votes from the Keystone State after the first few ballots have been cast." Earlier, the Philadelphia *Record* had reported that Clark was promised twenty-six Pennsylvania votes after the first ballot.[23] Wilson warned Palmer in mid-May of an attempt to win Pennsylvania delegates over to Clark.[24]

Colonel Guffey performed his last official act for the Pennsylvania Democratic party on June 24, when he voted for the Clark forces' candidate, Alton B. Parker, as temporary chairman of the convention. Later in the day, the Pennsylvania delegation, by acclamation, elected Palmer national committeeman in Guffey's place. Inspired by the idealistic spirit which pervaded the Wilson camp, Palmer accepted his post in a speech which would haunt him throughout his career as sovereign of the Pennsylvania Democracy. "I pledge my word," he proclaimed, "that so far as my influence extends, your action today has sounded the deathknell of the old tradition in Pennsylvania . . . that the National Committeeman shall be the boss of the party. It is undemocratic and un-American." [25]

That night, in a convention address, Palmer seconded Wilson's nomination for the Presidency. He declared that he spoke for the young men of America, whose aspirations, ideals, and hopes Wilson voiced. But in describing his candidate and his appeal to the young, he tried, as usual, to reassure the cautious political veterans. Wilson, he asserted, "promises fulfillment of their hopes with methods tested by time. He is a conservative on the move. He stands for radical measures to be accomplished in a conservative and orderly fashion." [26]

Before balloting began, Palmer fired his delegates with a pep talk about the momentous battle to come: "Pennsylvania is going to be the target of their attack today," he warned his men, "they are going to try to break our lines. If we falter our cause is lost. If we hold firm Wilson will win. We must stand together." Stand together they did. On the first ballot, which Clark led, Pennsylvania cast seventy-one votes for Wilson. From the third through the eighth ballots, Pennsylvania delegates gave Wilson seventy-three of their seventy-six votes.[27]

On the tenth ballot, Friday, June 29, Charles Murphy tried to set off a stampede for Clark by casting New York's ninety votes for the Missourian. If Guffey and his lieutenants had retained control over the Pennsylvania party, at this crucial point they would probably have attempted to swing Pennsylvania to Clark, thereby ensuring his nomination. With Palmer in command, however, Pennsylvania voted seventy-one to five for Wilson. Other important delegations also remained steadfast, and Clark was short of the necessary votes.[28]

Throughout the balloting, Palmer stood on the speaker's platform as field general of the Wilson forces. He kept a wary eye on Chairman Ollie James of Kentucky, elected largely because the Wilson leaders believed he would be less dangerous to them on the platform than on the floor, where he would have been Clark's most capable manager. When James announced at the end of the tenth ballot: "Mr. Clark, having received eleven more than a majority, is not the nominee until he receives two-thirds," Palmer interrupted and demanded to know why the chairman was giving out irrelevant information. James replied that he was only reminding the delegates that it required a two-thirds vote to nominate, but thereafter he was less partisan in his pronouncements.[29]

After the twenty-sixth ballot, Saturday, June 30, the convention was still deadlocked with Clark about sixty votes ahead. "Worn out by ten hours of continuous and sensational battling . . . on the point of exhaustion, adjournment seemed the only sensible step to take," the New York *World* observed.[30] Palmer, hearing that Clark was on his way to Baltimore to address the delegates, moved that the convention adjourn until Monday, and his motion was granted. A moment later, Burleson, McCombs, and Senator William Hughes of New Jersey were angrily shouting at Palmer. They had just won a promise from Roger Sullivan, Illinois Democratic boss, to throw his delegation's votes to Wilson on the next ballot. Sullivan was not sure he would still be able to make good his promise on Monday—he and his delegates faced a weekend of pressure from Clark and his managers.[31] McCombs, prepared a day before to withdraw Wilson's name,[32] was particularly irate. "It's a shameful mess and Mitchell Palmer got us into it," he remembered saying.[33] McCombs overlooked the fact that he had neglected to inform Palmer about the success of his negotiations with Sullivan; and he also forgot that Palmer's motion prevented Clark from making a dramatic entrance into the convention and an emotional appeal to the delegates.

By Saturday night, the political bosses from the large northern states who had been supporting Champ Clark realized that his nomination was almost impossible. These men did not want Wilson, who refused to make commitments to them; had criticized them and had ties to their enemies. Furthermore, they regarded him as a political ingrate. He had double-crossed Boss James Smith in New Jersey and set up his own state organization. The Democratic bosses decided that almost anyone else was preferable, if only they could help in his nomination. Nor was Clark averse to the nomination of a "dark horse"; he was intent upon stopping Wilson's nomination, as Wilson had prevented his.[34]

Earlier in the convention, the Clark managers had tried to wean Pennsylvania's votes from Wilson by offering the Vice-Presidential nomination to Palmer. They even went so far as to assure Palmer and McCormick that Clark had Bright's disease and would soon die.[35] Now the Democratic bosses decided they could swing the nomination if they obtained Pennsylvania's votes. On Saturday afternoon, a conference to explore means of ending the deadlock met in the rooms of Norman Mack of New York, chairman of the Democratic national committee. According to the New York *Times:* "Pressure was brought on Mr. Murphy by Congressman Palmer to have the Tammany chief desert Clark and come out in favor of Wilson." But Murphy could not be persuaded.[36] After three or four hours of fruitless discussion, Edwin Wood of Michigan pro-

posed Palmer as a compromise candidate; but when the Pennsylvanian reaffirmed his loyalty to Wilson, the party chiefs did
not make a formal offer of support. After the meeting Mack
told the press that Democratic leaders were trying to form a
new combination, but so far without success.[37]

About ten that evening, Roger Sullivan telephoned Burleson and asked him to bring Palmer to another meeting. The
two Wilson leaders agreed, apparently without knowing the
exact purpose of the conference. Burleson remembered that
Murphy, Fitzgerald, and Taggart were among those present,
but that the persuasive Judge Daniel F. Cohalan of New York
did most of the talking. They showed Palmer, by a careful
analysis of all the delegations, that neither Clark nor Wilson
could win. They told him he was madly defending a lost cause;
everyone was tired of the long, fruitless struggle; everyone was
clamoring for a "dark horse." Palmer's acceptance of the nomination would mean a victory for the Wilson cause. Wouldn't it
be better to nominate a true Wilson man than to have the
Democratic leaders agree upon someone else?

As Palmer listened to these arguments he rapidly calculated—or recalculated—his chances of being elected President in
1912. Perhaps Murphy, Taggart, and the other urban bosses
represented at the meeting, the Clark leaders, and the southerners could deliver enough delegates, especially if they offered
Underwood the Vice Presidential nomination. Palmer knew he
had made an excellent impression on the convention as Wilson's floor leader; he knew too that many of the delegates were
weary of the struggle and ready for a compromise. He or any
other progressive Democrat would have a better than even
chance of election against the divided Republicans. Nor was
his position without precedent. Thirty-two years before, in
1880, Congressman James A. Garfield, after acting as floor manager for Senator John Sherman, had accepted the Republican
nomination from a deadlocked convention, and Garfield had
been elected President.

Before him Mitchell Palmer saw the possibility of quickly
realizing his highest ambitions—and yet the risks were high.

No matter how he explained his defection, he would be damned as a traitor by the rabid Wilsonians; to the Bryanites he would replace Clark as a front man for the bosses. Many of the Pennsylvania delegates, deeply devoted to Wilson, might even repudiate him. He had already come a long way, quickly. Why endanger a future which could hardly be more promising? Why run the hazard of becoming a political outcast, when with patience and continued diligence the prize could be his, without such risks, four or eight years later? He was, after all, only forty years old. A reputation for integrity and for dedication to his candidate would be a useful asset in the future. All witnesses agreed that as soon as the proposition was made to Palmer, he turned it down flatly.[38]

On Monday, Palmer resumed his role as floor leader of the Wilson forces. He gave no indication that he had been affected in the slightest by the temptations to which he had been exposed, or by the possibility that the nomination might yet be his if Wilson failed. The following day, Sullivan finally kept his promise to swing the Illinois delegation to Wilson, and Senator Bankhead, under strong pressure from the Wilson managers, released Underwood's delegates, most of whom switched to Wilson. Wilson's nomination followed soon afterward to the great relief of most of the hot and weary delegates. The Democrats hardly bothered to listen as Palmer raced through a reading of their party platform, which was unanimously approved by delegates already headed for the exits.

Palmer might well have been nominated had he come to the convention less committed to Wilson's candidacy. McAdoo, no friend of Palmer's, later wrote of the plan to nominate him: "It was not, by any means, an illogical or chimerical scheme." [39] More important, Palmer believed that he could have been nominated if he had but nodded his head to Murphy. Josephus Daniels, a friend and a fellow member of Wilson's cabinet, held that ever afterward

Palmer had an air implying that Wilson owed him a great deal . . . [He] rarely mentioned it, but once or twice I heard him say that the nomination was offered or tendered him and that, if he listened to it, he might have been President. They say a man who gets the Presidential bee in his bonnet never gets rid of it, and I think it is equally true that a man who in the convention thought the nomination was in his grasp is ever afterward affected by it. Certainly the bee buzzed in Palmer's bonnet thereafter.[40]

After the Democratic convention, Palmer worked with a single goal in mind—the Presidency. If his rapid political rise was to continue, however, he would have to carry Pennsylvania for Wilson in 1912, or come close to it. Palmer's basic asset in national politics, his control over the state party, would be endangered if he failed for too long to deliver the promised victory. An overwhelming defeat would discourage amateur reformers drawn into politics by the reorganization movement and would greatly weaken Palmer's hold over professionals weaned from the old guard. Furthermore, the shrewd, opportunistic politicians who determined national nominations were not likely to risk defeat by choosing a man who could not even win his own state. On the other hand, the electoral votes of the second most populous state in the Union would be an impressive dowry to offer a convention in 1916 or 1920 in exchange for a nomination.

Aware of the effect the state election would have on his career, Palmer devoted himself almost entirely to winning Pennsylvania for Wilson. He used his position on Wilson's fourteen-man campaign advisory group—the so-called veranda committee [41]—to send many nationally known speakers and considerable amounts of money into Pennsylvania.[42]

However, Palmer did not altogether neglect the national campaign; he attended meetings of the policy-making committee in New York, and he helped arrange itineraries for out-of-state speakers. When the Ohio party leaders found it impossible to get the attention of National Chairman McCombs, Ohio gubernatorial candidate James M. Cox, familiar with Palmer's ability to get things done in Congress, cabled him for assistance. Palmer got some action from McCombs and then arranged a meeting with Wilson for the Ohio leaders. As a result of this conference Wilson went to Ohio to open the state's election campaign.[43]

Palmer found it easier to get help for Ohio than for Pennsylvania. His state had voted Republican in every national election since 1860, and many of Wilson's advisors believed that the candidate's time and the national committee's money would be wasted in the campaign there. On August 29, when Wilson visited his New York headquarters to confer with his campaign managers, Palmer called for a showdown. McAdoo, Palmer, Daniels, Henry Morgenthau, Sr., and Charles R. Crane discussed whether Wilson should visit Maine or Pennsylvania in the time still unscheduled. Maine voters went to the polls in September and a good showing there would boost party morale throughout the country. "There was considerable opposition in the committee to his going to Pennsylvania," Daniels recalled, "but A. Mitchell Palmer would not take no." Palmer maintained that it was possible for Wilson to carry the state and that his appearance there would help elect a number of Democratic congressmen. Reminding Wilson of the political debt he owed Pennsylvania's Democrats, Palmer finally carried the day.[44]

Wilson made three campaign trips to the Keystone state. On September 23, he traveled to Scranton to open the state Democratic campaign. Palmer saw to it that the route from Trenton to Scranton ran through the twenty-sixth Pennsylvania district. "Crowds greeted Wilson enthusiastically as he traveled towards Scranton," the New York *Times* reported. "But the reception that outdistanced all the others was at Stroudsburg." Despite a hard rain, some 4,000 people crowded around Wilson's railroad car, trying to shake the candidate's hand. Wilson performed the customary political amenity of blessing the local congressmen.

Out of the crowd and onto the rear platform of Gov. Wilson's car, A. Mitchell Palmer the young Pennsylvania leader, stepped into the arms of Gov. Wilson. "I want to tell you people confidentially," said Gov. Wilson, smiling as he patted the bulky Pennsylvania leader on the back, "that I don't see how your district could have a better Representative in Congress than Palmer. And for that matter, I don't think any Congressional district in the U. S. has a better one." This set the crowd yelling.[45]

At Scranton, Wilson delivered a hard-hitting address to 10,000 people jammed into the city's largest auditorium. Although warned to avoid discussing the protective tariff in Pennsylvania, where "even the Democrats loved it," Wilson devoted much of his speech to an attack upon protection.[46] Both Wilson and Palmer believed deeply that lower tariffs would benefit the great majority of the American people. Palmer knew that many more Pennsylvanians would have to be convinced of this fact before the Democrats could capture the state, and his opinion doubtless affected the subject selected for Wilson's Scranton address.

In mid-October, Wilson made two speeches in Pittsburgh. Later in the month, Palmer arranged a trip through southeastern Pennsylvania, with stops at West Chester and Media, and two important speeches in Philadelphia. The first of the Philadelphia addresses, delivered before an audience of progressive Republicans, Wilson dedicated to "This great middle class . . . [which] is being crushed between the upper and nether millstones" (organized capital and organized labor). After what has been called his "greatest campaign address," Wilson went to Philadelphia's Convention Hall, where he spoke before 15,000 cheering Democrats.[47]

Even more important to Palmer than bringing Wilson into the state was his own apparent success in patching up the feuds that divided Pennsylvania's Democrats. In an address before the Democratic state committee on July 17, Palmer applauded the new party harmony he professed to see. It was harmony "of the right kind," he declared, "coming as it does, from the acquiescence of the minority to the majority." The old guard may have felt that Palmer was rubbing salt rather than salve on their wounds; but all factions united in support of Palmer's climactic declaration: "I believe that we can carry Pennsylvania this year." Palmer's speech, the old guard Philadelphia *Record* observed, "wildly enthused the committeemen," and the *Rec-*

ord's politically active editor, John P. Dwyer, scenting victory
and national patronage, announced on July 19 that "factional
strife among our fellow Democrats has been ended." [48]

Palmer intended to leave his campaign for reelection to
Congress in the hands of local supporters, while he fulfilled his
obligations to the veranda committee and worked to win Pennsylvania for Wilson.[49] However, he was startled to discover that
his new national prominence and past services to his constituents were not enough to ensure his reelection. His opponent,
Francis A. March, Jr., was an attractive and capable candidate,
nominated by both the Republicans and Theodore Roosevelt's
Progressive Party, called the Washington Party in Pennsylvania.
March, a professor of political science at Lehigh University,
had served a highly successful term as mayor of Easton.

By mid-October Palmer was not only campaigning hard but
also vehemently attacking his opponent. He concentrated on
March's greatest advantage, his affiliation with both the Republicans and the Progressives. Accepting these nominations,
Palmer declared, was like riding two horses moving in opposite
directions. Did March adhere to Progressive party ideals or
to the principles of Boies Penrose's Republican party? When
March did not reply, Palmer accused him of hypocrisy and
opportunism.[50]

March retained an unusual degree of detachment from the
contest. At times he seemed amused and almost fascinated by
Palmer. In a major speech in Easton, he acknowledged: "I
really have a great deal of admiration for his [Palmer's] delight-
ful personal character and of respect for his eminent abilities.
. . . Mr. Palmer's eloquence is so great, his emphatic manner so
convincing, that as I listened some time ago to his denunciation
of me as a 'political acrobat' I really felt as if I were quite a
criminal, and was afraid to look the next policeman I met in
the face." [51]

To encourage his party workers, Palmer predicted that Wilson would win Pennsylvania by 100,000 votes.[52] But Pennsylvania's voters were not yet ready to subordinate their devotion
to the protective tariff. Furthermore, Roosevelt was a hero in
Pennsylvania, one of the most popular political figures ever to

campaign in the state. Everywhere he drew enormous, enthusiastic crowds. Fortunately for Palmer, Roosevelt's plurality was held to less than 50,000 votes; Democratic excuses, therefore, sounded plausible, and the state party's hopes remained alive for another two years. Wilson obtained more votes in Pennsylvania than Taft—the first time a Democratic Presidential candidate had outdrawn a Republican since James Buchanan's day. However, Roosevelt almost carried Northampton and Carbon counties, where the mining and manufacturing workers in Palmer's district were concentrated. Pennsylvania manufacturers might no longer need protection, but Pennsylvania workers were reluctant to take a chance.[53] Palmer was reelected to a third term in Congress by the surprisingly small margin of 18,201 to 14,451. In the previous election he had won twice as many votes as his opponent.[54]

Palmer apparently already realized that, for a time at least, he had reached the limits of his political power. In Congress he found his path upward blocked by a handful of seasoned southern and western representatives who monopolized the most important official positions. Many years would have to elapse before Palmer could become Speaker, or party leader, or chairman of an important committee. In national politics the outlook was dim for a Democrat in what seemed to be a permanently Republican state.

A place in Wilson's Cabinet, Palmer decided, would be an ideal solution to his political problems. From there he could build up a national following that might put him in the White House. He might even gain enough of a reputation to win a statewide election in Pennsylvania for governor or senator despite his opposition to protection.

It seemed likely, after the 1912 election, that the Attorney-General would be the most prominent if not the most important official in the new Cabinet. The chief election issue had been the control of giant corporations, and Wilson's program called for more vigorous prosecution under a strengthened anti-trust act. Responsibility for the execution of this program would rest with the Attorney-General. The position, Palmer decided, suited his talents and experience. Furthermore, the job of

Attorney-General seemed no more than a fair reward for his important part in making Wilson President and for his sacrifices at the convention, Palmer, of course, said nothing to Wilson. A reporter who asked the President-elect whether anyone had yet applied for a Cabinet position, was told grimly: "No one has yet committed that indiscretion." [55]

Unfortunately for Palmer, Wilson did not award the choicest prizes to those whose backing had come early, remained steady, and done most to make him President. He regarded support for his candidacy as the duty of all Democrats who had the welfare of their party and their country at heart. After the election, Wilson brushed off McCombs with the assertion that he owed his campaign manager nothing, allegedly stating: "God ordained that I should be the next President of the United States." [56] House and Tumulty had to convince Wilson that he should receive postelection visits from some of his leading campaign managers, Palmer among them.[57] Wilson thought of himself as a prime minister, seeking capable men to represent the various interests within the party rather than as a dispenser of rewards for personal service. He made a conscious effort to discount party work in selecting Cabinet officers, although he was finally forced to make a number of important appointments for primarily political reasons.[58]

For several months, the President-elect, with assistance from Colonel House, carefully deliberated the composition of his Cabinet. No announcements of appointments were made; Wilson repeatedly denied that any decisions had been reached.[59] On January 2, Wilson asked Burleson and Palmer to meet him in Trenton four days later.[60] These two men, heads of the delegations which contributed most to Wilson's nomination, may well have assumed they were in line for Cabinet posts. Actually, Wilson wanted to see neither man, but had been convinced by House and Tumulty that out of courtesy he ought to interview a few of the party leaders who helped run his campaign.[61] When they met, the three men discussed little more than the coming special session of Congress, especially the tariff bill, the chief reason for convening the legislators.[62]

Two weeks before, Wilson had told newsmen: "I have a

general principle that those who apply are least likely to be appointed" [63]; so Palmer avoided discussing his hopes. Made anxious by Wilson's failure to mention the cabinet, he interpreted his host's customary aloofness as hostility. He suspected that Wilson had heard McCombs' version of the efforts to make the Pennsylvanian a compromise choice at the convention.[64] According to McCombs, Palmer had wavered when the offer was made, and the national chairman hinted that Palmer solicited the proposal.[65]

Palmer stayed behind when Burleson left the meeting with Wilson, in an effort to clear up all misunderstandings and, if possible, to draw a hint about a place in the Cabinet. Finally, he departed, unsatisfied and despondent.[66] When reporters asked him to tell them what he knew about Wilson's plans, Palmer replied: "Tell you what I know? I am reminded of what a prominent statesman in Washington said after an interview with Governor Wilson. He said. 'If I were to tell you everything I know—everything, mind you, and nothing held back—they would set me down as an ignoramus.' " [67]

Despite his fears, Palmer was still very much in the running for appointment as Attorney-General. Wilson first thought of Louis F. Brandeis for the post, but Brandeis had made a host of powerful enemies; then House suggested New York attorney James C. McReynolds.[68] Soon, however, Palmer spread word of his availability, and House was bombarded with recommendations from eminent Democrats in support of the Pennsylvanian. McAdoo told House that Palmer certainly was better suited for the job than McReynolds. Senator Thomas Gore of Oklahoma also expressed approval of Palmer's nomination; Tumulty warned Wilson that if he left Palmer and Burleson out of his Cabinet, the old charges of ingratitude would be revived. Burleson assured House that Palmer had never flickered before turning down the proposal made to him at Baltimore; he asked the Colonel to pass this information along to the President-elect and House agreed.[69] Two weeks after his meeting with Wilson, Palmer became the leading candidate.[70]

In opposition to Palmer's nomination, Oscar Underwood asked Wilson not to remove such a capable administration man from the House; he depended upon Palmer, he said, as his "right arm." [71] For a week Wilson shared Underwood's opinion: Palmer would be most valuable to him in Congress. As a member of Wilson's projected "Congressional Cabinet," Palmer would be among those to meet frequently with the President to plan legislative campaigns. Then House suggested that the best way to increase the administration's influence in Congress was to put Palmer and Burleson, who had the respect of their colleagues, in the Cabinet; again Wilson changed his mind.[72]

On January 24, 1913, Wilson and House decided on Palmer for Attorney-General.[73] When Bryan was informed, he strongly opposed the choice, and House sent the Nebraskan's opinion to Wilson without comment.[74] Nevertheless, Palmer's name was included on the list of appointments House and Wilson drew up on February 14, at which time House considered the Cabinet "fairly definitely determined." [75] Wilson agreed to House's request that he name McReynolds Solicitor General, provided Palmer was willing. News of Palmer's impending appointment was so widespread that on February 15, Governor Charles R. Miller of Delaware introduced him to the Swarthmore Alumni Club of Philadelphia as "the next Attorney-General." [76]

Two weeks before the inauguration McReynolds informed his friend House that Palmer was unfit to be Attorney-General. First, Palmer had no experience as an administrator, or in the Justice Department. (McReynolds had served as an Assistant Attorney-General under Theodore Roosevelt.) More important, Palmer's law office still acted as counsel for the Lackawanna Railroad, then being prosecuted by the government for violations of the Sherman Act. Palmer also represented the Lehigh Coal and Navigation Company, scheduled to be indicted under the Sherman law within a week. Both cases would be tried by the next Attorney-General. In addition, McReynolds pointed out that Palmer had been charged on the House floor with soliciting and receiving campaign assistance from officials of the Lackawanna road. He related—accurately—that "Palmer's reply hardly met the direct charge." [77]

House asked McReynolds to prepare a written statement of these facts, and the same day told Wilson what had been uncovered. Wilson, who intended to open his administration on the highest possible moral tone, was "distressed" when he heard of Palmer's railroad connections, and said that it might "necessitate a rearrangement." [78] Palmer never had a chance to explain that he was only one of a multitude of local attorneys who represented the roads—they retained one in each county through which they ran. House took advantage of the opportunity to press his own man on Wilson, and McReynolds, although almost completely unknown to Wilson, received the appointment.[79]

About a week before the inauguration, Palmer was called to a meeting with Wilson, Tumulty, House, and Senator William Hughes of New Jersey, and was asked to be Secretary of War. Still bitterly disappointed at being passed over in favor of a man who had played no part in Wilson's election and whose qualifications were not especially imposing, Palmer turned down the offer, explaining that the post was incompatible with his religious beliefs. Tumulty and Hughes asked him to reconsider, maintaining that he would be occupied primarily with the legal aspects of the Philippine problem. Palmer agreed to withhold his final decision for a few days.[80]

Two days later, Palmer sent Wilson his regrets. He deeply appreciated the great honor done him, but his decision was final:

The more I think of it, the more impossible it becomes. I am a Quaker. As a Quaker War Secretary, I should consider myself a living illustration of a horrible incongruity. . . . In case our country should come to armed conflict with any other, I would go as far as any man in her defense; but I cannot, without violating every tradition of my people and going against every instinct of my nature, planted there by heredity, environment and training, sit down in cold blood in an executive position and use such talents as I possess to the work of preparing for such a conflict.[81]

Wilson apparently was touched by Palmer's show of idealism and perhaps embarrassed by the fact that he had not known that Palmer was a Quaker.[82]

"My Dear Friend," he replied, "Of course I understand, sorry as I am and disappointed that I shall not have the pleasure, as well as the benefit of being associated with you constantly in my immediate counsel, I understand perfectly and thank you with all my heart for your letter of yesterday. We shall have many talks over these things when I get to Washington." [83]

Colonel House, supersensitive to his associates' feelings and motives, completely discounted the pious reasons Palmer gave for his refusal. He wrote that Palmer was "visibly disappointed" when offered the War Department job: "His view is rather narrow and selfish. He wants to be Attorney-General in order to advance his own fortunes as he thinks it would be possible for him to obtain a lucrative practice after four years of service under the Government." [84] Possibly Palmer, called upon to explain his obvious disappointment, mentioned the law practice he might have obtained as a reason for his dejection. Somehow he fooled House. Palmer wanted wealth, but he wanted political power and prestige even more. Later, he willingly gave up a legal practice that brought him an annual six-figure income to take the job of Alien Property Custodian. Palmer wanted most of all to be President, and the Attorney-General's office provided an excellent stepping stone. He wished to be accorded the highest respect, and the position of Attorney-General would have brought both eminence and power. On the other hand, Palmer's religion cannot be discounted in explaining his refusal of the War Department portfolio. He was not especially devout, but his wife was; and more than forty-five years later, a close friend remembered the shock and dismay she and other Quakers had expressed upon hearing that a Friend had been offered the post of Secretary of War.[85]

Without a Cabinet position, Palmer was obliged to obtain higher office in a statewide election. In two years, Pennsylvania would elect a governor and a senator; meanwhile, Palmer's task was to make a record in Congress which would be satisfactory to both the national Democratic Party and the voters of Pennsylvania, an almost impossible undertaking.

CHAPTER V

THE CONGRESS OF ACHIEVEMENT

Few astute observers of American politics believed, early in the "progressive era," that the Democratic Party could carry out the political, social and economic reforms America badly needed. Herbert Croly, seer of the progressive movement, expressed a common sentiment in 1910 when he described the Democratic Party as impotent. It was indicative of this helplessness, Croly declared: "that the effective opposition to the traditional Republican policy has gradually developed within the ranks of the Republican party itself." [1]

Yet, when the battles of the progressive era were over and the results of the reform movement were appraised, it became evident that most of the reform legislation demanded by men like Croly had been passed by a Democratic Congress and approved by a Democratic President. A year and a half after Wilson took office, the *Nation*, previously sceptical of Democratic abilities and accomplishments, applauded the achievements of the first Wilsonian Congress: "The old cry that the Republican party is the only one fit to govern the country . . . will not be heard this year, or if heard, will provoke only a smile." [2]

Croly mistakenly based his conclusions about the party on its established leadership rather than upon the large, expanding group of young Democrats who in 1910 had not yet attained positions of national importance. "The generation that went Progressive was the generation that came of age in the nineties," [3] and many of the most politically active men in that generation, for a variety of economic, social, and sectional reasons, found their way into the Democratic Party. The progressive revolt within the Republican Party, which reached a climax with

Roosevelt's bolt in 1912, had its less noticed counterpart among the Democrats. When Croly's views of the party were printed in 1910, conservative Democratic state regimes throughout the country were on the brink of downfall. Even Tammany chieftain Charles Murphy would soon be forced to agree to the nominations of progressive Democrats for governor and senator.

In Congress, the complexion of the Democratic Party, heretofore predominantly southern, rural, and populist, shifted in the direction of northern, urban progressivism as scores of young Democrats entered Congress on the reform tide of 1910–12. In 1912, fifty-nine first-term Democrats were elected to the House from the eight densely populated northern states of Massachusetts, Connecticut, New York, New Jersey, Pennsylvania, Ohio, Indiana, and Illinois. These states alone elected 118 (over 40 percent) of the 290 Democrats in the Sixty-third House.[4]

Most of the new northern members proved eager to vote for social-welfare legislation, Daniel J. McGillicuddy, first elected from Maine in 1910, sponsored a bill establishing the first nationwide workmen's compensation system for federal employees. Raymond B. Stevens, who defeated an incumbent arch-conservative New Hampshire Republican in 1912, introduced legislation that set up the Federal Trade Commission. Edward Keating of Colorado, Robert Crosser of Ohio, and Warren Worth Bailey of Pennsylvania, all elected for the first time in 1912, advocated Henry George's single tax.[5] The New York *Evening Post* declared that eleven Democratic members of the Sixty-third House carried union cards, and scores of other Democratic representatives were considered friends of labor.[6]

Early in 1913, the New York *Times* and the *World* reported that a revolt among northern Democrats against southern domination of major committees was "under full headway":

During the long period in which the Republicans controlled the House there were very few northern Democrats in its membership. In the Sixty-third Congress . . . the northern Democrats will outnumber the southern ones, and they do not view with pleasure the prospect of having to content themselves with places in the rear.[7]

According to the *Times,* the rebels intended to organize themselves much as the Republican insurgents had done in their battle against Speaker Cannon and the Republican old guard in the
House: "The northern rebels are planning to start the fight in
a caucus to be held in the beginning of the extra session." [8]

Even before the 1912 election, signs of dissention had appeared. Representative J. Henry Goeke of Ohio complained to
Wilson in August, 1912, that Palmer, Burleson, and McGillicuddy were meeting secretly, planning a purge of anti-Wilson
congressmen. Allegedly, their primary objective was to replace
Champ Clark with a Speaker more friendly to Wilson's legislative objectives. Goeke named as his informants "members
from Texas, Arkansas and Missouri." [9]

By mid-January, 1913, Wilson had decided that he must
cooperate with the established Democratic leaders if his program was to pass Congress. Revolt, either by northern progressives or southern agrarian populists was discouraged.[10] In an effort to appease northerners, House leaders named Palmer as
chairman of the party caucus. The *World* observed, "For many
months the northern Democrats have been anxious to have one
of their number made [chairman] of the caucus. . . . The elevation of Mr. Palmer . . . is calculated to satisfy all factions
. . . and to restore complete harmony." [11] Because of the huge
Democratic majority, the fate of most legislation would be decided in caucus. The choice of Palmer assured northern progressives of a chance to speak and a fair vote, for his legislative
aims were the same as theirs. At the same time, veteran party
leaders knew that Palmer would not assist an attempt to overthrow their leadership, but would exert his influence to encourage unity. Administration supporters from all factions, remembering Palmer's skillful performance at the Baltimore
convention, were satisfied that the caucus chairmanship would
be in dependable hands.

On March 6, 1913, the Democratic caucus of the Sixty-third
House held its first meeting. It remained in session for six
hours so that every member could have his say. The possibility
of major committee assignments dawned for new congressmen

with the adoption of a resolution barring members of the eleven most important committees from sitting on other committees.[12] Wilson's desire for harmony among House Democrats dominated the meeting. Palmer was elected chairman, and Clark, nominated by Palmer, was named candidate for Speaker. Democrats agreed to be bound by all caucus decisions unless a member notified the majority leader that he would be violating a campaign promise to his constituents.[13]

A month after the opening of Congress, Palmer joined Democratic extremists in a move to open the party caucus to the public; he gave notice of his alignment henceforth with the most progressive wing of the party. Democratic leaders Underwood, Fitzgerald, and Swager Sherley of Kentucky vigorously opposed the plan. They pointed out that representatives were expected to side with the party majority on the floor of the House regardless of personal opinions. Only in the caucus could party members express diverse opinions and vote freely. If the public was admitted to caucus meetings such free expression would be inhibited; or else party solidarity on the floor might be destroyed by members ignoring caucus decisions rather than reverse views they had expressed in public. The proposal to open the caucus doors was tabled by a vote of 167 to 84.[14]

Wilson placed tariff reduction first in his administration's program. Democratic arguments that the tariff was a protector of privilege had played a crucial role in the party's return to power. Many Americans believed that the tariff was connected to the odious corruption beneath the surface of American life revealed by muckraking writers; tariff-making, according to contemporary critics, resembled the deals between city councilmen and local paving combines described by Lincoln Steffens. When the Republicans reneged on their 1908 promise of tariff reform, they stigmatized their party and thereby contributed enormously to Democratic triumphs in 1910 and 1912.[15]

The rapidly rising cost of living also heightened the tariff's importance as a political issue. Wholesale prices in 1912 were about 50 percent higher than in 1896. Democrats charged that greedy producers were able to raise prices because of the absence of foreign competition.[16]

Unfortunately for Palmer, nowhere in the country did arguments against protection produce less effect than in Pennsylvania. Palmer knew early in 1913 that in a year and a half he would run for office in a statewide election. At the opening of the Sixty-third Congress, therefore, he had to decide whether to appeal to the voters of his state by working for tariff compromise, or to help redeem his party's pledge of sharply lower rates. Disaffected, at least temporarily, by the Attorney-General debacle, Palmer did not feel bound by strong feelings of loyalty to the President. When Burleson told him that Wilson and House wanted his advice about an appointment, Palmer replied that his opinion was of no importance: "I am not one of the cards in the game, but one of the discards." [17]

Nevertheless, Palmer chose adherence to the ideals he had expressed since the beginning of his political career. He could be sure that Democratic leaders would appreciate his loyalty; but he could only hope that the breeze of reform fervor then swirling around the country would affect Pennsylvanians enough to make the Wilsonian policies palatable, if not popular in the Keystone State. Once Palmer decided in favor of lower tariffs, he led the fight—as was his wont—for that policy. He wrote Schedule C, which greatly reduced duties on most metals and metal products and placed many metals on the free list. He also helped prepare and push through the rest of the relatively low Underwood tariff bill, despite complaints from virtually every important Pennsylvania mining and manufacturing industry.

Palmer had no illusions about the political risk he ran. During hearings on the metals schedule, he frequently was warned of the effect that tariff reductions would have upon the fortunes of Pennsylvania workingmen. Early in the hearings, he engaged in a revealing exchange with John A. Topping, president of Republic Iron and Steel, one of the largest steel producers. Palmer first voiced the standard Democratic dogma that lower tariffs would adversely affect only the swollen profits of American manufacturers. Industrialists would be forced to reduce prices in order to meet the new foreign competition. Once made, however, these price reductions would prevent imports from rising; domestic production, employment, and wage rates would be unaffected.

Topping countered with the favorite doctrine of Pennsylvania protectionists: labor and not capital, he asserted, would pay for tariff reduction:

Mr. Topping: Our experience has been that when we cannot meet competition our first effort to convince labor that we cannot meet competition is to shut down. When you shut down and they get hungry they are anxious to make any terms that are satisfactory to you.

Mr. Palmer: What is your idea in convincing labor that you cannot meet competition? Do you want them to be against this tariff reduction?

Mr. Topping: I do not.

Mr. Palmer: You have no thought that you will have to do anything of that kind if this bill should become a law?

Mr. Topping: I think it will have a very serious disturbing effect. . . . But even if the experience will be expensive to us we believe it will result in a reaction that will create conditions later that will justify the expense that this bill may cost us if you put it through.

Mr. Palmer: You do not mean by that that labor is going to be taught a lesson by the steel manufacturers.

Mr. Topping: I do not. . . . I think there will be an object lesson. I think that the school of experience will be worth the cost, and I also think it is an unfortunate thing for labor, who must bear the brunt of it.[18]

After Topping's testimony, numerous witnesses and written protests warned Palmer of the terrible consequences in store for the workers of his district if the metal, chemical, or cement rates were appreciably lowered. A letter from the Baker and Adamson Chemical Company of Easton insisted that an advance in duty was needed for the types of chemicals produced by the firm.[19] A representative of the American Association of Portland Cement Manufacturers, aware that the largest cement mill in the world was in Palmer's district, alerted the

Committee that a drastic drop in employment in cement mills would follow reduction of tariff rates on that product.[20] The C. K. Williams Company of Easton submitted a brief, addressed to Palmer, reminding him that the mineral filler industry was an important one in his district and that it already was subject to strong foreign competition.[21] A memorial from the Glassworkers' Union of Philadelphia protested that lower protection meant reduced wages for its members.[22] Charles M. Schwab sent Palmer a final warning: "The inevitable result of tariff reduction would be lower wages and loss of employment to thousands of workmen, upon whom are dependent several millions of the population of the country." [23]

Apparently unimpressed by such dismal predictions, the Ways and Means Committee prepared a tariff bill which reduced rates in almost every classification. The schedule written by Palmer placed most forms of iron and steel and their products on the free list.[24]

By the time Wilson called Congress into special session to commence April 7, he already had a final draft of the committee's work. The President was not altogether satisfied. He felt that undue concessions had been made to wool, sugar, shoe, and agricultural interests, and he threatened to veto the entire measure unless these schedules were further reduced. The Ways and Means Committee immediately submitted to the President's wishes.[25] When he agreed to put wool on the free list, Palmer gave up his chief attempt to pacify protectionists within his district and state. He did not join a move in caucus to restore the wool duty.[26] His success in the 1914 elections would now depend largely upon continued prosperity, full employment, and the rapid reeducation of Pennsylvania protectionists.

Pressure from Wilson and whole-hearted support from the House leadership propelled the Underwood tariff bill through the Ways and Means Committee and won it a huge majority in the Democratic caucus.[27] To compensate for revenue lost through lower imports the Committee added a graduated income tax to the bill. When the measure reached the House floor it was suggested that the tax be applied to all income over

$1,000, rather than over $4,000, as the Committee had provided. Palmer replied: "The present consumption taxes bear most heavily upon the poor; it is right that the income tax should bear most heavily upon the rich." [28] Proud of the committee's handiwork, Palmer declared: "On the whole it is the best tariff law ever written." [29] These words were to plague him in 1914, when he tried to win the votes of Pennsylvanians who blamed the Underwood tariff for a good share of the state's economic difficulties.

Despite his disillusionment with Wilson, Palmer became one of the administration's leaders in Congress; he probably was closer to the President than any other representative. In part, this was because of Palmer's high place in the party organization, which obliged Wilson to deal with him on a variety of small matters. In June, 1913, the Democratic national committee appointed a five-man executive committee to supervise the party organization, raise funds, and conduct a national educational campaign. Previously, this work had been largely ignored between annual meetings of the full national committee. Palmer, appointed chairman of the new organization, represented the committee in directing the flow of patronage from the administration.[30]

Possessing an abundance of political knowhow, Palmer often made himself invaluable to Wilson. For example, his political insight spared Wilson a potentially damaging battle over the number of terms a President should be allowed. The Democratic platform in 1912 contained a plank, probably written by Bryan, demanding that the President be allowed to serve only one term. Mindful of the strong possibility that he would desire a second term in 1916, Wilson decided it was morally and politically necessary to repudiate the plank before the start of his administration. According to Palmer, Wilson wanted to renounce the one-term plank in his speech of acceptance to the Baltimore convention, but "some of us talked him out of it." [31]

On February 3, 1913, when the issue could no longer cost Wilson votes, Palmer wrote the President requesting his views about the single-term amendment which had just passed the Senate and seemed certain to pass the House. In a long letter, Wilson replied that the only limitation on Presidential terms should be that of the people's will. Voters would or would not elect the President to a second term, as they chose. Wilson proposed to publish this letter, and he asked Palmer's opinion.[32] Palmer quickly advised against immediate publication: he would stop the one-term resolution and yet avoid public controversy by showing Wilson's letter to as few people as possible —perhaps only to Representative Henry Clayton of Alabama, Chairman of the House Judiciary Committee, then considering the resolution. Palmer reminded the President that Bryan was responsible for the inclusion of the plank and had made much of it during the campaign. He assured Wilson, however, that the Nebraskan's opinion need not be a permanent obstacle:

My guess is that if you could get past the special session of Congress with a real democratic tariff law on the statute books, and monetary and anti-trust legislation on the way, I would have little fear of the result of a difference of opinion upon the matter between yourself and Mr. Bryan. The country would unquestionably sustain you.[33]

Palmer quietly used Wilson's letter to stifle the single-term resolution in the House Judiciary Committee.[32] Bryan made no objection while a member of the administration,[33] and when he left the Cabinet, other means were found of keeping the issue still.[36]

Early in 1914, the President again required Palmer's assistance in a delicate matter. Protests from English diplomats and advice from American experts on foreign policy convinced Wilson that exempting domestic coastwise shipping from payment of Panama Canal tolls was contrary to the provisions of the Hay-Pauncefote treaty, and that the exemption provision in the Canal Act ought to be repealed. The Democratic platform, however, had declared in favor of exemption, and Wilson and other leading party members had approved the declaration during the campaign. Wilson's new stand was an unpopular one in many parts of the country. Especially opposed were shippers and shipping interests, many nationalists, and several varieties of anglophobes, especially Irish-Americans. Influential Democratic congressmen felt they had little to gain and much to lose politically by backing the President's position.[37]

Palmer and other Democratic representatives upon whom Wilson relied to lead his fight, especially William C. Adamson of Georgia and Swagar Sherley of Kentucky, were called to the White House to discuss plans for accomplishing the repeal.[38] They informed Wilson that opposition within the party was so strong that only through personal intervention could he get what he wanted. As a consequence, the President decided to visit the Capitol again, and on March 5 he addressed a joint session of Congress, making a strong plea for repeal of the toll exemption. Four days later, Representative Thetus W. Sims of Tennessee introduced a bill for repeal.

Debate on Sims' measure began March 26. Democratic leaders Clark, Underwood, Kitchin, and Fitzgerald had already declared their opposition to the bill. Interest in the debate ran so high that the Senate adjourned for lack of a quorum—too many of its members were spectators in the House.[39] Burleson, McAdoo, Tumulty, and Vice-President Marshall, as well as loyal administration leaders in Congress, especially Henry, Adamson, Sherley, and Palmer, brought maximum pressure to bear on wavering Democratic representatives.[40] Although Adamson was administration leader on the floor, Palmer was considered liaison man with the White House and "the real spokesman for the President." [41]

Underwood made an effective attack upon the Sims bill the day after debate began. "The Democratic party, not I," he argued, "wrote this provision as to free tolls in its platform." Those Democrats who voted against repeal would be voting to sustain their platform.[42] Palmer replied, delivering an extemporaneous criticism of Underwood before reading a prepared speech in favor of repeal. It was the first time, he reminded the House, that he had differed in Congress with the man he proudly called "my leader upon this floor." He was "unaffectedly embarrassed" at having to reply to Underwood. However, in this crisis in the party's history, when the new administration's prestige would be severely damaged if the Sims bill was defeated, the congressional leader had forsaken his party. Underwood had forgotten the principle he had taught so many others: the principle of loyalty to the party majority. The House leader had even attacked the President. Not directly, Palmer acknowledged, but "by shadowy innuendo and intimation." Underwood, he declared, reminded him of one of his Quaker ancestors who, bitten by a dog, told the animal:

"If I were not a Quaker, and if I did not believe in peace and gentleness, I would kill thee; but since I do believe in these things and cannot be rude or cruel; I will simply call thee a bad name." So he went down the street shouting "Mad dog!" and other persons, without his sweetness of disposition and kindliness of character, attended to the dog.[43]

House Democrats chose to follow the President, and the Sims bill passed on March 31 by a vote of 247 to 162.[44]

Wilson enjoyed a long honeymoon with the Sixty-third House. For a year and a half, Democratic congressmen gave large majorities to all measures backed by the administration, and important legislation was shaped to suit Wilson's desires. In mid-1914, the President felt that his major objectives had been achieved. Tariff walls had been lowered, the banking and currency system reformed, and by early August, the Federal Trade Commission bill had passed the Senate and was about to be accepted by the House.

Yet, while the Wilson administration could boast of important economic reforms, the question of social justice for large masses of the people remained largely ignored. In his inaugural address Wilson had spoken of perfecting the "means by which government may be put at the service of humanity in safeguarding . . . the health of its men and its women and its children." The people, he insisted, must be "shielded in their lives, their very vitality, from the consequences of great industrial and social processes which they cannot alter, control or singly cope with." [45]

Attempts to translate these humanitarian sentiments into legislation, however, received scant support from the President.

After the first great rush of New Freedom legislation passed, advanced progressives within the Democratic Party in Congress began to respond to the clamor of social reformers for laws protecting women and children and extending the rights of laborers. But when public pressure for social-welfare legislation was strongest, and when Congress contained more members favorable to such measures than ever before, Wilson showed little interest. Although aware that new legislation was needed, the President never decided upon specific measures. He reacted to most social welfare proposals by protesting that under the Constitution such laws could be passed only by the states.

Wilson believed in 1914 that his program had been carried out and that no more federal reform measures were necessary. He wrote in October, 1914, "The reconstruction legislation which for the last two decades the opinion of the country has demanded . . . has now been enacted. That programme is practically completed." He told McAdoo that when the Democrats came to power in 1912 there were "real wrongs which cried out to be righted. . . . The legislation of the past year and a half has in a very large measure done away with these things." [46]

Palmer was one of those who did not agree with the President. He introduced two major social reform measures in 1914, neither of which became law, chiefly because the President would do nothing to help them. The first of these was a woman-suffrage amendment to the Constitution, the second a child-labor law.

Wilson was put under great pressure to declare himself in favor of national woman-suffrage legislation. He received visits from a series of suffrage delegations, including a group of four hundred working women who insisted the vote was the only way they could win fair economic treatment. All were put off, however, at first with equivocation, later with declarations in favor of states' rights.[47] The House Democratic caucus also shunted the issue aside by resolving overwhelmingly in February, 1914, that woman suffrage was a matter for the states, not the national government to decide. According to the New

York *Times*, "practically all the Democratic leaders" took this view. "Among them were Speaker Clark, Mr. Underwood and A. Mitchell Palmer of Pennsylvania, Chairman of the caucus."[48]

Only two months later, however, Palmer introduced a resolution which, if passed, would have offered a woman-suffrage amendment to the states for ratification.[49] Palmer's sudden espousal of female rights, despite the opposition of Wilson and party leaders, may be partially explained by his decision to go before the Pennsylvania electorate in November as the image of progressivism. Palmer hoped that his record as a reformer would outweigh his tariff views among a considerable number of Pennsylvania protectionists. His probable opponent, the incumbent Boies Penrose, was a rabid protectionist, and an arch-conservative.

Palmer may also have been under pressure from his wife and Quaker friends. He called his wife a "born suffragist" because of her Quaker ideals of equality of the sexes.[50] Whether his own principles or his wife's ideals or both moved Palmer to sponsor legislation for women's rights, he made the most of the issue politically. In a speech about woman suffrage delivered during the fall campaign, he declared, "I shall stand upon the side where my mother would have had me stand. . . . Every instinct of my nature, planted there by heredity, education and training requires that I shall do it. I am a Quaker. My people came here with William Penn. Quakers have been the pioneers in every movement which has guaranteed to women equal rights with men." [51]

Heredity, education, and training must have been slow to work upon Palmer, however, for according to his Swarthmore classmates, young Palmer was hardly enthusiastic about equal rights for women. Hannah Clothier, later an active suffragette, told in her senior class prophecy of a vision in which she saw an account of Palmer's later career. She found good news: "The study of law had apparently broadened the mind and somewhat changed the views of our honored [class] president, for he had become very actively engaged in lecturing upon the great importance of 'Higher Education for Women.' " [52] Not until pushed into the race against Penrose in 1914 did Palmer suddenly become an advocate of female voting.

Palmer's woman-suffrage bill never got past the House Judiciary Committee, which decided to report instead a suffrage resolution introduced by Representative Franklin W. Mondell of Wyoming. On the House floor, Mondell's measure suffered attacks by leading congressmen of both parties, including Majority Leader Underwood, as an invasion of states' rights.[53] Representative Carl Hayden of Arizona suggested that states' rights could be protected and the cause of women's suffrage advanced if Palmer's bill were substituted for Mondell's. Palmer's version, Hayden pointed out, would not impose woman suffrage on any state that did not want it. Eight percent of a state's voters would have to petition for a state-wide referendum, and a majority vote would then decide the question. Hayden reminded the House that a measure similar to Mondell's resolution had already been defeated in the Senate, while one based on the same principle as Palmer's had been favorably reported and was on the upper house's calendar.[54] Hayden's speech had no effect; Palmer's bill never reached the floor, and a majority voted against the Mondell resolution.[55]

Early in 1914, Palmer introduced a bill designed to end child labor in most American mines and factories, demonstrating emphatically that he could be counted among the most advanced progressives. The bill, making it a misdemeanor for a producer or dealer to put products of child labor into interstate commerce, has been called "the most momentous measure of the progressive era. . . . The champions and opponents of the Palmer bill . . . recognized the measure for what it actually was—the first step toward a potentially comprehensive national social and economic regulation under the commerce power." [56] Nowhere in the North was child labor legislation more bitterly opposed than in Pennsylvania. Less than a year before, Pennsylvania businessmen, especially coal, glass, and textile producers, and representatives of the Pennsylvania Manufacturers'

Association, had descended on Harrisburg and smothered a proposed state child-labor measure.[57]

Palmer's bill was primarily the work of Owen R. Lovejoy, Secretary of the National Child Labor Committee. Although the congressman helped word the bill so that it would be within the bounds of constitutionality, his primary responsibility was to guide it through Congress.[58] Lovejoy's effective organization had been responsible for the passage of dozens of state child-labor laws between 1904 and 1914. Officers and advisors of the committee included many of the leading reformers, religious leaders, editors and business men of the day.[59] Until 1914, the National Child Labor Committee attempted to allay the constitutional scruples of many Americans, including some of its members, by working for state action only.[60]

By 1913, however, the organization found its efforts stymied in many states legislatures. Strong and increasingly concerted opposition came from industrial interests, who complained that child-labor laws would put them at a disadvantage in competition with industry in states that allowed cheap child labor. By 1913, also, public opinion was more favorable to national social-welfare legislation. The committee's Board of Trustees changed its position. A bill was drafted by Lovejoy, who was advised by attorneys sympathetic with the organization's aims. On the advice of A. J. McKelway, the committee's contact man with Congress, Palmer was asked to present the measure and push it through the House. After editing Lovejoy's work somewhat, Palmer introduced the bill on January 26, 1914.[61]

Hearings on Palmer's bill opened before the House Committee on Labor on February 27. Palmer made a lengthy speech describing the terrible plight of child workers—there were almost two million of them in the country—and the inability or unwillingness of the states to end this exploitation. He assured the committee that Congress had the constitutional authority to enact the law he recommended. He then led a parade of witnesses before the sympathetic congressmen: social workers, educators, women's-club representatives, a lawyer to attest

further to the bill's constitutionality, and a union official to assure the committee of the AF of L's approval. The Labor Committee altered a few details in the measure, then gave it unanimous approval.[62]

Palmer finally brought the measure to the House floor on
February 15, 1915, where it set off a determined filibuster attempt by James F. Byrnes of South Carolina and other southern
congressmen. Palmer checked the attempt, with some aid from
Minority Leader James Mann, and the measure passed 233 to
43.[63] Southerners threatened another filibuster in the Senate,
where Palmer's bill was introduced by Robert L. Owen of Oklahoma. With the end of the Sixty-third Congress near and
other pressing business still at hand, Senate leaders did not
force a floor test.[64]

The bill's failure probably resulted more from Wilson's
antipathy than from southern threats. When McKelway and
Lovejoy asked the President to support Palmer's measure in
February, 1914, Wilson replied that in his opinion the bill was
unconstitutional and potentially dangerous; it would remove all
limitations upon regulation of the economy by the federal government. Wilson remained inert while the measure was stalled
in the Senate, and Democratic leaders, faced with the strong
possibility of a Presidential veto, were reluctant to push the bill
ahead of other important legislation.[65]

There is no clearer illustration of Wilson's dominant role
in the passage of his administration's legislative program than
the way in which he forced a child-labor bill through the Senate only a year after he allowed Palmer's measure to die. In
1916, as he planned his campaign for reelection, the President
was finally convinced that it was politically imperative to pass a
child-labor law. He went to the Senate and insisted that party
leaders take action. Owen's bill was promptly brought to the
floor and put to a vote. Only twelve Senators voted against it—
ten southerners, and Boies Penrose and George T. Oliver, Republicans from Pennsylvania.[66]

Penrose and Oliver's votes against the child-labor bill
pointed up the irony in Palmer's progressivism. His loyalty to

Wilson's program, his hard work on behalf of advanced reform measures, and the abilities he displayed made him a leader among progressives in the Democratic Party. But Palmer's career depended chiefly upon his popularity in Pennsylvania, and most Pennsylvanians believed that their prosperity was endangered by tariff reform and social-welfare legislation. The further Palmer went in the direction of progressive reform, the more votes he lost in Pennsylvania.

CHAPTER VI

THE "SIEGE OF PENROSE"

By 1914, most Pennsylvanians were aware that their state and many of their city governments were models of corrupt administration. In 1895, James Bryce had described the Pennsylvania legislature as "such a Witches' Sabbath of jobbing, bribing, thieving, and prostitution of legislative power to private interest as the world has seldom seen," and subsequent investigations showed, if anything, further deterioration. Early in the twentieth century the state became a happy hunting ground for muckraking journalists. Lincoln Steffens justifiably dubbed Philadelphia "Corrupt and Contented," and "the worst governed city in the country;" Pittsburgh was "A City Ashamed." [1]

One shocking scandal succeeded another in the late nineteenth and early twentieth centuries. Reform movements waxed and waned, but the Republican masters of Pennsylvania remained virtually unchallenged, except for occasional predatory raids on one another. Of the many reasons for public acquiescence to the long Republican domination, the most powerful was the protective tariff. "What if they do rob and plunder us," a Pennsylvania manufacturer defiantly told Steffens. "It can't hurt me unless they raise the tax rates, and even that won't ruin me. Our party keeps up the tariff. If they should reduce that, my business would be ruined." [2]

Ida Tarbell, a native Pennsylvanian, wrote in 1912 that her state's attachment to the Republican Party was due to the "training in selfishness which for sixty years her Congressmen have given her. Throughout this period, those who sought her suffrage have held up the promise of protecting taxes. Vote for us and we will take care of you." [3] Most Pennsylvania businessmen as well as the state's thousands of miners and factory workers, were convinced that their economic well-being depended upon the prosperity of the manufacturers. Pennsylvania's well-to-do farmers also believed that anything that harmed industry in the state would be detrimental to their own sales and prices.[4]

It was not unreasonable to argue in the middle, or even in the late nineteenth century, that growing Pennsylvania industries like coal, glass, petroleum, chemicals, and steel needed protection. Steel rail imports, for example, were 505,000 tons in 1871 despite a high tariff, while American output was only 692,000 tons. As late as the 1880's and 1890's, the United States sometimes imported as much as one-quarter of its steel requirements.[5] By the early twentieth century, however, Pennsylvania's most important industries no longer needed tariff protection. They undersold their foreign competition in this country and held their own abroad. High American tariffs only enabled manufacturers to raise prices when supplies were short, confident that they could still undersell highly taxed imports.[6]

Nevertheless, Republican politicians and newspapers continued to remind their audiences that the tariff had made Pennsylvania prosperous and would keep the state affluent so long as the voters returned high-tariff Republicans to office. As the 1914 campaign began, the Philadelphia *Press* asserted, "Republican supremacy at Washington has always meant the humming of the wheels and the spindles, the noise of the steady tread of industry. . . . Under other political supremacy the picture is reversed. This is not a coincidence, it is a fixed fact." Senator Penrose opened his fight for renomination with a warning: "Pennsylvania will suffer more than any other state from the Underwood tariff measure," and he continued with a plea for the "restoration of the Republican economic policies under which the country had such a long period of splendid prosperity."[7]

The Democrats also commanded effective issues in 1914. Foremost among these was the old charge of dishonesty in high places; and the charge hit home that year especially, for the

Republican senatorial candidate was Boies Penrose, known throughout the country as a symbol of corruption in government.

Nevertheless, Democrats knew from experience in the elections of 1908 and 1910 that it would take more than charges of graft, bribery, and fraud, no matter how well substantiated, to defeat their opponents. In 1906, a series of scandals involving financial misbehavior by Republican officials was capped by the disclosure that the new State Capitol, originally supposed to cost $4,000,000 had actually cost $13,000,000. Despite a number of suicides and some jail sentences for minor officials, Republican power was hardly disturbed.[8] Again in 1910, evidence of Republicans' misdeeds abounded and the party nominated a weak gubernatorial candidate; but the Democrats were unable to win. Palmer complained that whenever the people of Pennsylvania were asked to turn the Republican thieves out of office: "We are met always with the answer that the sacred cause of protection requires them to stand by the party of their fathers." [9]

Yet the Democrats learned some lessons in 1910 which they believed would enable them to triumph in 1914. Berry, who uncovered the Capitol scandal, almost won. Therefore, the progressive movement had taken hold even in Pennsylvania, and the Democrats might win if they nominated known reformers; candidates who could maximize charges that Republican leaders were corrupt and arch-conservative. But even Berry had lost because his party was split and disorganized; clearly the party must be united and disciplined. Once Democratic politicians were impressed with these points the reorganizers were able to seize power and Palmer was given a chance to construct a political machine capable of challenging the Republicans for state control.[10]

In creating an efficient Democratic organization, Palmer indulged the impulse which caused him so much trouble in Congress: he gathered into his own hands all the power and responsibility he could. He obtained nearly complete control over the state party machinery and operated it with a ruthlessness unsurpassed by the urban bosses so despised by progressives.[11]

Palmer's most potent weapon was his absolute command over the federal patronage in Pennsylvania. Wilson and his Cabinet members generally cooperated with the established heads of the state parties. Furthermore, the President depended on Palmer for important assistance in Congress. Early in the Wilson administration, therefore, orders went out from Presidential secretary Joe Tumulty that no federal appointments were to be made in Pennsylvania until cleared with Palmer or Morris, whom Palmer had chosen to succeed Guthrie as state chairman.[12]

As a result of Palmer's importuning, desirable government positions were awarded to many of the leaders of the reorganization movement. In some cases, these appointments temporarily weakened the new party leadership by taking valuable men out of the state. Guthrie, for example was named Ambassador to Japan, and Samuel Graham, a reorganizer leader in Pittsburgh, became Assistant Attorney-General. These impressive rewards, however, also ensured loyalty and stimulated party activity among other ambitious Pennsylvania Democrats.

At Palmer's insistence, and often against bitter opposition from the old guard, the President appointed reorganizer leaders to positions from which they could control access to government jobs within the state. Kane became United States Attorney for the Eastern District of Pennsylvania. Berry was handed the key post of Collector of the Port of Philadelphia. Blakeslee obtained an important position as assistant to Postmaster General Burleson, a job dealing chiefly with patronage matters. William W. Roper was appointed Collector of Customs at Philadelphia.[13] Each of these men influenced the hiring of a multitude of lesser officials. Hundreds of Pennsylvania Democrats were rewarded with federal patronage, and in almost all cases the appointments were channelled through Palmer. Judges, revenue officers, postal officials, and Justice Department representatives were chosen from among those who gave political support to the new regime.

When Palmer discovered that Morris was sometimes inept in dealing with local politicians, he came to depend increasingly upon Joe Guffey for advice. Soon there were complaints that no Pennsylvanian could be appointed to a federal job without first seeing Guffey.[14] If a Republican or uncooperative Democrat was named to the most obscure government position in the state, Guffey would complain and Palmer would quickly take the matter up with top officials. "[Comptroller John Skelton] Williams has been at it again," Guffey cried to Palmer in 1915, "by appointing a Republican lawyer for a piece of special work . . . I have complained about this sort of thing . . . so often that I have grown sick and tired." Palmer rushed the complaint to the President's office with an urgent request for action, and Tumulty replied that he and Burleson deplored the situation and were already working to correct it.[15] When a United States Marshal in Pittsburgh refused to make an appointment requested by Guffey, he was first visited by investigators from Washington, then fired for "inefficiency." [16]

Despite violent protests from disgruntled Pennsylvanians about Palmer's use of the patronage,[17] Wilson was content to have the national committeeman control federal appointments in Pennsylvania. He knew Palmer used his power to advance progressive state legislation in Pennsylvania and to assist Wilson's program in Congress. In May, 1913, the President expressed concern when Democratic members of the Pennsylvania legislature helped defeat a corrupt-practices act and other reform measures. Palmer replied that he was going to Harrisburg the following day to deal with the recalcitrants. He arranged to have Secretary of State Bryan address the legislature in the afternoon and to have both Bryan and Secretary of Labor Wilson speak at a dinner meeting for Democratic representatives in the evening. The President expressed "warm appreciation of your good work at Harrisburg." [18]

In an effort to keep Pennsylvania Democrats in line, Palmer made an example of Congressman Michael Donohue of Philadelphia, the only Democrat from the state to vote against the Underwood tariff. In September, 1913, Donohue endorsed a constituent for the post of Collector of Internal Revenue in his district. Palmer recommended another man, observing that Donohue's "influence with the administration is not what it would be if he had more loyalty." Amid howls of protest from the Philadelphia old guard Palmer's man was appointed.[19]

In using patronage to weld together an effective progressive machine, Palmer antagonized many who were disappointed with the distribution of spoils. Some resented the party chief's high-handed manner. "Much of the discord in the Democratic delegation from Pennsylvania," the Philadelphia *North American* declared, "is due to Mr. Palmer's control of the patronage and his refusal to share either responsibility or political profit with any of the other members." [20] Moreover, many professional politicians who respected Palmer resented the power wielded by newcomers to politics—the well-educated professional and business men suddenly elevated by Palmer into positions of party leadership. Democratic leaders in Philadelphia's Irish wards, for example, despised such gentlemen as Morris, Kane, and Roper. One veteran party worker dismissed Morris as a "Sunday School orator." Most of Palmer's "fool friends," he asserted with some disgust, were all right for "pink tea functions," but were of no use in politics.[21]

Palmer's basic difficulty, however, was that the number of applicants for federal patronage greatly exceeded the number of positions available. Characteristically, he made as much as he could out of what he had to offer by refusing to fill posts until after the July, 1913, meeting of the state committee. Anxious county chairmen were told that Palmer would pass out the prizes only after the committee elected Roland Morris to complete Ambassador Guthrie's unexpired term as state chairman.[22]

Even after Morris' election, however, Palmer found it necessary to stall the office-hungry politicians. Addressing the state committee, he praised the members for being more than just place-seekers, and called upon them to continue their "disinterested, unselfish and patriotic devotion to the underlying and fundamental principles of the party." Nevertheless, Palmer was besieged by supplicants. One grumbled: "Speeches like Palmer's don't get me anything for working in my district sixteen years without reward." At the meeting's conclusion, Palmer reputedly looked as though he had "gone through a wringer." [23]

When Palmer finally announced his patronage decisions, there were angry objections from all over the state. He had expected disappointment among members of the old bipartisan machine and was ready to gamble on losing these men. What troubled him most was that in trying to please as many of his supporters as possible, he antagonized others whose friendship he wanted and needed. Congressman Warren Worth Bailey protested against Palmer's choice for United States Attorney in Bailey's district.[24] Representative John J. Casey virtually broke with Palmer when the party leader neglected to consult him before arranging the appointment of a deputy revenue collector in Casey's district. Even minor appointments were important to Casey, who found his seat endangered by his support of the Underwood tariff in spite of the fact that he was a union leader with a predominantly labor constituency.[25]

Several congressmen from eastern Pennsylvania objected to Palmer's nominees for positions in the Philadelphia customs house and post office.[26] In one important case, Palmer had to contend with a dozen aspirants for a federal judgeship in the Pittsburgh area, all of whom had influential support.[27] In Philadelphia, where the reorganizers had established an organization outside Charles Donnelly's regular group, W. Horace Hoskins, erstwhile president of the reformer's club, set up a third organization when Palmer chose another candidate for superintendent of the Philadelphia mint.[28]

Palmer and his opponents had their showdown in the state primary campaign of 1914, in which nominations for governor and senator were at stake. Politicians who objected to Palmer's leadership knew that if they opposed his bid for a nomination, they risked the complete loss of federal patronage. In the end, all but the most hostile members of the old guard supported him.

Palmer chose the race for governor, in which the tariff issue would be of least importance, and a Palmer-for-Governor Committee was formed in December, 1913. The other party leaders had trouble deciding which of them would pluck Penrose's senate seat. Among the avowed candidates were Berry; William T. "Farmer" Creasy, Grand Master of the State Grange; and State Supreme Court Justice Leslie Mestrezat, who was prepared to resign his seat in order to run. Some thought that McCormick, the state's wealthiest Democrat, would be the best choice, while Palmer wanted Secretary of Labor W. B. Wilson as a running mate. To avoid a disruptive primary battle, all the Democratic senatorial prospects met in late January, 1914. Berry and Mestrezat were induced to withdraw, and Creasy was promised the nomination for lieutenent governor. Finally, all agreed that Secretary Wilson would be the strongest candidate. Wilson, although reluctant, agreed to enter the race if the President approved.[29]

Palmer and Morris visited the White House and asked permission to enter the Labor Secretary against Penrose. The President requested a week to think the matter over; but a day later he was implored of AF of L President Samuel Gompers not to let the Labor Secretary resign:

He is the right man in the right place. . . . His retirement . . . to enter into the hopeless race . . . will disappoint and dishearten the men in the labor movement of America. . . . Unless a political revolution takes place in the minds of the people of Pennsylvania, the nomination of any Democrat in Pennsylvania for the United States Senatorship is doomed to failure. . . . It is neither fair nor just to lead Mr. Wilson to political slaughter.[30]

Palmer and Morris returned on February 4, this time bringing McCormick and Blakeslee with them. The President told the group that he believed it would be much easier for Pennsylvania Democrats to choose another Senate candidate than it would be for him to find another Secretary of Labor. Nevertheless, he went on, Palmer and McCormick had deeply impressed him with their arguments about the necessity of beating Penrose. The strongest possible candidate had to be entered in the senatorial contest—Palmer. For an hour the men argued; finally Palmer capitulated.[31] According to newspaper reports, Wilson promised Palmer a place in the administration if he was defeated by Penrose.[32]

A strong candidate for the Democratic gubernatorial nomination was already in the field. City Solicitor Michael J. Ryan of Philadelphia, backed by Charles Donnelly's city machine, had expected to encounter Palmer in what one newspaper termed "a war of political extermination" between the reform leaders and the patronage-starved old guard.[33] Even after Palmer left the contest for governor the reorganized state organization could not accept Ryan. Inasmuch as a tough primary fight as well as a general election was in store for the gubernatorial candidate, party leaders chose the man best able to finance his own campaign, Vance McCormick.[34]

McCormick was utterly incapable of meeting the vitriolic attack launched against the Democratic state leadership by Ryan and his campaign manager, Judge Eugene C. Bonniwell. Moreover, Ryan's assault was directed from the start not against his official opponent, but chiefly at Palmer. As a result, McCormick toured the state lecturing against Republican misgovernment, while Palmer and Ryan traded charges and countercharges.

Ryan shrewdly took advantage of the inordinate sensitivity to criticism which compelled Palmer to answer almost every accusation made against him. In attempting to refute charges that he had accepted and not reported a 1910 campaign contribution from the late State Senator James Hall, Palmer completely exposed his weakness. His first reply was that Hall, a leader of James Guffey's organization, offered him a contribution in 1910, but that he refused it. His opponents then produced a letter, dated June 17, 1910, in which Palmer thanked Hall for his gift of $500. They also charged Palmer with withdrawing his statement of 1910 campaign contributions from Monroe County's record office, signing for it in his own distinctive handwriting and never returning it. Two men swore they saw Palmer's account before it disappeared, and both declared that it contained no reference to Hall's contribution.

Palmer then changed his story. The day after publication of

his correspondence with Hall, Palmer remembered that when he refused Hall's offer of a contribution, the old guard leader sent a check anyhow. He had not reported the gift, Palmer explained, because he used it only to cover his out-of-state travel expenses for the Democratic congressional campaign committee. He denied knowing anything about the missing records.[35] Bonniwell tried to heighten the issue by announcing that Palmer had received $4,000, not $500, but he produced no new evidence.[36]

Other accusations against Palmer included: taking money from the nearly bankrupt state party for personal expenses; opposing the election of a judge because he had convicted a member of Palmer's organization; and accepting bribes in return for loans from his Stroudsburg bank.[37] Needless to say, Palmer did not accept such charges passively. In response, he charged Ryan with being a front man for the old Guffey-Hall-Donnelly bipartisan machine and a traitor to his party; Ryan had been asked to campaign for Wilson in 1912, Palmer charged, and had refused. Just before the primary election, Palmer accused Ryan and his managers of hiring detectives to investigate his personal and business affairs. All they found, Palmer observed scornfully, was material his opponents had been using against him unsuccessfully for years.[38] Goaded by Palmer's replies, Ryan gave vent to the fury felt by so many of Palmer's adversaries: "The state is now weary of his strutting, arrogant, insulting bossism, coupled as it is with his petty meanness." [39]

Bonniwell and Donnelly tried desperately to find a candidate to run against Palmer, hoping to draw some of his fire away from Ryan. The first man named as Ryan's running mate withdrew on February 6, immediately after Palmer announced his candidacy.[40] Attempts to persuade other eminent Pennsylvania Democrats to oppose the state party leader failed,[41] until April 7, when one Henry Budd, an unsuccessful candidate for a judgeship in Philadelphia, agreed to run.[42] Palmer continued to campaign against Ryan.

McCormick seemed to need all the help Palmer could give him. Enemies of the reform leadership throughout the state

united behind Ryan. Twenty-five hundred Democrats paid to
attend a Ryan-for-Governor dinner in Philadelphia early in
April.[43] Boss Mutchler of Northampton announced that Ryan
would certainly carry his county.[44] The state's well-organized
and wealthy liquor interests, warned that McCormick was a
militant prohibitionist, went all out to defeat him.[45]

Even more dangerous opposition to McCormick's candidacy
arose among Pennsylvania working men. McCormick, a man
of great wealth, had antagonized workers when as mayor of
Harrisburg he opposed a minimum—wage law for city employees. A prolabor Democratic candidate for Congress from Potter
county, L. B. Siebert, charged that McCormick's nomination
proved that groups hostile to labor and agriculture dominated
the state party. He predicted that Palmer would be dragged
down to defeat by a running mate unacceptable to working
men, adding:

I shall, of course, be glad to do all I can for Palmer. . . . Politically
speaking, the defeat of A. Mitchell Palmer will go further towards
discrediting the national Democracy than the defeat of a score of
other prominent Democrats in the north; for it is generally understood and known that Mr. Palmer is recognized as the direct representative of the national administration in the House. . . . Nothing,
of course, would delight the interests more than the defeat of this
real Democrat.

But, Siebert concluded, he would support the only gubernatorial candidate with a chance of winning—Michael J. Ryan.[46]

News of this dissatisfaction reached Palmer and he asked
Labor Secretary Wilson to help McCormick. Wilson met with
Siebert, but without success. The Labor Secretary also wrote
his friend James Purcell, Vice-President of the Pennsylvania
United Mine Workers, defending McCormick's labor record,[47]
and campaigned with McCormick and Palmer in several sections
of the state.[48] Near the end of the campaign, Palmer brought
Secretary of State Bryan to Pennsylvania, and Bryan told an
enthusiastic throng in Wilkes Barre that he was there to support
"progressive democracy" against "reactionary democracy." [49]

On May 19, Pennsylvania Democrats showed their approval

of Palmer's leadership as well as their determination to keep the party progressive, giving Palmer a majority in sixty-five of the state's sixty-seven counties. McCormick did almost as well, Democratic leaders were disturbed, however, by one aspect of their easy triumph. The old guard swept the city of Philadelphia by a margin of better than two to one, demonstrating convincingly that it still controlled the city's Democratic wards and could ruin the party ticket in November.[50]

Most political observers agreed, early in 1914, that for the first time since the Civil War the Democrats were likely to elect a United States senator from Pennsylvania. One reason for this optimism was Woodrow Wilson's good showing in 1912; he had defeated Taft easily and lost to Roosevelt by less than 50,000 votes. After the 1912 election, the state Progressive Party practically disintegrated, and many of those who voted for Roosevelt were expected to turn Democratic.

Certainly Penrose did not seem likely to win back a majority of Roosevelt's supporters, for by 1914, he was identified with corrupt ties between business and government, and between organized vice and local and state officials. His name was synonymous with bribery, graft, absolute bossism, and rigged elections. "It is the siege of Penrose that is on," proclaimed a writer in *Harper's Weekly,* "which is to say that the issue in Pennsylvania is that of the people against the predatory interests; the moral sense of the community against the forces of political corruption, government debauchery and social decay." [51] The Republicans could not have chosen a candidate against whom the Democrats could more effectively level their charges of dishonest government and resistance to necessary change.

Progressives in all parties joined the crusade against Penrose. Republican Senator George W. Norris of Nebraska wrote the Anti-Penrose Republican League of Pennsylvania that nothing would help the party more than the defeat of the Pennsylvania senator. He said he would campaign against the man himself, and Republican Senator William S. Kenyon of Iowa declared himself ready to do the same.[52] The gubernatorial candidate on Penrose's own ticket refused to campaign with him and did all he could to disassociate himself from the senator's candidacy. Pennsylvania's leading Republican Journal, the Philadelphia *Public Ledger*, strongly opposed Penrose's reelection, although the newspaper's editors could not bring themselves to endorse one of his non-Republican opponents.[53] Not a single important Republican leader from another state entered Pennsylvania to help Penrose.

A confidential report drawn up for Progressive Party leader Gifford Pinchot in December, 1913, advised him that veteran newspapermen and politicians throughout the state believed that the Democrats had the best chance of winning the coming election. According to the report, Pennsylvania Democrats had strong candidates and abundant confidence, while many Republicans felt that they would rather not vote than vote for Penrose. Progressive Party success was "generally regarded as impossible." [54]

Penrose's position, however, was not as hopeless as his highly vocal opponents made it appear. He had several important advantages. Foremost among them was the economic recession which began in the fall of 1913, severely affecting Pennsylvania's major industries, especially iron and steel manufacturing. Republican orators, including Penrose, had predicted that a business decline would follow passage of the Underwood tariff. In 1914, Penrose solemnly declared the prophesies confirmed. In some cases, the evidence was exaggerated, as when the *Public Ledger* reported in December, 1913, that over 700 unemployed Bethlehem Steel workers had written a letter to Palmer demanding that he do something to help them regain their jobs. Palmer replied in Congress that he had received no such letter and that his inquiries revealed no unusual layoffs at the Bethlehem works.[55] Penrose also magnified the effect of the depression when he compared conditions in early 1914 with his recollections of Pennsylvania after the last Democratic tariff reduction, the Wilson-Gorman bill of 1894 (passed after a depression began in 1893):

I shall never forget [he told a Pittsburgh audience] the scenes of desolation, of poverty and distress which presented themselves in every town that I visited. Mills closed tight and thousands of men thrown into the streets, absolutely in distress for food and necessities. . . . With the election of McKinley prosperity returned as at the touch of a magician's wand.[56]

Palmer, on the other hand, tried to persuade his audiences that most of the recession was taking place in Penrose's imagination, and that Pennsylvania manufacturers intentionally were creating the rest. He warned a crowd of Pittsburgh steel workers that some of them might suffer pay cuts and layoffs, not because of the tariff, but because of the election. He also charged that railroads were holding back equipment orders in an attempt to impress the ICC with their need for rate increases.[57]

Unfortunately for Palmer, Pennsylvania industry really was depressed; unemployment was high and increasing, and Democratic denials of these facts were not convincing to hungry workers. Republican warnings that industrial disaster would follow if tariff rates were lowered seemed, in the fall of 1914, to be tragically accurate, and Penrose's gloomy forecasts of disaster unless the party of protection was returned to power had a powerful effect.

Nor were the layoffs due primarily to the coming election, although some manufacturers probably cut their work forces sooner and deeper than they would have otherwise.[58] Unfilled orders of the United States Steel Company fell in September, 1914 to 3,787,667 tons. A year before the figure had been 5,003,785 tons, and that in turn was a decrease from the 6,551,507-ton backlog of September 12, 1912. Smaller steel manufacturers suffered even more. The Lackawanna Steel Company's backlog on September 30, 1914 was down to 166,344 tons compared to 255,945 on the same date a year earlier and 569,977 in September, 1912.[59]

As industrial activity fell off, railroad loadings and profits dropped precipitously. By the end of March, 1914, the Pennsylvania Railroad had laid off 15,000 men with 10,000 more scheduled to be furloughed over the next few weeks. The railroad had been expected to order 15,000 tons ($4,200,000 worth) of rails from Pennsylvania mills, but four months after the orders were scheduled to be placed, not a single rail had been purchased.[60] Charles Schwab frankly told an interviewer from the New York *Evening Post:*

The iron and steel industry is in the worst condition that I have ever known it to be. I make no exception for any previous year. The present output is below one-half of the normal capacity of our factories. . . . The number of employees in the Bethlehem works is the lowest in nine years.

Significantly, despite his strong protectionist views, Schwab did not blame the tariff for these difficulties.[61]

Few Pennsylvania Republicans were as candid as the Bethlehem executive. President John A. Topping of Republic Steel had also predicted that the Underwood tariff would bring heavy unemployment to steel workers. In January, 1914, he announced that his prophecy had come true: 25,000 men were idle because low tariff rates allowed foreign producers to flood the eastern seaboard with their metal.[62] Official figures, however, do not show the increase in imports described by Topping, Penrose, chairman Elbert H. Gary of United States Steel, and other Republicans.[63] For example, one of the chief causes of distress in the steel industry was the sharp drop in production of steel rails; but rail imports declined also, remaining at the negligible level of one-nineteenth of domestic output.[64]

The main cause of the drop in production, never mentioned by the moaning manufacturers, was that exports of iron and steel fell by $47,000,000 in the fiscal year ending June 30, 1914.[65] European firms cut back expenditures during the period of great uncertainty and tight money which preceded the outbreak of war. Also, domestic sales decreased as credit stringency in Europe affected money markets here. The sharp fall in sales to Europe coincided with a decrease in American capital spending to produce a brief but painful recession which lasted throughout the 1914 election campaign.[66]

Penrose benefitted also from a split in the progressive vote. Washington Party leaders thought of themselves as Republicans, temporarily forced out of their party by a reactionary leadership. Fusion with the Democrats was unthinkable for most of them; yet they could not, in good conscience, support

Penrose. Party leaders, therefore, decided to nominate their own men for governor and senator, although the Democrats were certain to run progressive candidates, and the two platforms were almost identical except for their tariff planks.[67]

Early in the campaign, Roosevelt persuaded the Washington candidate for governor to withdraw in favor of McCormick; but the move dismayed many party members. After the election, one Washington Party official wrote: "My greatest regret is that we permitted ourselves to tie up with the weaker arm of a bipartisan combination in an effort to defeat the stronger arm." Another grumbled, "Our leaders made a great error in allowing Mr. [William Draper] Lewis to withdraw. Thousands of our voters who had been lifelong Republicans said: 'well, they can't tell me to vote the Democratic ticket.' "[68]

Washington senatorial candidate Gifford Pinchot stayed in the race,[69] basing his campaign against Penrose upon the same charges of corruption made by the Democrats. State Chairman William Flinn explained that the Washington Party could not support a Democrat for senator: "We believe in the protective policy and there can be no compromise on the principle." Roosevelt even proclaimed Pinchot a better protectionist than Penrose; the Senator's stubbornness he asserted, stood in the way of compromise and was the real cause of the "ruinous" Democratic tariff.[70]

Pinchot and his friend Roosevelt, who spent much more time in Pennsylvania than in any other state during the campaign,[71] hardly mentioned Palmer until about two weeks before the election. Until then they had hoped that the Democratic candidate would quit the race in order to make Penrose's defeat certain.[72] Palmer, meanwhile, had been hoping that Pinchot would give up.[73] Late in October, the Washington leaders began a determined effort to convince Pennsylvania progressives that Palmer could not win. "Don't forget," Roosevelt told an audience of 12,000 in Uniontown, "there is no use wasting your votes on Mr. Palmer. He's a good fellow, I have no doubt, and an honest gentleman. But he has no show." [74]

A week before the election, when reports indicated that

Penrose and Palmer were running neck and neck, Roosevelt spent a hectic four days campaigning through Pennsylvania, making at least fifty speeches.[75] At the same time, 1,200,000 postcards were mailed from Oyster Bay, Roosevelt's home, to Pennsylvania voters with a message written in a facsimile of Roosevelt's handwriting: "I am writing to ask you personally for your support of Gifford Pinchot against Boies Penrose. . . . [He is] fighting for the same thing for which we fought in 1912." [76] The large crowds that flocked to hear Roosevelt in Pennsylvania heard the same message: "Every man who voted for me two years ago and is not ashamed of it owes it to himself to vote for Pinchot this year. . . . We are fighting for the same principles and against the same foes." [77] Impartial observers estimated that Roosevelt's strenuous Pennsylvania campaign took many more votes from Palmer than it won from Penrose.[78]

In addition, Penrose had the advantage of dissension within the Democratic Party. Donnelly's Philadelphia organization sat out the election. Early in October, McCormick and Morris swallowed their pride and visited the city solicitor's office to ask Ryan's assistance in the campaign. They received a polite but frosty reception. Ryan told reporters: "We had a pleasant interview and I have nothing further to say." Five days later the state committee held a fund-raising dinner in Philadalphia, and Ryan and his supporters, although invited, refused to attend.[79]

In Northampton, Boss Mutchler also had his revenge on Palmer. He helped Henry J. Steele, an Easton attorney and one of the largest slate producers in the state, win the primary contest over the man Palmer chose as his successor in Congress. Then, in the fall, Mutchler's organization ignored Palmer and McCormick, and worked only for Steele's election.[80]

Palmer tried to reduce the antagonism engendered by his patronage decisions, as well as the drain on his time, by announcing early in May that until the election was over all such matters would be handled by State Chairman Morris. At the time, about two hundred postmasters were to be appointed, as well as a federal judge, Surveyor of the Port of Philadelphia,

and other officials. The new system may even have added to
Palmer's troubles. Men who had responded to their party
leader's solicitations and had worked for Palmer's nomination
expected him to grant suitable rewards, or at least to listen to
their recommendations. Now they found themselves shunted off
to Morris. Furthermore, politicians knew very well that Palmer,
not Morris, was responsible for final decisions.[81]

Even with all Penrose's advantages—the tariff, the recession, a divided progressive vote, and squabbling Democrats—
he might have been beaten but for one surprising asset which
his opponents never dreamed he possessed: Penrose turned out
to be a magnificent campaigner. Previously, he had been sent
to the Senate by obedient Republican majorities in the state
legislature, and even these victories were not easily arranged.
After Penrose's first election, four hundred leading Pennsylvania business men met in Philadelphia and passed a resolution declaring: "A large majority of the members of the Assembly of 1897 were nominated and elected by questionable
methods, the chief end in view being the election of Boies
Penrose as United States Senator. . . ."[82]

When the Seventeenth Amendment, providing for the direct
election of United States senators, was ratified in 1913, Penrose concluded that his career was over. He told friends that
he was retiring, but Joseph R. Grundy, head of the Pennsylvania Manufacturers' Association, talked him into making the
race. In defense of his seat Penrose waged a dynamic campaign,
one of the most colorful the state had ever seen. He traveled
over 50,000 miles, stopping frequently for short speeches, driv-
ing slowly so that he could wave to the crowds who recognized
his bright red open touring car. When it broke down he bought
another, even brighter and redder.[83]

Pennsylvanians were curious to see this huge man (he
weighed over 300 pounds), whose handsome picture was so familiar to them. Journalists had written of his voracious appe-
tites for wine, women, and food, and even for song when he
had the time; they portrayed him as a relative of the devil—
corrupt, immoral, and reactionary. Penrose wisely stopped in

almost every village in the state to show the surprised inhabitants that he was a "regular guy." His friends knew that he hated crowds, despised the public, and could not be approached by strangers. Yet, in the words of one awed newspaperman, Penrose "walked down the congested avenues, shaking the hands extended to him from every direction and chatting with all, not failing to compliment the proud mothers of babies held up for his inspection." [84]

Fortunately for him, although he was the symbol of the political corruption which disgraced Pennsylvania under his leadership, Penrose was also identified with the protective tariff. He encouraged this favorable association by stressing it in all his speeches. He flooded the state with posters and large highway signs, some with pictures of himself over such captions as "Prosperity and Protection to the Wage Earner," and "The Full Dinner Pail." One showed Penrose shielding a Pennsylvania family with his wide cloak while they securely ate their dinner. As champion of the state's manufacturers and liquor dealers, Penrose commanded almost unlimited campaign funds, enabling him to travel continually and to print a phenomenal amount of posters and campaign literature.[85]

In farm areas, where the Democrats were strongest, Penrose combined the tariff issue with an appeal to old Civil War and Reconstruction enmities. He asserted that the Underwood bill, by allowing free importations of foodstuffs, sacrificed Pennsylvania farmers to southern cotton and tobacco planters who were not troubled by foreign competition. This was no accident, he averred, but part of the Democratic policy of favoring the South and southerners. "Not a single Union veteran has been appointed to office in this state under the Wilson administration. On the other hand, scores of Union veterans have been discouraged. . . . Many Confederate veterans have been appointed to federal offices." [86]

Penrose sensibly refused to answer the sensational accusations of financial and political dishonesty made against him. He ignored Pinchot, except to observe that the man knew nothing about fostering business or meeting a payroll.[87] Palmer he denounced as "the Benedict Arnold of Pennsylvania" for having written and secured passage of the metal tariff, which according to Penrose caused the unemployment of thousands of Pennsylvanians. Palmer, he charged, was unable to explain this treachery, so the Democrat resorted to untruthful abuse of his opponent.[88]

Palmer waged a hard campaign, speaking in six or seven towns a day. Early in the race, he tried to identify himself as completely as possible with the record of the Wilson administration. "I approve every part of that record—I glory in it," he declared. He wrote Wilson: "Before long I shall want to talk to you about plans for helping us. The opportunity to carry Pennsylvania is too good and success will mean so much for the administration that I am hopeful we can count upon your active cooperation."[89]

After some debate within the administration, however, Wilson decided to follow the tradition that the President, once elected, was above partisan politics.[90] His "active cooperation" consisted of a letter to Powell Evans of Philadelphia, a Republican Wilson supporter, who came out for Palmer. "I have seen Mr. Palmer tested," Wilson wrote, "I know his quality. Pennsylvania ought to accept and trust him and through him play her proper role in the constructive policies of a new generation." Late in October, after considerable urging from the man he had sent off to battle Penrose, Wilson visited Pittsburgh where he addressed a YMCA convention, without mentioning politics.[91]

At first, Palmer minimized the tariff issue, justifying the Underwood bill as a boon to farmers and workers, but maintaining that most voters were not concerned about the question. Everywhere, he declared, the wave of moral indignation against Penrose was growing higher.[92] He announced that he would make a sensational expose of Penrose's crimes against the commonwealth in a series of fifty speeches beginning September 8. Palmer reviewed all the old charges against the Senator, most of them backed by good evidence; Penrose had been bribed by corporations, had introduced special interest legislation, and had helped fix elections. The Senator consistently opposed efforts to promote human welfare; he had even voted against a bill to grant much-needed medical assistance to Eskimos and Indians in Alaska.[93]

The AF of L, in a move then unusual for that organization, called for Penrose's defeat. Samuel Gompers announced that Penrose had never voted for a single bill benefitting wage-earners. Palmer's record, according to an AF of L spokesman, was "quite satisfactory." [94] The National Popular Government League, which later plagued Palmer, published a resolution opposing Penrose's reelection because of his opposition to democratic principles. At a most inopportune time for Penrose, a gigantic voting fraud involving registration lists padded up to three times their normal size was uncovered in several Republican-controlled townships in Luzerne county. Evidence also was produced of a huge unreported campaign fund collected for Penrose from the state's manufacturers and liquor dealers.[95]

Penrose finally felt obliged to talk about something besides the tariff. He astounded his political enemies, and probably his friends, by announcing himself in favor of higher taxation of trusts, wage-and-hour-laws for women and children, a graduated income tax, and a referendum on woman suffrage.[96]

As Penrose blossomed forth as a reformer, Palmer stopped trying to move the Pennsylvania public to his position and became instead a convert to moderate protectionism. He cancelled Bryan's scheduled visit to Pennsylvania early in October, and asked other Cabinet members to stay away for fear that they would remind voters of Democratic tariff policy.[97] "I believe," Palmer proclaimed on October 13, "in a competitive tariff, based on the difference in the cost of production at home and abroad." This was precisely what Penrose demanded. A Republican leader taunted that Palmer was trying to "make us believe now that he is in favor of Republican tariff principles." [98]

Despite the camouflage attempts by Palmer and Penrose, most Pennsylvania voters knew what the three senatorial candidates stood for. The campaign aroused intense interest, not only in Pennsylvania, but throughout the country, and newspapers and national magazines covered it especially well. Furthermore, each of the candidates spoke many times in every part of the state. Palmer was closely associated with the Wilson administration and its program, and Pinchot with Theodore Roosevelt and his policies. Penrose tried to offset his reputation for corruption by stressing protectionism as necessary for high profits and employment; and he was a notorious wet competing in a largely urban state against Pinchot, a dry, and Palmer, uncommitted on the question.

Given this choice of candidates, in a year of business depression, Pennsylvanians made an emphatic decision. Penrose received almost as many votes as Palmer and Pinchot put together. Pinchot won three thousand more votes than Palmer, probably because of Roosevelt's vigorous campaign in late October.[99] Almost as disturbing as defeat to Palmer were the huge majorities Penrose received in wards where workingmen predominated. Palmer felt entitled to these votes because of his record in Congress and in his district. Even Northampton County went to Penrose by a wide margin, as the steel, cement, quarry, and mine workers, whom Palmer had striven so long to please, deserted him. Carbon County, easily swept by Palmer in past elections, gave Penrose only nine fewer votes than it gave its congressman.[100]

Penrose originally had agreed with his critics that the Seventeenth Amendment would be his political ruin. By the time he won his second easy popular victory in 1920, the Senator knew that he had misjudged Pennsylvania's voting public. "Give me the people every time," he was heard to rhapsodize. "No legislature would have dared to elect me to the Senate . . . but the people, the dear people . . . elected me by over half a million." [101]

CHAPTER VII

A POLITICIAN OUT OF OFFICE

The political future looked bleak to A. Mitchell Palmer after
the election of 1914. If the infamous Penrose could defeat him
so overwhelmingly, there seemed no chance that he could ever
win a majority in Pennsylvania. Nor did there appear to be
any substance to the persistent reports, heard during and after
the campaign, that Wilson intended to find a high administrative post for the man he had forced to run against Penrose.[1]
For several months after the election, no offer was forthcoming.
Palmer even tried to prod Wilson a bit. Early in March, 1915,
he wrote requesting a government position for former Congressman Robert Lee: "Pennsylvania has not received many
places in the federal service at Washington," he reminded the
President.[2] Three weeks later, he asked that a certain post be
given to another defeated Pennsylvania congressman. When
Tumulty replied that the job was already taken, Palmer wrote
back sadly that such positions ought to be kept open long
enough for deserving Democrats to experience at least "the
joys of anticipation . . . they can hope for little more." [3]

Until late February, Palmer retained some faint hope that
the Senate would void Penrose's election because of voting
frauds and huge unreported campaign contributions. Before
the election, Palmer and Representative Arthur R. Rupley of
the Washington Party presented evidence which convinced a
majority of the Senate Committee on Privileges and Elections
that an official inquiry was necessary. However, when an investigation of Democrat Roger Sullivan's campaign for the Senate
in Illinois was approved at the same time, administration leaders worked successfully to kill the whole inquiry.[4]

In February, 1915, Palmer made his charges again, this time on the House floor. Again several congressmen demanded an investigation. Penrose then announced that his friends possessed incriminating evidence not only against Sullivan, but against Senator-elect Underwood of Alabama and other successful Democratic candidates in California, Indiana, and Nevada. Once more the investigation was called off.[5]

In deep despair because of the complete frustration of his high ambitions, Palmer decided to retire from politics. On March 13, 1915, he told Tumulty that he would like to be appointed to a newly created post on the Court of Claims, a lifetime position with the moderate salary of $6,500 a year. Wilson quickly agreed to this easy means of settling his political debt.[6]

When other leading Pennsylvania reorganizers heard of Palmer's impending retirement, they foresaw another bitter struggle with the old guard for control of the state party, and realized more clearly than ever how essential a role Palmer played. They needed a leader who shared their reform objectives and yet could dominate the professional politicians. Morris, McCormick, and their friends pleaded with Palmer to refuse the post, unaware that he had asked for it.[7]

Members of the old guard rejoiced at the news that Palmer would soon leave politics for the bench, and they did what they could to hasten his abdication. Bonniwell pointed to the anomaly of an appointed judge holding a high partisan political position and demanded Palmer's immediate resignation as national committeeman. It was high time too, he declared: "One thing is certain, that another year of the Palmer-Morris management will reduce the ranking of the Democratic Party to that of a fourth or fifth rate party." [8] John Dwyer of the Philadelphia *Record*, asked President Wilson to help Pennsylvania Democrats choose a new leader who would "reunify" the party; in other words, a leader who was not a reorganizer.[9]

Wilson did suggest to Palmer the advisability of resigning his position as chairman of the executive committee of the democratic national committee, and he recommended to the committee, through Palmer, that Frederick B. Lynch of Minnesota be appointed in his place. Palmer surrendered his chairmanship willingly enough, but he balked at demands that he immediately yield his post as national committeeman. "While a place upon the bench is very much to my liking and I am sure I shall enjoy the service," he wrote Wilson early in April, "I cannot help but regret that it will be necessary for me to quit active politics." [10] Not only was Palmer becoming increasingly reluctant to give up his most cherished ambitions, but he was aware that his retirement might diminish the authority of the Pennsylvania reorganizers and invite a resurgence of the old guard.

Storm warnings were already flying. Congressman-elect Michael Liebel of Erie, one of Ryan's leading supporters in 1914, insisted in February, 1915, on his right to name five new postmasters when the terms of the incumbents in his district expired in March. Postmaster-General Burleson cautiously avoided antagonizing the new congressman, but Palmer still held the reins of the state party. Burleson told Liebel that he could do nothing for him until he took office, and Wilson appointed men named by Palmer.[11] Liebel's demands for recognition were certain to grow more insistent, however, when the administration began to ask for his vote in Congress. Furthermore, three of the other five House seats the Pennsylvania Democrats salvaged from the Republican landslide in 1914 were held by potential enemies of the state regime. Henry J. Steele, sponsored by Mutchler in Palmer's old district, was certain to cause trouble; John J. Casey remained estranged from the regular organization; and the other new Democratic representative, former State Chairman Arthur G. Dewalt, had long been a leader of the old guard faction.

Fortunately, Palmer found an excuse to issue himself a temporary reprieve. Morris was obliged to go to Europe for personal reasons, and Palmer's resignation would have left the state party without officers. Palmer therefore suggested to Wilson that he defer moving to the bench until Morris returned. The other judges of the Court agreed to the arrangement and Wilson gave his approval.[12]

Even as he procrastinated about retirement, Palmer took advantage of a new opportunity to remind the President of his value as an active politician. On June 8, 1915, William Jennings Bryan created a major crisis within the administration by resigning from the Cabinet in protest against the President's stern note to Germany about the sinking of the *Lusitania*. Shortly thereafter, Wilson called Palmer to a conference at Sea Girt. The President had already decided to run for a second term and he feared that Bryan would lead or join a campaign in opposition. This fear was reinforced by the recollection that Bryan had sponsored a plank in the 1912 platform limiting the Presidency to one term, while Wilson's letter to Palmer repudiating that plank was never made public.[13] The President suspected that his opponents might insist that he abide by the platform resolution he apparently had accepted.

In June, 1914, Palmer had told Tumulty and Thomas J. Pence, secretary of the national committee, of a letter from Bryan to Representative Henry Clayton of Alabama, chairman of the Judiciary Committee, in which Bryan agreed that there was no immediate need for single-term legislation, and that in any case such a law should not apply to Wilson. Palmer tried unsuccessfully to get the letter from Clayton, and he remarked to Tumulty at the time that it might "become a very much more important piece of literature later." [14] The letter doubtless provided a major subject of discussion when Wilson and Palmer met at Sea Girt.

Soon after his conference with Wilson, Palmer telegraphed Clayton, again requesting a copy of Bryan's letter; this time Palmer made it plain that the President himself wanted the document. Clayton found himself in a difficult position: a devoted supporter of Bryan, he owed his position as federal judge to Wilson. Clayton unhappily wired Palmer that he would search his files for the correspondence with Bryan; but even if he found the letter, he would not feel "entirely free to give it out or to say anything about it under the present circumstances." The letter, Clayton protested, was sent as "friendly, personal correspondence":

You remember that when you appeared before the Democratic members of the Committee you asked us to treat the letter of the President which you read to us, as confidential; and not until after it was so accepted and read, did I say anything about Mr. Bryan's attitude. . . . I hope I may be able to see the President before very long. In the freedom of friendship and with entire confidence in his good judgment and high sense of propriety, I shall tell him all that I know.

Clayton's wire was forwarded to Wilson by Palmer with the notation that it would be wise for the President to see Clayton. To allay any compunctions the President might have, Palmer added:

While it was a personal and confidential letter to Clayton, I know that Mr. Bryan desired that all of us who were particularly interested in the matter at the time should know his views. This certainly included you. The letter was written for that purpose.[15]

Wilson met with Clayton and prevailed upon him to hand over his correspondence with Bryan. When rumors spread in February, 1916, that Bryan would oppose Wilson's renomination, reporters were informed of the letter's existence and told that it would be made public if Bryan attacked Wilson on the single-term issue. Perhaps because the President held his letter to Clayton, Bryan never raised the question.[16]

As Palmer's discouragement abated, he became increasingly reluctant to retire into the shelter of the judiciary. Not only did he still feel compelled to fight for political power, he already enjoyed financial success in his private legal practice. Palmer's clients valued his knowledge of the law and his exceptional skill in argument and negotiation; but they were even more aware that he had been an influential congressman and national committeeman, and that he had easy access to high government officials. It is difficult to tell just when Palmer's income began to spurt upward, but by mid-1915 he must have known that he could be a very wealthy man if he chose to remain in private practice. The Washington *Star* estimated that before Palmer became Alien Property Custodian in late 1917 his annual income from his law practice alone was $200,000.[17]

Late in July, 1915, Palmer finally decided that he did not

want to be a judge. "My roots are down too deep in the ground," he announced, "and I am too much of a going concern to suddenly cut off my activities by the acceptance of a place for life upon the Federal bench." [18] Palmer's decision was not due primarily to his prospective wealth; he had never been content to be cut off from the road to political power. Even before he told Wilson of his decision, Palmer informed his friends that he wanted a place in the administration, and Democrats as influential as House, Tumulty, and Burleson set about finding him a suitable job.

Palmer's benefactors acted not only because of their high regard for him—House, indeed, apparently distrusted the Pennsylvania leader—but perhaps even more out of awareness that many northern Democrats would be heartened if Palmer received an important government post. He had served the party well in Congress and in election campaigns, and he had been one of the most effective of Wilson's early supporters for the Presidency. Furthermore, many Democrats believed that Palmer sacrificed his political life for the President by running against Penrose. Naming him to high office would help dispel the prevalent feeling that the President was ungrateful to those who served him best. It would also answer complaints that the administration favored southerners in its major appointments. The northern wing of the Democratic party had suffered many serious defeats in 1914; party leaders knew that northern Democrats must be rallied and brought to wholehearted support of the President if he was to be reelected in 1916.

Several fairly important positions were open in mid-1915, but the job Palmer wanted and the one his friends made the most concerted effort to obtain for him was the councellorship in the State Department. From this office Robert Lansing had recently resigned to succeed Bryan as Secretary of State. Lansing was not a man who could be induced to make a major appointment for reasons which were largely political. Nevertheless, House and Burleson, especially, put considerable pressure on him to choose Palmer. The new Secretary held a long conference with Palmer on July 21, but afterward he refused to commit himself.[19] A few days later, House talked to Lansing and reported to Burleson, "He feels that he does not know Palmer well enough to altogether approve the suggestion. The truth of the matter is his heart is set on [Solicitor General John W.] Davis and he hopes some arrangement can be made by which that can be brought about." [20] Tumulty and Thomas J. Pence, secretary of the national committee, did their best to boost Palmer and to convince Lansing that Davis was needed in the Justice Department. After receiving reports on the situation, House tried again. He informed Pence: "I have communicated with Secretary Lansing and told him that in my opinion Mr. Davis should not be taken from the Department of Justice. Albert [Burleson] thought this would be sufficient. He is to see Mr. Lansing in person on Monday." [21]

Burleson's mission failed. "Lansing will not give his approval to the appointment of Palmer," he wrote House. "I regret this very much, as Palmer rendered great service to the President in the pre-convention contest, and for that reason I think was entitled to consideration." [22] The strong support Palmer commanded among top Democrats did not win him the assignment he wanted in mid-1916. But two and a half years later, similar assistance from influential party leaders would obtain for him the Attorney-Generalship.

Without such impressive backing, Palmer might have been a victim of the surge of patriotism which accompanied the entry of the United States into World War I. A few hours after news of the sinking of the Lusitania arrived on May 8, 1915, the New York *Times* telegraphed dozens of prominent Americans, asking their reaction to the tragedy. Of the replies printed the following morning Palmer's was among the most pacifistic. No action was required, he asserted, since passengers were warned not to travel on munition-bearing ships. Those who made the perilous trip assumed a risk "for which the entire nation ought not be asked to suffer. . . . It certainly should not embroil us in this foreign war." [23] Palmer's sentiments, probably common among his fellow Quakers, were not in accord with the shock and rage felt by most Americans. Despite subsequent evidence of Palmer's fervent patriotism, Republican Senator Theodore Frelinghuysen of New Jersey tried, in 1919, to use the Pennsylvanian's statement against him. Frelinghuysen proclaimed to the upper house: "I will say that I distrusted Mr. Palmer from the very bottom of my heart from the time that his weasel words about the sinking of the *Lusitania* were published in the New York *Times*." [24]

A few months after the *Lusitania* episode, Palmer was involved in a more serious controversy which might have ruined the reputation of a politician with less opportunity to prove his loyalty. On August 23, the New York *World* printed a front-page story about "M.P.," an American with high government connections who seemed to be serving German government agents. The story was based on German documents uncovered by the newspaper, especially a reported conversation among "M.P.," John Simon, a New York cotton broker, and a man identified in the report as "Legal Agent Levy." Simon and Dr. Heinrich F. Albert, a top German agent in the United States, wanted to ship American food and cotton to Germany. The success of their scheme depended heavily upon approval, if not support from the United States government. The President, who had sent a sharp note to Germany about the *Lusitania* sinking, was reported ready to send one to Britain about her interference with our trade and to take severe action against both sides. Albert and his associates sought to ascertain the President's plans, in the hope that they could turn his wrath against England while winning his support for trade with Germany.

According to the document written for transmission to Berlin, "M.P.," at the request of German agents, saw both the President and the Secretary of State. He told Wilson and Lansing that a syndicate, planning to ship large quantities of American cotton to Germany, had requested that he determine for it the views of the administration toward the belligerents' interference with our trade.[25] Wilson's reply, as allegedly reported by "M.P." to Simon and Levy, was surprisingly favorable to Germany. A strong protest would be sent to England,

whether the German answer to the *Lusitania* note were satisfactory or not. The President reportedly declared that he
"could hardly hope for a positive statement that the submarine
warfare would be discontinued," and that "Americans who in
the present situation take passage on a munition-laden ship
take their lives in their own hands." Wilson also expressed a
willingness to discuss his next note to Germany with "M.P."
before it was drafted, and "eventually to so influence it that
there will be agreement for its reception and also to be ready
to influence the press through a wink." [26]

The *World* pointed out that if the reported conferences between Wilson and "M.P." actually took place, it must have
been between July 19, when Wilson returned to Washington
from his summer home in Cornish, New Hampshire, and July
23, when he left for New Hampshire again. Among those who
visited the President while he was in Washington was one
man with the initials M.P.—Mitchell Palmer, who saw Wilson
on July 22. Palmer also conferred with Lansing July 21.[27]

A statement by Palmer headed "Palmer Denies He is M.P."
appeared on the front page of the *World,* August 24, the day
after publication of the original "M.P." story. Palmer declared:

The story printed in the *World* this morning which indicates,
though it does not say, that I am the mysterious "M.P." referred to
in somebody's report of an alleged conversation with the President,
is all a fairy-tale as far as I am concerned.

Palmer said his conversation with Wilson on July 22 dealt
with only two things: his resignation as a judge, and a request
from a friend, attorney John B. Stanchfield of New York, that
Palmer obtain for clients of Stanchfield's the President's opinion
of a plan to ship noncontraband goods to neutral European
ports. Wilson replied that he could only say what he already
had announced: he intended to protest to England against that
country's interference with our shipping. Palmer said he relayed this message to Stanchfield.[28]

The New York *Times* also printed Palmer's statement, with
the comment: "It did not take Mr. Palmer's denial . . . to
acquit him in the minds of people who know him of any sus-

picion that he had gone to President Wilson for the purpose of getting information desired by pro-German agents." [29] In its haste to exonerate Palmer, the *Times* did not notice—nor did the *World*—that Palmer never denied he was "M.P."; he only denied saying what "M.P." was alleged to have said by the German reports.

Not until 1919 did a special Senate subcommittee attempt to discern the truth about the "M.P." story. Palmer acknowledged in a closed session of the subcommittee that he undoubtedly was "M.P." He insisted, however, that he had obtained information for Stanchfield without knowing whom the New Yorker represented, and without receiving a fee for his work. The printed report of "M.P.'s" conversation with Wilson, Palmer testified, was "a garbled, exaggerated and entirely different statement of what I had told Mr. Stanchfield." [30]

Palmer admitted that Levy, Stanchfield's law partner, and Simon had visited him in Stroudsburg; but he did not speculate, nor was he asked, whether the "garbled, exaggerated" account of his conversation with Stanchfield could have been a description of the information he gave Simon and Levy, whose report appeared in the *World*. Palmer's opinions about German submarine warfare and Americans who traveled on munition-laden ships, as recorded in his statement following the *Lusitania* sinking, resembled very closely the statements ascribed to Wilson in the "M.P." memorandum. It seems likely that Palmer gave Simon and Levy his interpretation of Wilson's remarks, colored by his own attitudes, and that Palmer's words, in turn, were tailored for the German Foreign Office. It is also possible that Wilson spoke differently to Palmer than he would have had he known that his words were destined for publication in the *World*. In any case, the President never considered the matter important, and he showed no hesitation because of it in appointing Palmer to high government office.

The "M.P." incident, however, armed Palmer's enemies with new accusations, and it planted suspicion of Palmer's patriotism in the public mind. Some of his actions between 1918 and 1920, when he held positions of national prominence, were motivated, in part, by the necessity of erasing those lingering doubts.

Before he consolidated his position in Pennsylvania by obtaining an influential position in the administration, Palmer encountered two more threats to his leadership of the state party. First came the almost inevitable challenge from Mutchler's ally, Representative Steele. The battle took place quietly over what appeared to be a small matter, the appointment of a postmaster; but to politicians throughout Pennsylvania the issue was pregnant with meaning. After he took office in March, 1915, Steele followed the old congressional custom of recommending men to fill vacant federal positions in his district. From the beginning of the Wilson administration, federal appointments in Pennsylvania had been made only with the approval of Palmer or Morris. But with Morris abroad and Palmer out of Congress—apparently on the verge of retirement —Steele's recommendations were accepted; a number of his choices, including four postmasters, received appointments.[31]

Shortly after his renomination as congressman in May, 1916, Steele nominated Warren Roberts, a member of the Mutchler organization, for postmaster at Bethlehem. Palmer, on the other hand, asked that the leader of his supporters in the city, Allen H. Barthold, be appointed. Burleson balanced Palmer's power against the congressman's—and decided to appoint Steele's man. Congress would probably be divided fairly evenly after the next election, Burleson reasoned, and Steele's vote would be needed.

When Palmer learned from Blakeslee of Burleson's decision, he took his case to Wilson. "I can only plead by way of excuse that this is absolutely the first time I have brought any Pennsylvania patronage troubles direct to you," he pointed out. Steele's recommendation of Roberts, declared Palmer, was "intended to be a direct slap at me and it would be so construed by all the citizens of the district." Wilson, who heard of the matter for the first time, asked Burleson for advice, observing: "Evidently Mitchell Palmer's feeling in the matter is exceedingly deep." Debate continued within the administration for several months without decision. Palmer worded his next letter as strongly as he could, yet he made it dignified and reasonable enough to command Wilson's respect. Both candidates, he assured the President, were admirably qualified. What Wilson had to decide was whether to support Palmer or Steele. The Congressman, Palmer pointed out, was one of two Democrats to vote against the Adamson Eight-Hour bill, and one of three or four Democrats to vote against establishment of a government factory to manufacture armor plate. The latter vote, especially, Palmer charged, was proof that Steele's chief role in Congress was as servant for the Bethlehem Steel Company, a major producer of armor plate.

After reading the letter the President concluded to Burleson: "Palmer has convinced me." Despite warnings that Steele might avenge himself by being absent or even by voting with the enemy on key bills, Palmer's man was appointed.[32]

Another challenge came from Congressman Liebel, who took the field in mid-1916 as the old guard's champion in the contest for national committeeman. This fight was decided by a popular vote in the May Democratic primary. Liebel attacked Palmer's "dictatorial methods" and argued, as Palmer himself had done five years before, that only a change in leadership was needed to assure party victory. Palmer, however, remained by far the most popular Democrat in Pennsylvania. He carried sixty-three out of sixty-seven counties, and even came close in Philadelphia.[33]

Palmer's influence among leaders of the national party increased not only as a result of his easy reelection, but also because his friend Vance McCormick was named chairman of the Democratic national committee. McCormick owed his election largely to a last-minute plea from Palmer to Wilson. The President had asked Colonel House to find a new national chairman to manage his campaign for reelection; preferably a known progressive who could help win the votes of those who had supported Theodore Roosevelt in 1912.[34] McCormick, among the first candidates approached by House, told the President's emissary that he could not accept the job, both for per-

sonal reasons and because liquor interests so violently opposed
him that his selection might bring them into the campaign
against Wilson.[35]

McCormick probably did not mean to give House a definite
refusal; more likely he wanted the President to understand fully
that if chosen he might prove a handicap. Nevertheless, House's
interest passed to other men, finally settling on Homer Cummings, national committeeman from Connecticut.[36] Initially
House had doubts about Cummings, who had been divorced
after a notorious breach-of-promise suit, and, even more damaging, served as attorney for the New Haven Railroad. A few
days before the convention, however, House decided that Cummings was the best choice. He sent Wilson a laudatory memorandum about the Connecticut committeeman written by
Frank Cobb, editor of the *World,* who knew him well. House
concluded that nothing more serious could be proven against
Cummings than that he was a successful, well-paid corporation lawyer.[37]

The day after House's recommendation of Cummings,
Palmer wired the President from St. Louis, where the national
committee was meeting.

Chairmanship of the National Committee ought to be settled immediately. Members of the Committee are organizing for Cummings
whose election would be a mistake. Chairman ought to be man
who can make strong appeal to Progressives. Best man in my judgment is Vance C. McCormick. . . . If you will indicate preference
for McCormick now campaign will immediately start right.[38]

Informed in this fashion of McCormick's availability, Wilson notified party leaders that the Pennsylvanian was his choice.
Palmer assured the committee that McCormick would do a
superb job; "I know him as a brother knows a brother." Cummings joined Palmer in pushing through McCormick's election
despite strenuous opposition led by Committeeman Edward H.
Moore of Ohio, who insisted that McCormick was ineligible
for the chairmanship because he was not a member of the committee.[39]

During the campaign, Palmer labored once again at the

hapless task of trying to win his state for the Democrats. This time Wilson, detained in Washington until October by negotiations to end a major railroad strike, could not be induced to speak in Pennsylvania. In an effort to rally discouraged party workers, several thousand Pennsylvania Democrats were herded aboard a special train in Philadelphia on October 14 and transported to Long Branch, New Jersey. The politicians then marched eight abreast for over a mile to Wilson's home at Shadow Lawn, carrying banners and pennants, and singing and cheering most of the way to the accompaniment of half a dozen loud brass bands.

Wilson greeted them from his front porch. After an introductory speech by Palmer, the President tried to cheer the tired pilgrims with a reminder that New Jersey progressives also had fought unsuccessfully for many years before they displaced the entrenched political bosses. It must have been scant comfort to Palmer and his followers that six years after Wilson had won New Jersey their own prospects were still too meager to warrant a Presidential visit to their state. The Pennsylvanians were sufficiently inspired, however, to march back to the station in Long Branch with banners still flying and brass bands blaring.[40]

Pennsylvania did receive a visit from the junior member of the ticket, however. Just before the election, Vice President Thomas Marshall addressed a large audience in the Philadelphia Academy of Music. A reporter for a Republican newspaper observed that Palmer, "who delivered a stirring address in defense of the President's foreign policies and of the Adamson Eight-Hour bill, received an ovation which equaled that accorded the Vice President." [41]

Charles Evans Hughes, the Republican Presidential candidate, took no chances with Pennsylvania's large block of electoral votes. He campaigned through the state twice, almost always concentrating on the tariff. In Pittsburgh he warned that unless Republican tariff policies were adopted, "when the world war ends the industrial war will begin, conducted by countries which have protected themselves behind high tariff walls, which will flood this country with their cheap labor products." [42] Businessmen received copies of a letter signed by Penrose charging Wilson with putting the country "virtually on a free trade basis." [43]

Nevertheless, Palmer probably cherished some hope of victory. The European war provided Pennsylvania industry with all the protection it needed; profits were high, unemployment low. Democratic orators stressed the fact that the Wilson administration had kept us out of war and that its legislation helped the workingman. Palmer remained closely in touch with leaders of the railroad brotherhoods. These unions, which benefited from the Adamson Eight-Hour law, were expected to make large contributions in votes and money to the Democratic campaign. Brotherhood officials joined the squads of Democratic speakers sent by Palmer to tour Pennsylvania's major industrial areas in October and November. [44]

The Democrats organized their campaign far more effectively than in the past, largely because Joe Guffey replaced the absent Morris as State Chairman. Palmer and Guffey, usually traveling together, visited party leaders in every county, invigorating the local politicians and arranging a series of mass meetings. [45]

On November 1, Palmer optimistically announced that the result in Pennsylvania remained in doubt. [46] A week later, Pennsylvania returned its customary large Republican majority, this time about 180,000 votes. If Palmer still thought of himself as the workingman's friend, he must have been disillusioned by the support Republican candidates received in the state's labor districts; even Congressmen Casey and Warren Worth Bailey were defeated. [47] By this time, Palmer could hardly help but feel that labor, in Pennsylvania at least, was ungrateful to its political friends. [48] Stymied within his own state, Palmer turned again to the national administration for an opportunity to win political power.

CHAPTER VIII

ALIEN PROPERTY CUSTODIAN

On April 2, 1917, Woodrow Wilson went before a joint session of Congress and asked for a declaration of war against Germany. The previous day, in one of the most sagacious prophesies ever made by an American political leader, Wilson had said to Frank S. Cobb of the New York *World:*

Once lead this country into war . . . and they'll forget there ever was such a thing as tolerance. To fight you must be brutal and ruthless, and the spirit of ruthless brutality will enter into every fibre of our national life, infecting Congress, the courts, the policeman on the beat, the man on the street. Conformity would be the only virtue . . . and every man who refused to conform would have to pay the penalty.[1]

As the martial spirit swept America early in 1917, Palmer found himself with an unenviable reputation: an acknowledged pacifist, he was also suspected of collaboration with German agents. As soon as the United States declared war, Palmer underwent a startling metamorphosis; the former pacifist became one of the most aggressive belligerents. A national magazine reported that when America entered the war, Palmer told a friend, "I made up my mind that I just must get into it somehow, even if I had to carry a gun as a private." [2] Two days after we declared war, the Quaker politician visited the White House and offered his services "in any capacity without compensation." [3] In part, Palmer's transformation can be attributed to an abiding and genuine pride in his country. But Palmer's actions henceforth were motivated also by a desire to protect his political future. Wilson was not the only one to sense the change in America's temper.

Palmer's first wartime job as chairman of his district draft board fell short of his aspirations. His friends, however, continued to work for his elevation to a more responsible position. In September, 1917, Herbert Hoover, director of the newly established Food Administration, asked Tumulty to recommend a lawyer to direct the agency's controls over the meat-packing industry. Tumulty reported to McCormick: "He said he wanted a big, progressive, upstanding fellow who could handle this big problem. I suggested Mitchell Palmer." McCormick enthusiastically offered to follow up the suggestion, but Hoover could not be persuaded to appoint Palmer.[5]

In October, 1917, Wilson created the office of Alien Property Custodian to take over and administer enemy-owned property in the United States. Palmer, whose experience as a lawyer and a banker qualified him for the position, was named Custodian. Fortunately for him, Congress was too busy with other matters to hold up his appointment while it investigated his role in the "M.P." affair, and the *World* did not bring up the matter again until Palmer's nomination as Attorney-General in 1919. Nevertheless, many Americans wondered why a man suspected of dealing with German agents was given control over all German property here. A Fairfield, Illinois, resident protested against the appointment, complaining to Tumulty of rumors that Palmer had made daily reports to the German ambassador about his confidential talks with the President.[6] Doubts about Palmer's patriotism did not disappear until he began his crusade against radicals in 1919–1920.

No one in the administration realized what an enormous task the new Custodian had been given. At first, Palmer recalled, "I was shoved off into a little back room behind a tailor shop with nothing to begin work with except a lead pencil and a colored messenger at the door." [7] As it turned out, German property holdings in the United States were extensive and valuable. Palmer told the New York City Bar Association in December, 1918, that his office was administering 29,753 trusts worth $506,400,500.94 and that 9,000 additional trusts with an approximate value of $300,000,000 had not yet been officially evaluated.[8] By mid-November Palmer's fast-growing staff was spread over parts of four Washington buildings, and early in January, 1918, he converted a large uncompleted apartment house into an office building for his 300 Washington employees.[9] Soon afterward, Palmer opened a New York office as well.

The job required broad business knowledge and superior executive abilities. Palmer managed a wide variety of properties, including many firms producing goods essential to the armed forces. "When the armistice was signed," Palmer reported to Congress:

the Alien Property Custodian was supplying the Government with magnetos for aeroplane and automobile motors, with cloth to make uniforms for the soldiers and the dyes with which the cloth was dyed, with medicines, surgical instruments and dressings, with musical instruments, with ball bearings, telescopes, optical instruments and engineering instruments, with charcoal for the making of gas masks, with glycerin for the making of high explosives, and a large number of other and varied products. In some instances the enemy-owned corporations . . . were running 100 per cent of their capacity on Government business.[10]

Palmer's agency also engaged in the lumbering and shipbuilding industries; companies under his control raised sugar, cotton, tobacco, and chicory; published newspapers; mined and smelted lead, zinc, copper, silver, and tungsten; manufactured iron and steel products, brewed beer, and produced chocolate, machinery, and munitions.[11]

As a model for the organization he rapidly established Palmer used the large commercial trust company, whose function, like that of the Custodian's office, was to supervise a large variety of businesses.[12] There were some important differences, however, between Palmer's organization and the ordinary trust company. Most important, the Alien Property Custodian was obliged to uncover by investigation a large proportion of the trust estates which belonged in his hands. The Germans, who foresaw the declaration of war and had had experience with alien property offices in England, France, and Germany, took measures to hide their assets. In an effort to ferret out enemy-owned property, Palmer established a sizable Bureau of Investigation.[13]

Unlike the ordinary trust company, the Custodian received the property he was to administer before he could establish an efficient organization. Therefore Palmer needed immediately a large number of experienced executives and attorneys, capable of accepting great responsibilities. Wisely, Palmer ignored political obligations in making most of his early appointments. He manned the key posts in his agency largely with financiers and attorneys of impeccable reputation and high-level business experience. The managing director was J. Lionberger Davis, a nationally respected St. Louis banker and vice president of the St. Louis Chamber of Commerce. To head his Bureau of Trusts Palmer named Ralph Stone, president of the Detroit Trust Company, and as general counsel Moritz Rosenthal, partner in a large New York banking firm and previously an attorney retained by some of the nation's largest corporations.[14]

For the vital post of director of his Bureau of Investigation, Palmer chose Francis P. Garvan, chief of the Homicide, Insurance, and Business Division in the New York district attorney's office—a superior sleuth and a clever interrogator. "Work with Garvan," Palmer ordered one of his young assistants, "he has a way of breaking down these German fellows and making them confess the truth." [15] Garvan, who eventually exerted enormous influence on Palmer's policies and succeeded his chief as Custodian, was described by an acquaintance as a "warm-hearted, nimble-witted, pugnacious Irishman." Another associate found that despite Garvan's great wealth and Yale education, this son of an immigrant contractor "had a coarse streak about him which was a bit puzzling." Yet Palmer apparently valued his advice very highly. The two men shared an aversion to certain types of "foreigners," a feeling that dangerous internal enemies were plotting against the country, and a powerful devotion to Palmer's political career.[16]

Palmer also brought two of his closest personal associates into the new organization. He appointed Norman Dreher, his personal assistant for twenty years, director of the Bureau of Administration. Palmer's young Stroudsburg law partner, Allan R. Bensinger, became his personal secretary.[17] These two assistants Palmer knew he could trust completely—and they would do his bidding without question.

The new Custodian worked hard; he wore out secretaries, dictating letters, directives, speeches and publicity releases at a furious pace. His anteroom was always crowded with supplicants: officers of German-owned firms or their lawyers, or American businessmen who had German partners. All hoped to stave off action by the Custodian, who, by law, acted as judge and jury in deciding whether a company should be taken over. Other visitors desired the lucrative directorships and legal positions which the Custodian had to offer, or they wanted to lease German-owned factories and patents.

Palmer talked to scores of people daily, apparently without fatigue. He was stubborn, occasionally impatient and angry with those who tried to hide enemy ownership of their firms or to avoid compliance with his orders to surrender property. Most visitors and employees, however, found him friendly and relaxed. When he wanted to discuss something with an assistant, Palmer would walk down the hall to the man's office, pull up a chair, and after preliminary casual conversation come directly to the point. Palmer was accustomed to an arduous routine, and his habits were those of a small-town lawyer and rising politician. Inclined to be arrogant toward his enemies, he depended upon his charm and tact to win the cooperation of his associates.[18]

The demands of Palmer's job coincided to a large extent with those of his ambitions. He appointed many capable assistants partly because he feared that lesser men's mistakes would injure his reputation. The enormous effort he invested in publicizing his agency's duties and achievements contributed greatly to his performance as Custodian. Publicity was a vital part of Palmer's job—he needed the assistance of informants to unearth hidden enemy assets. So assiduously did the Custodian work at obtaining newspaper and magazine publicity, however, that the President was obliged to insist that Palmer leave such matters to George Creel, head of the government's Committee on Public Education.[19] Palmer fed a steady stream of information to Creel, who eventually did almost as good a job of advertising the Custodian's work as Palmer's office had done.[20]

Palmer also used other means of reaching the public. In the course of an immense official correspondence aimed chiefly at uncovering enemy-owned property, Palmer informed well over 100,000 influential Americans of his agency's work. By mail, he requested information from every lawyer in the United States, and he received replies from 35,000. Every probate judge in the country received an inquiry, as did each of the nation's banks and building and loan associations. Palmer also sought aid from 56,000 postmasters, and from heads of many federal agencies.[21]

However, Palmer's political ambitions sometimes damaged his performance as Custodian. The vast number of jobs at his disposal, in the Custodian's office and in the firms under his control, gave him the long-awaited opportunity to build a nation-wide political organization. Below the top level, Palmer considered appointments largely as political patronage.

Of the fifty-one state counsels the Custodian retained in 1917 and 1918 to advise on state laws and to help litigate in state courts, seventeen attended the Democratic national conventions of 1916 or 1920 as delegates or national committeemen, or were relatives or law partners of delegates or committeemen.[22] Several others ranked high in the national party. Among the Custodian's state attorneys were National Committeemen E. D. Smith of Alabama, Isidor B. Dockweiler of California, Arthur F. Mullen of Nebraska and Angus W. McLean of North Carolina. Others included Boetius H. Sullivan, son of Illinois Democratic boss Roger Sullivan; Frank A. Morey, law partner of Congressman McGillicuddy of Maine; Alfred C. Kremer, law partner of Montana National Committeeman J. Bruce Kremer; and former congressmen J. Henry Goeke of Ohio and J. Harry Covington of Maryland, both still very influential in party affairs.[23]

Some of these men also served as directors of or attorneys

for companies taken over by the Custodian. Covington, for example, who helped manage Palmer's campaign for the Democratic Presidential nomination in 1920, received about $17,500 in fees for legal services to the Bayer Chemical Company, $3,000 from the Berlin Aniline Works and $26,000 from the Bosch Magneto Company. Sullivan was awarded $12,500 for services to the Schoenhofen Brewing Company.[24]

Palmer appointed National Committeeman Homer Cummings of Connecticut as counsel for the International Textile Company of Bridgeport and as a director and counsel for Stollwerck Brothers, Stamford. He named National Committeeman Frederick B. Lynch of Minnesota president of Botany Mills and vice president of the American Trans-Atlantic Shipping Line. Former congressman John J. Fitzgerald, who had retired to private law practice in 1917 after eighteen years as leader of the Tammany delegation in Congress, received $37,000 from three companies under Palmer's control. Palmer appointed former congressman Arsene P. Pujo of Louisiana a director of H. Koppers and Company, large Pittsburgh-based chemical firm; and Palmer's old political associate and adversary, J. Davis Brodhead, was employed first on Palmer's regular staff of attorneys, then as counsel and as a director of a number of enemy-owned firms. James C. MacCloskey, Jr., son of a Democratic leader in Pittsburgh, received lucrative positions as attorney for the Orenstein and Koppel Corporation, which paid him $20,323.59, and the Passaic Worsted Spinning Company, Garfield Woolen Mills, and Gera Mills, each of which awarded him $1,059.08.

Jersey Democratic leader Mark Sullivan served as director for several companies, as did influential Jersey politicians William E. Tuttle, a former congressman; Edward Grosscup, former state treasurer; and James F. Fiedler, former governor. In addition, Palmer assigned positions to Robert F. Wagner, Alfred E. Smith, Dudley Field Malone, and former governor Martin J. Glynn, all of New York, and to former national committeeman Joseph E. Davies of Wisconsin. William J. Harris of Georgia was made supervisor and liquidator of a

German-owned firm while he was United States senator-elect. Two of the largest financial contributors to Woodrow Wilson's campaigns, Henry Morgenthau, Sr., and Abram I. Elkus of New York, received assignments from Palmer. Elkus received over $16,000 in fees. Harris and Davies earned $5,000 each for very brief service.[25] With such appointments as these Palmer went a long way toward making himself the Democratic politicians' choice for the Presidential nomination in 1920.

The real prizes among the positions Palmer had to offer, however, went to four New York City attorneys who were appointed solely because of their exceptional abilities. James A. Delehanty, John Quinn, John L. Crocker, and Isidor J. Kresel each received fees totaling over $100,000 for work done for the Alien Property Custodian.[26] But of the four, only Quinn was connected with the Tammany organization. Palmer, who had built his Pennsylvania machine with the assistance of federal patronage, recognized his own obligation to help fellow Democrats. He also understood, however, that for the sake of his political future he must avoid scandals arising either from dishonesty or incompetence, and therefore he tried to choose men of proven capabilities for the key positions in his agency.

Delehanty was an independent, highly respected judge in the New York Court of General Sessions, but lost his campaign for reelection in 1916 to a Tammany-backed candidate.[27] Crocker, a graduate of Harvard Law School, and a corporation lawyer of some distinction, was a Democrat, but a friend and occasional supporter of William Church Osborne, leader of the upstate opposition to Boss Murphy. Although Crocker's law firm served as counsel for 150 enemy-owned companies, he worked without a fee in ninety percent of these cases. "The total amounts received by us," Crocker reported to Garvan in 1920, "have not been equal to the overhead expenses of my office directly chargeable to the work done for the Alien Property Custodian." [28]

Kresel, an investigator of extraordinary ability—keen, ruthless, and perservering—had worked with Garvan in the New York District Attorney's office before Kresel entered private practice. On Garvan's recommendation, he received the task of ferreting out hidden German investments in the metal industries. He did such a superb job that Palmer called upon him again in 1919 to take charge of the Justice Department's investigation of the major meat packers, a probe which resulted in successful antitrust action. Another of Kresel's investigations enabled Palmer, as Attorney-General, to bring suit against the leading cement manufacturers.[29]

Quinn, who received $174,000 in fees—far more than any other attorney—for work assigned by Palmer, enjoyed a close relationship with Tammany leaders.[30] But by 1918, Quinn was too occupied with his legal practice and his career as a leading patron of the arts to have time for politics. A recognized authority on banking law, he acted as attorney for some of New York's largest financial institutions. Before Palmer's appointment as Custodian, Quinn published a treatise on the significance for banks of the new Trading-with-the-Enemy Act, giving special attention to the problem of alien property. In a case tried before the United States Supreme Court, Quinn won the decision which established the constitutionality of Palmer's seizures under the Trading-with-the-Enemy Act.[31]

There were few public complaints about the size of fees awarded to Custodian-appointed attorneys, possibly because Palmer and Garvan never fully complied with congressional instructions to turn over information about these payments. However, even after the fees were published in 1922, no cry went up for investigation. Perhaps congressmen were satisfied with the knowledge that eminent attorneys like Quinn, Crocker, Cummings, Elkus, and Delehanty obtained equally high, or even higher fees from their other corporate clients. Then too, most congressmen were lawyers themselves, and many must have seen the dangers in a long debate on the proper compensation for legal work.

Most of the criticism that centered for years on Palmer's administration of the Alien Property Custodian's office arose not from his appointments or the fees allowed, but from his sales of enemy property. To some it seemed that Palmer was passing around a gigantic gravy bowl to his friends and political associates. With his extravagant enthusiasm for selling German property, his occasional recklessness, and his stubbornness when criticized, Palmer encouraged such beliefs.

The original Trading-with-the-Enemy Act gave the Custodian the right of sale only in exceptional cases, such as the threat of spoilage, and apparently Palmer was satisfied, at first, to be what he called a "mere conservator" of enemy-owned property. But the period in 1918 during which Palmer and Garvan became aware of the extent of German investments in this country was one of rising nationwide hatred of everything German. Government agencies helped disseminate tales of German undercover plots to gain world domination; the popular image of hordes of insidious German agents at work gave rise to a great deal of hysterical fear. At the same time that Kresel and Garvan's other investigators began to report their findings, Attorney-General Thomas Watt Gregory informed a friend: "We not infrequently receive as many as fifteen hundred letters in a single day suggesting disloyalty and the making of investigations." [32] He advised another correspondent:

Keep your shirt on and don't accept as true the utterly baseless statements constantly being made, such as that gas masks are being intentionally made defective; that arms and munitions are being shipped to Germany, that the efforts to investigate and enforce the law are utterly inadequate, and that munition plants are being blown up and destroyed all over the country. [33]

Palmer and Garvan were receptive to stories of foreign plots, and they were susceptible to the national fear of German agents. Evidence of German investments in American industry they took as proof of a "great industrial and commercial army which Germany planted here with hostile intent." [34] Palmer had always felt hostility to recent immigrants—taking advantage of American freedom, he felt, without adopting American ways. [35] When he discovered the German "plot," he determined that at least this noxious foreign influence would soon be eliminated.

In his first report to Congress, early in 1918, Palmer pleaded with the legislators to "make the Trading-with-the-Enemy Act a fighting force in the war" by allowing the custodian to sell all enemy-owned industrial and commercial property. He assured Congress:

Great and permanent good will result to this country from the Americanization of these enemy-owned concerns. A hybrid Americanization is no less dangerous in industry than in individuals. Foreign capital ought to be welcomed here, but only if it becomes promptly naturalized and remains loyal to the country of its adoption.[36]

Palmer's enthusiasm for the "Americanization" of enemy assets here was probably heightened by the knowledge that many Americans shared his hatred of the enemy, and that consequently his actions would be extremely popular. Doubtless the Custodian also understood that his offensive against German economic power would go far toward allaying the suspicions of those who questioned his patriotism.

Palmer took his demand for unrestricted power of sale to the President. Wilson, not yet caught up in the most virulent form of war fever, found Palmer's request unnecessarily drastic. Palmer acknowledged: "He called my attention to the fact that I had issued immediately after becoming Alien Property Custodian, a public statement . . . to the effect that the Alien Property Custodian was a mere conservator of these enemy properties." [37]

There were ways of appealing to Wilson, however, and Palmer knew his man. Colonel House had advised a friend that Wilson could be won only through his emotions: "Never begin by arguing. Discover a common hate, exploit it, get the President warmed up and then start your business." [38] His investigations, Palmer told the President, revealed enormous investments in American industry by the German ruling classes—he referred to them as "the Junker class." These men, known to be militarists and monopolists, were a group that Wilson could despise. Experts who studied the German investments agreed, Palmer continued, that they were "part of the deliberate plan of Germany to conquer the world by trade." To Palmer—and he hoped the President would agree—it seemed an "absolutely unmoral proposition" for the American government to continue, at great expense, to collect enormous wartime profits which would eventually be returned to the very Germans who caused the war.

Concluding with a burst of eloquence, Palmer asserted that the confidence of German leaders was buoyed by knowledge that no matter what happened in the war, they could still win America through industrial invasion. Now it was necessary to strike at that confidence. The Germans were riding high; there were reports that Paris was about to fall. As Palmer recalled his closing words:

I asked the President to let me go down to the Congress and ask Congress to hit the Germans where it would hurt, to strike a blow from which they knew they could never recover, and let them know right now, as an act of war, that we proposed to Americanize this property.

Wilson's belief in the sacredness of private property failed to withstand such salesmanship; he promised to support Palmer's plan.[39]

Eager to separate German owners from their property here and at the same time to exploit the possibilities for augmented personal power, Palmer demanded the right to dispose of enemy-owned property at private sale rather than through public auction. He warned Congress that German agents might buy companies which produced essential war goods if the firms were sold at auction. Nevertheless, Senator Frelinghuysen, who suspected that Palmer would use private sales to enrich his friends, insisted upon public bidding, and his amendment to that effect was accepted by Congress.[40]

The power of sale was a mixed blessing to Palmer. It enabled him to eliminate the German investments he found so threatening to the economy, and it earned him a national reputation as a dynamic champion of "Americanism." On the other hand, the rich prizes under his control attracted the attention of greedy, unscrupulous men and placed temptation in

the path of some of the Custodian's friends and political associates. Inevitably, Palmer faced numerous charges of dishonesty,
some of which resulted from disappointment and envy, some of
which he brought upon himself with his highhandedness. Then
too, there is reason to believe that Palmer closed his eyes to
the manipulations and dishonesty of some of his friends; although, as always, he himself seems to have walked successfully
the fine line which separates the legal from the illegal.

His first move was to protect himself against charges of corruption or favoritism by setting up an Advisory Sales Committee composed of four distinguished bankers and an eminent
jurist. No sale was to be final until this board, which would
meet weekly, approved the terms and method of sale and the
integrity of the buyer. The five members were Otto T. Bannard, chairman of the board of directors of the New York
Trust Company; George L. Ingraham, former presiding judge
of the Appelate Division, New York State Supreme Court; Cleveland H. Dodge, vice president of Phelps Dodge Corporation,
director of the National City Bank and other financial institutions, and one of Woodrow Wilson's most trusted friends;
Benjamin H. Griswald, Jr., head of the banking firm of Alexander Brown and Sons, Baltimore, also an attorney and judge
advocate of Maryland; and Ralph Stone, president of the Detroit Trust Company, who was familiar with the operation of
Palmer's agency because of his former service as director of
the Bureau of Trusts in the Custodian's office. Palmer assured
a Senate committee in 1919:

With all the millions and millions of dollars worth of property
which I sold while I was Alien Property Custodian, I never put my
hand to an instrument that approved a single one of those sales
until this committee of five of the most distinguished men in America had put their stamp of approval upon it unanimously.[41]

Bannard, Ingraham, Dodge, Griswald, and Stone were con-
scientious, incorruptible, and proud of their reputations. They
would not be mere figureheads, as Palmer must have known
when he asked them to serve. Indeed, Palmer may have appointed such men not only as protection against criticism, but

as a check on himself; for he may have foreseen that he would be subjected to pressures beyond his power to resist. On a number of occasions the Advisory Board canceled sales or refused to permit private sales which might have resulted in severe criticism for the Custodian.[42]

There were scandals nevertheless. Palmer's first serious mistake was to choose Joe Guffey as director of sales. Guffey had proven himself a reliable if ruthless political lieutenant, but he was not the man to assume responsibility for selling hundreds of millions of dollars worth of property held in trust. The post required a judicious public servant of extraordinary integrity, and Guffey was an opportunist, deeply involved in oil speculations.

Guffey soon learned that his predecessor, Joseph Bower, had used proceeds from enemy property sales (allowed under the old regulations to prevent spoilage) to benefit a bank with which he had been connected before the war. Bower customarily deposited large sums in the bank for three or four weeks at a time, enabling it to increase its loans in a period of industrial and commercial expansion and high demand for capital. According to the law, proceeds from sales of enemy property were to be transferred immediately to the United States Treasury for conversion into government bonds; but Bower never was reprimanded for his dilatoriness.[43]

Shortly after he took office, Guffey began depositing sales proceeds in trust accounts in various New York banks. Eventually, most of the money in his control found its way into the Guaranty Trust Company, which received about $42,000,000 during Guffey's regime. Another $1,600,000 was deposited in the American Trust Company, and large amounts went to the Harriman National Bank. This money usually remained on deposit for several months. From time to time Guffey made large withdrawals for his personal use, sometimes keeping the money for weeks. Guffey also negotiated personal loans totaling $2,147,774 from the banks in which he maintained these accounts, pledging as collateral the highly speculative common stock of two oil companies he controlled. Evidently he utilized the money to increase his oil stock holdings. In one case Guffey used $275,000 of the government's money, which he had deposited under his own name in the American Trust Company, as security for a personal loan.

Guffey neither reported the interest earned by funds he deposited nor remitted the interest to Washington. The accounting division in Washington and Guffey's sales office exchanged correspondence on the matter in mid-1920; but not until March, 1921, when the Democrats were about to leave office, did Garvan protect himself by insisting that Guffey turn over the interest, which by that time amounted to over $400,000.[44] It is difficult to believe that Garvan, head of the New York office and Guffey's direct superior until he became Custodian in March 1919, did not know in 1918 that funds were being retained for long periods in New York banks. It is equally unlikely that Palmer, who was chairman of the board of one bank and director of another, failed to realize that Guffey was holding back both the sales proceeds and the interest earned by his accounts. A federal grand jury indicted Guffey in December, 1922, on twelve counts of embezzlement from the government; But Palmer was not held responsible in any way for the actions of his employee and close political associate.[45]

Palmer erred a second time in 1918 when he chose Governor-General of the Philippine Islands Francis Burton Harrison as managing director of the Alien Property Office there. Before Wilson appointed him to the Philippine post in 1915, Harrison had served five terms in Congress where he was associated with Palmer on the Ways and Means Committee.[46] Harrison delegated most of his alien property duties to his brother Archibald, secretary of the Philippine National Bank in Manila. The most valuable enemy-owned properties seized by the Harrisons were placed in the hands of a few of their friends and business associates. After these cronies received extravagant fees for several months, they were allowed to buy the companies under their management with money borrowed from the Philippine National Bank. The properties were sold by sealed bids called for on very short notice.[47]

When Palmer received information about these sales, he tried to avert a gigantic scandal that would cloud his reputation and perhaps ruin his political career. After a series of urgent warnings failed to affect Harrison's policies, Palmer ordered him to discontinue the sales and cancel those already made even if the property had been transferred. Harrison responded by dispatching his personal secretary, Fred N. Berry, and another assistant to Washington to seek aid from his friends in the Custodian's office and to plead with Palmer to suspend judgment. The worried Custodian replied: "My decision disapproving sales is final, nothing Quinn or Berry could say will alter it. . . ." Harrison promptly resigned as the Custodian's representative. "I consider your instructions to cancel sales . . . unreasonable, unjust, illegal and impracticable," he cabled Palmer, and he released the text of his message to the press.[48]

Anxious to end the matter before it brought on a congressional investigation, Palmer appealed to the President for a decision, and on July 22, Wilson notified the Governor-General: "I am clearly of the opinion that Palmer is right." Harrison then agreed to revoke the sales.[49] Palmer's chief concern, after the cancellations, was to keep the affair quiet. As one of Harrison's emissaries in Washington reported: "You cannot realize the delicacy of alien property matters here and caution necessary to protect against coming attacks and partisan investigations." Palmer sent New York attorney Douglas M. Moffat to replace Harrison with instructions to "keep the lid on." Moffat, he assured the Governor-General, was a man "who I am sure you will like." [50]

Moffat proceeded to approve the resale to the original purchasers of all the properties, except one, whose sale had been canceled. In almost every case, Berry was dispatched to visit the internment camps in which the German owners were held, and to offer these men their freedom if they agreed to sell their property. Not only did members of the Custodian's staff assist Berry in this scheme, but Palmer and Moffat were completely aware of his activities.[51] Once again, although abundant evidence of fraud was uncovered by the Republican administrations of the 1920's, no one was brought to trial.[52]

In two other cases Palmer did not escape so easily. His most serious difficulties arose from the sale of the Bosch Magneto Company, largest producer of magnetos in the United States. When Palmer took over this firm he appointed a new team of executives. As general manager in charge of operations he named Arthur T. Murray, president of Bethlehem Motors Company, a truck manufacturing firm in Allentown, Pennsylvania. Murray was chosen, Palmer admitted, because "he happened to be one automobile manufacturer whom I personally knew. . . . I had known him for years." [53] Palmer also appointed George A. MacDonald as treasurer, John A. MacMartin as assistant secretary, and J. Harry Covington as associate counsel.[54] Later the Justice Department charged these four men with participating in a conspiracy to defraud the government.

In December, 1918, Bosch Magneto was sold at auction to Martin E. Kern, of Allentown, Pennsylvania, who was the chief stockholder in Bethlehem Motors and a friend and client of Palmer's. Covington represented Kern as counsel in arranging the sale, and five of the firm's chief executives, including Murray, MacDonald, and MacMartin, became the top company officials after Kern reorganized it. Murray was named president, MacDonald vice president and treasurer, and MacMartin secretary and assistant treasurer. In addition, all four men received large stock bonuses.[55]

Immediately after the sale, rumors circulated in the business world that the auction had been rigged, and substantial evidence indicates that the rumors were correct. Kern had formed Bethlehem Motors soon after his release from Sing Sing penitentiary, where he had been imprisoned for jewel theft. After diverting enough money from the firm to buy a newspaper, a bank, a brewery, real estate, and other property in the Allentown area, he allowed it to declare bankruptcy, settling with creditors for ten cents on the dollar. It was discovered that the company, whose liquid assets totaled $621,000, had borrowed $1,700,000 from banks in various parts of the country.[56]

Palmer helped Kern win control of Bosch Magneto by making it difficult for anyone outside the company to obtain accurate information about its value. Soon after the Custodian took

over, independent accountants audited the firm's books, calcu-
lating the net value of its assets over its liabilities at $8,587,-
547.68. Five profitable months later, MacMartin was authorized
by his fellow executives to conduct another audit; the result
this time showed a net value of only $5,699,667. MacMartin's
figures were published by Palmer in a prospectus sent to potential bidders for the company.[57] Palmer assured a Senate committee that MacMartin's audit had been checked by A. W.
Anthony of the large New York accounting firm Haskins and
Sells, and that MacMartin's figures were high rather than low.[58]
Anthony, however, was not an impartial investigator. Although
ostensibly employed by Haskins and Sells and assigned to accounting work in the Custodian's New York office, he served
as one of Guffey's principal aides. Anthony received large payments from Guffey's office for unexplained travel expenses and
for work done on cases completed before he was assigned to the
office. None of these payments, even those for work he actually
did, should have been made; Anthony's salary and expenses
were paid by Haskins and Sells, whose rules and contracts forbade compensation to its employees by clients. Anthony was so
securely in Guffey's confidence that when the Custodian's audit-
ing division inquired in 1919 about the interest collected by
the sales director but never remitted, it was Anthony who replied, effectively postponing an accounting.[59]

In other ways Palmer acted to discourage potential purchasers of Bosch Magneto. When he put the company up for
sale, he decreed that only those who deposited bonds of $50,000
with the Custodian could examine the corporation's books; an
additional bond of $50,000 was required in order to enter a bid.
Palmer acknowledged when questioned that these were by far
the highest bonds he ever required. Although the firm's main
offices were in New York, the Custodian held the bidding at
the company's plant in the small city of Chicopee in central
Massachusetts.[60]

Only four bidders deposited the required bonds and appeared in Chicopee on December 7, 1918. Two dropped out
when the bids jumped from $350,000 to $3,500,000, and the

company finally went to H. E. Griffiths of New York City for
$4,150,000.[61] This was an extremely low price for a concern
that had already proven itself capable of consistently earning
over a million dollars a year and had about two million dollars
in cash and government securities in its treasury.[62] Almost immediately after the sale was completed, the new owners issued
$1,800,000 worth of bonds, and their prospectus informed the
public that "Based on a report made by Messrs. Ernst & Ernst,
Certified Public Accountants, the net quick assets alone as of
September 30, 1918, were $4,367,767. . . . [In addition] The
value of the plant and equipment as certified by the Manufacturers' Appraisal Company as of September 30, 1918, was $2,-
363,300." Two of the three unsuccessful bidders, Charles B.
Fisk of the Fisk Rubber Tire Company, and the Chase Securities Company, were allowed to share in the purchase, and Chase
Securities was given a lucrative part in the reorganization.[63]

Palmer, of course, denied all charges that officers of the firm
had conspired with bankers to gain control of Bosch Magneto.
In a statement before the Senate Judiciary Committee in 1919,
he declared:

When Mr. Griffiths who bought the property and Hornblower and
Weeks and the Chase Corporation and a large list of persons who
were the real purchasers came to reorganize the company they asked
Mr. Murray if he would stay. . . . They were not automobile manufacturers, these purchasers. It really was bought as an investment
proposition by a lot of New England people who joined with Hornblower and Weeks to buy this property.

According to Palmer, when Murray and the other Custodian-appointed officials were asked by the New England financiers to remain with the company, they asked him if they would
be violating any law if they continued to serve the firm and accepted a "small block" of stock, totaling "twenty-five or thirty
shares," as a bonus. The Custodian assured them, he said, that
they would be blameless. Palmer told this outright lie with
great sincerity and he apparently convinced the Senators.[64]

As a matter of fact, when Bosch Magneto was sold, Palmer
knew full well that his friend Martin E. Kern rather than a

group of New England bankers would be the real owner. Although the New Englanders supplied Kern with money, they obtained only a minor share of the ownership. Garvan, in a report on the sale made only a little over a month before Palmer testified, declared:

I have made a complete investigation into the circumstances surrounding the sale of the Bosch Magneto Company, and the character of the purchaser. I have examined the letters of Hornblower and Weeks, and the letter of J. Harry Covington, counsel for Martin E. Kern, delivered January 6, 1919, and in view of my investigation and the filing of these letters, I beg to recommend that the Bureau of Sales approve the same to H. E. Griffiths, agent of Martin E. Kern, of Allentown, Pennsylvania.[65]

The "small block" of twenty-five or thirty shares of stock received as a bonus by Murray, MacDonald, and MacMartin, was already worth a small fortune when Palmer mentioned it so casually to his interrogators. Bosch Magneto's entire capitalization was two hundred and fifty shares of common stock, as the Custodian's prospectus of sale plainly declared.[66]

Kern quickly reorganized Bosch Magneto as the American Bosch Magneto Company, and offered securities to the public through a syndicate headed by Hornblower and Weeks. Kern's immediate paper profit was calculated by a Justice Department accountant at $302,246; Murray's profit was $275,584 and MacDonald's $168,500. Within six months of its sale to the public, furthermore, the price of American Bosch Magneto stock almost doubled, so the real profits of the new managers may have been much higher. Hornblower and Weeks earned $351,946 from commissions and a stock bonus, while Chase Securities made $210,000.[67]

Palmer, Kern, Covington, and three officers of American Bosch were charged, in 1926, with defrauding the government, and the case was put before a Boston grand jury in October, 1926. However, no indictments were obtained; the Justice Department could not prove that Palmer or any member of his staff benefitted from the sale. Kern testified that he no longer retained his correspondence with Palmer, Murray, or Hornblower and Weeks. Three of the four Justice Department agents assigned to the investigation reported to the Attorney-General that they could not find sufficient evidence to warrant further prosecution, and early in 1930 the case was dropped.[68]

Palmer encountered further difficulties because of his sale of over 5,000 German chemical patents to the Chemical Foundation, a private corporation formed to purchase them. The transaction occasioned little unfavorable criticism when it took place, early in 1919; but when the facts were reviewed in the calmer atmosphere of the mid-1920's, Palmer was implicated in what threatened to be another major scandal. One newspaper proclaimed, "Nothing in any oil transaction, not even the acts of Albert B. Fall, has any more sinister aspect." And Attorney-General Harlan Fiske Stone, who sued for return of the patents, wrote a friend: "You would hardly believe that such things could happen in our government." [69] In this case, Palmer's critics exaggerated his guilt. His actions broke no law; he engaged in no conspiracy; he showed no favoritism to any individual, corporation, or group of corporations within the chemical industry. Nevertheless, he again revealed a tendency to take important public matters into his own hands and to act as though any means were justified if the end was desirable.

Before 1914, German firms dominated the segment of the chemical industry based on coal-tar derivatives, especially manufacture of drugs and dyes. It seemed probable, in 1918, that after the war German producers would use their superior technical skill and strong patent positions to win back their U.S. chemical markets at the expense of the war-born American coal-tar chemical industry.[70] Palmer decided to save the new industry. His first solution was to sell the German branch houses here with all their patents and equipment. The Bayer Company's subsidiary, first to go on the auction block, was purchased on December 12, 1918, by the Sterling Products Company, highest of seven bidders, for $5,310,000. However, Sterling wanted only the medicinal patents, especially the one for aspirin. All other Bayer patents and the Bayer dye-producing plant were sold to the Grasselli Chemical Company; thus one firm obtained control of 1,200 of the most important coal-tar chemical patents. Palmer was flooded with complaints that he had destroyed a German monopoly only to set up an American one in its place.[71]

Garvan then devised a plan for an independent, nonprofit corporation which would purchase the Custodian-held chemical patents and license all American chemical producers to use them. Inasmuch as the proposed Chemical Foundation would receive rights to German patents applied for as recently as 1917, it promised to keep out German competition for many years. Garvan presented his idea to representatives of the chemical industry and, as Palmer proudly told Congress, "The suggestion . . . met with an instantaneous and enthusiastic approval." [72]

In order to establish the Foundation Palmer had to convince Woodrow Wilson of its great value to the country, for only the President could waive the requirement that enemy-owned property be sold at auction. Palmer talked with Wilson for about an hour on March 3, 1919. Once again, according to his own account, he did a superb sales job on his chief. Even though Palmer had incorporated the Chemical Foundation before he sought the President's approval, and Garvan, slated to replace Palmer as Custodian, was also to head the Foundation, Wilson agreed to have the auction provision disregarded.[73]

Later, Palmer was criticized for selling the patents too cheaply. "Who shall say that these men have the right to throw this property away?" Attorney-General Stone asked during his suit against the Foundation. Certainly the patents were worth much more than Palmer demanded for them and the chemical industry would gladly have paid a higher price. This money was lost not only to the German owners but to the American government as well, for our peace treaty with Germany provided that such funds could be used to pay indemnities owed the United States by Germany. Nevertheless, three federal courts, including the United States Supreme Court, decreed the sale legitimate.[74]

What is most questionable about Palmer's sale of the chemical patents, and about his entire career as Custodian, is not the illegality of his acts—he may well have remained within the law at all times, even in his sale of Bosch Magneto—but rather his broad interpretation of his powers. Palmer apparently believed that any action which protected the nation in any way was justified in time of emergency, and the Custodian had a very loose definition of an emergency. For example, he defended his seizure and sale of German property here after the enemy's surrender in Europe by pointing to the threat of post-war German economic competition. This threat was sufficient, he asserted, to justify continued use of the government's war-time powers. What were the limits of that government power? Palmer told an audience of New York attorneys, a month after the armistice: "The war power is of necessity an inherent power in every sovereign nation. It is the power of self preservation and that power has no limits other than the extent of the emergency." [75]

Armed with this philosophy, Palmer was impatient with legal barriers. He complained early in 1919 that "lawyers who, while the war was on, would have been unwilling to play any part in resisting the just demands of the Government in the taking of enemy property," were now opposing the Custodian's demands and even invoking the aid of the courts to do so.[76]

Palmer's precipitate use of his power led him into many conflicts with the more scrupulous Wilson. In most cases the President's cooler judgment prevailed. For example, he checked Palmer's inordinate efforts to obtain publicity. In September, 1918, Wilson warned Palmer: "Certain of my friends have reported to me a certain degree of uneasiness in the business world among men who want to purchase what you sell." When Wilson advised the Custodian to use his right of private sale—permissible for property worth less than $10,000—in the "most sparing manner and only when no other sort of sale is possible," Palmer promised compliance.[77] Again, when Palmer prepared to sell the Busch Brewery Company, despite strong evidence that the owner was an American citizen, Wilson forced him to abandon his plan: "I am sorry to differ with you in your judgment about the Busch property. . . . My advice, therefore, is that you release it as soon as possible." [78]

In other cases, Palmer convinced the President to let him move full speed ahead, Wilson's misgivings notwithstanding. Late in November, 1918, Wilson advised the Custodian:

It seems to me that it would not be wise to add just now to the list of alien names, in view of the virtual cessation of hostilities. . . . Misapprehensions . . . would arise if we seemed to be taking advantage of the technical continuation of the war to get hold of this property.[79]

But Palmer convinced the President that Germany had not abandoned her plans for the industrial conquest of this country, and the Custodian was allowed to continue his attempt to divorce German capital from American industry. Palmer earlier had obtained the right of unrestricted sale despite Wilson's original objections, and later he won authority to establish the Chemical Foundation. The President, preoccupied with problems of war and then of peace-making, might in other circumstances have detected a pattern in his conflicts with Palmer, and he might have sensed the danger in giving the Pennsylvanian even more power.

Attorney-General Gregory began to talk privately about retirement hardly two years after he succeeded McReynolds in August, 1914. He found the satisfactions of high office insufficient compensation for the financial sacrifices he made. Wilson managed to keep him in the cabinet until late 1918; then, with the war over, Gregory decided to reenter private legal practice. He recommended his exceptionally capable assistant, Caroll Todd, as successor.[80] The position immediately became the prize in a political tug-of-war, and Todd, whose only qualifications were experience, proven abilities, and the high recommendation of his chief, never had a chance.

The question of the Attorney-Generalship commanded especially great interest among northern Democratic leaders such as Tumulty, National Chairman McCormick, and Vice Chairman Cummings. After the shattering defeat their party suffered in the North in the 1918 elections, these men took steps

to revitalize the northern wing of the party in preparation for
the 1920 presidential contest. They found they had to combat
the belief, common among northern Democrats, that the administration was dominated by southerners who received a dis-
proportionate share of major appointments. Tumulty, and the
leaders of the national committee saw their big chance to
change this attitude with the Attorney-Generalship. Todd,
from the South, as were McReynolds and Gregory, would not
do. Tumulty, Cummings, and their friends needed a prominent northerner for the job.[81]

At first the leading candidates were believed to be Frank
L. Polk of New York, Counsellor of the State Department, and
Senator James Hamilton Lewis of Illinois, whose term was to
expire in 1919. When Assistant Attorney-General Samuel J.
Graham was suggested for the place, the New York *World* observed: "But Mr. Graham is a Pennsylvanian, and there would
be no political point in naming a Pennsylvania Democrat." [82]

Palmer, however, was more than just a Pennsylvania Democrat. For ten years, in Congress, as national committeeman,
and Alien Property Custodian, he had been closely associated
with the most influential leaders in the party. Many of these
men were his friends, and a considerable number were politically indebted to him. Chairman McCormick owed his position to Palmer; Vice Chairman Cummings, who had served
under Palmer on the executive committee of the national committee, had earned large fees from positions given him by the
Custodian, as had other party leaders.

Perhaps most important to key northern Democrats was
their certain knowledge that Palmer understood the facts of
political life—that he would use the power of his office to help
the party in every way possible. This was not an asset likely to
prove decisive with Wilson; nevertheless, Tumulty pointed out
to the President that the Attorney-General's office had "great
power politically. We should not trust it to any one who is not
heart and soul with us." [83]

Furthermore, Wilson himself was indebted. Palmer had
played a large part in Wilson's first nomination and had proven

his loyalty in the 1912 convention. He had been one of the President's most effective supporters in the Sixty-third Congress, which approved almost all Wilson's legislative objectives. At Wilson's insistence, Palmer had given up his House seat to run in what proved to be a hopeless race for the Senate against Boies Penrose. Also, when the members of the Pennsylvania Supreme Court were asked by Governor Martin Brumbaugh in 1918 to recommend the man best qualified to fill a vacancy on their court, the Republican-appointed Justices selected Palmer and the Republican Governor offered him the post. Palmer declined, because, he said, he felt obliged to continue his service to his country for the duration of the war, and he saw to it that Wilson was informed of his sacrifice.[84]

Despite his impressive support, Palmer had powerful opposition. Gregory continued to insist that Todd was the best man for the job, and he reminded Wilson of the various charges against Palmer.[85] Even more dangerous to Palmer's candidacy was Colonel House's desire to select Gregory's replacement. House had proposed McReynolds to Wilson in 1913, after talking the President out of nominating Palmer, and he had been responsible also for Gregory's elevation.[86] Now he decided that the new Attorney-General should be Sherman Whipple, a Massachusetts corporation attorney who had never held an important public office.[87] House remained Wilson's most trusted advisor, and he was in Paris with his chief while the President was mulling over the problem of a successor for Gregory. In mid-February, just before he left the peace conference for a short visit to the United States, Wilson decided to take House's advice once more. He cabled Tumulty to prepare an official commission appointing Whipple Attorney-General.[88]

Palmer's supporters had not been idle while the President was in France. McCormick, who resigned as chairman of the national committee in order to go to Paris as international trade advisor to the peace commission, kept prodding Wilson about Palmer.[89] He reported to another Pennsylvania politician early in February, 1919: "I have been doing my best to put Mitchell over for Attorney-General but have not yet succeeded." [90] So anxious were the leaders of the national committee to have Palmer nominated that they pressed McCormick to work even harder for his friend. W. R. Hollister, assistant secretary of the executive committee, informed McCormick:

There is a very lively interest among members of the Committee and a number of Senators and Congressmen with whom I have talked, in the probability of Mr. Palmer's appointment as Attorney-General. It would be a very satisfactory appointment, judging by the expressions I have heard from all quarters. There is considerable apprehension lest Todd be named. His geography is bad, and his appointment would seriously hurt, while the appointment of Palmer would not only be a generally popular one, but would be well received among lawyers all through the country. We hope that you are pushing the matter as strongly as you can. If you think it will do any good to have sent some cablegrams from a few strong men, we will arrange to have this done.[91]

Most influential in bringing about Palmer's nomination were Tumulty and Cummings. As soon as Gregory resigned, Tumulty moved to counter the Attorney-General's strong recommendation of Todd. He cabled Wilson:

This vacancy gives chance to realign independents who have been critical of Southern domination. Recognition of Palmer, who stands before the country as antagonist of Penrose, would be most helpful and cheering to young men of the party. Palmer our friend in 1912 and has been loyal throughout. He is most accessible and Democratic. His ability as a lawyer beyond question. You will make no mistake if appointment is made. It will give us all heart and new courage. Party now in need of tonic like this.[92]

And two weeks later Tumulty warned the President:

Your attitude toward the future of our Party will be measured by this appointment. Palmer young, militant, progressive and fearless. Stands well with country, Congress, appeals to young voter; effective on stump. McCormick, Cummings and whole Democratic Committee in favor his selection. . . . Our enemies and some of our friends have the feeling that you do not care to recognize the services of those who stood by us in the dark days. . . . The ignoring of men of high type of Palmer who have been faithful throughout will accentuate this feeling.[93]

Tumulty complied with Wilson's instructions to prepare a commission for Whipple, but when he met the President's ship at Boston, the secretary also carried a nomination with Palmer's name on it. Tumulty repeated in Boston his argument for Palmer's appointment, and this time, without House to present an opposing view, Wilson was swayed.[94] When the President reached Washington, the first man to talk with him about domestic politics was Cummings, whom Wilson had designated to succeed McCormick as national chairman. Cummings also pressed hard for the selection of Palmer.[95] Wilson capitulated. The following day, he wrote Gregory:

I have been thinking and thinking hard and in many directions, about the appointment of your successor, and each time my mind comes back to Mitchell Palmer. I think that on the whole he is my most available man. I have looked into some of the matters you mentioned to me in our last talk and think that they clear themselves up quite satisfactorily.[96]

That same day the White House announced that the name of A. Mitchell Palmer would be sent to the Senate immediately as the President's nomination for Attorney-General of the United States.[97]

CHAPTER IX

THE HIGH COST OF LIVING

Americans were slow to recover from the unsettling effects of World War I. "This country," Senator James Reed of Missouri observed in August, 1919, "is still suffering from shell shock. Hardly anyone is in a normal state of mind. . . . A great storm has swept over the intellectual world and its ravages and disturbances still exist." [1] The wartime "shell shock" robbed many Americans of the psychological resilience needed to cope with such postwar social and economic disturbances as runaway prices, great strikes, a brief but sharp depression, revolutions throughout Europe, the threat of revolt here, bomb explosions, and an outpouring of radical literature. The most obvious evidence of general anxiety was the fear, which afflicted millions of Americans in 1919, that a widespread internal conspiracy threatened the government. Serious economic difficulties—rising prices, scarcity of goods, strikes—also were attributed to sinister plots. Americans had experienced great social disruption and severe economic crises before, but never had the people as a whole responded more unrealistically to the problems they faced. [2]

Conditioned by the New Freedom and their wartime experience to depend upon the federal government for solutions to national problems, Americans looked to Washington, and especially to Woodrow Wilson, for action in 1919. After the war, however, the President first devoted himself almost exclusively to the peace treaty and then suffered a disabling stroke.

A vacuum of power existed within the administration, therefore, when Palmer entered the Cabinet. The President's assistants did not rush to fill the void. When Secretary of the

Interior Franklin K. Lane retired in March, 1920, he complained in a letter to Wilson that government officials shrank from taking responsibilities and from making controversial decisions: "Everyone seems to be afraid of everyone. The self-protective sense is developed abnormally, the creative sense atrophies." [3] Lane could not have been thinking of Palmer, however. Slow at first to intrude upon the prerogatives of his increasingly sensitive chief, the Attorney-General eventually took all the power he could. A man with lofty political ambitions and only a negligible national following, Palmer could not afford to hesitate for long when presented with an opportunity to stand in the spotlight. By the end of 1919 he had taken charge, with much fanfare, of the government's efforts to cope with a series of difficult postwar problems, and a reporter observed that Palmer "has within six months become the outstanding member of President Wilson's Cabinet." [4]

This is not to say that Palmer simply grabbed the reins of power and rode off toward the Presidency. Rather, the American public and press joined Congress in demanding that the government use its vast wartime powers to alleviate postwar troubles, and most of these powers came under the jurisdiction of the Justice Department. Wilson's condition and the Cabinet's attitude forced the ambitious Attorney-General to ride or be dragged. In most cases he required little urging once he ascertained the public's wishes.

The country wanted fast action, quick results; but even if a large portion of the public, the press, and Congress had not been so impatient, even if the atmosphere in which he worked had not been one of critical emergency, Palmer would have had no time for the slow, careful working out of national difficulties. He became Attorney-General fifteen months before the 1920 national convention, and the pattern of postwar troubles did not become clear until several months after he took office. If Palmer was to attract a national following, he had no time to pick up radical aliens one by one as he collected proof of individual wrongdoing; no time to let an antitrust action against the major meat packers, brought as a result of public insistence, crawl its laborious way through the courts; no time for patient negotiations while popular clamor against a coal strike increased; no time to await the inevitable postwar deflation. Unable to respond immediately to the public's demands, he compensated for his tardiness by dramatic action.

Of the major postwar domestic issues, the administration grappled first with the high cost of living. Retail prices more than doubled between 1915 and 1920.[5] Food prices, most noticeable to the public, rose from an average index figure of 101 in 1915 to 219 in June, 1920.[6] This fast ascent brought serious economic difficulty to Americans with relatively stable incomes, and they cried to the federal government for help.[7] By late July, 1919, complaints of exorbitant prices for necessities were flooding Congress and the White House.[8] Democratic National Chairman Homer Cummings returned to Washington from a trip around the country and warned Wilson that the American people demanded government action to bring down living costs. The Democratic state chairmen agreed with his diagnosis of public opinion, Cummings reported.[9] The Washington *Post*, early in August, called the cost of living "the burning domestic issue, [which has] temporarily blotted out from the councils of the Capitol" the great international questions of the League and the peace treaty. When Wilson promised to attack high prices, the Philadelphia *Public Ledger* observed that the administration had "come rather tardily to a realization of what is uppermost in the minds of the American people." [10]

Actually, the great price rise was a world-wide phenomenon. French prices in March, 1919, were more than three times their 1913 average and by May, 1920, they were over five times the prewar figure. The cost of living in Germany also tripled between 1913 and early 1919 and by March, 1920, German prices had soared to thirteen times their 1913 average. Most of the former combatant nations, including the United States, continued currency inflation for six or eight months after the war. This increase in the money supply occurred during a period of high demand for many kinds of goods, some of which were in short supply. The last obstacle to a rising price level was removed when all governments relaxed wartime controls over materials, credit, and prices. Then, as businessmen and consumers saw prices moving steadily upward, they began increasingly to stock up on goods for their own protection as well as for speculation. Under these conditions only a stringent system of allocations, price, wage, and credit controls, similar to the late wartime controls, might have held the price line until government expenditures fell off—as they did after mid-1919—and supply and demand were brought into better balance.[11]

President Wilson showed no inclination to take on the knotty problem. Probably he begrudged time and public attention taken from the League issue. When his energetic Attorney-General demonstrated a willingness to bear responsibility for the cost-of-living question, Wilson allowed him to take charge. As in most of his other assumptions of extraordinary power, it should be noted, Palmer acted only in response to an insistent public demand for action.

Palmer had done nothing about high prices during his first five months in office. Although the government's wartime food control powers remained in existence—Wilson refused to proclaim the war over until the Senate ratified the peace treaty—Palmer acted as though they had expired with the fighting. Nor did Congress object, at first, to his inactivity. Living costs rose only slightly in early 1919 and the legislators even denied Herbert Hoover's Food Administration an appropriation, forcing that agency out of operation in June.

During the second quarter of 1919, however, prices began to skyrocket, and in July Republican congressmen started complaining about the administration's apathy toward the high cost of living. Then, in late July, the full force of the public outcry over prices reached Congress, and the Republican majority immediately launched a concerted attack upon the Attorney-General for his failure to enforce wartime food control laws. "Capital Demands Action by Palmer to Cut Living Costs," a headline in the *World* proclaimed. In speeches and resolutions, congressmen demanded prosecution of speculators, profiteers, and the meat packers.[12] Palmer refused to commit himself to the use of the wartime statutes, but he prudently announced his intention to act immediately:

I am open to any suggestion looking to the solution of the question of the high cost-of-living . . . I received a letter from a man in West Virginia recently telling me that if I would reduce the cost-of-living fifty per cent I could be elected President. I think that suggestion is entirely impersonal; I think any man who can reduce the cost-of-living fifty per cent can be elected President.[13]

With Wilson's approval, Palmer called eight high government officials to a meeting in his office on July 31.[14] For over three hours, the secretaries of the Treasury, Agriculture, Labor, and Commerce, the Director General of Railroads, and the Chairman of the Federal Trade Commission, tried to agree on a comprehensive plan to fight high prices. Palmer reported to the press that progress had been made, and a second meeting was scheduled for five days later.[15] The White House announced that the committee's report would be the basis for a legislative program which the President would present personally in a speech to a joint session of Congress.[16]

Republicans met the flurry of administration activity with a volley of criticism. "Republican members of Congress charge that the Attorney-General has been slow or slack in his efforts to break up food monopolies or profiteering," a Democratic newspaper reported.[17] Representative Gilbert N. Haugen of Iowa, chairman of the House Agriculture Committee, which would receive any new cost-of-living legislation, declared: "We have plenty of laws now, but they are not being enforced. The Department of Justice should see to it that the laws are enforced." [18]

Obviously, the Democratic Party would have paid a heavy political penalty if the President and his Attorney-General had refused to use the government's wartime powers. The committee of government officials met again in Palmer's office on August 5, and immediately afterward Palmer held a long conference with Wilson. When he emerged from the White House Palmer announced to newsmen: "The Department of Justice

will use all of its agents throughout the nation to hunt down
the hoarders of and profiteers in food," and he promised to use
all available laws, including the wartime acts.[19] The following
day, Palmer ordered an antitrust suit filed against the five huge
meat-packing corporations, and in a telegram sent to all Justice
Department agents he pointed out that since the President had
not yet proclaimed the war to be over, the wartime food-control
law was still in effect. The Attorney-General ordered his agents
to enforce especially section six of that act, which made hoarding of necessities a crime.[20]

Apparently Palmer never seriously considered recommending that the government impose a comprehensive system of economic controls, like those which had worked fairly successfully
during the last year of the war. He was inhibited, in part, by an
aversion, shared with most other leaders of the New Freedom,
to large-scale government interference with individual economic freedom in peacetime. But he had political motives as
well for limiting his program. If broad powers were granted,
either a new supervisory agency would be established outside
his authority or the Attorney-General would have to face the
political consequences of arbitrating Americans' postwar economic relationships. The crusade he planned against hoarders,
profiteers, and the meat trust was politically safer, if less likely
to hold down prices.

While Palmer formulated his plans, Wilson ostentatiously
canceled all appointments, including some with senators to discuss the peace treaty. Instead, he held a series of conferences on
living costs in preparation for his address to Congress. A reporter for the *World* observed the President, Congress, and the
Cabinet working on schemes to cut prices, and commented:
"The whole system of the government tackled the high cost-of-
living today." [21]

In a thirty-four-minute speech to Congress on August 8,
1919, Wilson promised to do everything legally possible to
bring down prices. He announced government plans to sell surplus stocks of food and clothing and to limit exports of wheat.
Palmer, he declared, would immediately commence prosecution

of hoarders and combinations in restraint of trade. Wilson warned, however, that the administration's program would be ineffective unless Congress provided additional legislation. Most important, he demanded that the wartime food-control bill, the Lever Act, be extended, and that other commodities, especially clothing, be placed under its jurisdiction. He asked also for an amendment providing stiff penalties for individual profiteers. Under the wartime law, Wilson pointed out, the Justice Department could not prosecute profiteers unless they were involved in a conspiracy.[22]

The Republican-controlled Congress gladly offered the administration the additional powers, knowing that if prices continued to rise voters would blame the President and his Attorney-General. Indeed, in committee hearings, it took all of Palmer's persuasiveness to convince eager members of the House Committee on Agriculture and the Senate Committee on Agriculture and Forestry that they should not provide the administration with power to fix prices outright.[23]

Despite the nation-wide fervor for lowering prices, a few congressmen inquired cautiously into the constitutionality of using a statute passed expressly for wartime purposes. Palmer himself was uncertain, but, characteristically, he assured the legislators: "Given this penalty, we can break the backbone of this profiteering in sixty days, and then you won't have to worry about constitutionality." [24]

Both agriculture committees quickly reported the bills favorably; but Republicans delayed final passage while they exploited the past inactivity of the President and his Attorney-General. In the House, Representative William A. Rodenberg of Illinois launched the chief attack. Rodenberg arose to enthusiastic applause and was frequently interrupted by the loud approval of his fellow party members. His first target was Palmer: "I do not regard this legislation as necessary to enable our inactive and incompetent Department of Justice to do that which they have so flagrantly and persistently refused to do during the last six months. . . . " Rodenberg then turned on Wilson, ridiculing his passionate concern with the League of Nations. "I want to say to him [Wilson] in all good faith that now where there is one man in a thousand who cares a rap about the League of Nations, there are nine hundred and ninety-nine who are vitally and distressingly concerned about the high cost of living." [25]

In the House, where debate could easily be limited, the Lever Act amendment was adopted a few weeks after its introduction. Senate Republicans, some of whom doubted the advisability of giving more power to a possible Democratic candidate for President, postponed a final decision until October 16. Neither house produced much opposition when the matter finally came to a vote. [26]

While waiting for additional power and money, Palmer initiated a well-publicized assault on high prices. On August 11, he dispatched telegrams to the forty-eight former federal food administrators, who had been in charge of the wartime Food Administration's state organizations, calling on them to resume their posts and to reorganize the county Fair Price committees. [27] During the war, these local boards, composed of wholesalers, retailers, and representatives of organized labor and the public, had set "fair prices," enforcing them by means of a licensing system under which wholesalers could be deprived of the right to engage in interstate commerce. Offending retailers were cut off from supplies through pressure on licensed wholesalers, although the threat of this drastic action usually sufficed. [28] Now Palmer asked the food administrators to hold the price line through use of "merciless publicity" for profiteers, and the threat of prosecution by the Justice Department after the food-control amendment was passed. [29] Apparently it had not occurred to Palmer that prices might rise considerably without a corresponding surge in profits.

Palmer also pushed his campaign against hoarders; by mid-August his district attornies had taken over huge stores of foodstuffs. On August 16, for example, the Department announced seizure of over 10,000,000 eggs in Detroit, 1,000,000 eggs in Nashville, 200,000 pounds of sugar in Canton, Ohio. The next day there were confiscations of 100,000 pounds of beans in Kansas City, Missouri, 5,000,000 eggs in Chattanooga, 16,569,360 eggs in St. Louis, and 300,000 pounds of butter in Detroit.[30] All large quantities of stored foodstuffs were subject to seizure, Palmer announced, unless the owner could prove that he was not holding them for speculation.[31] The Department usually returned expropriated goods to their owners, subject to sale within a specified time at a "reasonable" price under the supervision of the district United States Attorney.[32]

By mid-October, the Department had taken hundreds of millions of eggs, 1,427,062 pounds of butter, 4,500,000 pounds of sugar, 765,615 pounds of dry salt pork, and large quantities of miscellaneous foodstuffs including 11,653 pig's ears and 5,700 cases of salmon.[33] As one result of the offensive, banks throughout the country refused to lend money to dealers who had always stored seasonable commodities like poultry, apples, and sweet potatoes in the fall for release at higher prices during the winter, for fear that the Justice Department would seize the goods. It required Palmer's intervention to reopen the credit lines.[34]

Palmer also established a Division of Women's Activities to disseminate information about prices and to campaign against consumer spending.[35] Leaders of influential women's organizations were appointed to head the state and local branches. Letters and pamphlets in large quantities went to women's clubs, and meetings of clubwomen throughout the country heard addresses by speakers sent from Washington and by local Division representatives.[36]

Palmer acknowledged on several occasions that the great postwar rise in prices was due chiefly to world-wide conditions beyond his control.[37] Nevertheless, he maintained:

I am one of those who believe that a large part of the high cost of everything is due to the fact that a number of unconscionable men in the ranks of the dealers have taken advantage of these other conditions which we may term the abnormal causes, to gouge the public. If we can make a few conspicuous examples of gougers and give the widest sort of publicity to the fact that such gougers have been and will be punished, in the future there will be little inclination to profiteer in this country.[38]

Palmer promised, in effect, that once he obtained the necessary legislation, he would produce a quick remedy for the high cost of living. He probably did the best job possible, considering the weapons he selected. About 70 percent of the former federal food administrators responded to the new call to duty, and state governors recommended administrators for most of the other states. In a few cases, United States attorneys temporarily took over the job. About 50 percent of the former county Fair Price committees were reorganized, and these covered almost all the important urban areas.[39]

The county committees set "fair prices" on the basis of local costs. Any wholesaler or retailer who sold goods at higher than the listed price was advised of his violation, and, if he persisted, was liable to prosecution by the United States Attorney. Palmer admitted that a "fair price" was hard to determine; but the Justice Department's policy, as he described it, was to "dump into the lap of a jury the same evidence which convinced the representative men upon the fair-price committee . . . " on the assumption that the evidence would "likewise convince the representative men in a jury box in that community." [40]

Within two months, the Department instituted 179 prosecutions for violations of the amended Lever Act. But most violators quietly conformed to the Fair Price committees' demands —trials for Lever Act violations were especially long and expensive because of the vagueness of the statute, and juries were hostile toward defendants. More important, customers usually did not await a verdict before they sought a new source of supply. Palmer observed: "I would just as leave be convicted as indicted by a Federal grand jury, and most people would." [41]

The High Cost of Living Division had a low payroll in most areas, with only a state administrator and a state women's chairman as paid personnel. County committees were made up of volunteers, although they received assistance from investigators attached to the district attorneys' offices and from the Department's Bureau of Investigation. In large cities, however, HCL and Women's Division offices were staffed with well-paid investigators, writers, and office help.[42]

Investigators in Washington, D. C., for example, followed

up every complaint, even the most trivial, of hoarding or profiteering. Special Assistant to the Attorney-General Howard E.
Figg, in charge of the Division, sent one investigator to calcu-
late the cost of a cup of coffee in Childs' Restaurant, and was
informed that each five-cent cup cost the restaurant three and
one-half cents. Another sleuth spent a day checking the weight,
cost, and sales price of bread in twenty retail stores in various
parts of Washington. Many others investigated complaints
about small grocers, clothiers, and restaurants. One of Figg's
men recommended that an increase in the price of coffee at a
local luncheonette be disallowed; it was poor coffee, he reported, served in thick mugs and the "waiter unclean in person." Few clear-cut cases of profiteering were discovered, although Figg claimed he could show an unreasonable increase
in the price of meat on the part of the big packers.[43]

Palmer's attempt to control the price of sugar, the commod-
ity most associated with profiteering in the public mind, clearly
illustrates the difficulties which beset his entire campaign. During the war, the Food Administration and the Sugar Equalization Board controlled the importation and distribution of
sugar and prevented any sizable increase in prices.[44] After the
Food Administration discontinued its supervision in June,
1919, the price of sugar began to rise, accompanied by widespread complaints of hoarding and profiteering. One of Palmer's
first acts in his attack on the high cost of living was to order all
United States attorneys to enforce the "fair prices" set by the
Sugar Board.[45] Within a week, a small retail grocer in Bing-
hamton, New York, was fined $500 for selling sugar at a profit
of five cents a pound.[46]

Suspected cases of sugar hoarding and profiteering were
carefully investigated; wholesalers were allowed a profit of one
cent a pound and retailers two cents. The Justice Department
strictly enforced these maximum margins, bringing suits for
profiteering against some of the largest sugar brokers as well
as small grocers. When the situation threatened to get out of
hand, most of the leading sugar refiners were called to Washington, where they were threatened and cajoled by Figg.[47]

Unfortunately, Palmer's tools were not adequate for the

task at hand. The price of sugar doubled in 1919–20 and kept on rising. The Attorney-General had no control over costs or foreign producers. Speculative buying or holding of sugar was often impossible to detect—there was a fine line between hoarding and maintaining a full inventory. Most important, the Attorney-General could not combat public willingness to pay higher prices for sweets.

The second quarter of 1919 saw a great upsurge in public demand for sugar and sugar products. Some attributed this unusual demand to high incomes and the demobilization of military personnel; others saw the onset of prohibition as the chief cause. Speculation played an important part once the basic consumer demand became apparent. Candy and soda manufacturers, whose supply of sugar had been limited during the war, responded to high consumption and the relaxation of controls by placing large orders. As sugar supplies suddenly tightened, a longshoreman's strike cut off imports. Then rumors spread that the British were making large purchases of sugar in Cuba and that the Louisiana crop was far below normal. Panic resulted. Many sugar refiners and users intentionally over-ordered; brokers began buying up available sugar. Even though sugar supplies increased as fast as final consumer demand, some sugar purchasers were unable to fill their normal needs. Newspaper reports of a severe sugar shortage encouraged the general tendency to overstock.[48]

Confusion within the sugar industry was compounded by conflicts among government agencies. Until mid-November, 1919, the Justice Department, the Sugar Equalization Board, and beet sugar refiners bickered over a "fair price" for beet sugar.[49] Meanwhile, Wilson argued with Republican congressmen about the President's power to buy and distribute the Cuban crop. As a result, beet sugar producers held their crop off the market and the Cubans began to sell their sugar to the highest bidder.[50]

In 1918–19, the Sugar Board had purchased the entire Cuban and domestic crop for less than nine cents a pound, and retailers were permitted to charge eleven cents. By September,

1919, refiners were paying as much as eleven and one-half cents a pound, and in November, anxious users offered over twenty cents a pound for sugar from the short Louisiana crop. The "fair" retail price reached twenty-four cents a pound in New York early in December, and Figg acknowledged to his chief that the American sugar market was in a "chaotic" condition.[51]

Palmer's political reputation suffered not only from his complete lack of success in holding down sugar prices, but also from charges that he had illegally fixed the price of Louisiana sugar. In negotiations with representatives of the Louisiana planters during late October and early November, 1919, Palmer insisted, at first, that he would allow the producers to charge no more than fifteen cents a pound. Then he was shown evidence that the crop was less than half the size of the year before and that many planters would be ruined if they had to sell at fifteen cents. On the advice of Figg and the United States Attorney at New Orleans, who also acted as food administrator, Palmer finally agreed to raise the "fair price" to seventeen cents.[52]

Republican congressmen intent upon proving that the opposition party favored southern interests, hauled the Democratic Presidential hopeful before an investigating committee, accusing him both of illegally fixing the price of sugar and of fixing it too high.[53] Palmer denied both counts. He demonstrated that because of the small crop many planters had been unable to make a profit even at the seventeen-cent rate. He went on to deny that his announcement of the "fair price" amounted to price-fixing:

I would have hated myself, Mr. Chairman, and I would have despised the methods pursued by this great, free Government of ours, if, having determined in my heart that 17 cents was a fair price, I had held it locked in my own bosom and refused to tell the public in Louisiana that that was what the Department of Justice would hold.[54]

Palmer was severely censured by the Republican members of the Judiciary Committee—the chairman, Representative

George H. Tinkham of Massachusetts, demanded that Palmer resign or be impeached—but the Attorney-General was praised by Democratic members.[55] Sugar prices continued to rise until the wholesale price reached twenty-three cents a pound in June and July, 1920. Then the world-wide speculative bubble collapsed and the price of sugar plummeted with prices of all commodities. By February, 1921, sugar was wholesaling for six and three-quarter cents a pound.[56]

Palmer met with little more success in holding down prices of other commodities. Although the Attorney-General made periodic announcements that prices were falling because of his policies,[57] these statements invariably were followed by the appearance of statistics showing a continued rise in the cost of living. The rise even accelerated in 1920; retail food prices soared 5 percent (8 percent in some large cities) between March 15 and April 15 alone, a crucial month in Palmer's campaign for the Presidential nomination.[58]

To some extent international currency inflation and high demand for goods after World War I made Palmer's attempt to hold down prices an impossible task. Yet the transition to a peacetime economy could probably have been accomplished more smoothly, with less strain in many areas of American life, if the federal government had been more farsighted and thorough in its planning. Palmer's choice of methods was a mistake, one which was in many ways typical of the Wilson administration.

The Attorney-General actually was attempting to enforce a moral code—to battle those old-age public enemies, the engrosser and the forestaller—rather than taking practical steps, such as the broad system of controls tested during World War I, to stabilize the price level. His efforts to bring down prices by attacking excess profits had only a minor effect; because although prices rose fast in 1919–20, profits did not. Palmer's difficulties were graphically illustrated when the Louisiana sugar planters threatened to sell their crop for twenty-five cents a pound regardless of the "fair price." The small crop, their representatives argued, meant that few of them would make a profit at the higher price and therefore hardly any would be open to prosecution for profiteering. When New York Food Administrator Williams was called upon to investigate complaints that sugar, which nine months before had retailed for eleven cents a pound, was selling in December, 1919 for twenty-four cents, he acknowledged that the charges were true; but there was nothing he could do about them. Because of the scarcity, high-priced Javan sugar was being brought to New York. Costs of handling, transportation, storage, and sales were uncontrolled and rising fast. Consequently, even at the twenty-four-cent rate wholesalers were making no more than one-half cent a pound profit and retailers one cent. There was nobody to prosecute.[59]

Palmer was frequently accused of directing his attacks on food and clothing prices chiefly at small retailers and whole-salers, while he ignored the swollen profits of the big manufacturers. However, even though the large corporations raised their prices in 1919–20, their profits fell. National Bureau of Economic Research statistics show that net income of a sample of thirty-one major manufacturers, in a wide variety of fields, fell 11 percent between 1918 and 1919, and another 5 percent in 1920, placing earnings for these corporations at less than half the 1916 level, a depth not plumbed again until the bottom of the Great Depression. Costs of all kinds, especially for raw materials, interest charges, and labor, were rising faster than prices. Productivity was diminished by rapid labor turnover and strikes.[60] Profits in the industries Palmer tried hardest to control—food and clothing—suffered as much as any. A sample group of 215 large food manufacturers, for example, earned only 4 percent on sales in 1919, and even this was squeezed to less than 2 percent in 1920.[61]

Herbert Hoover warned Palmer in September, 1919: "Until shipping, credits and production become normal there is no effective control of the cost of living that can be set up that is not based on an absolute control of price and distribution of the great underlying staple commodities." [62] Such an alternative evidently never was considered by Palmer or proposed to

Wilson, despite the government's satisfactory experience with wartime controls. For reasons both of political expediency and personal belief, Palmer chose a moral crusade rather than the kind of comprehensive action which might have eased the post-war pressures on the American people.

CHAPTER X

BETWEEN CAPITAL AND LABOR

Palmer described himself in 1920 as a "radical friend" of labor: "All of my political life I have been fighting for labor. . . . I have fought the battles of the coal miners in my state, and of the steel workers in Bethlehem." [1] Palmer's record in Congress confirmed his assertion; an AF of L dossier of his congressional career shows that during three terms in office Palmer never voted against what organized labor believed to be its interests.[2] He wrote a child labor bill and pushed it through the House of Representatives, and helped win passage of quarry inspection legislation. He sided with the Bethlehem Steel strikers in 1910, thereby winning political assistance from the strike leaders. When he ran for the Senate in 1914, the chief national officers of the AF of L applauded his record.[3]

Yet, as Attorney-General, Palmer became the administration's leading opponent of labor's demands—the most notorious violator of the rights of labor, as labor defined them. To some extent Palmer's apparent transformation derived from a feeling that labor had let him down in the past and therefore could not be depended upon for political support in the future. Pennsylvania's labor districts had favored Theodore Roosevelt over Wilson in 1912, despite the prolabor record of the Democratic-controlled Sixty-second House, and the campaigning of Palmer and a number of union leaders. In the same election Congressman William B. Wilson, former Secretary-Treasurer of the United Mine Workers, suffered defeat in one of the state's strong labor districts. Wilson recalled that when he heard the news his first thought was: "Father, forgive them, for they know not what they do." [4] Palmer lost most of the labor wards within his own district in 1912; two years later, in the senatorial election, Boies Penrose swept the areas in which mine and factory workers predominated, despite the AF of L's high praise for Palmer and Gompers' denunciation of Penrose. In 1916, the Republicans won an even more pronounced victory in Pennsylvania's labor districts. Democratic Senator Thomas J. Walsh of Montana, known as a friend of workingmen, replied to a critic of Palmer's policies in 1919: "I should feel much more concerned . . . if I agree with you that the so-called labor vote came to us . . . at the 1916 election." Walsh sent a copy of his letter to Palmer who answered, "I think your reply . . . covers the matter." [5]

Palmer's disillusionment was not the only reason for his postwar clash with labor. A good politician, he reflected the changed attitude of the group whose support he needed most—the middle-class progressives comprising the backbone of Woodrow Wilson's strength within the Democratic Party. Much of the sympathy labor had received from this source was dissipated by the rapid wartime and postwar rise in wages, apparently a major cause of soaring prices, and by the great industrial strikes of 1919. Protested the *New Republic* in 1919: "Between organized labor, on the one hand, and organized capital on the other, the large class which lives by rendering services to both stands an excellent chance of being crushed as between the upper and nether millstones." [6] Additional hostility to union demands arose out of the conviction, held by many Americans (including Palmer's leading advisers), that the postwar strikes were in some way associated with a world-wide Communist conspiracy. An Oklahoma businessman, acclaiming the government's stand against the coal miners, placed Palmer in exactly the role he sought: "The unorganized middle classes need but your clarion voice to quickly follow your command in repelling mob rule in this country." [7]

Actually, Palmer's new attitude toward labor did not require much of an intellectual adjustment. As a college student, he had been inspired by the call to reform that affected so many of his generation. He believed, perhaps as strongly as did Woodrow Wilson, that every American deserved a fair chance for economic success. But Palmer's idealism was always subordinate to his more powerful ambitions. Early in his political career, Palmer's opportunism and altruistic drives served each other. Reform was popular when Palmer ran for Congress. Furthermore, as a rebel against the established political leaders in his district, Palmer was obliged to appeal not only to the long-established, old-American voters who dominated political life in the area, but also to immigrant mine and factory workers.[8]

Even in the period when he appeared most prolabor, however, Palmer thought of himself not as a partisan, but as a referee between opposing economic forces. In 1910, when labor support was essential to Palmer's success, one of his campaign managers introduced him to an audience composed partly of Bethlehem Steel strikers as a man "who stands . . . equally poised on the great question of capital and labor—not giving way to either extreme for the purpose of winning votes. . . ." Palmer described himself in similar terms during the campaign.[9] When he discovered that he could not count upon workers for political support, and when middle-class voters demanded that union power be curbed, Palmer's "friendship" for labor cooled.

Nevertheless, he hesitated to commit himself to antilabor policies. He did not intervene in the series of violent strikes between February and November, 1919. He refused to add to the charges, made by businessmen, newspapers, and congressmen, that radicals were instigating the labor disturbances. Not until others had proven the political potency of antilabor activity, and criticism of Palmer's inactivity became so intense that it endangered his career, did he take the field against strikers.

Palmer's hesitancy was not due to lack of opportunity. The year 1919 was a vintage year for strikes; there were more than 3,600, involving over 4,000,000 workers. More employees walked out than did in the ten-year period 1923–32.[10] Public apprehension ran high and a large proportion of the American people apparently approved government intervention in major strikes.

In February a general strike paralyzed the city of Seattle for five days. Mayor Ole Hanson, formerly a prolabor state legislator, won national fame when he defied the strikers, called in federal troops and threatened to use them as strikebreakers. Next, the Boston police strike made a hero of Governor Calvin Coolidge, who refused to compromise with the policemen. When he sent his famous wire: "There is no right to strike against the public safety by anybody, anywhere, anytime," Coolidge became a political figure of national prominence almost overnight, and politicians throughout the country thus discovered an easy road to popularity.[11]

Many Americans feared that the wave of strikes was but a prelude to a general industrial breakdown, similar to the one which had brought on the Russian Revolution. The alarm increased when a nation-wide steel strike followed close upon the Boston police walkout. Steel companies encouraged fears that the strikers harbored revolutionary objectives, and newspapers printed uncritically the unwarranted allegations of employers. Military intelligence officers also contributed to the picture of a "Red" conspiracy. They raided radical centers in Gary, Indiana, then informed the press and Congress that they had discovered evidence linking strike leaders to a nation-wide bomb plot and to representatives of Soviet Russia. Only later did military spokesmen acknowledge that although there were both strikers and dangerous radicals in Gary, intelligence agents had found hardly any connection between the two groups. Meanwhile, the army's activities produced yet another antilabor, antiradical hero, General Leonard Wood, commander of the soldiers at Gary.[12]

Congress also did its part to spread the idea that revolutionists inspired the steel strike. A Senate committee investigating the walkout heard sensational evidence of radical influence. Much of this evidence concerned the syndicalist beliefs of William Z. Foster, one of the leaders of the AF of L committee that organized the steel workers.[13] Actually, Foster, always something of a lone wolf, was distrusted by the IWW and denounced by the Communists in 1919 for aiding the AF of L, which the radicals considered a decadent enemy of the workers. Foster undoubtedly retained his revolutionary ideas, but during the steel tie-up he acted so discreetly that he had to be urged by a veteran AF of L leader to add a few fighting words about the class struggle to a strike pamphlet.[14] Nevertheless, in its final report the Senate committee declared: "Behind this strike there is massed a considerable element of IWWs, anarchists, revolutionists, and Russian Soviets, and . . . some radical men not in harmony with the conservative elements of the American Federation of Labor are attempting to use the strike as a means of elevating themselves to power within the ranks of organized labor." [15]

The Congressmen failed to see not only the real motives of almost all the strikers and their leaders, but also the true strength of the radical organizations. The IWW exerted practically no influence on the strike, although some members took part. In the key Pittsburgh area, the "wobblies" tried to discourage strikers with a pamphlet predicting the walkout's failure, and a leading IWW journal acknowledged later: "The steel strike caught us unprepared." [16]

The Communist parties were totally inept throughout the great strike wave of 1919–20. Communist writers jeered at Foster for cooperating with the AF of L and for leading a strike which had as its objective not revolution but higher wages and the check-off system of union dues collection. Investigators for the Interchurch World Movement, after spending weeks in the strike areas, saw only one sample of Communist literature: a bundle of pamphlets confiscated by strike leaders from a would-be distributor who was thrown out of a union hall. Charles E. Ruthenberg, leader of the Communist Party in 1919, admitted several years later: "In the Communist Party and the Communist Labor Party conventions of 1919 it would have been difficult to gather together a half-dozen delegates who knew anything about the trade-union movement." [17]

Palmer remained on the sidelines throughout the strike, still reluctant to risk the enmity of organized labor. He warned that radicals urging workers to seize the steel mills faced arrest. But Justice Department officials refused to corroborate Army charges that Gary strikers were involved in a nation-wide plot, and a military intelligence officer complained that the Attorney-General took no action after receiving evidence of a relationship between strike leaders and Soviet agents.[18] Early in 1920, Palmer declared that the steel strike had been part of a radical conspiracy and he arrested hundreds of alien workers in steel towns for deportation; but he did not make these moves until months after the strike ended.

By late October, 1919, pressure on Palmer was mounting rapidly. Public fear of revolution or economic disaster was aggravated by news that nation-wide coal and railroad strikes were scheduled to begin November 1. With winter weather on the way, and coal and food already in short supply, popular sentiment for drastic action against strikes reached such a pitch that a Presidential candidate in a position of power could ignore it only at great peril to his career.[19]

Only eight months before the Democratic national convention, with his campaign against high prices lagging,[20] Palmer was in no position to sit and wait for labor strife to end. Furthermore, on October 17, the Senate dealt his political hopes another blow by demanding that Palmer explain why he had taken no important steps against the radicals threatening to overthrow the government.[21]

At last Palmer made up his mind to act; he would take a firm stand against the imminent coal and rail strikes, risking the antagonism of some union leaders and of workers in some industries. He was confident that the great majority of the public would back him wholeheartedly, as they had sustained Hanson, Coolidge, and Wood, and he believed that the conservative heads of the AF of L, cowed by public opinion, would supply only weak opposition. He had the complete support of Lansing and Tumulty, who took the lead in such policy-making as occurred during Wilson's illness, and backing also from Vice-

President Marshall, Postmaster-General Burleson, Treasury Secretary Glass, Director-General of Railroads Walker D. Hines, and Fuel Administrator Harry Garfield.[22]

Secretary of Labor William B. Wilson led the Cabinet minority which opposed coercive labor policies. He understood the pressure on union leaders from their memberships and he sympathized with the determination of workers to raise their living standards. Wilson received little active support, however, from the Cabinet members who leaned toward his position: Secretary of the Navy Daniels, Secretary of the Interior Lane, and Secretary of War Baker. Even Secretary Wilson felt unable to champion the unions' cause aggressively. He agreed with Palmer and Hines that the railroad brotherhoods had no right to strike as long as the roads were under government control. Early in the coal negotiations, he asked only that the government encourage continued meetings between the operators and the union, and "if they result in a break with the probability of tying up the fuel supply, take such steps as the situation at that time would warrant." [23]

Members of the railroad brotherhoods probably needed a pay raise even more than the bituminous coal miners, although wages of both groups had fallen behind rising consumer prices. Nevertheless, the well-established brotherhood leaders felt better able to control their rank and file than did the new president of the United Mine Workers, John L. Lewis.[24] Informed that both Cabinet and Congress were determined to break a rail strike and convinced that the public would support any government action, Brotherhood executives postponed their walkout.[25]

Lewis, however, felt obliged to defy the government. With a strike almost certain, Tumulty and Hines prepared a statement warning the miners that such action would be "a grave moral and legal wrong against the government and the people of the United States" and that means would be found "to protect the interests of the nation." This statement was approved by the Cabinet and then sent to the President.[26] It may never have passed Mrs. Wilson, who received all communications to the White House in an effort to protect her husband from emotional stress. "Every time you take him a new anxiety or problem to excite him," a nerve specialist warned her, "you are turning a knife in an open wound. His nerves are crying out for rest, and any excitement is torture to him." If Wilson did see the statement, he may not have fully understood its implications, for it was issued on October 25, the day that the President's physician, Rear Admiral Cary Grayson, informed a close friend: "He is still traveling on thin ice. I am doing my best and hoping for the best." [27]

The executive board of the United Mine Workers held one last conference with the union's district representatives, and finding that worker sentiment was stronger than ever in favor of a walkout, the board refused to recall its strike order. John L. Lewis, in awe of no man, addressed to Woodrow Wilson a sermon haughty as any that later Presidents brought down upon themselves: "The President of the United States is the servant and not the master of the Constitution. . . . His statement of October 25 . . . proclaims a refusal [to work] to be a crime when no such crime exists, nor can such a crime be defined under the Constitution." [28]

By the time Lewis issued his dictum, Palmer had already announced that a strike would fall under the provision in the Lever Act which prohibited interference with production or transportation of necessities.[29] Union leaders who had applauded when Palmer applied the statute to profiteers and hoarders now protested that it was a wartime law, no longer valid. Gompers declared also that he had been assured by President Wilson, Gregory, and members of Congress that the act would not be used to prevent strikes, and that these promises had been kept during the war. Palmer replied that Congress, not the President, made the law, and the House of Representatives had voted down an amendment exempting labor unions by a vote of 152–45; furthermore, Gregory denied that he had entered into any such agreement.[30]

Plans for use of the Lever Act took shape at a Cabinet meeting held October 28; by this time, as Cabinet members knew from a flood of letters, popular sentiment had turned strongly against the mine workers.[31] Details of the government's course were worked out at a meeting held the following night, presided over by Palmer and attended by Tumulty, Hines, Garfield, Secretary Wilson and Assistant Attorneys-General Garvan and Ames. Emerging from the conference, Palmer addressed the assembled Washington press corps. "The Attorney-General," the New York *Times* related, "was very solemn when he made his announcement. His every feature showed his great earnestness and full determination to maintain the law. . . ." Palmer declared: "Every resource of the Government will be brought to bear to prevent a national disaster which would inevitably result from the cessation of mining operations." Ames left immediately for Indianapolis, where Federal District Judge Albert B. Anderson openly prepared to grant an injunction.[32]

On the afternoon of October 30, Palmer visited the President; Dr. Grayson was the only other person present. Wilson, susceptible to Palmer's powers of persuasion even when his mental faculties were sharpest, probably offered little resistance to the Attorney-General's plans. Approached by reporters as he left the White House, Palmer said only: "I went over the whole situation with the President and the President gave his approval to what has been done up to this time." [33]

On October 31, Judge Anderson issued a temporary injunction, forbidding officers of the United Mine Workers to take any part in the proposed strike. The next day, about 400,000 soft-coal workers ignored the court order against their leaders and refused to report for work. Immediately after the injunction was issued, Gompers and AF of L Vice-President Matthew Woll hurried to the Justice Department for a long, stormy meeting with Palmer. A delegation from the railroad brotherhoods delivered a protest only slightly less bitter.[34] Palmer, already assured of the backing of almost all major newspapers and of the leaders of both parties, refused to budge.[35] He did, however, warn coal operators and dealers that he would apply the Lever law to them too, if they raised prices. When the Wholesale Coal Trade Association protested against government price fixing, Palmer, still the self-proclaimed referee between capital and labor, replied: "You ought to be quite as willing as other citizens to cooperate in the general public welfare in this emergency, even to the extent of sacrificing profits." [36]

Gompers and Palmer held four conferences on November 7, in a final effort to reach a compromise. Palmer agreed to postpone the government's plea for a mandatory injunction, which would force the union leaders to withdraw the original strike order, if Lewis would halt the strike while negotiations based on Gompers' proposals were held. Lewis refused, and Palmer, equally stubborn, obtained the stronger injunction the next day.

Gompers was furious. For a generation he had fiercely resisted the use of labor injunctions, demanding labor's freedom to use its most powerful weapon—the strike—in its conflicts with capital. He believed that the period of federal intervention in peacetime industrial disputes was finally over and that the Wilson administration, pledged to fair play for workers, would not use the courts to break a strike. He had no intention of meekly surrendering labor's right to strike; for once, the cautious Gompers seemed prepared to battle with every weapon at his command. He called the executive committee of the AF of L into a special session and obtained approval for action in support of the miners. After the meeting, Gompers issued a statement denouncing the coal injunction as "so autocratic as to stagger the human mind." He urged continued resistance by the mine workers and called upon all labor unions to support their oppressed brethren.[37]

When this challenge was relayed to Palmer, the Attorney-General sensed, apparently for the first time, that he had sowed the seeds of his political destruction. A reporter who interviewed him soon afterward observed: "It was apparent that the extreme stand . . . was a surprise to Mr. Palmer." Gompers' threat sent the Attorney-General to the White House again; after conferring with Wilson, however, Palmer announced: "All I can say is that the law will be enforced." [38]

Gompers reiterated his determination to back the strikers in a fiery address before the International Labor Conference on November 10. Lewis, however, decided that Gompers' support was not enough. Faced with the threat of criminal charges for contempt, he surprised and perhaps disappointed the AF of L chief by recalling the strike order.[39]

Lewis' capitulation did not end the deadlock; most of the miners ignored the public statements of their leaders and refused to return to work. Labor Secretary Wilson drew up a compromise proposal which the union approved, but it was turned down by the operators. Another, recommended by Fuel Administrator Garfield, satisfied the operators but was rejected by the miners. Most of the Cabinet, disturbed by the fast-rising cost of living, supported Garfield's plan which held the wage increase to 14 percent, allowed no increase in prices, and provided for a commission to study work rules and wages and to make further recommendations.[40]

As the strike dragged on, the political advantages of the administration's position began to evaporate. Because coal was rationed, industrial and commercial firms were obliged to cut back operations. Consumer supplies fell dangerously low. Palmer had particular cause for concern when former Treasury Secretary McAdoo, one of his strongest rivals for the Presidential nomination, stated publicly that the miners' demands were fair and that the operators could meet them without raising prices.[41] If the strike continued, Palmer realized, he would be cast in the role of the villain, responsible for its awful consequences.

Palmer and Tumulty decided to force a settlement on whatever terms they could get. By December, Lansing also agreed to accept higher coal prices rather than "have the critical state of industry continue and millions added to the financial loss. . . ."[42] Lewis and William Green, Secretary-Treasurer of the UMW, were invited to Washington on December 5 to meet with Palmer and Tumulty the following day. By this time the labor leaders were under enormous pressure to settle. To defy the government at a time when men were being beaten in the streets for showing "disrespect" for the American flag—a time when labor unions were widely suspected of revolutionary designs—was foolhardy. The mine workers remained willing, and many were even eager to fight on; but by December, Lewis and Green clearly recognized that an overwhelming majority of Americans would support any government measures to break the strike.

On the afternoon of December 6, the union leaders again were presented with Garfield's plan, this time in the form of a letter from Woodrow Wilson, and delivered in the Attorney-General's finest style.[43] Palmer recalled:

I impressed upon them the fact that the Government of the United States never could surrender unless it met a power greater than itself, and that I did not believe they would like to have it go out to the world that the United Mine Workers was a greater power than the United States. I told them the result would be a continuous fight in which the Government was bound to win.[44]

Lewis and Green were encouraged to believe that they were really dealing with the President. As Green described the situation to a miners' convention:

We . . . met the Attorney-General . . . and the Secretary to the President. They acted as messengers between us and the President himself. And it was then we were told again that no longer could the government wait, that the condition of the country was such that the people must have fuel and have it immediately. The Attorney-General read to us a letter prepared by the President of the United States that was to be given to the public immediately, and we realized that when that was given to the public the rising tide of public sentiment, that had so strongly set in against us, would rally behind the President as never before and that it would reach such an acute stage that if they had taken the local officers and the leaders of your organization out against some stone wall and shot them to death the public would have applauded and said 'Amen.'[45]

The union leaders demanded one important concession before they would accept the once-rejected proposal. The commission of inquiry, they insisted, must have the power not merely to suggest increases in wages and prices, but to make binding decisions on these matters. Although Palmer and Tumulty agreed, the meeting adjourned for dinner without a final settlement.

During the recess, Lewis and Green conferred with Secretary Wilson, who urged them to accept the government's plan. Meanwhile, Palmer and Tumulty met at Palmer's home with Garfield, Glass, Houston, and Hines. Garfield, unaware of the concession already made by Palmer, received a "distinct impression that the Attorney-General was weakening in his stand against the mine workers." Both Garfield and Glass stood adamant against any settlement that would allow a price increase. Nevertheless, when negotiations with Lewis and Green resumed that night, the strong commission demanded by the labor leaders was included in the compact they agreed to recommend to their union's Scale Committee.[46]

Garfield learned of the accord the following day at a meeting in Palmer's home. Immediately thereafter he appealed to the President. Wilson's first reaction was to support the Fuel Administrator's contention that the commission should not have authority to raise coal prices. Tumulty and Lansing, on behalf of the Cabinet, however, convinced Wilson that a settlement could not be reached on Garfield's terms, and he withdrew his support.[47] The miners' Scale Committee violently debated the proposals Palmer read to them, and the operators also threatened to reject the agreement their representatives had approved; but both sides finally accepted the plan.[48]

Palmer had good reason to believe, immediately after the coal strike, that he had scored a political coup. Scores of letters praising his actions came from business and professional men throughout the nation—from people whose judgment he respected and whose backing, he believed, could make him President: "The Asheville [North Carolina] Board of Trade, composed of a thousand of Asheville's leading business men, desire to commend you . . . on the stand you have taken in the matter of the coal strike." "I have heard a great many people who did not know you heretofore say that your splendid work in this connection made you a strong Presidential possibility." "I feel certain that you have the backing of all 100% Americans."

"You are injecting into the Administration the very thing they needed, a firm hand." "A lion-hearted man, with a great nation behind him, has brought order out of chaos. You have shown . . . that the United States is not a myth, but a virile, mighty power which shows itself when a man who measures up to the duties of the hour is at the helm." To this last message Palmer replied: "You have stated the issue with great clearness." [49]

With such acclaim ringing in his ears, Palmer was all but deaf to labor's complaints. In December, 1919, he wrote: "I shall be very sorry if our treatment of the coal strike situation has alienated any large body of voters, but I am so convinced that the course was right that I can not believe it will lose politically in the end." [50] Palmer was so convinced that he held to his course until he had given an exhibition of antilabor activity unmatched since Richard Olney used the Justice Department to harry Coxey's Army and smash the Pullman strike in 1894.

Palmer next took on a group of unions even more politically powerful than the United Mine Workers. The "Big Four" railroad brotherhoods had appealed twice to President Wilson in 1919 for higher wages and were rebuffed both times. They refrained from walking out on November 1—the day the soft coal workers quit work—only out of certainty that the government would stop at nothing to break their strike. When the coal miners obtained a sizable pay boost, however, the railroad workers put almost irresistible pressure on their leaders to win similar gains. Rail union spokesmen then dispatched a new plea to the President, who still controlled the railroads, and rescheduled the strike for February 17, 1920.[51]

Talks between officials of the brotherhoods and Railroad Director Hines collapsed because Hines could offer no concessions. Palmer then stepped in and threatened the union leaders with an injunction. Allen E. Barker, president of the Brotherhood of Maintenance of Way Employees and Railway Shop Laborers, replied that his organization would ignore a court order, and another great industrial battle appeared in the offing. The Washington *Post* declared that the situation seemed "even more serious than that with which he [Palmer] dealt so firmly and successfully in the strike of the bituminous coal miners a few weeks ago." The Justice Department prepared a bill of complaint against Barker and other union officials; but the brotherhoods again gave in, rescinding the strike order in exchange for Woodrow Wilson's promise of "justice to all." [52]

By this time the railroad workers were straining at the leash. After six weeks passed with no indication that Wilson meant to take action, the brotherhood leaders lost control of their members. The discharge of John Gruneau, a yard conductor attempting to organize a new switchmen's union in Chicago, set off a rapid chain reaction: within a week, at least 25,000 railroad workers, from New York to Los Angeles, quit work. On April 11, a Justice Department agent reported that only 20 percent of the scheduled trains in the Chicago area operated, despite the strikers' willingness to allow shipments of consumer necessities.[53]

Palmer went all out to crush the walkout. As soon as its scope became apparent, he announced the likelihood of federal intervention. Palmer discussed his plans with Tumulty on April 12, and the following day a number of strike leaders in New Orleans were arrested for alleged violations of the Lever Act. A Cabinet meeting discussed the strike on April 14. Once again, Palmer met only weak opposition to his plans. On April 15, Gruneau, then acting as chief spokesman for the strikers, was arrested with other instigators of the walkout, for violating the Lever Act and interfering with transportation of the mails. Palmer's agent in Cleveland was so carried away with the spirit of the hour that he gathered together fifteen strike leaders and threatened to arrest them and every other striker in Cleveland who did not report for work the next day. Five hundred of the fifteen hundred strikers in the area held a mass meeting and shouted their readiness to go to jail rather than to work. Palmer promptly repudiated his agent.[54]

Intimidation and arrests were not the only weapons Palmer used against the railroad workers; he added a new dimension to his antilabor activity when he attempted to defeat the strike by identifying the strikers as radicals and the walkout as an attempt at revolution. On April 13, Palmer and Garvan charged that the strike leaders were members of the IWW, with Communists providing most of their funds. A day later, Palmer paralyzed Cabinet opposition by informing a meeting that he had conclusive proof that the strike was part of a world-wide Communist conspiracy and that the walkout's real leader was none other than the notorious William Z. Foster.[55]

What should have been an adequate antidote to Palmer's slanders was provided by the strike leaders themselves. On April 20, they disclosed their objectives in a petition to the Railroad Labor Board. Their chief demands were for a minimum wage of $150 a month; time-and-a-half for overtime, Sunday, and holiday work; and twenty-minute lunch periods. Even before Palmer made his accusations, however, he was told by Charles B. Ames, his assistant in charge of the Lever Act's enforcement, that wages were the only substantial issue in the strike and that consideration of that question by the Railroad Board probably would end the tie-up.[56]

Palmer later gave a congressional committee evidence collected against thirty-eight strike leaders charged with violating the Lever Act. A few statements made during meetings of the strikers and overheard by Justice Department agents constituted the only signs of radicalism. One striker reportedly declared that "the IWW was not as bad as it was supposed to be." Another was overheard stating that "in his opinion Mr. Palmer . . . was the greatest Red in the United States. . . ." The chairman of a strike meeting in Chicago allegedly permitted a speaker to assert that railroad workers "would not stand for being called Bolsheviki just because they wanted a living wage." These were the most incendiary of the reported statements.[57]

Frank Morrison, Secretary of the AF of L, pointed out: "If there were enough revolutionary power in the United States to create such an outbreak as this, the condition would be serious indeed. There is no such power. The absolute failure of the Attorney-General to grasp the true situation is amazing." [58] In fact, the Communists, as usual, were almost completely isolated from an important industrial crisis. Only after a long theoretical debate in their Central Executive Committee did the Communist Party even issue a manifesto calling upon the strikers to revolt against the government. Like the IWW literature distributed to strikers, the Communist pamphlet was published long after the strike began and it probably had its greatest effect in the Justice Department. Members of the IWW took part in the strike; but the organization's leaders were completely surprised by the walkout and unable to take advantage of it. An IWW periodical lamented: "The steel strike caught us unprepared. So did the railway strike. What next?" [59]

In insisting that revolutionists kindled the rail strike, Palmer was not merely a victim of hallucination. To a large extent he gambled on policies which seemed likely to win him the Presidency. Already the leading symbol of the government's fight against both Reds and strikers, Palmer attempted to combine these groups into one gigantic enemy. In so doing he hoped to gratify that large portion of the nation which detested both, and to frighten those otherwise patriotic Americans who still doubted the existence of the "Red Menace." His intention was to accent the need for an experienced battler against Bolshevism in the White House, while emphasizing his own availability.

Furthermore, Palmer received some evidence of a connection between radicals and the rail strike, and blinded by his own political interests, he may have been misled into believing that he was telling the truth. Railroad managements furnished the Justice Department with long lists of allegedly radical strikers at the Attorney-General's request.[60] More important to Palmer, two days before his accusations against the strikers, officials of the railroad brotherhoods (who knew they would be discredited by a successful strike), denounced the insurgents as radicals anxious to establish "one big union," and they urged members of the brotherhoods to serve as strikebreakers.[61]

Nevertheless, if Palmer really believed that revolutionists

instigated and managed the rail walkout, it was not primarily because of the union allegations, the railroad reports, or the Communist pamphlets. Even at the height of his fear of revolution, Palmer could not have been taken in by these alone. He had established a General Intelligence Division in the Justice Department to provide him with reliable information about such matters, and the Division's report stressed radical tendencies among the strike leaders.[62] Division chief, J. Edgar Hoover, even went so far as to declare in a public hearing on April 24 that at least 50 percent of the influence behind the recent strikes was traceable directly to Communist organizations.[63]

After the walkout ended, the brotherhoods repudiated their charges that radicalism played a part in it.[64] Nevertheless, the Attorney-General's description of the rail strike changed not at all. In mid-May he called it an attempt "to win the workers over to social and industrial revolt," [65] and he joined Hoover in applying this thesis to other strikes. In October, Palmer had taken almost no part in the attempts of business groups, newspapers, the military intelligence organization, and a Senate committee to prove radical influence on the steel strike.[66] Neither had he given encouragement to Ole Hanson, T. T. Brewster, the coal operators' chief bargaining representative, and others who charged that Lenin and Trotsky brought about the coal strike.[67] In May, 1920, however, Palmer lumped together the coal, steel, and rail strikes as "three signal failures to promote economic and social revolution through the medium of general strikes of an outlaw nature . . . which were directed against the people and had little or no concern with the grievances of employees against employers." [68]

The enthusiasm Palmer brought to his battles against workers in late 1919 and early 1920 was missing from his actions against businessmen. With the latter he was more reasonable and inclined to compromise; no important principles appeared to be involved. Palmer's treatment of antitrust cases illustrates these differences. Under his administration the Department diligently pressed most of the suits brought by his predecessors, and won several important cases. A Supreme Court decision obliged the Lehigh Valley Railroad to end its monopoly of the coal trade along its route. Major victories were also recorded against the Reading Company, Eastman Kodak, and the Southern Pacific Railroad. On the other hand, Palmer surprised businessmen by dropping several cases because they resembled suits decided against the government.[69]

Palmer instituted a sizable number of antitrust actions—sixteen in the fiscal year ending June 30, 1919 alone.[70] The nation-wide "cement trust" was sued in August, 1919, and Colgate was brought to court soon afterward. The Justice Department instituted a long-deferred action against the United Shoe Machinery Company in November, 1919.[71] Palmer's polite letter advising the intransigent president of the latter firm of the Department's decision to sue contrasted sharply with his intemperate treatment of the coal miners at the same time.[72] The Attorney-General took little part in these antitrust cases;[73] they were tried and won by the Justice Department with little fanfare and without proclamations that the nation had been saved from dangerous enemies.

Palmer undertook only one antitrust prosecution with the same vigor that marked his attacks on labor and radicals; that was his suit against the five giants of the meat packing industry —Swift, Armour, Wilson, Morris, and Cudahy. The packers, long subjected to intense criticism from cattlemen, farmers, consumer groups, and muckraking journalists, had lost an antitrust case in 1904 with no apparent effect on their business practices. In 1917, Wilson ordered the Federal Trade Commission to investigate the packers' operations thoroughly. By mid-1918, with the preliminary results of this investigation widely publicized, public demand that the packers be placed under government control became more intense than ever. The FTC's new evidence was sent to Gregory and the Justice Department began preparing an antitrust suit.[74]

After Palmer took over the Justice Department, talk of immediate prosecution ceased; at first he moved cautiously in all areas, waiting to discover the direction of postwar political winds. He hired Isidor J. Kresel, his favorite sleuth, to take charge of the Department's investigation of the packers; but with no pressure for immediate results, Kresel limited himself to a perfunctory probe; as late as June, 1919, his investigation consisted of analyzing the FTC's findings.[75]

Then, in July, the situation changed. Food prices began a rapid ascent. At the same time, the FTC issued its final report on the packers, containing sensational evidence that consumers, as well as livestock producers, were being victimized by the Big Five's domination of the meat industry.[76] The packers became the first scapegoats of the general anxiety about rising prices. Farmers, consumer groups, and labor unions joined to establish a strong lobby in Washington to press for regulatory legislation. Congress, already under strong pressure from the public, seemed certain to pass restrictive legislation.[77]

The ambitious Attorney-General, of course, could not afford to be left behind. He ordered his investigators to speed up their work, and early in August announced that as part of his wide campaign against the high cost of living, he would begin antitrust action against the packers immediately. He borrowed seven members of the FTC staff to assist in the prosecution and hired John H. Atwood to help present the Justice Department's case to a grand jury.[78]

The suit promised to be a long one. Throughout September evidence was heard by a Chicago grand jury, then Palmer decided to develop the case further before a New York jury. Early in October, an Armour representative requested a conference with the Attorney-General; the packers wanted an agreement which would end the suit, ease public hostility, and perhaps lift pressure in Congress for restrictive legislation. Palmer, just as eager to close the case as were the packers, agreed to meet if the companies would surrender in advance on the most essential point, if they would consent to get out of all businesses except meat packing and closely related lines.[79] The packers met Palmer's conditions.

For the next two months the Attorney-General took direct charge of negotiations. During this period he also was occupied with lengthy coal strike negotiations, a threatened nation-wide rail strike, the high-cost-of-living campaign, the first of the "Palmer Raids," and the planning of the great January raids. Because of the time he devoted to meetings with packer representatives, Palmer could not give sufficient attention to other important affairs. Furthermore, if the suit remained unsettled much longer it would handicap his campaign for the Presidential nomination. In an effort to hurry a settlement, Palmer kept pressure on the meat firms by encouraging the public enmity they had already incurred. He told a New York audience that the packers were carrying on a "conspiracy directed against the American table" and that if the people could see the evidence collected by the Justice Department, their wrath would compel a conviction.[80]

Finally, Palmer and the packers' representatives hammered out an agreement, announced December 17, that took from the firms their stockyard, newspaper, wholesale grocery, public warehouse, and all retail businesses, but allowed them to retain their poultry and dairy lines and to manufacture but not distribute cereals. The decree had to be obeyed within two years, but no special provisions were included for enforcement. According to Palmer the agreement made "butchers of these five great packers, and nothing else." [81] But Francis J. Heney, who had been in charge of the FTC inquiry, complained that the settlement would "accomplish less than nothing," and that it amounted to "complete surrender of the rights of the general public." Twelve western cattlemen's associations also joined in protest, pointing out that although the decree obliged the packers to sell their stockyard holdings, there were no potential purchasers. These organizations demanded a new prosecution with Heney in charge.[82]

Palmer established an efficient system to compel compliance. All United States attorneys were ordered to report to Atwood, who set up headquarters in Chicago, on relevant steps taken by the packers in their districts. Atwood, intent upon enforcing the decree, pressed the packers to take action. Plans for disposal of their stockyards were sent by the companies to the Department of Justice for approval; some properties were sold and some lines were dropped.[83]

Nevertheless, critics of the decree turned out to be almost entirely correct. Meat and other food prices fell sharply after mid-1920, and the public lost interest in the packers. Even the cattlemen stopped protesting after the stockyards were placed under federal control in 1921. The Republican administrations of the 1920s seldom were vigilant or severe in enforcing the decree and the packers managed to drag the few suits that were brought through the courts for years. In fact, until the New Deal era, the packers evaded most of the decree's terms.[84]

Criticism of Palmer's settlement with the meat packers amounted to little compared to the storm of protest which greeted his refusal to appeal a suit over oil lands against the Southern Pacific Railroad. This case aroused the conservationists, led by Palmer's old antagonist Gifford Pinchot.[85] Pinchot might not have been so quick to sense a vile conspiracy had another man been Attorney-General, and Palmer probably would have been more responsive had the burst of public criticism originated from another source.

The land in question was purchased by the railroad at low prices under an act passed by Congress in the 1870s as an inducement to construction. Both the original act and the land patents issued by the Interior Department excluded all lands on which minerals were found. This provision was partly nullified, however, by a 1914 Supreme Court decision that mineral lands did not have to be returned unless they were obtained fraudulently.

Around the turn of the century, huge quantities of oil were discovered on land patented by the Southern Pacific, and in 1910 the government instituted suits to recover title. In one case, involving 6,560 acres in the Elk Hills region of California, the Justice Department proved that company officials knew the lands were oil-bearing when they applied for patents. A California district judge decided in favor of the government, and although this decision was reversed by a superior court, the

United States Supreme Court, in November, 1919, finally ordered the lands returned.[86]

Six other cases, involving 160,000 acres of California oil lands, were consolidated and tried in district court soon after Palmer became Attorney-General. The case was heard by District Judge Benjamin F. Bledsoe, who had ruled in favor of the government in the earlier Elk Hills suit. J. Crawford Biggs, who argued the Elk Hills case in the Supreme Court after Bledsoe's decision was reversed by the Circuit Court of Appeals, again represented the Justice Department.

This time Judge Bledsoe decided against the government. He found vast differences between the two cases. The Elk Hills property, which Bledsoe had ordered the Southern Pacific to return to the government, had been obtained by the company in 1904, five years after the California oil rush began; while the 160,000 acres involved in the later suit were applied for in the 1880s and 1890s, before oil was discovered in the area. Furthermore, correspondence in the company's files showed that Southern Pacific executives knew they were buying oil lands when they applied for title to the Elk Hills tracts, and after receiving the land the railroad turned it over to a subsidiary mineral company for development. The acreage obtained earlier, however, was aggressively sold to the public at low prices, and purchasers who fell behind in their payments were usually given extensions.[87]

The question of whether to appeal was left primarily to Biggs, who had recommended an appeal in the Elk Hills suit. This time Biggs concluded: "It is hopeless to appeal this case. . . . This case is as different from the Elk Hills case as black is from white." After Biggs sent his opinion to the Justice Department, he was called to Washington and spent two days going over the matter with Assistant Attorney-General Frank Nebeker, the man in charge of public land litigation. Both Nebeker and Solicitor-General Alexander King concurred in Biggs' opinion, and on their recommendations Palmer dropped the case.[88]

When Palmer announced his decision, the first protest—
mild compared with what was to come—arose from Navy Secretary Daniels, who had expected the oil lands to be added to the
naval reserves. Daniels requested "that you take no steps toward
abandoning these suits, at least until we have had an opportunity to take the matter up with the President." Palmer replied
that "had there been even a remote chance of success on appeal
I would have directed appeals to be taken." In February,
Daniels conferred at length with Palmer and King and apparently was convinced that no grounds existed for further action.[89]

Gifford Pinchot was not so easily satisfied. Early in January,
1920, he wrote Palmer, protesting that lands of such great importance to the nation should not be abandoned without trying
every possible remedy no matter how small the chances of success. The government had carried the matter this far, Pinchot
argued, why not take one more step?[90] Palmer should have
known what was in store for him—he had been in Congress
when Pinchot devastated the reputation of Richard A. Ballinger, Taft's Secretary of the Interior, with accusations that
Ballinger was giving away the government's Alaskan coal lands
—yet the Attorney-General, perhaps because of the current
Red Raids, did not even bother to answer his old adversary.

After waiting almost a month for Palmer's reply, Pinchot
sent his charges to the President. Palmer, he declared, refused
to protect the public interest, and he attributed the Attorney-
General's neglect to ties with large oil companies, which Palmer
had once represented. Pinchot also found a sinister meaning in
Palmer's replacement of Assistant Attorney-General F. J. Kearful, who had helped win the Elk Hills case.[91] Pinchot's accusations were as absurd as those made by Palmer in 1909, when he
tried to connect Pinchot with lumber magnates in explaining
the conservationist's opposition to lower lumber tariffs.[92] Although Palmer had indeed represented a group of independent,
Pennsylvania-owned oil companies in a 1915 suit involving
Oklahoma oil leases, there was no evidence of a relationship
between these firms and the Southern Pacific or the California
oil lands. Also, after Kearful's resignation, Palmer left the

Southern Pacific suit in the hands of Biggs, who had been most responsible for the government's successful appeal of the Elk Hills case.

Nevertheless, when Tumulty read Pinchot's letter he sensed the possibility of a major scandal. Immediately, he forwarded it to Mrs. Wilson, with a request that since the matter was "vitally important" the letter be read to the President.[93] Wilson made no reply; possibly he never saw the message. Pinchot, however, did not fight his battles privately. He distributed copies of his letter by the score, and his charges appeared prominently in newspapers and magazines throughout the country.[94]

As in the Pinchot-Ballinger controversy, the matter was finally fought out before a congressional investigating committee. Palmer and his assistants in the Justice Department showed that it was reasonable to believe that an appeal would fail.[95] Nevertheless, Pinchot's bitter accusation and the inflated value placed upon the lands by those who favored an appeal [96] made Palmer's explanation that he was trying to save the government the expense of unnecessary litigation seem a lame excuse. The case dulled the image Palmer was trying to create of himself as the defender of middle-class Americans.

Palmer's cautious approach to suits against large business firms points up even more clearly the fervor of his attacks upon labor and radicals. The latter served as popular villains in 1919–20 and to Palmer his course seemed politically sound as well as necessary for the nation's safety. But in appealing to the majority, he antagonized several minority groups; and one of these, organized labor, fought back with great effectiveness. Palmer took a calculated risk when he chose policies likely to alienate workers; but he guessed wrong about the depth of the antagonism he would arouse, and about labor's strength within the Democratic Party. Organized labor was a minority, and in the eyes of many Democratic politicians a discredited one; yet Palmer was to find, as other American political leaders have discovered to their sorrow, that a determined minority can exercise a potent veto.

CHAPTER XI

THE RED SCARE

At a victory loan pageant in the District of Columbia May 6, 1919, a man refused to rise for the playing of the "Star Spangled Banner." As soon as the national anthem was completed, an enraged sailor fired three revolver shots into the unpatriotic spectator's back. When the man fell, according to the Washington *Post,* the crowd "burst into cheering and hand-clapping." In February of the same year a jury in Hammond, Indiana, took two minutes to acquit the assassin of an alien who yelled: "To hell with the United States." Early in 1920, a clothing store salesman in Waterbury, Connecticut, was sentenced to six months in jail for having remarked to a customer that Lenin was "the brainiest," or "one of the brainiest" of the world's political leaders.[1]

Dramatic incidents like these, or the better-known Centralia Massacre, Palmer Raids, or May Day riots, were not everyday occurrences, even at the height of the Red Scare. But the fanatical 100-percent Americanism reflected by the Washington crowd, the Hammond jury and the Waterbury judge, pervaded a large part of our society between early 1919 and mid-1920.[2] A West Virginia wholesaler, with offices throughout the state, informed Palmer in October, 1919: "There is hardly a respectable citizen of my acquaintance who does not believe that we are on the verge of armed conflict in this country." When William G. McAdoo asked a friend what he should speak about in Chicago, he was told: "Chicago, which has always been a very liberal-minded place, seems to me to have gone mad on the question of the Reds." [3] "Never before," wrote a leading student of American nativism, "had antiradical nativism stirred

the public mind so profoundly." "Never before," concluded another historian of the Red Scare, "had the nation been so overwhelmed with fear." [4]

Palmer has an unenviable place in our history as the leading
symbol of the great Red Scare of 1919–20. "As Clemenceau
slew the liberal dream in Paris, so Palmer slew it in America"
is the opinion of many historians.[5] To a large extent, Palmer
deserves this reputation. He encouraged the public's fears,
partly because he expected to ride them to the Presidency; he
showed little concern for Constitutional rights when he finally
responded to the popular clamor for deportation of allegedly
subversive aliens. His career and his role in our history can be
understood, however, only if it is recognized that Palmer hesitated to comply with the public's demand for action against
radicals; that at the height of the Red Scare he received more
criticism for inactivity than for violations of civil liberties; that
when he finally attacked the Red Menace, he moved as much
because he shared the current fears and hostilities as from an
intention to exploit popular feelings.

Palmer was at least as susceptible as most Americans to the
nativism—directed largely at immigrants from southern and
eastern Europe—which served as the basic element of the Red
Scare. Raised in Monroe County, a hotbed of nativism, he nat-
urally imbibed the local attitudes.[7] As a college student in the
early 1890s, Palmer shared the widespread hostility against recent immigrants. In his commencement address he excused
what he termed an "aristocratic" mob which had recently
lynched eleven Italians in New Orleans; the mob acted, Palmer
declared, only after "justice" had been denied by a jury which
refused to convict the Italians of murder. Taking it for granted
that the new immigrants were criminally inclined, Palmer criticized those Americans who showed leniency toward unassim-
ilated aliens: "The boasted freedom of America has not half so
much to fear from the foreigners who seek our shores as from
the American citizens who from the jury box connive at their
crimes." Palmer recommended jury reform, which, he said,
would "insure justice . . . to the lowest foreigner who comes to

our free land, as well as to the highborn American through whose veins courses the blood of the Pilgrim fathers." [8] Palmer's feelings about southern and eastern European immigrants changed little during his career as a lawyer and politician. Addressing Congress in 1912 on behalf of quarry workers, he complained of 232 recent fatal quarry accidents in Northampton County alone. These deaths were a real loss to the nation, Palmer asserted, for the victims were mostly Welsh immigrants: "They are a high class of workman—not cheap foreign labor."[9]

In 1919, the xenophobia common in America before the war was greatly exacerbated, and Palmer, like many others, was caught up in the powerful upsurge of feeling against recent immigrants. He wrote of the alien radicals arrested during the Palmer Raids: "Out of the sly and crafty eyes of many of them leap cupidity, cruelty, insanity, and crime; from their lopsided faces, sloping brows, and misshapen features may be recognized the unmistakable criminal type." [10] The Bolshevik revolution, Palmer declared, was managed by "a small clique of outcasts from the East Side of New York. . . . Because a disreputable alien—Leon Bronstein, the man who now calls himself Trotsky —can inaugurate a reign of terror from his throne room in the Kremlin; because this lowest of all types known to New York can sleep in the Czar's bed . . . should America be swayed by such doctrines?" [11]

Of course, Palmer was more than a victim of his prejudices. He knew that by crusading against alien radicals he could win political support, just as he had with his moralistic attack on high prices, his antilabor activities, and, earlier, his wartime offensive against German property in this country. In each of these cases, however, Palmer found it easier to follow the policies he chose because they were in accord with his own proclivities.

Nevertheless, early in Palmer's administration of the Justice Department, he continued the liberal policies toward radicals instituted by Gregory and even reversed some repressive policies inaugurated by his predecessor. Probably Palmer did not sense, at first, the political possibilities of super-patriotism or the feverish nativism with which Americans responded to post-war difficulties. Nor did he fear revolution early in 1919; his severe attacks on radicals began only after he considered that possibility much more seriously. When he joined the Cabinet, Palmer leaned toward the idea that it was time to return to the progressive ideals which had brought the Wilson administration—and Palmer—to power. He was ready to promote again the government's role as defender of individual rights. Consequently, Palmer initially resisted powerful pressure from Congress, the press, and the public for decisive action against the Reds.

In March, 1919, Attorney-General Gregory had been sharply criticized by Congress for his failure to check radical agitators. The *World* reported in January: "The activities of the 'Reds' in New York, Philadelphia and other cities may cause an outbreak in Congress at any time. Congressmen are waiting to see what the Department of Justice will do." [12] In mid-February, the Labor Department's Bureau of Immigration shipped thirty-nine radical aliens from the West Coast, where they had been arrested over a period of months, to Ellis Island for deportation. As this move was being enthusiastically applauded by most of the nation's press, the Justice Department finally announced that it would round up an "army of undesirable aliens" for deportation by the Labor Department. "The United States is to be swept clean of its alien anarchists and trouble makers," the *World* disclosed. At least 7,000 to 8,000 radicals were expected to go.[13]

After Palmer took office, however, there were no further reports of impending large-scale roundups by the Justice Department. The new Attorney-General also refused to take advantage of other opportunities to add to the public hysteria about radicals. In an abrupt shift of policy early in 1919, Gregory had ordered the dissolution of the Justice Department's ties to the American Protective League, an organization of perhaps 250,000 members which assisted the Department's Bureau of Investigation during the war and for several months thereafter.[14] Palmer affirmed the Justice Department's wish to have the League disband. A few weeks after he became Attorney-General he declared: "Espionage conducted by private individuals or organizations is entirely at variance with our theories of government, and its operation in any community constitutes a grave menace to that feeling of public confidence which is the chief force making for the maintenance of good order." Three weeks later, in an interview in Cleveland, Palmer even asked the association to stop sending him information about radical activities: "Their continued work of watching meetings of Socialists, Bolsheviki, and other antigovernment bodies is unnecessary and is fully covered by the United States Secret Service. . . . There is no way to prevent them sending the reports, but they are not wanted." "The Attorney-General," complained the New York *Times*, "has perhaps been a little hasty in telling the patriotic and defensive societies that their help in guarding the Republic is neither needed nor welcome." [15]

Soon after Palmer's inauguration, Governor James M. Cox of Ohio requested permission to examine material, collected by the American Protective League and turned over to the Justice Department, dealing with German wartime propaganda in Ohio schools. Palmer refused the request, explaining that the files contained mainly "gossip, hearsay information, conclusions, and inferences," and that it was "our opinion that information of this character could not be used without danger of doing serious wrong to individuals who were probably innocent." [16]

The new Attorney-General continued the policy, instituted near the end of Gregory's administration, of reviewing the cases of all those convicted under the wartime Espionage Act and of recommending clemency where the verdict seemed unjust or the sentence unnecessarily severe. He also asked all United States attorneys for advice on dropping cases pending in their districts. Hundreds of suits were abandoned, and in 1919, on Palmer's recommendation, Wilson granted clemency to over 100 of the 239 still imprisoned for Espionage Act violations when the Department began reviewing cases in February. [17]
A month after he became Attorney-General Palmer ordered the

release from parole of over 10,000 enemy aliens arrested during the war and subsequently paroled.[18]

Palmer's willingness, early in his administration, to free violators of the wartime security laws, has been obscured both by his sharp reversal in policy once the Red Menace seemed real to him and by his refusal from the beginning to recommend clemency for Eugene V. Debs, most famous of all those convicted for obstructing the war effort. Palmer seriously considered releasing Debs. A few days after taking office he asked Judge D. C. Westenhaven, who had presided over Debs' trial, for his recommendation. At first Westenhaven refused to comment on the case; error proceedings were before the United States Supreme Court, he said, and he might be called upon to preside over a new trial. After the Supreme Court unanimously upheld the conviction, Westenhaven was approached again. In his answer, the trial judge cited evidence that Debs had not only urged his followers to oppose the war effort but had assured them that after the war they would be released from prison. "I earnestly recommend," the Judge concluded, "that he be not pardoned and that his sentence be not commuted." [19]

Palmer also requested an opinion from Alfred Bettman, who, with John Lord O'Brian, had been in charge of prosecutions under the Espionage Act. Bettman sincerely believed that it was the Justice Department's duty to protect civil liberties— as a Justice Department official and later he bitterly opposed prosecution of men for membership in groups rather than for their individual actions. Nevertheless, Bettman informed Palmer on March 25, 1919, that Debs had been guilty of a clear violation of the law and that the ten-year sentence was not excessive.[20] Undoubtedly, Palmer also consulted O'Brian, who had argued the case for the Justice Department and who was therefore in an even better position than Bettman to give an opinion. O'Brian, a justly famous defender of civil rights, stated unequivocally early in the spring of 1919, that Debs' sentence was fair and that there was no reason for clemency.[21]

On March 26, President Wilson cabled from Paris that he

had received suggestions that Debs be released, but he added: "I doubt the wisdom and public effect of such an action." He asked Tumulty to discuss the matter with Palmer and to let him know the result of their conference. Only a few days before, Palmer had been advised by Westenhaven and Bettman, and almost certainly by O'Brian, that clemency was not warranted. Debs had received a fair trial, Palmer declared, and since the trial he had publicly denounced the government, the courts, and the law. In view of Debs' attitude it was "imperative" that no respite be given. Tumulty cabled the President, expressing his agreement with the Attorney-General.[22]

In July, 1919, after promising Clarence Darrow that he would take up the matter again, Palmer conceded, in a message to Wilson, that he believed Debs' sentence was "too long and ought to be commuted." Public opinion, however, was bitterly opposed to clemency, and Debs' release, he feared, would help the opponents of the peace treaty. In his judgment, it was best to keep Debs in prison until after ratification of the treaty. Although Wilson repeatedly expressed a desire to have Espionage Act violators released, he agreed with the Attorney-General's policy.[23] In August, 1920, and again in October, 1920, Palmer argued for Debs' release; but each time the President overruled him, and clemency was not granted until Harding took office.[24]

As Palmer implied in his July 30 letter to Wilson, the government's amnesty program was unpopular. A large segment of the public believed there were too few Espionage Act violators in jail rather than too many. When representatives of the Socialist Party met with Palmer in May, 1920, Seymour Stedman, the Party's Vice-Presidential candidate and chief spokesman, acknowledged that the public had pressed harder for enforcement of the wartime security measures than had officials of the Justice Department, most district attorneys, or judges. Stedman, attorney for a considerable number of the prisoners in question, told the Attorney-General: "I want the record to show that when I say the country went wild, I do not mean either the courts or the Department of Justice. . . . I want to say this frankly, that the courts of the country . . . in a sense stood between a raging, unreasoning mob in this country and the people who were the defendants." [25]

Most of the imprisoned foes of the war were radicals, and all of them were associated with the Reds in the public mind. In 1919 public feeling ran strongly against a policy of tolerance toward these prisoners. Labor unions, radicals, and a good many liberals protested when Palmer announced his opposition to the release of Debs; but when the National Civil Liberties Bureau attempted to organize local committees to work for a general amnesty, the Bureau was swamped with angry criticism and it abandoned the plan. Meetings held in major cities to demand release of the so-called "political prisoners" were sparsely attended.[26] More enthusiasm probably could have been aroused in 1919 for the policy advocated by a county judge in Austin, Texas, who advised Palmer: "I believe he [Debs] should have been shot instead of simply being sent to the pen for ten years." [27] Certainly only a foolhardy or extraordinarily brave politician would have adopted or continued liberal policies toward imprisoned radicals in mid-1919.

As Palmer became aware of the widespread popular hostility toward radicals, his interest in civil liberties abated. Nevertheless, he did not shift toward a more repressive course until alarmed by the bombs and riots of May and June, 1919. By August, however, he was prosecuting rather than releasing violators of the wartime Espionage Act.[28]

On May 1, 1919, the nation was shocked to read, in glaring headlines, of a plot to assassinate some of the most prominent men in America, including Cabinet members Palmer, Burleson, and Wilson; Supreme Court Justice Oliver W. Holmes, Jr.; and business leaders John D. Rockefeller and J. P. Morgan. Thirty-six bombs mailed from New York and timed to arrive on May Day were wrapped to explode when opened. Fortunately, the New York Post Office detained about half the parcels because of insufficient postage, and almost all the others were intercepted before delivery. Only one bomb exploded, blowing off the hands of a maid in the home of Senator Thomas W. Hardwick of Georgia.

New York police officials immediately asserted that the bombing attempts bore all the earmarks of an IWW-Bolshevik plot. Justice Department officers theorized that the bombs were intended to signal a May Day reign of terror. These statements and others like them appeared in newspapers on May 1.[29] There might have been riots that day in any case—a considerable number of radical meetings and parades were scheduled—but many of the "patriots" participating in the May Day street fights must have been stimulated by news of the bombs and by the oppobrium thrust on radicals by the hasty statements of law enforcement officials.

In New York City mobs broke up every radical gathering but one, and 1,700 club-swinging police were needed to prevent invasion of a radical mass meeting in Madison Square Garden. In other cities police assisted mobs in their attacks on radical meetings and parades. After a battle in Boston, a parade was stopped and 112 radicals were arrested. Mounted policemen charged and dispersed paraders in Chicago, Detroit, and other cities. In Cleveland, where the worst riots occurred, army tanks and trucks joined police and civilians in attacking an assemblage of 20,000 who were listening to speeches in the public square. Surprisingly, only two men died in the ensuing battle, although well over 100 were shot or badly beaten.[30]

For many Americans the May Day riots provided evidence both of the strength of American radicalism and of radicals' willingness to use force to achieve their ends. Palmer, however, was not yet ready to become an apostle for the superpatriots. In his sole comment on the riots he reminded the nation that all men had the legal right to urge changes in American laws and institutions and that radicals violated the law only when they advocated use of violence. The Justice Department, he added, was reviewing speeches made at May Day celebrations and would take action if it found evidence of conspiracy to use force.[31] Congress, at this point, was much more impressed than Palmer by the menace of radicalism and the magnitude of the popular nativistic response. The New York *Times* reported on May 4:

The May Day riots, the bomb outrages and preceding occurrences in different parts of the country, have convinced members of the House that the policy of tolerance which has marked the attitude of the Department of Justice . . . must be dropped for one of vigorous prosecution if the Bolshevist movement is to be held in check.[32]

Palmer did not long remain immune to the increasing popular fear of violent upheaval. At 11:15 on the night of June 2, 1919, as the Attorney-General and his wife prepared for bed, he heard a crash downstairs, as though something had been thrown against the front door, then a deafening explosion. Broken glass showered Palmer's head and a huge elk's head fell from the wall and landed at his feet.

Assistant Secretary of the Navy Franklin D. Roosevelt and his wife Eleanor entered their house across the street about three minutes before the blast. They had driven home early from a dinner party, parked their car in a garage a few blocks away and walked to their house without noticing anything suspicious at the Palmers'. The terrific explosion shattered windows in the Roosevelt home; their cook began shouting: "The world is coming to an end!" Roosevelt's first reaction was to rush upstairs to make sure that his young son James was all right. He found the boy standing at the window staring at the wreckage across the street. James later remembered: "He grabbed me in an embrace that almost cracked my ribs."

While Mrs. Roosevelt tried to get James back to sleep her husband hurried to the Palmer's. He found the front of his neighbors' house badly damaged—the front door and all the windows were blown in. Had the Attorney-General been downstairs when the explosion occurred, he might have been badly injured, or killed if the bomb had been thrown through a front window. Although he tried not to show it, Palmer was frightened. A newspaperman described him the next morning as "the coolest and most collected person" in the neighborhood, but Roosevelt told his family that in his excitement Palmer reverted to the Quaker usage: "He was 'theeing' and 'thouing' me all over the place—'thank thee, Franklin!' and all that."

Roosevelt and Palmer searched the premises and discovered parts of at least one body. Apparently the man lit a short fuse, then tripped over a rise in the Palmer's walk as he hurried forward to throw the bomb into the house. Limbs and pieces of bone and flesh were later found on front lawns up and down the block. About fifty copies of an anarchist pamphlet titled "Plain Words" were also scattered through the neighborhood. This warned: "Class war is on and cannot cease but with a complete victory for the international proletariat. . . . There will have to be murder; we will kill . . . there will have to be destruction; we will destroy . . . we are ready to do anything and everything to suppress the capitalist class. . . ." [33]

One of Roosevelt's biographers observed that the future President's experience on June 2 "might well have made a confirmed Red-baiter out of a more timid or perturbable man." [34] Palmer was not timid but he certainly was very much perturbed. The bomb, after all, had been aimed at him and his family, and it was clearly the work of organized conspirators. Although the attack on Palmer captured most of the public attention, bombs similar to the one thrown against the Attorney-General's home blasted public buildings and houses of government officials and businessmen in eight cities—all within an hour of the attack on him.[35] "Plain Words" presented evidence enough that there would be similar violence in the future.

Now there was additional pressure on Palmer to take drastic action. The Attorney-General later told a Senate investigating committee:

I remember . . . the morning after my house was blown up, I stood in the middle of the wreckage of my library with Congressmen and Senators, and without a dissenting voice they called upon me in strong terms to exercise all the power that was possible . . . to run to earth the criminals who were behind that kind of outrage. . . . [36]

After the bombings Palmer's first move was to change sharply the complexion of the Justice Department. Bettman and O'Brian, who had agreed only to emergency wartime service, had already resigned; so had Gregory's Director of the Bureau of Investigation, A. Bruce Bielaski. Immediately, Palmer appointed Garvan Assistant Attorney-General in charge of all investigation and prosecution of radicals. He chose William J. Flynn, former chief of the Treasury Department's Secret Service, to replace Bielaski. Flynn, he declared, was the nation's foremost expert on radicalism. Frank Burke, manager of the Secret Service's New York office and its Russian Division, became Flynn's assistant.[37]

On August 1, Palmer created a General Intelligence Division, whose sole function was to collect information about radicals and coordinate the results of its own investigations with intelligence transmitted by the Bureau of Investigation and other government investigative agencies. Under the leadership of J. Edgar Hoover, chosen by Palmer on Garvan's recommendation, the GID set up an index file of over 200,000 cards on radical leaders, publications, and organizations, as well as on radical activities in various localities. The GID regularly checked 625 radical newspapers, including 251 designated as "ultra-radical" by the Division. Hoover also made a thorough study of the world-wide Communist movement, using not only information gathered by the GID, but reading Marx, Engels, Lenin, Trotsky, and other radical and Communist authors.[38] In effect, the GID became, as it was often called, the Anti-Radical Division of the Justice Department, and its twenty-four-year-old director had the crucial responsibility of interpreting the purposes and gauging the strength of American radical organizations for Garvan and Palmer.

Unfortunately for Palmer, the men he depended upon to inform him about American radicalism and to help establish antiradical policies were extraordinarily susceptible to the fear and extravagant patriotism so prevalent in 1919. Furthermore, they were often careless about the language they used in evaluating the danger of revolution. For example, when asked by a congressman, late in June, 1919, whether there really was a dangerous, organized effort under way to destroy the federal government, Garvan replied, "Certainly." [39] Flynn, after a month's intensive investigation, announced, on July 2, that the men who had committed the recent bomb atrocities were "connected with Russian Bolshevism, aided by Hun money," although he apparently had not a shred of evidence to back his assertion.[40] During hearings in April, 1920, to determine whether membership in the Communist Labor Party was sufficient grounds for deportation (Secretary Wilson ruled that it was not), Hoover testified that the party was "a gang of cut-throat aliens who have come to this country to overthrow the government by force." [41] Palmer, of course, would not have appointed such assistants to replace more careful men like Bettman and O'Brian if by June, 1919, he had not come to share their attitudes almost completely.

Actually, there was not even a remote possibility of a serious uprising in 1919–20. Most of the evidence which convinced Justice Department officials that the government was in danger, consisted of printed matter collected by the GID. After the Bolshevik triumph in Russia, American radicals became unduly optimistic; scores of new foreign-language communist and anarchist journals began publication. Palmer's reply, in 1921, to suggestions that his advisers had intentionally misled him was:

I was not imposed upon. . . . I saw the evidence. I have personally read and examined hundreds and hundreds—possibly thousands—of the pamphlets and literature. . . . There was a well defined, basic and dangerous propaganda abroad in the country, which was bound, if unchecked . . . to result in serious violence and disturbance throughout the country.[42]

However, such calls to revolt, as a recent historian of American Communism pointed out, "belonged to the realm of literary make-believe. No preparations accompanied them; no consequences followed them. The Communist factions were talking to themselves." [43] During an investigation of the Palmer Raids, Senator Thomas J. Walsh remarked caustically: "Noth-

ing, so far as the evidence here has described, has evinced anything in the nature of preparation for a military uprising. No
guns, no munitions of war were accumulated; there was no
drilling of soldiers or anything of that kind. . . ." [44] Furthermore, American workers were indifferent if not hostile to
Communist or any other kind of radical propaganda, and the
Communists had practically no contacts in 1919–20 with the
trade unions. Even the new Bolshevik regime in Russia was
not yet in a position to offer leadership or funds to the disorganized American Communists.[45]

Nor did any other radical organizations provide a serious
threat to national institutions. American anarchists were capable of isolated bomb atrocities, but a more ambitious organized
attempt was far beyond them. According to Palmer, the GID
found in the summer of 1919 that there were three especially
dangerous anarchist groups: the Union of Russian Workers,
El Ariete, and L'era Nuovo. By 1919, however, the revolutionary founders of the largest of these, the Union, had returned to
their homeland. Some radical propagandists remained, but most
members of the almost completely autonomous branches of the
organization were young, unmarried Russian males, who used
the meeting houses as social clubs and educational institutions,
and who were uninterested in revolutionary activity. No violence or disturbance of any kind was ever shown to have been
caused by a group connected with the Russian Workers. El
Ariete and L'era Nuovo were much less benign, but their total
combined membership in 1919, according to the GID was
thirty-seven.[46] The IWW, after the war, was a strife-ridden
organization, with its most effective leaders in jail or in hid-
ing, and its prestige among workers was low. Some "wobblies"
took part in the major strikes of 1919–20, lending a tinge of
credibility to the myth that the strikes were radical-inspired.
But a number of historians who have studied the IWW agree
that by 1919 whatever power it had before the war was rapidly
declining.[47]

Nevertheless, Palmer and his advisers in the Justice Department were not the only high government officials who be-

lieved that revolution threatened America. Public and private statements by Palmer's fellow Cabinet members placed additional pressure on the Attorney-General to exercise his powers against the Reds. Lansing, as well-informed as anyone in the government, declared in a private memorandum, entitled "The Spread of Bolshevism in the United States," written in July, 1919: "It is no time to temporize or compromise; no time to be timid or undecided; no time to remain passive. We are face to face with an inveterate enemy of the present social order." A month later, he wrote: "I wonder how long we can tolerate the radical propaganda which is being carried on in this country . . . without a disaster? The peril seems to me very great." [48] Daniels praised Mayor Hanson of Seattle in February, 1919, and pledged that the government would act against Bolsheviks and anarchists: "There are enough jails in America to accommodate all those who would bring about chaos. . . . The Red flag shall not menace America." Baker assured the Ohio State Federation of Women's Clubs in October that he had ordered army commanders to respond "instantly" to state calls for help in quelling radical outbursts. Baker's speech, the New York *Times* observed, was "the first declaration by an administration official of a policy to meet the disturbances of recent times." [49]

Secretary Wilson, who later took a more skeptical view of the Red Menace, replied to criticism of the Labor Department's deportation policies by proclaiming in February, 1919: "Any foreigner who comes to this country and advocates the overthrow of our form of government by force is an invading enemy, who is treated with great leniency when he is simply deported." Two days later, Wilson told a Chamber of Commerce meeting in New York City that recent major strikes had been instituted by the Bolsheviks and the IWW for the sole purpose of bringing about a nation-wide revolution in the United States.[50]

During his last speaking tour in September, 1919, President Wilson repeatedly warned against the danger of revolution both in the United States and abroad. In one speech he exclaimed that "the poison of disorder, the poison of revolt, the poison of chaos," had already forced their way "into the veins of this free people." [51] In May, 1919, six months before the first Palmer Raids, Vice-President Marshall spoke in favor of the immediate deportation of alien radicals, and the barring of all immigration to this country for an indefinite period.[52]

Soon after he reorganized his Bureau of Investigation, Palmer decided to act against radicals. On June 17, the Attorney-General held an all-day conference with Garvan, Flynn, and their assistants; they discussed the Bureau of Investigation's report on the bombings and agreed upon a broad policy for the elimination of dangerous radicals.[53] Earlier in the week, Palmer had asked Congress to add $500,000, earmarked for the investigation of radicals, to the $1,500,000 requested earlier for investigations and prosecutions in fiscal 1920. After meeting with his chief investigators Palmer warned the House Appropriations Committee: "We have received so many notices and got so much information that it has almost come to be accepted as a fact that on a certain day, which we have been advised of, there will be another . . . [attempt] to rise up and destroy the government at one fell swoop." [54] When House Republicans balked at granting Palmer the amount he asked, Garvan went before the Senate Appropriations Committee to explain why the full $2,000,000 was needed. "We have every reason to believe," declared Palmer's chief lieutenant, "that the Russian Bolsheviki are pouring money in here at the rate of that much a month." [55]

The primary policy decided upon at the all-day meeting of June 17 was the mass roundup and deportation of alien radicals.[56] However, Palmer hesitated to put this plan into operation. First of all, it was difficult to decide whom to deport. The Communists had not yet withdrawn from the Socialist Party—a meeting of the Socialist left wing, in late June, 1919, voted heavily against formation of a Communist organization—and the Socialists were unquestionably dedicated to peaceful change.[57] All efforts by the Bureau of Investigation to track down the participants in the bomb conspiracies and to connect them with radical organizations failed. There were also indications that the Labor Department, charged by law with enforcing the deportation statutes, might not cooperate. Secretary Wilson had already decided that membership in the IWW did not constitute a deportable offense.[58]

Moreover, Palmer was not yet entirely committed to the idea of an impending revolution. He may have become even more cautious, temporarily, when appropriate calamities failed to follow the dire predictions made by Flynn and Garvan. Despite Flynn's assertion early in June that there were "more bombs to come"—and soon—no more explosions occurred.[59] The nation-wide uprising Palmer's assistants warned of did not take place.

According to the prophets in the Bureau of Investigation, the Bolsheviks planned to make July 4, 1919, a day of terror in America. On June 29 Flynn met with the police chiefs of major cities and arranged for the collaboration of federal, state and municipal law enforcement agencies. In New York City every man on the police force, a total of over 11,000, was mobilized for continual duty throughout Independence Day. A heavy guard protected all public buildings and homes of prominent citizens, and the state militia was alerted for action should disturbances prove too much for city police.

Radicals could not have been unaware of the uprising they allegedly had plotted; the daily newspapers reported it fully. Communists especially would hardly have been put off by the prospect of additional clashes between proletariat and police. Yet July 4 passed quietly, except for the usual patriotic fireworks and speeches, and a bloody case of mayhem in Toledo, Ohio, where Jack Dempsey beat Jess Willard to a pulp to win the heavyweight boxing championship.[60] Palmer may have been sobered slightly by the mistaken predictions of his seers, and some of his countrymen may have begun to question the strength of the Reds; but so deeply rooted was fear that America stood on the brink of catastrophe that the idea survived with undiminished power after July 4, 1919.

Nevertheless, the summer of 1919 went by, then September

and October, without Justice Department raids or mass deportations or widespread arrests for radical activities. Meanwhile,
public dread of a social upheaval increased. Great race riots,
leaving scores dead and hundreds wounded, flared in Washington and Chicago during July. Police reported radical agitators
among Negroes in those cities, but Palmer announced that he
possessed no evidence of radical influence and he refused to
intervene.[61] A nation-wide steel strike broke out in September;
newspapers, Congressmen and other public officials joined
businessmen in telling the nation that the walkout was inspired
and led by radicals. Even before settlement of the steel strike,
nationwide coal and rail tie-ups were threatened. Major newspapers printed startling exposes of a Bolshevik plot to engulf
the world, including the United States, in class warfare.[62]
American Communists broke with the Socialists in September
and formed the Communist and Communist Labor parties,
both dedicated to the downfall of national political and economic institutions. Still the Attorney-General took no action
against radicals and seemed to have none planned.

In the fall of 1919, a storm of criticism broke around
Palmer because of his inability—some believed it was his unwillingness—to stamp out the threatening fires of revolution.
Palmer provided ammunition for his critics by injecting a bit
of old-fashioned liberalism into an address delivered October
15 at Lafayette College, Easton, Pennsylvania, where he was
awarded an honorary LL.D. degree. He opposed the proposals
for immigration restriction then being urged upon Congress.
"We cannot back-track on the policy hallowed by more than a
century of usefulness," the Attorney-General asserted. "We
cannot be less willing now than we have always been that the
oppressed of every clime shall find here a refuge from disorder
and distress." [63]

With Wilson ill, Palmer sought to inherit the President's
political support among liberal Democrats. Perhaps the Lafayette speech pleased some liberals; but Palmer's sentiments
certainly were obnoxious to the great majority of Americans
and he did not repeat them.[64] The circumspect editors of the

New York *Times,* hitherto lenient in their treatment of the Attorney-General, now lost their patience. A *Times* editorial complained that in his address at Lafayette on October 17

Attorney-General Palmer expressed ancient and outworn views on immigration; views which, coming from the head of the Department of Justice are not too pleasant to hear when, all over the country, alien or foreign-born agitators are carrying on in many languages, in five hundred or more papers and magazines, the Bolshevist and IWW propaganda for the overthrow of the Government. . . .

Some of these enthusiasts of destruction tried to kill Mr. Palmer himself. The sound of their bombs is still in our ears. From Seattle and Gary to New York, their campaign of murder reaches. . . . The resolve of Americans to defend the American policy against Bolshevism, against all its aiders and abetters, is growing sterner every day. And here is the Attorney-General of the United States, whose official duty it is to have these alien seditionaries, anarchists, plotters against the Government of the United States arrested, punished, deported, talking this pre-Adamite sentimentality. . . .[65]

Denunciations of the Attorney-General's inactivity poured into the Justice Department. From a New York patriotic society: "We protest . . . to the loose manner in which the Department of Justice is conducting the campaign against Bolshevism, anarchists, and traitors, who are seeking to destroy the Government. . . ." A midwesterner: "Unfortunately there is widespread feeling throughout the country that the Administration has been especially tender in its treatment of the disloyal elements." And from the Pacific coast: "It is unnecessary to tell you that the people of the Pacific northwest have about reached the end of the road of patience in the matter of extreme radicalism. . . . They have hoped that the government would come to their aid. . . ."[66]

Many of the critics implied that Palmer was timid, if not cowardly, in the face of great danger to his country. The most damaging attack came from the Senate. On October 14, Senator Miles Poindexter of Washington warned: "If the Government continues in that supine and indifferent attitude . . . there is real danger that the government will fall."[67] Poindexter thereupon introduced a resolution demanding that

Palmer inform the Senate whether he had yet begun legal proceedings against those who preached anarchy and sedition, advised defiance of the law, and advocated the destruction of property, "and if not, why not, and if so, to what extent." In addition, the resolution asked whether the Attorney-General had "taken legal proceedings for the arrest and deportation of aliens who, it is alleged, have . . . committed the acts aforesaid, and if not, why not, and if so, to what extent." Poindexter's resolution passed the Senate without a dissenting vote.[68]

Even Palmer's close friends and political supporters found it difficult to defend him. Senator Duncan Fletcher of Florida, who argued alone for softening the Poindexter resolution, would make no stronger declaration than: "It is possible that the assumption that there has been a total failure to act is not justified. There may be steps taken which we are not informed of." Senator Kenneth McKellar of Tennessee visited the Justice Department to hear Palmer's side of the story. "The trouble is," McKellar reported to a Senate committee, "that we have got a very liberal provision in our Constitution about the freedom of the press and freedom of speech." [69]

Palmer later described the coercion he felt in the fall of 1919 to take drastic action against radicals:

I say that I was shouted at from every editorial sanctum in America from sea to sea; I was preached upon from every pulpit; I was urged—I could feel it dinned into my ears—throughout the country to do something and do it now, and do it quick, and do it in a way that would bring results to stop this sort of thing in the United States.[70]

Other pressures were imposed upon Palmer in the autumn of 1919. By this time, his friends on the Democratic national committee were mentioning his name for the Presidential nomination. The prize he wanted seemed within reach, especially after Woodrow Wilson fell ill; but Palmer was under attack for his failure to hold down the rising cost of living, and the furious criticism of his failure to protect the nation from the Red Menace was more than he could bear. After passage of the Poindexter resolution Palmer decided that the "very liberal" provisions of the Bill of Rights were expendable, that in a time of emergency there were, as he had put it in December, 1918, "no limits" on the power of the government "other than the extent of the emergency." [71] By mid-fall, 1919, Palmer had completely accepted the idea that the emergency was indeed very grave.

CHAPTER XII

THE PALMER RAIDS

Those who cried for drastic government action against the Red Menace in 1919 demanded one remedy above all others; deportation of alien radicals. Fully 90 percent of the members of the American Communist and anarchist organizations were foreign born. The overwhelming majority of them were southern and eastern Europeans, and nativistic feeling ran high against these groups even before the Red Scare. If only the menacing foreigners could be eliminated, many Americans believed, our nation would be cleansed, our differences mitigated. "In 1919," Higham found, "the clamor of the one hundred percenters for applying deportation as a purgative rose to an hysterical howl." [1]

Palmer decided upon deportation as his solution to the radical problem as early as June, 1919. But even if he had not preferred that remedy, he soon discovered that it was the only legal action he could take successfully against most radicals. At first Palmer tried to use section six of the criminal code, written in 1861 to cope with a genuine danger of civil war. Using GID-collected information about the American radical organizations, Palmer brought a test case against three members of the El Ariete society of Buffalo, which proclaimed its dedication to the destruction of organized society. However, Federal Judge John Raymond Hazel found the Civil War statute inapplicable; nothing in the El Ariete manifesto, he decided, advocated the overthrow of our institutions by violent means. "Congress in passing it," declared Hazel, "did not have in mind, in my judgment, the overthrow of the Government . . . by the use of propaganda." [2]

Deportation laws, on the other hand, could not be construed so narrowly. According to the Immigration Act of 1917,
as amended in October 1918, any alien anarchist, no matter
how pacific his beliefs, was deportable. So was any alien advo-
cating use of violence against property, public officials, or the
government; or who belonged to an organization which advocated the use of violence. The deportation statutes, however,
gave no authority to the Justice Department. Alien violators
could be arrested only on warrants issued by the Secretary of
Labor; their cases were heard by an immigration inspector and
they could be deported only on orders signed by the Labor
Secretary.[3]

After the bombings and riots of May and June, 1919, when
public agitation for government moves against radicals became
extremely intense, both the Justice and Labor Departments
asked Congress for additional funds to wage campaigns against
subversives. The Justice Department, which already operated
a huge network of investigators, received a large extra appropriation; the Labor Department, whose regular staff was inadequate for large-scale investigation and apprehension of radical
aliens, was denied additional money. Consequently, when
Palmer suggested, in the fall of 1919, that the two departments
cooperate in the enforcement of the deportation laws, Secretary Wilson agreed.[4]

On Wilson's orders three Labor Department officials—Commissioner General of Immigration Anthony Caminetti, Solicitor General of the Department John W. Abercrombie, and A.
W. Parker, chief legal advisor of the Bureau of Immigration—
met with Justice Department officers to plan the arrest and deportation of alien revolutionists. The conferees agreed to con-
centrate first on the Union of Russian Workers, a nation-wide
organization of perhaps 4,000 Russian immigrants. Names of
alien members were to be provided by Justice Department investigators, next the Department of Labor would issue warrants of arrest, then the Justice Department would round up
the aliens and turn them over to the Labor Department for
deportation.[5]

According to its own manifesto, the Union of Russian Workers advocated revolution and anarchy. Its "Fundamental Principles" contained such radical statements as: "We must teach the working class to take the initiative . . . in order to bring about the necessary and inevitable strike to abolish government." Even before deportation of radical aliens was facilitated by the legislation of October, 1918, Caminetti, Parker, and Abercrombie agreed that membership in the Russian Workers Union was sufficient grounds for expulsion of an alien.[6]

Unfortunately, Justice and Labor departments' investigators apparently did little more than read the Russian Workers manifesto and pamphlets. A sociologist and a social worker, each of whom studied the organization carefully—interviewing members as well as others familiar with the group—both concluded that it was not dangerous. Always a loose confederation, the Union's branches became almost completely autonomous when the radical founders returned to Russia after the revolution. A few members continued to give radical lectures and distribute revolutionary propaganda; but by 1919 the organization served chiefly as a social club for the lonely and an educational institution for the ambitious. Members were not required to read the Union's principles and testimony at deportation proceedings showed that many had never seen them. Furthermore, as Kate Holladay Claghorn pointed out, "no disorder, no crime, no preparation for crime, even, has been traced to any group of the Union of Russian Workers."[7]

On November 7, 1919, the second anniversary of the Russian Revolution, Department of Justice agents carrying arrest warrants signed by Caminetti swooped down on Russian Workers meeting places in twelve cities. In New York, Justice operatives and city police surrounded the Russian People's House and at a prearranged signal charged into the building and rounded up everyone on the premises. Only two rooms in the People's House were occupied by the Union; other tenants included a steamship company, and a dock workers school which offered Russian-language courses in mathematics, mechanical trades, music, and literature. There was also a clubroom, open to the public. All those found in the building were lined up and searched. When some protested a policeman silenced them shouting, according to a New York *Times* reporter: "Shut up there, you, if you know what's good for you." Later, the police declared that they had protected themselves against violent resistance; many of the Russians, however, claimed they were beaten without provocation and forced to run a gauntlet of blackjacks on their way downstairs. According to the *Times:* "A number of those in the building were badly beaten up by the police during the raid, their heads wrapped in bandages testifying to the rough manner in which they had been handled."

Although the Bureau of Investigation had obtained only 27 arrest warrants in New York, about 200 men and women were removed from the People's House, herded into trucks and taken to Justice Department headquarters. Some of the captives proved to be citizens and many were neither members of the Russian Workers Union nor radicals of any other persuasion. Police questioned a number of men who walked by the People's House during the raid and detained some who admitted they were Russians. Government agents eventually released these men when no further evidence against them could be found. Only thirty-nine of the two hundred or more arrested at the People's House were held for deportation hearings, and many of these cases were dismissed for lack of evidence.

Other raids took place all over New York City. Homes were invaded without search warrants and men taken into custody because they roomed with suspects or lived in an apartment formerly occupied by party members. Altogether, the Justice Department arrested about 650 people in New York, releasing most of them after questioning. Finally, only forty-three New York members of the Russian Workers were deported.[8]

Even more flagrant violations of civil liberties occurred in other cities. Everywhere Palmer's agents made arrests without warrants; the Labor Department issued thirty-six warrants in

Newark, but 150 people were taken into custody there. In at least two Pennsylvania towns, men were apprehended on charges by a steel company undercover agent, some allegedly because they maligned the Bethlehem Steel Company. A Labor Department investigator discovered in March, 1920, that some members of the Russian Workers Union had been imprisoned in Hartford, Connecticut, without a deportation hearing since November 7. Many of the aliens arrested in the November raids and later released swore they were beaten and threatened while being questioned by Department of Justice agents.[9]

Palmer and his assistants operated, in late 1919 and early 1920, under the theory that the United States stood on the brink of revolution, and that in such an emergency national safety took precedence over fine concern for Constitutional rights. Department officials ignored protests against overcrowding of detention centers, and they turned their backs on arrests and searches made without warrants. When Isaac Shorr, an attorney for the National Civil Liberties Bureau, complained to Palmer that men had been beaten and property destroyed during the raid on the New York People's House, no investigation ensued. J. Edgar Hoover, liaison man between the Department and its field agents during the roundups, informed his superiors that he had heard of no such violence, and he advised against a reply to Shorr lest it be used to continue the controversy.[10]

Despite some annoying criticism, Palmer, for the first time in his administration, basked in the warm glow of public approval. Newspapers almost unanimously applauded the raids. When the transport *Buford*, dubbed the "Soviet Ark," sailed from New York on December 21 carrying 249 anarchists bound for Russia, most of the nation's press was ecstatic. The Cleveland *Plain Dealer* voiced a typical comment: "It is to be hoped and expected that other vessels, larger, more commodious, carrying similar cargoes, will follow in her wake." Palmer also had the pleasure of pointing to his raids on the Russian Workers when he finally replied on November 14 to the Poindexter Resolution, passed by the Senate a month earlier. He could now declare, self-righteously, that the lag in the government's attack against the Reds derived from Congress' failure to provide needed legislation, not from timidity in the Justice Department.[11]

Confident that his assistants would effectively carry out his policy of mass arrests, Palmer hardly supervised the men he chose to manage his antiradical campaign. Instead, the Attorney-General divided his time and energy among a number of other important tasks. With prices of food and clothing still rising, Palmer determined to establish a nation-wide price-fixing organization. Conferences about the price of sugar especially occupied his time. Early in October, representatives of the meat packers entered negotiations with Palmer about a consent decree, and he guided these meetings until an agreement was reached in mid-December. All his activities were interrupted on November 1 by the coal strike. When the raid on the Russian Workers took place, the Attorney-General had just obtained one injunction against leaders of the United Mine Workers and was seeking a second.[12]

Palmer's health gave way in mid-November, when plans were being made for the vast raids of January 2. His private secretary, Robert Scott, denied reports of a complete collapse: "The Attorney-General has been working under heavy pressure during the last three or four years and his doctor has advised him that it would be the part of wisdom for Mr. Palmer to lay off for about a week for rest and recuperation." Another report declared that Palmer was leaving Washington for a two-week rest.[13] By December 6, though, Palmer was ready to begin strenuous negotiations with William Green and John L. Lewis of the United Mine Workers, and on December 17 he announced that he had finally worked out a consent agreement with the meat packers. Meanwhile, his subordinates continued to organize the Palmer Raids.

Palmer's assistants did learn a few lessons from the November roundups. One was the danger of allowing arrested aliens to speak to their attorneys before being interrogated. After receiving legal advice, many radicals refused to talk about their beliefs or associations and consequently had to be released because of insufficient evidence. The chief reason so many arrested aliens exercised their right to counsel was the observance by Labor officials of a section of Rule 22 of the immigration regulations which read: "At the beginning of the hearing under the warrant of arrest the alien shall be allowed to inspect the warrant of arrest and all the evidence on which it was issued, and shall be apprised that he may be represented by counsel."

On November 19, J. Edgar Hoover, who bore the major burden of organizing the January raids, wrote to Caminetti recommending a change in Rule 22. When the Immigration Commissioner failed to reply, Hoover again urged the revision on December 17, concluding: "In view of the difficulty in proving the cases against persons known to be members of the Union of Russian Workers, due to the arbitrary tactics of persons employed by such members, I would appreciate an early reply to my letter of the nineteenth, in order that the same condition may not arise when future arrests are made of undesirable aliens." [14] Caminetti presented a memorandum to Abercrombie, Secretary Wilson's officer in charge of deportation matters, calling for the modification of Rule 22 and on December 31, Abercrombie agreed. Caminetti then sent all immigration agents copies of the new version, which began: "Preferably at the beginning of the hearing . . . or at any rate as soon as such hearing has proceeded sufficiently in the development of the facts to protect the Government's interests, the alien shall be . . . [advised of his right to counsel]." [15]

The Justice Department next turned to its primary target among radical groups—the Communist and the Communist Labor parties. These remained separate organizations chiefly because neither set of leaders would agree to surrender its power; but they differed hardly a whit in their revolutionary principles, and each party was composed largely of Slavic immigrants.[16] Before Palmer's men could round up the Communists, however, they needed approval from the Department of Labor, which was responsible for issuing warrants and for final decisions in deportation cases. Again, Hoover set out to win compliance. He sent a memorandum on the Communist Party to Caminetti—a man as hostile to all forms of radicalism as anyone in the Justice Department—and the Immigration Commissioner used it as the basis for a brief recommending the deportation of one Marion Bieznuk solely because of his membership in the Communist Party.[17]

On December 24, Caminetti reported: "In company with Acting Secretary John W. Abercrombie, a conference took place with the Secretary of Labor, who agreed with the view expressed that members of that [Communist] 'Party' and the 'Russian Workers Union' aim to reach the same objective, only by different methods." [18] Hoover, knowing that the Communist and Communist Labor parties had similar aims, then rashly decided not to ask the Labor Department's opinion on the deportability of Communist Labor Party members. Instead, as soon as he received Caminetti's note of December 24, the GID chief replied:

The Communist Party . . . is exactly similar to the Communist Labor Party, members of both being pledged to the principles and tactics of the Third International. . . . It is therefore the intention of this office to treat the members of the Communist Labor Party in the same category as those of the Communist Party.[19]

Evidently Palmer never learned that the round-up of Communist Labor Party members was based on Hoover's assumption that membership was a deportable offense, and that the Labor Department had made no statement to that effect. Questioned about the matter a year later by the Senate Judiciary Committee, Palmer conferred with Hoover, who sat beside him, and then asserted:

Mr. Hoover, who was in charge of this in the Bureau of Investigation, is more familiar with the history of it than I am. It appears that Mr. Abercrombie, Acting Secretary, held that the Communist Labor Party and the Communist Party were alike in their views and principles and that membership in each made out a prima facie case and it was with that understanding that the arrests of both Communist and Communist Labor Party members were made.[20]

Immediately after Hoover passed word that both communist organizations had been proscribed, the Department of Justice began casting its enormous dragnet. A request for about 3,000 warrants was sent to Caminetti only a few hours after Hoover and the Immigration Commissioner exchanged messages. Upon examination of the attached affidavits, certifying cause for the warrants, Abercrombie found that in almost every case the only evidence cited was membership in the Communist or Communist Labor Party. He refused to sign the warrants; instead he brought the affidavits to Secretary Wilson and asked him for a decision.[21]

Wilson called Post, Caminetti, and Abercrombie to a conference. The Labor Secretary and his Assistant opposed another series of mass arrests and Abercrombie was reluctant to sign the warrants; only Caminetti wanted to go ahead. Yet, as Abercrombie observed later: "The country was wild on the subject of the suppression of anarchy, every newspaper was full of it." And suppose the nation really was on the brink of revolution? According to Post, the Labor Department heads decided to continue cooperating with the Department of Justice

upon the faith of assurances by the Attorney-General and his official coadjutors in the secret service adjunct of his Department that resident aliens in large numbers and of a desperate type were positively known to be engaged in a conspiracy to overthrow our Government . . . and that the danger was both extreme and imminent.[22]

Wilson instructed Abercrombie to issue the warrants called for by the Justice Department only if evidence of wrongdoing other than party membership was submitted—and then the Solicitor was to judge each case on its own merits. Five days later, Wilson sent the Attorney-General a mild protest against the planned mass arrests. Even the smaller-scale roundup of Russian Workers had placed a severe strain on the Immigration Bureau, Wilson asserted, and he warned of long delays and crowded conditions if Palmer went ahead with his raids.[23]

Wilson did nothing to ascertain that his instructions to Abercrombie were followed.[24] Nor did Abercrombie insist upon compliance by the Justice Department. When Post later examined Justice Department affidavits in support of its demand for warrants, he discovered:

They were mimeographed forms filled in and sworn to by supervising detectives. The affiants seldom had any other information; their informants often had none at all. . . . Some were not even signed by the affiant. Some were as blank as when they were ground out by the mimeographing machine, except for names and wear and tear.

Nevertheless . . . warrants were accordingly drafted by an obedient clerical force in the Bureau of Immigration and transmitted wholesale to the Solicitor of the Department of Labor for his signature as Acting Secretary of Labor. . . . The Acting Secretary thereupon signed the warrants. Most of them he signed perfunctorily, depending upon the assurance of the Bureau of Immigration.[25]

As soon as they were sure that Abercrombie would issue the warrants, the Justice Department's radical-chasers completed preparations for their raids. On December 27, instructions signed by Burke went out to all United States District Attorneys. The Fourth Amendment to the Constitution forbids arrest or search without warrant, and it furthermore stipulates: "No warrants shall issue, but upon probable cause, supported by oath or affirmation, and particularly describing the place to be searched, and the persons or things to be seized." Various courts had already decided that aliens arrested in deportation proceedings enjoyed the protection of the Fourth Amendment. An 1899 decision established the fact that papers illegally obtained could not be used as evidence against aliens in expulsion hearings.[26] Yet, Burke's cablegram not only instructed the District Attorneys to thoroughly search meeting places and homes of Communist and Communist Labor Party members ("All literature, books, papers and anything hanging on the walls should be gathered up."); but it went on:

I leave it entirely to your discretion as to the method by which you should gain access to such places. If, due to local conditions in your territory, you will find that it is absolutely necessary for you to obtain a search warrant for the premises you should communicate with the local authorities a few hours before the time for the arrests is set and request a warrant to search the premises.[27]

Questioned later by Senator Walsh about his Department's use of search warrants, Palmer confessed his ignorance about much that occurred during the raids, and he finally suggested:

"I can not tell you Senator, personally. If you would like to ask Mr. Hoover who was in charge of this matter, he can tell you." Hoover then asserted that he had left the question of obtaining warrants up to local Bureau of Investigation officials, and that although a year had gone by since the raids, he had not ascertained the number of search warrants.[28]

Furthermore, thousands of arrests were made without warrants. Burke instructed his agents to "take into custody all persons for whom warrants have been issued," but the method of making arrests made an orderly and legal procedure improbable if not impossible. Immigration inspectors, holding the warrants issued by Abercrombie, waited in detention centers while Justice agents rounded up all persons attending Communist meetings. Captives were then brought in and matched against the warrants. Asked why he adopted such cumbersome procedures, one immigration officer replied that he had obeyed instructions received at "a conference in Washington in the Department of Labor with Mr. Hoover and another gentleman of the Department of Justice." [29]

Tho most spectacular of the Palmer Raids swept up radicals in dozens of cities on January 2, 1920. Mopping-up operations continued for several days thereafter, and smaller raids were carried on sporadically in many parts of the country over the next six weeks. During this period over 3,000 radicals were arrested, and at least as many other suspects were taken into custody, held for periods ranging from a few hours to several months, and then released without ever having been officially arrested.

All the worst features of the November raids reoccurred, but on a much larger scale. There was the knock on the door, the rush of police. In meeting houses, all were lined up to be searched; those who resisted often suffered brutal treatment. Except for a few who carried documentary proof of citizenship all were taken to police headquarters for intensive questioning; usually they received a confession to sign, and often were threatened or beaten if they refused to comply. Prisoners were put in overcrowded jails or detention centers where they remained, frequently under the most abominable conditions, until called for deportation hearings, or until their captors decided their evidence was insufficient.

Police searched the homes of many of those arrested; books and papers, as well as many people found in these residences were carried off to headquarters. Policemen also sought those whose names appeared on seized membership lists; they captured many of these suspects in bed or at work, searching their homes, confiscating their possessions, almost always without warrants.[30] An immigration inspector in the Boston area described under oath police methods of obtaining evidence in suspects' homes. Asked if any search warrants were issued in his district, he replied: "Not to my knowledge." Pressed further, he admitted that if any warrants had been applied for he "would have heard of it." The same inspector testified that Justice agents, after thoroughly examining their prisoners on the night of January 2, decided that about a hundred of them should be deported; but when these suspects came before an Immigration official, he was unable to connect any of them with the ten arrest warrants he held. An immigration inspector from Seattle told an astonished Congressional committee how Justice agents and police in his area rounded up several hundred radicals in one evening: "They went to various pool rooms, etc., in which foreigners congregated, and they simply sent up in trucks all of them that happened to be there." [31]

In most cases, Department of Justice operatives avoided violence, as Burke's instructions ordered. However, because of the vast scale of the raids the Department commissioned local police assistance; in many areas police rounded up radicals and Justice agents interrogated prisoners as they were brought in. Frequently, members of private patriotic organizations helped conduct the raids; [32] although only nine months before, Palmer had publicly declared that help from such sources was "entirely at variance with our theories of government." These assistants, along with agents added temporarily to the Bureau of Investigation's staff probably inflicted a large share of the beatings reported. J. Edgar Hoover stated: "I was sent up to New York later by Assistant Attorney-General Garvan and reported back that there had been clear cases of brutality in the raids." [33]

The violence, however, did not distress prisoners as much as the overcrowded, insanitary condition of many of the detention centers. The Labor Department had little time to prepare facilities for the thousands of captives; Byron H. Uhl, Immigration Commissioner in New York, who was wholeheartedly in favor of the deportation of alien radicals, pleaded unsuccessfully with the Justice Department to postpone its raids until he had more room on Ellis Island. A Department of Labor investigator reported that in Detroit "conditions could not have been worse" but ample evidence suggests that conditions were at least as bad in Hartford and on Deer Island in Boston Harbor.[34]

Inevitably there were mistakes. Many citizens remained in custody for considerable periods before they could prove their citizenship. Even among aliens arrested at party meetings, a fair number were not members. Some whose names appeared on membership lists turned out to be completely illiterate and totally devoid of interest in communism; most belonged to one of the Russian social organizations whose leaders decided to affiliate their group with one of the new Communist parties. Many branches of the Socialist Party also transferred their allegiance to the Communists without the knowledge of all members. Thirty-nine men, arrested and held overnight in Lynn, Massachusetts, had come together, in a meeting hall often used by radicals, solely for the purpose of forming a cooperative bakery. It was not uncommon for aliens mistakenly arrested to remain incarcerated for several weeks, and in some cases a month or more, awaiting a hearing. Meanwhile, families of these unfortunate immigrants suffered not only anxiety but, often, economic hardship.[35]

The public knew only that thousands of supposedly dangerous alien radicals had been rounded up for deportation. Apparently, most Americans enthusiastically approved the raids. Flattering letters poured into the Justice Department and a large proportion of the nation's press cheered. The New York *Times* practically apologized for the aspersions it had cast upon

Palmer: "If some or any of us," acknowledged a *Times* editorial on January 5, "impatient for the swift confusion of the Reds, have ever questioned the alacrity, resolute will, and fruitful intelligent vigor of the Department of Justice in hunting down those enemies of the United States, the questioners and the doubters have now cause to approve and applaud." [36] Later, Cabinet members Daniels, Lane, and Wilson declared that they had opposed Palmer's actions; but in January, 1920, they kept their opinions to themselves. At a Cabinet meeting January 6, when stories of the raids crowded the newspapers, there was, according to Lansing, "No real business. All politics." [37]

The first telling protest against the raids came from within the Justice Department. Francis Fisher Kane, United States Attorney in Philadelphia, owed his position largely to close political association with Palmer. But Kane, one of the wealthy, idealistic reformers who entered politics during the Progressive era, had been disturbed by the November raids. Having no further political ambitions, he decided, after seeing Burke's instructions of December 27, to follow the dictates of his conscience. In a letter to Palmer, Kane warned of the injustices inevitable during mass arrests and he threatened to resign rather than participate in such violations of men's rights. Palmer did not reply until January 3, when he explained that the District Attorney's letter had been received too late for consideration. Kane thereupon wrote letters of resignation to Palmer and the President, repeating at length his objections to the raids; these he released to the press on January 12.[38] Kane's response provided the first indication from a responsible public official— and a fairly important member of the Justice Department at that—that laws had been violated during the raids and that not all of those arrested were engaged in a revolutionary plot.

Other scattered protests followed. A few newspapers wondered whether large-scale roundups provided the best weapon against Bolshevism. Liberal magazines like the *Nation* and the *New Republic* continued to criticize the Attorney-General. Most of the early criticism, however, was as ambiguous as that delivered by William Allen White, who wrote in his Emporia

[Kansas] *Gazette* on January 8: "The deportation business is going to make martyrs of a lot of idiots whose cause is not worth it." But White declared in the same editorial that if a man "preaches violence he is disturbing the peace and should be put in jail." [39]

Early in March, 1920, Palmer's nemesis appeared on the scene. At that time Abercrombie suddenly left the Labor Department to run for the Senate in Alabama. With Secretary Wilson ill, Assistant Secretary Louis F. Post became Acting Secretary, in charge of all deportation matters.

It was easy to underestimate Post. A slight man, seventy-one years of age, he had a long, sad face framed by an old-fashioned pointed beard at one end and a wild mop of grey hair at the other. Although unsympathetic with the theories of the radicals in his charge—he had long opposed all forms of socialism—Post himself professed some unpopular beliefs. He advocated easy divorce and Henry George's single tax, and he invariably took the side of the poor and helpless. Occasionally, he expressed a populistic fear of the "money power." Late in 1918 he complained to Secretary Wilson that Justice Department agents in the West were persecuting critics of "certain financial interests." Even in his careful testimony before the House Rules Committee in May, 1920 Post spoke of "big business interests that are trying to run the country," and "the newspaper drive that was made to create a great terroristic scare in the country." [40] When he engaged in controversy with the more conventional Attorney-General, Post found it difficult to win support from Congressmen and newspapermen, and his appearance and background may have aroused suspicion in most newspaper readers as well.

Nevertheless, Post proved to be a tough antagonist. He had the advantage of a keen mind and a remarkable memory. During seven years as Assistant Secretary he had thoroughly mastered the intricacies of immigration law and procedure; as an attorney he spoke confidently about Constitutional precedents and even about the Justice Department's duties—he once served as Assistant United States Attorney in New York City. When called before a Congressional committee, he turned out to be a convincing speaker with a caustic tongue.

By the time Post assumed responsibility for deportation cases, Secretary Wilson had already announced that the Communist Party fell within the deportation statute. Post said he agreed with his superior's decision; [41] but even if he did not, the Assistant Secretary had no alternative but to approve Immigration Bureau recommendations of deportation for Communists.

Post, however, thought of the aliens as human beings, not merely cases. "Administrative process is a very dangerous institution for a country like ours to adopt with reference to personal liberty," he cautioned; "and it is pretty near time that some check was put upon its development in so far as it affects the rights of personal liberty." [42] During his first day as Acting Secretary, Post discovered that some men had been imprisoned for two months, and that attendance at a meeting was the only evidence against them. After demanding the records piling up in the Immigration Commissioner's office, he worked day and night, seven days a week, canceling warrants where evidence seemed obviously insufficient.

Post dismissed all cases of "automatic" membership—men transferred without their knowledge from other organizations. He followed a recent court decision, as well as earlier precedent, in releasing aliens held on illegally seized evidence,[43] but he did order the deportation of aliens unequivocally members of the Communist Party even when they appeared to have little understanding of Communist doctrines. By April 10, Post had decided 1,600 cases, canceling arrest warrants in 1,141, or 71 percent of them. He also ordered the release of numerous others for whom warrants had not been obtained, and in many cases he reduced the amount required for bail.[44]

Certainly Post made mistakes. He freed aliens whose testimony indicated they were deportable, merely because the men had made incriminating statements before being informed of their right to counsel. Yet Post was aware of a court decision to the effect that aliens in expulsion cases did not have to be granted counsel even if they requested such assistance. Post also released all members of the Communist Labor Party despite the fact that the organization's principles were almost identical with those of the Communists.[45] Nevertheless, for every legal error Post made, he restored freedom to many innocent men.

Post's actions enraged Palmer. Presidential primaries had begun and as the Pittsburgh *Post* observed: "Much of the campaign material that Attorney-General Palmer has been using in his very active campaign for the Presidency concerns his efforts against the Reds." Palmer counted upon the spectacle of thousands of deported radicals to establish his image as guardian of the commonweal. Late in February, 1920 the Attorney-General promised an audience of New York clubwomen that they would soon be treated to the sight of a "second, third and fourth Soviet Ark," sailing from their beautiful harbor. Now one small, stubborn old man stood between Palmer and his reward. Post, Palmer told Lansing, was a "Bolshevik himself." The Attorney-General spread the word to congressmen who wondered what was holding up the deportations they demanded; he also enlightened the press.[46]

Hoover was as angry as his chief; he thought he had shattered the Communist threat. On January 26, he assured newspapermen that least 3,000 of the 3,600 aliens arrested by the Justice Department were "perfect" deportation cases. Now Hoover fired memorandum after memorandum at the helpless Caminetti. Why was a dangerous anarchist released on $1,000 bail when Hoover had recommended $5,000? How could Caminetti justify the cancellation of warrants for six proven anarchists? Why was a certain case stayed for three months? [47] Finally, before a subcommittee of the House Committee on Immigration and Naturalization, a Justice Department representative recited the Department's woes, and that group obtained Post's permission to scrutinize his records. The subcommittee's report became the basis for impeachment proceedings.[48]

When Post appeared before the House Committee on Rules, to which the impeachment resolution was referred, he confounded his inquisitors with a quick wit and ready knowledge of his subject. In a staunch defense of his actions, he reviewed the cases his accusers had used against him and showed that in each instance he had made a difficult decision over which, as he put it, honest men might disagree. As Post rehearsed these cases, it became clear that few of the aliens in question were in any way dangerous. Indeed, Thomas Truss, whose case Post's opponents selected as the best example of his culpability, turned out to be a highly respected elder in a Baltimore Presbyterian church, with a good job, a wife, and three American-born children. A Socialist, he had been talked into transferring with his small group to the new Communist Party. Truss said he understood that the new party also was a peaceful socialistic organization. His group dissolved in October, 1919 after a few meetings, before receiving a copy of the Communist Party's constitution.[49]

Post's testimony alone might have done little more than detract from the glamor of the Palmer Raids—to many Americans, a single-taxer with a Vandyke beard was not a reliable judge of whether radicals were dangerous or whether the Justice Department had arrested them illegally. But the defense was delivered at a propitious time. Less than a week before the Assistant Secretary confronted the Rules Committee, Palmer's own reputation as an authority on radicalism suffered irreparable damage: his predictions of a May Day reign of terror had proved completely unfounded. This fiasco gave credence to Post's charges that the Justice Department was abusing rather than protecting the rights of Americans.

Palmer's information about the May Day threat came largely from the omnivorous readers in the General Intelligence Division. In mid-April, the GID discovered a common theme in the handful of anarchist pamphlets which came into its possession —a call for revolt and general strikes on May 1. Late in April, 1920, the Central Executive Committee of what was left of the Communist Party issued a proclamation calling to American workers: "Show your power on May Day." The official organ of the remnants of the Communist Labor Party headlined its May Day issue: "Down Tools May 1, 1920." [50]

By this time, the Justice Department had interrogated thousands of radicals captured in the raids, and its undercover-agents had infiltrated many branches of the radical organizations. The Department, therefore, possessed abundant evidence of the wide gulf between the words of revolutionary pamphleteers and the actions of American radicals. True, there had been riots on May 1, 1919, but these were caused, with few exceptions, by citizens who invaded radical meeting halls and interrupted parades. Nevertheless, when the summons to revolt were brought to Palmer's attention in April, 1920, he instructed the GID to warn the nation of the gigantic conspiracy they had uncovered.

For at least ten days before May 1, Hoover's division alarmed Americans with bulletins about the general strikes, assassinations, and bombings planned for May Day. On April 28, Palmer added his personal warning: many federal and state officials and other prominent Americans were marked for death, he asserted. "Radical literature of all kinds . . . predicts the general May Day strike." Newspapers throughout the country repeated in bold headlines the predictions of calamity: "Terror Reign by Radicals, says Palmer." "Nation-wide Uprising on Saturday." [51]

Major cities ordered their police forces to prepare for the emergency. Some state militia were called up, federal troops prepared for action, and private patriotic organizations mobilized with official approval. In New York, the *Times* reported: "Stirred by Attorney-General Palmer's warning of an international plot in the interest of Soviet Russia . . . every force of law and order . . . was made ready last night." The entire police force of 11,000 remained on duty from midnight, April 30, to 8:00 A.M., May 2. Heavy guards covered public buildings and the homes of public officials. In Boston, every available law enforcement officer, including court officials, stood guard assisted by seven machine guns mounted on automobiles and stationed in various sections of the city.[52]

Nothing happened. No bombs, no riots, no assassinations. Not even a noisy meeting. Radicals were even quieter than on

July 4, 1919, the last time the Justice Department had prophesied a reign of terror. Even the customary May Day speeches lacked their usual fire. On May 2, the New York *Times* printed comments from newspapers around the country indicating that the Attorney-General was now widely regarded as subject to hallucinations. A cartoon in the May 4 Chicago *Tribune* showed Palmer walking down the street, wearing a heavy overcoat and shivering, although it was a fine spring day. All around him children played and mothers strolled with babies. But Palmer saw only radicals; little girls jumping rope wore beards and held firebrands, and the mailman concealed a bomb in his pouch.[53]

By spring, 1920, most of the American public was ready for a reconsideration of the Red Menace. To a large degree, the fears contributing to the extraordinary popular anxiety of 1919 and early 1920 evaporated. The European revolutions died out and Bolshevism seemed isolated in Russia; bombings had abruptly ceased after the explosion in Palmer's house; prices of food and clothing began to recede; important industries were relatively free from labor strife. Furthermore, many Americans who had acquiesced, at first, in the crusade against radical aliens became disturbed when the policies of the "one-hundred percenters" threatened traditional liberties. Among such excesses were the New York State Assembly's refusal in January, 1920 to seat five duly elected Socialist legislators, and the introduction in Congress of a number of draconic peacetime sedition bills. Probably the Red Scare was on its way out by May, 1920, but Post's testimony and the May Day fiasco gave it two hard pushes.

As public sentiment shifted, the man who had made himself the leading symbol of the Red Scare became the chief victim of the reaction. One reverse followed another for Palmer in the spring of 1920. The President apparently sided with William B. Wilson when the Labor Secretary defended Post in a Cabinet meeting on April 14. "Palmer, do not let this country see red!" the President allegedly admonished, as though the country had not been doing so for well over a year.[54]

Some of the most damaging criticism arose out of a trial in Boston's federal court, *Colyer et al. v. Skiffington,* in which eighteen aliens, arrested during the January raids, sought release on writs of habeas corpus. Judge George W. Anderson, who heard the case, had exclaimed in court fourteen months

from the Chicago *Tribune,* 1920

A. MITCHELL PALMER OUT FOR A STROLL

before: "This is no time to whittle down the rights of American liberty, whether it be against anarchists or not." [55] Now, as Anderson heard Justice and Labor Department agents describe under cross examination how they had violated fundamental rights in hundreds of cases, he registered first shock, then anger.

Finally, he burst out: "A more lawless proceeding it is hard for anyone to conceive. Talk about Americanization! What we need is to Americanize people that are carrying on such proceedings as this." Both the testimony introduced at the trial and Judge Anderson's comments bolstered Palmer's critics.[56]

In mid-April, 1920, representatives of a group of liberal organizations meeting in Washington decided to conduct an investigation of the Palmer Raids and publish their findings. The National Popular Government League took charge of the project, although members of the National Civil Liberties Bureau provided a good deal of the material. However, most of the editorial work was undertaken by Jackson Ralston, attorney for Post in the impeachment hearings, in the expectation that the exposé would help his client. The booklet ultimately produced was comprised largely of two kinds of materials: affidavits from aliens who swore they had been arrested illegally and mistreated during the raids, and testimony and documents presented in the Colyer case.

Before its public distribution, copies of the booklet were sent to a small number of eminent attorneys, most of whom had appeared as counsel for aliens taken in the raids, with a request that they endorse the charges. Among those who signed the report were Felix Frankfurter and Zechariah Chafee, Jr., professors at Harvard Law School, who had served in the Colyer case. (Frankfurter conducted the cross examination of George E. Kelleher, head of the Bureau of Investigation office in Boston, which elicited Burke's instructions.) Roscoe Pound, Dean of the Harvard Law School, who had heard much of the Colyer testimony and frequently discussed the case with Frankfurter and Chafee, also signed, apparently without being asked to do so. Other endorsers included Ernst Freund of the University of Chicago Law School, Tyrell Williams, Professor of Law at Washington University of St. Louis, Frank P. Walsh of New York City, and Francis Fisher Kane.[57] All twelve signers commanded considerable respect in the legal profession. Frankfurter, Chafee, Pound, and Freund rank among the most illustrious figures in the history of American law.

The sixty-seven page booklet, issued late in May by the National Popular Government League, was skillfully prepared, its sober, ponderous tone served to emphasize the sensational charges. It began: "For more than six months we, the undersigned lawyers, whose sworn duty it is to uphold the Constitution and Laws of the United States, have seen with growing apprehension the continued violation of that Constitution and breaking of these laws by the Department of Justice of the United States government." [58] Newspapers that had skimmed over Post's charges accorded much more respectful treatment to this new indictment. Perhaps more important, the booklet persuaded other influential Americans, like Charles Evans Hughes and Harlan Fiske Stone, to speak out against Palmer's activities.[59]

Powerful industrialists and business organizations also attacked the Justice Department in the hope that they could bring the Red Scare to an end. These businessmen, some of whom contributed earlier to the hysteria, now feared that unless nativists were curbed, immigration restrictions would soon be invoked, stopping the flow of cheap labor.[60] As a result of business efforts, by May even those newspapers which applauded the Palmer Raids were publishing articles about the value of immigrants to American industry.[61] Charles Schwab, frequently accused of importing workers for his Bethlehem Steel works, called the radical menace a "bogcy" and predicted that Palmer's Raids would create more Reds than they eliminated. Schwab's charges were echoed by T. Coleman du Pont, who declared that those who persecuted aliens suffered from "sheer Red hysteria, nothing more." [62]

Palmer continued to insist that real danger of a radical uprising existed. He acknowledged that the government could not be overthrown, but he warned that revolutionists still thought that it could be. Even after May Day, he foresaw bloody attempts at revolt unless radicals were kept in check by a vigilant Department of Justice, and he continued to demand new and stringent sedition legislation.[63] Palmer was running for President as his country's protector; only if the peril seemed great would his past efforts be fully appreciated and his future services appear needed.

There were other reasons, too, for Palmer's continued agitation of the radical issue. Finally the spotlight focused upon him, and he was reluctant to give up his place. Furthermore, Palmer and his assistants continued to be convinced that they had discovered a deadly plot against the nation and that only their activities safeguarded America against catastrophe.[65] During his career Palmer often became obstinate once he committed himself to a policy. In this case both he and his associates simply refused to acknowledge abundant evidence that American radicals were hopelessly divided, poorly led, and almost without support among American workers.[66]

Certain that he was right, Palmer defended himself aggressively against his accusers. He tried to dismiss Post as a man with "habitually tender solicitude for social revolutionists and perverted sympathy for the criminal anarchists of the country." As for the address to the American people by "twelve gentlemen said to be lawyers," Palmer retorted, "I do not know all of these gentlemen. Such of them as I do know I am not much impressed by." He hinted that Post, Judge Anderson, labor leaders, the Interchurch World Movement, and all his other critics, were enemies of the republic: "We find at the present time that not only have the 'borers-from-within' been able to gain headway in the American Federation of Labor, but they are likewise to be noted in the church, on the bench, and even in high government offices." Charges that he was trying to make political capital out of the Red Scare Palmer attributed to "the pale-pink parlor Bolsheviks and . . . the friends of the radicals." [67]

However, Palmer did not depend wholly upon epithets and accusations for his self-defense; he sought also to dispose of the weighty criticisms by denying that his department acted illegally during the raids. He admitted that aliens were taken into custody without warrants, but "detention does not constitute imprisonment, nor even deprivation of liberty without due process of law." If men remained in detention for considerable periods of time, he asserted, complaints should be addressed to the Labor Department. Palmer admitted that in some cases visitors to those "detained" during the raids were also "detained." But those who visited radicals, Palmer explained, were "practically the same as a person found in an active meeting of the organization." Palmer also produced a number of cases in which men who confessed their anarchist beliefs or who were almost certainly Communists were released by Post, and he intimated that these were not exceptional cases.[68]

In his appearance on June 1 before the Rules Committee, Palmer adamantly defended himself and vigorously indicted his opponents—but this time he was not convincing. Even the Indianapolis *News,* hostile to Post and his "spirit of speculative radicalism," declared on June 2: "The country will be slow to accept at face value everything that Mr. Palmer says, not because it doubts his veracity, but because it has come to feel that, on the Red question, he is something of an alarmist." The Rules Committee decided to drop the whole matter without censuring either Palmer or Post, and the impeachment resolution was quietly buried.

One of the most important casualties of the reaction against the Red Scare was the peacetime sedition law that Congress appeared ready to pass early in 1920. Palmer had asked for a new statute in July, 1919, following the bombings and May Day riots. He made a more urgent request in November as part of his reply to the Poindexter resolution.[69] Popular enthusiasm for this type of legislation soared after mid-1919; most states passed drastic laws or strengthened existing ones, and congressmen vied with one another to attach their names to a federal sedition act. By mid-November, 1919, congressmen could choose from about seventy such measures.[70]

After the great raids of January, 1920, Palmer released to newspapers much of the revolutionary propaganda his agents captured; at the same time he demanded in the most insistent tone he had yet adopted, a sedition law which would enable him to prosecute native radical leaders. The arrest of thousands of alleged anarchists and Communists and publication of excerpts from captured revolutionary literature apparently called forth a final burst of extreme fear and patriotism in the nation. Even the New York *World,* a resolute foe of peacetime sedition legislation, despaired of blocking the "new and drastic laws . . . urged on every hand." Later, the *World* saw no excuse for a new law; but in the post-raid excitement, it put the blame for such legislation on Bolshevism, "a tyrannizer of mankind. By its very lawlessness it [Bolshevism] compels the adoption of measures which restrict the privileges of freemen everywhere." [71]

The Senate responded to Palmer's new demand by passing the severe Sterling Bill on January 10. This measure prohibited advocacy of violence against the government or private property, it forbade display of radical flags, and it enabled the Postmaster General to prevent the mailing of seditious material. On January 5, House leaders agreed to prompt consideration of the Graham Bill, which strongly resembled the measure before the Senate.[72]

Palmer had already declared his opposition to the Sterling Bill; he warned the Senate Judiciary Committee that the measure would do more harm than good. The Justice Department had prepared a milder piece of legislation, introduced in the House by Representative Martin L. Davey of Ohio; but House leaders decided to push the more stringent bill despite the Attorney General's preferences. Palmer declined to appear at hearings on the Graham measure, nor would he send a Justice Department representative.[73]

Liberals like Bettman and Chafee, and labor-union representatives including Gompers, established a convincing case against the bill. They rejoiced when the Rules Committee sent it back to the House Judiciary Committee with instructions to prepare a less objectionable measure. Labor periodicals, certain that Palmer intended to use a sedition law chiefly against workers, jeered at him. A usually conservative railroad brotherhood journal boasted that organized labor had killed the sedition bill and declared that it did so fearing that, if Palmer gained the power he sought, "free discussion of political, industrial, or social problems would be at an end." [74]

Labor's opposition probably did squelch the Graham bill, but Palmer had opposed it also. Palmer's real test came when the Rules Committee considered the Justice Department's measure, the Davey Bill. The Attorney-General opened hearings on February 4 with a vigorous attack on the Graham and Sterling measures; thus defending himself against accusations that he was an enemy of labor and of civil rights. The Graham Bill, he asserted, "makes me shudder a little." He pointed to one especially nefarious provision which outlawed speeches resulting in injury to private property. A speech inciting men to strike, Palmer complained, might indirectly cause injury to property and would therefore come under the law. He had intentionally omitted anything about oral statements from the Davey Bill, he said; the act covered only the written summons to violence. Palmer also opposed the censorship power created by the Graham and Sterling measures.

Indeed Palmer may have startled Congress with his vigorous defense of the right to agitate for radical change:

It is perfectly proper for a man to stand on a soap box here on Pennsylvania Avenue and harangue a crowd to the effect that he believes the Government of the United States is wrong, built upon the wrong principle, and that the Congress is a useless appendage in this Nation. It is perfectly proper for him to say that he favors the abolition of the Congress of the United States. . . . Yes; or of the Constitution . . . and the substitution of a Communist form of government. That is all right. He ought to be protected in that kind of speech by all the power of the government.

The Davey Bill, argued Palmer, was written by the Justice Department "for the purpose of meeting this one hiatus in the law—the individual advocacy of the forcible injury or overthrow of the government." As far as Palmer's opponents were concerned, however, the Davey Bill left the Attorney-General and the courts much too much latitude in deciding who was guilty of sedition.[75] Palmer declared during the hearings that the IWW, which advocated large-scale strikes and other economic pressure on the government, would be deemed a seditious organization under the Davey Act. Labor leaders and liberals wondered whether the bill could not be stretched a little in practice to include them also. Gompers, Chafee, Ralston (this time appearing as counsel for the AF of L), Kane, and Judson King of the National Popular Government League assured the committee that sedition legislation was unnecessary, and they warned that it might have unfortunate consequences.[76]

The Judiciary Committee tabled Davey's Bill, waiting for the controversy aroused by the Palmer Raids to be settled. Instead of considering a new sedition law, the Rules Committee interrogated first Post, then Palmer. The House adjourned in June without having settled either the Post–Palmer dispute or the matter of sedition legislation. By that time Congress, like the rest of the country, desperately wanted to forget the problems and recurrent crises of the preceding decade. The great Red Scare was over.

Palmer's name is indelibly associated with violations of civil liberties, and to a great extent his reputation is deserved. He decided to combat the Red Menace with large-scale round-ups of alien radicals, despite warnings that many innocent men would be caught in his dragnet. He took insufficient precautions against violence by his agents or their assistants, or against infringements of civil liberties.[77] Palmer's negligence is especially inexcusable in view of the fact that even while the January raids were being planned, he ignored complaints of illegal procedures during the November arrests of Russian Workers. True, he was under massive pressure to take drastic action. But government officials have been known to resist the demands of a hysterical public; to some degree, Attorney-General Gregory did so during the wartime panic over German subversion.

On the other hand, an evaluation of Palmer's actions must take into consideration his belief that the nation faced a real danger. His most trusted advisers—and he had no reason to question their competence—informed him that radical organizations wielded immense power, enough to bring about a violent uprising in the country. The character and attitudes of the Attorney-General's assistants—Garvan, Flynn, Hoover, and Burke—helped determine Palmer's political fate and later reputation. Because he was overburdened with work and ill, and so unable to supervise closely the assistants he chose, Palmer's reckless policies had the worst possible effect.

Furthermore, it should be remembered that Palmer was slower than many, if not most Americans, to be caught up in the nativistic excitement which swept the land in 1919. He did not act against alien radicals until most Cabinet members had declared themselves in favor of combating the Red Menace with a big stick, and until Congress demanded in unequivocal terms that he take immediate action.

CHAPTER XIII

THE CAMPAIGN FOR THE PRESIDENCY— AND AFTERWARD

The veteran politicians who managed the Democratic Party favored Palmer for the Presidency in 1920. Political columnist Mark Sullivan described Palmer's position shortly before the opening of the 1920 Convention:

The Democratic leaders like Palmer best because he is more nearly of them. He has been a member of the Democratic National Committee for years and also of that inner arcanum of the party—the Executive Committee. In this official party position, Palmer has won the affection of his associates for his personal qualities and their respect by his wisdom. . . . In his appointments, Palmer has always honored party obligations.[1]

National committeemen, almost all of whom had great influence in their state parties, provided the core of Palmer's support. According to Homer Cummings, chairman of the Democratic national committee in 1920, a majority of the committee members worked for the Attorney-General's nomination. Chairman Cummings and Vice-Chairman J. Bruce Kremer of Montana both backed Palmer; although Cummings —himself a Presidential aspirant—gave Palmer only limited support.[2] Wilbur B. Marsh of Iowa, treasurer of the national committee, served as the Attorney-General's campaign manager in the West. Frederick B. Lynch of Minnesota, Norman E. Mack of New York, Cordell Hull of Tennessee, Edward F. Goltra of Missouri, William F. Connelly of Michigan, Clark Howell of Georgia, and A. R. Titlow of Washington were among the other powerful national committeemen to take an active part in Palmer's campaign. Former committeeman Tom

Taggart of Indiana, still one of the most respected men in the Democratic Party, also backed Palmer early in the race.[3]

Palmer received further support from many Democratic politicians indebted to him for lucrative jobs which he had bestowed as Alien Property Custodian. Lynch, who managed and financed Palmer's campaign in Minnesota, had been appointed president of Botany Mills and vice-president of a large shipping line. Palmer's campaign treasurer in 1920 was former Congressman J. Harry Covington of Maryland, who received over $46,000 in fees for work assigned to him. The Attorney-General's most enthusiastic backer among New York Democratic leaders, former Congressman John J. Fitzgerald, had been awarded a total of $37,000 in fees.[4] Roger Sullivan, who ruled the Democratic Party in Illinois, openly favored Palmer's nomination early in 1920; during the war he bought, at a bargain price, a German-owned beer company about to be taken over by the Alien Property Custodian. Sullivan's son Boetius, furthermore, served as the Custodian's counsel in Illinois; he and other Illinois Democrats earned large fees from work assigned by the Custodian.[5]

Palmer benefitted also from his distribution of Justice Department patronage. At least half of New England's votes were promised to the Attorney-General, most of them in exchange for Justice Department patronage. His emissary to that section, Assistant Attorney-General Thomas J. Spellacy, a genial Connecticut politician, traveled through the area early in 1920, promising positions in return for votes. From Connecticut he reported that fourteen delegates had been named, "at least eight of which will be my close political and personal associates. The State may be safely counted for Mr. Palmer under any and every circumstance." Spellacy urged the Attorney-General to appoint Fred J. Brown, then United States Attorney for New Hampshire, to a better paying job as Special Assistant to the Attorney-General. He pointed out that this would give National Committeeman R. C. Murchie another desirable post to fill, "in addition to the two places he would have in the Bureau of Investigation." Furthermore, Brown (elected Governor in

1922), had political power of his own. Spellacy persuaded his friend, Thomas J. Boynton, to step down as United States Attorney in Massachusetts, so that a crony of influential Massachusetts politicians could be named as his successor. Boynton, a former Chairman of the Democratic State Committee in Vermont, with many friends in Maine, was then appointed Special Assistant to the Attorney-General and paid $1,000 a month. Together Boynton and Spellacy toured Maine and Vermont, gathering votes for Palmer.[6]

Many of Palmer's most effective supporters, as Mark Sullivan observed, were "old congressional comrades of his, now scattered throughout the country and filling positions of power in the local Democratic organizations."[7] Goltra, Hull, and Frank Doremus of Michigan had been junior congressmen when Palmer first worked with them in the House, but by 1920 they were leaders of their state parties. Palmer's friendship with Covington and Fitzgerald also dated back to their days in Congress. Covington had represented a Maryland district for ten years when Wilson appointed him Chief Justice of the District of Columbia Supreme Court, and Fitzgerald had long been the leader of the Tammany delegation in the House.

Influential southerners also prepared to jump on the Palmer bandwagon. Early in February, 1920 the New York *Times* reported: "Sentiment among strong southern members of Congress seems to be turning toward Attorney-General Palmer."[8] Palmer had been on intimate terms with most of the veteran southern leaders from the time he served as Underwood's "right arm" on the Ways and Means Committee. Underwood, retained considerable influence in several southern delegations, and led the southern contingent for Palmer. Congressmen James F. Byrnes of South Carolina and Thomas M. Bell of Georgia also worked for the nomination of their former associate. Charles C. Carlin of Virginia, who had served seven terms in the House, became Palmer's campaign manager.[9]

However, it was in Pennsylvania, with its seventy-six convention votes—more than any other state except New York and Illinois—that Palmer laid the cornerstone of his campaign.

Palmer's lieutenants exerted such pressure on Pennsylvania politicians that almost every important Democrat in the state lined up behind the Attorney-General. Only Palmer's most bitter enemies—Samuel Shull (who still remembered his father's defeat in the savage 1908 primary election), former Congressman Liebel, and Judge Bonniwell—resisted the steamroller.[10]

Palmer's friends throughout the country probably could have mustered enough votes to nominate their man, and early in the campaign it looked as though they would. Mark Sullivan reported that in February "a majority of the more powerful leaders among the Democrats had an almost crystallized intention to nominate Palmer." [11] However, party leaders hesitated to risk their prestige and patronage by backing a candidate who might not win the national election. In Palmer's case the risk was especially great; for the Attorney-General had failed to carry his own state in the last two Presidential contests and in the senatorial race of 1914. Boss Murphy of New York was swayed by associates who backed Palmer, and was pleased when the Attorney-General joined him in a battle with McAdoo's friends over an upstate federal judgeship. But he shrank from antagonizing the labor unions, which were strong in New York. Furthermore, Murphy believed that only an outright "wet" could carry New York; and Palmer, who did not want to concede the "dry" areas to McAdoo, refused to make a positive statement about the repeal of prohibition.[12]

Roger Sullivan died in mid-April, and although his successors, led by George E. Brennan, probably preferred to honor their late chief's commitment to Palmer, they doubted his ability to capture big city votes. Taggart liked Palmer; but because he was running for the United States Senate in 1920 he wanted the strongest possible presidential candidate to lead the ticket. After sounding out experienced politicians, Taggart concluded: "All these charges that various persons are making against him seem to be taking effect." [13] Nevertheless, as late as June 22, when delegates began streaming into San Francisco, the political columnist for a newspaper hostile to Palmer reported: "Could Democrats be convinced that Attorney-General Palmer could be elected in November there would not be much doubt about his nomination." [14]

Neither Palmer nor his rivals for the Democratic Presidential nomination attempted to win popular support by recommending bold new programs or even by suggesting important extensions of the New Freedom. Palmer spoke vaguely of continuing Wilsonian policies—once or twice he advocated compulsory federal arbitration of major industrial disputes—but generally he ignored legislative matters. Nor did his leading opponents present more definite plans. The Wilsonians had achieved their original aims; indeed in some areas they had gone beyond their expectations. The wartime experience suggested new programs—government developments of power sites and other natural resources, federal operation of railroads and public utilities—to leaders like Woodrow Wilson, William McAdoo, and Newton Baker. But by 1920 these men, like most other Americans, were weary of agitating for reform and preaching sacrifice. McAdoo gave expression to a popular attitude when he retired from government service after the armistice to make money. Most of the crusading zeal left in America by late 1919 was channelled into the League fight or the Red Scare, and even the excitement aroused by these issues abated by mid-1920.

In courting the national following which would guarantee his nomination, Palmer took advantage of the postwar frenzy for 100-percent Americanism, the movement which had given such impetus to the political careers of Hanson, Coolidge, and Wood. At the Democratic Party's annual Jackson Day dinner in January, 1920, Vice-Chairman Kremer introduced Palmer as "an American whose Americanism cannot be misunderstood." This was the image Palmer tried to project in his campaign speeches and in his attacks against strikers, profiteers, and alien radicals. In an address delivered in Georgia shortly before the primary election there, Palmer asserted: "I am myself an American and I love to preach my doctrine before undiluted one hundred percent Americans, because my platform is, in a word, undiluted Americanism and undying loyalty to the republic." The same theme predominated in the address made by Palmer's old friend John H. Bigelow of Hazleton, Pennsylvania, when he placed the Attorney-General's name in nomination at the 1920 National Convention. Proclaimed Bigelow:

No party could survive today that did not write into its platform the magic word 'Americanism'. . . . The Attorney-General of the United States has not merely professed, but he has proved his true Americanism. . . . Behind him I see a solid phalanx of true Americanism that knows no divided allegiance.[15]

Palmer also made a strong bid for the support of those loyal Wilsonians who backed the President on the League of Nations issue. In announcing his candidacy on March 1, Palmer declared that the people "should have the opportunity to directly pass upon the record made by the present Administration. The candidacy of one who supports that record in every phase presents that opportunity." Palmer's managers told reporters that their candidate believed that the League question was more important than any other and that he would carry it aggressively into the campaign. In his first speech as a candidate, Palmer demanded early ratification of the peace treaty; none of the other major problems facing the world could be solved, he averred, until it was signed. In an interview two days later, the Attorney-General declared that the League would be "the issue upon which they [the Presidential candidates] will have to face the nation." [16]

As the campaign progressed, Palmer's enthusiasm for Wilsonian internationalism waned. He discovered powerful anti-League sentiment on his speaking tours. When he visited Georgia early in April Palmer began to hedge on the question; in his first speech there he called for prompt ratification of the treaty but added: "I would not object to substantial reservations, if friendly and really designed to save the treaty and the covenant." [17] In a Cabinet meeting on April 20, he agreed with Burleson that the Democrats should stress issues other than the League.[18] By convention time, the Attorney-General was regarded by party leaders as "half on the Administration reservation and half off" on international questions. Upon arriving at the convention, Palmer gladly imparted to reporters his views on Americanism and the necessity for strict enforcement of the law, but he refused to comment about prohibition or the League of Nations.[19]

When he talked about the peace treaty and in fact, about most campaign issues, Palmer had to consider the effect of his words on both the public and the President. From start to finish, Palmer's campaign was profoundly influenced by his hope for Wilson's support and his fear that the President would seek another term or back another candidate. He knew from two visits to the President in November, 1919, that Wilson's health had failed, and other visitors to the White House confirmed his knowledge. In January, 1920, therefore, Palmer confidently assured a reporter that Wilson would not be a candidate again: "His personal friends know he will not even consider it." [20] But the President would not announce his plans, and as long as Wilson remained silent, Palmer's efforts on his own behalf were constricted. He could not enter the race officially until he obtained his leader's consent; he could not expect open support from the President's close associates or from Wilson's many admirers in the party; nor could he drop the League issue until he was certain that the President would not endorse his candidacy.

Twice Palmer tried to force Wilson's hand. He persuaded Vance McCormick, whom the President liked and trusted, to visit the White House late in January, 1920. But McCormick got no further than Mrs. Wilson; she asked him to lunch with her but refused to allow him into the sick-room. When McCormick described Palmer's embarrassment and suggested that the President make a statement about the 1920 nomination, Mrs. Wilson replied that her husband had not yet made up his mind and might feel obliged to run again.[21] A month later, Palmer sent word through Tumulty that he planned to announce his candidacy soon. He offered to hold off if the President objected or to support any man that Wilson named. The Chief Executive replied ambiguously that Palmer was free to do as he chose.[22]

Wilson probably expressed his true feelings about the nomination in a conversation reported by Dr. Cary Grayson, the President's personal physician and, except for Mrs. Wilson, his only confidante during his illness. On the morning of March 25, according to Grayson, Wilson launched into a lengthy monologue on the 1920 campaign, asserting in part:

The Democratic Convention in San Francisco may get into a hopeless tie-up, and it may, by the time of the Convention, become imperative that the League of Nations and the Peace Treaty be made the dominant issue. The Convention may come to a deadlock as to candidates, and there may be practically a universal demand for the selection of someone to lead them out of the wilderness. The members of the Convention may feel that I am the logical one to lead—perhaps the only one to champion this cause. In such circumstances I would feel obliged to accept the nomination even if I thought it would cost me my life.

Grayson, knowing that the President could not withstand another campaign, but unwilling to destroy his morale, listened to Wilson's dream without comment.[23]

McAdoo, who probably wanted to be President as badly as Palmer did, was even more restrained; he was married to Wilson's daughter, and she apparently dreaded the possibility that her husband might usurp the nomination from her father. Consequently, McAdoo denied any interest in becoming President, although continuing to speak publicly on major issues. He refused to enter primaries, but urged his friends to work for unpledged delegations. Although the other strong candidate, Governor Cox of Ohio, could not boast of association with the administration, he did not suffer the disadvantages incurred by Palmer and McAdoo. Cox had no hesitation about declaring his candidacy when the time was ripe, and he openly appealed for support from all elements within the party, including Wilson's enemies.[24]

Palmer knew that his aggressive attempts to obtain wide public support for the nomination involved grave political risks. Nevertheless, once he decided on a course of action, he sought to carry it out—as was his habit—with the utmost vigor. Not until the preconvention campaign was well along did

Palmer discover that he had guessed wrong. His fervent approval of the administration made him suspect among political bosses like Murphy and Brennan; furthermore, it failed to win him the backing either of the President or his supporters, most of whom remained loyal to Wilson or supported McAdoo. Palmer's attacks on profiteers and hoarders and his frequent promises that prices would fall brought him more jeers than cheers; despite evidence of an imminent world-wide collapse in prices, the cost of living continued to skyrocket. Worst of all for Palmer, the Red Scare petered out; apparently most Americans wanted to forget the experience, but Palmer's enemies remembered.

Probably Palmer could have won support from many of Wilson's enemies; he was willing to compromise on prohibition and the League, and he had already proven his readiness to cooperate with the established party leaders. Even the high-cost-of-living issue would not, in itself, have greatly diminished his chances; many Americans admired the Attorney-General's vigorous policies if not his results; and those who had mocked his prophesies fell quiet when a sharp drop in prices began about a month before the Convention. However, the considerable number of Americans that Palmer had offended with his attacks on labor and by the excesses of the Palmer Raids were not so easily pacified.

In fact, organized labor provided Palmer's major obstacle to success; he had earned an indelible reputation as labor's enemy.[25] In 1920, even conservative leaders of the AF of L and the railroad brotherhoods were convinced that the Attorney-General's nomination would be a tragedy for workingmen. *The Brotherhood of Locomotive Firemen and Enginemen's Magazine* indicted Palmer on February 1: "Clearly he has favored the powers of wealth and privilege, while handling labor with the mailed fist of the autocratic tyrant." Timothy Healy, President of the Brotherhood of Stationary Firemen and Oilers, described Palmer's antiradical activities as "part of a despicable propaganda against labor," and "undoubtedly for the purpose of aiding in the campaign of certain employers . . . to secure laws establishing involuntary servitude." [26] In Palmer's own state, a special convention of the Pennsylvania Federation of Labor, an affiliate of the AF of L, resolved that the coal injunction was "one of the most vicious assaults that has ever been made upon labor." At the annual meeting of the Pennsylvania Federation in May, 1920, President James H. Maurer denounced "Pontius Palmer" and his "government by injunction." [27]

Most damaging to Palmer was the enmity of Samuel Gompers. As the campaign approached, the AF of L chieftain continued his bitter condemnation of the coal injunction, and he excused the stricken President from any responsibility for the actions Palmer had taken in his name. Gompers also arraigned the Justice Department head for refusing to use his price-control powers against giant corporations, complaining: "The Attorney-General has found it possible to indict corner grocers and small haberdashers." [28] Moved by an extravagant suspicion of Palmer, Gompers felt certain that the Attorney-General wanted sedition legislation primarily for use against organized labor. Testifying before the House Judiciary Committee, Gompers demanded to know: "What kind of violence, what kind of terrorism . . . was in the mind of the Attorney-General when he framed the Davey bill?" Did the Attorney-General mean to apply the act only to those who used physical force in their attempt to change the government, or was it aimed also at those who used moral force? Would not Palmer twist the meaning of a sedition law, just as he had misused the Lever Act? [29]

Gompers' invective took on added political effectiveness when the AF of L finally agreed to take part in a national election campaign. To counteract the influence of the newly formed National Labor Party, Gompers announced that an AF of L committee would organize the union's 40,000 locals and 4,000,-000 members into an unaffiliated political body which would seek to reward labor's friends and defeat its enemies. [30] However, Gompers made it clear that if the Democrats nominated an acceptable candidate and wrote a satisfactory platform they could expect the AF of L's full support. The only Democratic candidate known to be unacceptable to Gompers was Palmer.[31]

To show party leaders that he could win despite labor's opposition, Palmer entered two primary races—in Michigan and Georgia. All the Democratic candidates appeared on the ballot in Michigan—a state law prevented even McAdoo and Herbert Hoover, who had recently declared himself a Republican, from withdrawing—but none except Palmer campaigned on his own behalf or enlisted support among state party leaders.

Michigan was not an ideal testing ground for Palmer. The state had long been a Republican stronghold, and Democrats were clustered in the large industrial cities where the labor vote was important. The sizable group of radicals in Detroit could hardly be expected to welcome the Attorney-General warmly. Palmer spent three days traveling in central Michigan, meeting voters and conferring with politicians. He made five major speeches, three in Detroit and one each in Battle Creek and Lansing. The state Democratic leaders came out solidly behind him. National Committeeman Connelly and Congressman Doremus, who had been chairman of the Democratic congressional campaign committee when Palmer was vice-chairman, announced that their man was a sure winner. Even Palmer's opponents conceded the state to him.[32]

Democratic politicians throughout the country registered shock when Palmer was swamped in Michigan. Herbert Hoover won the Democratic primary and promptly declared that he would not take the Democratic nomination if it were offered to him. Governor Edward I. Edwards of New Jersey, the leading symbol of repeal, finished second, followed by McAdoo and Bryan. Palmer ran a very poor fifth. Labor, most politicians believed, had defeated the Attorney-General. The Cleveland *Plain Dealer* called the election "little short of a stunning blow at the Palmer chances," and the Cincinnati *Enquirer* stated unequivocally: "The returns mean the elimination of Attorney-General Palmer." The first response from the Palmer camp issued, in typical fashion, from Garvan, who told a Treasury Department official: "My man certainly got a blow in the face in Michigan." Palmer, just beginning his Georgia campaign, offered no comment. Soon after news of the disaster reached him, he canceled all engagements and took to bed with an acute attack of indigestion.[33]

Palmer recovered in time to address a Savannah audience. Attempting to excuse the Michigan debacle he declared, "I went into a state with a great pro-German element, and there is not a German or a pro-German in America who has any use for me. . . . Detroit is the largest city in America in population of alien reds or radicals and revolutionists, whose friends played the political game." Michigan, Palmer pointed out, had never supported the administration. Wilson suffered severe defeat there in 1912 and the Republicans swept the state with a huge majority in 1916.[34]

Palmer himself may not have believed these excuses, but they followed the main themes of his campaign in Georgia: Americanism and Wilsonianism.[35] Palmer had even greater reason to be anxious about the result in Georgia than he had had in Michigan. In Georgia, as in Michigan, he commanded the support of most of the dominant political organization; but this time his opponents did not sit quietly elsewhere. He was forced to compete with the two best vote-getters in the state, Tom Watson and Senator Hoke Smith, neither of whom had entered the race when Palmer first decided to run. Watson made no speeches; the old Populist leader was still the most powerful politician in the state, and everyone knew where he stood. The columns of the Columbia *Sentinel*, a paper owned by Watson and widely read throughout rural Georgia, daily ridiculed Palmer's vaunted Americanism. Watson, threatened with prosecution in 1918 because of his opposition to the war, had no sympathy with the antiradical crusade. Palmer, he gibed, was one of "the one hundred percent idiots." "The Attorney-General would have me clawed out of bed at midnight; and I would have been aboard a steamer, off Brunswick, before my wife would have known that I was a Red bound for Russia." [36]

Smith, twice elected to the Senate, opposed Wilson on the League; and his foes, led by National Committeeman Howell, exploited the conflict in the hope of ruining him politically. "The issue in this race is clearly drawn," Howell's editorial spokesman asserted: "it is loyalty against disloyalty." "So the issue is plain." Palmer echoed in Savannah: "I support the leadership of Woodrow Wilson, Senator Smith repudiates it." In contrast to Palmer's three speeches in Georgia and Watson's newspaper offensive, Smith spoke in every part of the state and waged "the most arduous campaign of his life." [37]

Although Palmer was hindered by his position as an outsider involved in internecine warfare, he benefited from the support of a Georgia Democratic organization which had a large stake in the election. Whereas his backers in Michigan did little more than talk to newspapermen,[38] in Georgia they excited the voters and brought them to the polls. Palmer did remarkably well. He finished a close second to Watson in the popular vote, despite the fact that in some rural counties more ballots were cast for Watson than for Palmer and Smith combined. And Palmer edged out Smith in the county unit vote, winning the right to name all Georgia's delegates.[39]

Palmer had won a majority of the Michigan delegation, too. The preferential primary in which he had been badly beaten was only a popularity contest; in most districts the Palmer delegates put up by the regular organization met with no opposition. Even though some of his Michigan supporters defected just before the convention, Palmer emerged on the first ballot at San Francisco with forty of the fifty-eight votes cast by Michigan and Georgia, and he retained thirty-seven of these votes as late as the thirty-seventh ballot.

If Palmer had been trying only to win delegates, his campaigns in Michigan and Georgia would have been deemed successful. What Palmer really sought, however, was to convince party leaders that he could win in November. In this he had failed dismally. His showing in the primaries buttressed the warnings of union leaders and the results of the *Literary Digest* poll completed in June, in which Palmer ranked far down on the list of candidates, only slightly ahead of the imprisoned Debs.[40]

Nevertheless, the Attorney-General played the convention game to the end. He made a last-minute attempt to pacify labor with large-scale prosecutions of coal profiteers, and he won a strike for New York railroad dock workers by invoking the Adamson Act.[41] He pointed to the vulnerable labor record of the Republican nominee, Senator Warren G. Harding of Ohio, as evidence that workers could expect nothing from the opposing party and would have to support him if he were nominated.[42]

When the delegates poured into San Francisco late in June, 1920, they were forced once more to take Palmer's hopes seriously. Large poster portraits of Palmer, his face strong and dignified, yet friendly, covered the city. He held a book in one hand and admonished the public with the index finger of the other, and the legend read: "The Fighting Quaker—laying down the law."

At Cox's headquarters in San Francisco the atmosphere was restrained, the visitors few. McAdoo had no official representatives in the city. But Palmer's magnificent offices on the ground floor of the St. Francis hotel held the visiting delegates' attention. A huge colorful banner, strung across the outside of the hotel, announced the headquarters. Inside, according to a reporter, the rooms were "redolent with flowers, plastered with posters, littered with literature and loud with enthusiasm." Passing delegates, virtually shanghaied by the Pennsylvanian's supporters, were obliged to listen to mixed quartets, orators, and a private sales talk from a Palmer manager before they could escape. A reporter who wandered in observed: "One is greeted with tremendous enthusiasm on entering the Palmer camp. A hearty handshake and an openhanded smash between the shoulder blades is the least one may expect."[43]

The Palmer forces received periodic encouragement from McAdoo's repeated assertions that he did not choose to run. An especially emphatic declaration from the President's son-in-law followed the national publication on June 18 of an interview with Wilson, in which the President gave the illusion of being in excellent health, ready to campaign for a third term. McAdoo's statement the following day that he would not allow his name to be presented to the convention, disturbed many of his less knowledgeable supporters and even drove some of them into the Palmer camp.[44]

On June 23, five days before the opening of the convention, McAdoo wired the Reverend Burris Jenkins, chosen by the McAdoo managers to nominate their candidate, that he could not allow his name to be used. When Jenkins announced that he would make the nomination anyhow, McAdoo asked newspapermen plaintively: "What more can I do?" But Secretary Glass, who had discussed the nomination with McAdoo just before the telegram to Jenkins, observed wryly that the ostensibly reluctant candidate had never declared that he would turn down the nomination if it were offered him.[45]

McAdoo's friends understood his game. And if such tactics left the McAdoo camp leaderless and unorganized in San Francisco, that only bolstered the impression that the movement for Wilson's son-in-law was a spontaneous popular uprising. Indeed, the choice of Jenkins, a political unknown, to make the nominating speech, was calculated to strengthen this impression. And as the convention opened, McAdoo, obeisance to his wife and father-in-law completed, finally made plain his availability. He agreed to his friends' request to say no more about his unwillingness to be nominated, and his correspondence took on a new note: "If I am drawn into this fight. . . . " "If I have to take up the fight. . . . " "If by chance I should be recalled. . . . " "My friends tell me there is no escape and if I am drawn back into public life. . . . "[46] Had McAdoo pulled out of the contest, Palmer would have become the leading administration candidate and possibly the nominee. This last chance disappeared when McAdoo agreed to maintain silence while his backers moved ahead.

By the eve of the Democratic convention Palmer, despite his show of confidence, was hopelessly beaten. McAdoo had captured most of the Wilsonians, the labor delegates, and the "drys." A reporter who noted Palmer's popularity among the "regulars" in the New York and Illinois delegations a week before the convention observed that these politicians gave Cox a much better chance of winning the election. "It will take the arrival of delegations bringing word from home to tell the tale," the reporter concluded. "If they bring news of a possibility of winning with Palmer his is the big chance. If they bring the opposite word, which has been the word here to date, the first big chance goes to Governor Cox." [47] As the delegates arrived, they brought news fatal to the Attorney-General's hopes —labor would not abide his nomination; he could not be elected.

Labor leaders circulated among the delegates in San Francisco, hinting at union support for the party, if the candidate and platform were satisfactory.[48] Although National Committeeman Titlow of Washington had worked zealously for Palmer in early spring, a delegate from his state declared after the convention: "There was no sentiment and no votes in our delegation for Palmer. Labor would have fought Palmer and we knew it, although he is a brilliant man, a great orator, and really is presidential timber." [49]

Tom Taggart had given up in mid-June. "I don't think he has much chance," he told an interviewer. The Michigan and Illinois delegates began to move toward more probable winners soon after they reached the convention. There were signs that even Lynch could not hold his men in line; the Minnesota delegates arrived in San Francisco shouting and waving banners for McAdoo. Marsh, Palmer's campaign manager in the West, indicated his willingness to switch, and his Iowa delegation went over almost completely to McAdoo.[50]

Despite the loss of delegates eager to desert a sinking candidacy, Palmer did well on the first ballot, held July 2. He drew 256 votes, only ten less than McAdoo and over a hundred more than Cox. He received the expected support from Pennsylvania, Georgia, and New England, more than half of Illinois' votes, and almost half of Michigan's. His friends in Missouri and Tennessee gave him nineteen votes, and the Colorado party leaders turned over eight of their state's twelve ballots, despite the fact that Palmer had not entered the Colorado primary. Carlin and Covington, both attorneys in the District of Columbia, obtained the District's six votes for him.[51]

Palmer showed only his minimum strength on the first ballot; but his vote total rose no higher than 267½ on the seventh roll call, then dropped sharply as his political friends, having fulfilled their obligations, sought a winner. When neither McAdoo nor Cox proved able to break the deadlock, Palmer obtained a final chance to get a bandwagon rolling after the thirtieth ballot on July 5. Ten Illinois votes were handed over and most of the Tennessee, Alabama, and Virginia delegations transferred to Palmer; nevertheless, he managed to gather a total of only 241 votes.[52]

After the thirty-sixth ballot, Lynch moved that the convention recess for three and one-half hours. During the recess, party leaders informed Palmer that he was through. If he persisted in the race, even his closest friends would be forced to desert him. The friendships and party loyalty which had served Palmer so well no longer availed; Democratic leaders urged him to save his party from a disruptive deadlock by withdrawing from the contest. Palmer was still considering these pleas when the recess ended; but his delegates began to disaffect. One third of his votes were gone by the thirty-eighth ballot. At the end of that roll call, Carlin rose and released Palmer's delegates. Later in the evening, the convention nominated Cox.[53]

A. Mitchell Palmer's political career ended with the national convention. Although he had planned to campaign for Cox, the candidate found it necessary to repudiate the Attorney-General's labor and antiradical policies, and Palmer withdrew to Stroudsburg, emerging only at Tumulty's request for a few speeches late in the campaign.[54] He was ready for an easier, more luxurious life, a desire always strong in him, but stifled during his drive for power. Significantly, he gave up his Stroudsburg newspapers to his political opponents without a fight in June, 1920, but he battled fiercely in July to keep control of the city's largest bank. Palmer had already chosen Joe Guffey to succeed him as national committeeman, and Guffey was elected to that post in the primary election which gave Palmer control of the Pennsylvania delegation. Late in 1920, Palmer made plans for the establishment of a Washington law firm in partnership with former Justice Department and Alien Property Custodian subordinates.[55]

Perhaps Palmer might have wearied of political retirement, as he had in 1915. After his discouragement abated, he might once more have utilized the Pennsylvania party for a come-back to national political prominence. But early in 1922 Palmer suffered a heart attack while golfing near Palm Beach, Florida. A series of similar attacks followed, cutting his activity to a minimum and ending any possibility of a return to polit-ical life. During the 1924 Presidential campaign he made sev-eral speeches on behalf of John W. Davis, with whom he had served both in Congress and in the Wilson administration. In 1928, he tried to help Al Smith in the South. But between Pres-idential elections, Palmer remained in political hibernation.[56]

Palmer played one last brief but important role in national politics. He had continued his friendship with his former neighbor, Franklin D. Roosevelt, and after Roosevelt was elected governor of New York in 1928 he tendered his political services: "If I can help you any time and anywhere, command me." [57] Only eight years before, Palmer had been one of the Democratic Party's greatest orators and one of the party's most skillful parliamentarians. He had commanded powerful sup-porters in every state. By the time he volunteered to help Roo-sevelt, however, Palmer's poor health and long absence from politics left him little to offer a Presidential candidate.

Nevertheless, Roosevelt seldom wasted his assets, however moderate their value. He decided, early in 1932, to have a party platform prepared so that his forces could unite behind it at the convention. Remembering Palmer's masterful speeches and his work on the 1916 platform, Roosevelt asked him to do the job. The Governor had already exchanged platform ideas with veteran Senate leaders like Hull, Glass, Thomas J. Walsh, and Pat Harrison of Mississippi. When he spoke to Palmer he informed him of the planks he wanted and their general content. He also requested that the document be brief, succinct, and easily understandable, so that it could be used effectively in the campaign.[58]

With help from Hull, Palmer prepared a rough draft which he took to Roosevelt. The two men spent most of a beautiful June day below deck on the state yacht *Inspector II* rewriting the platform, while their wives watched the Poughkeepsie regatta. By early evening, they had worked out a draft which, except for the farm, labor, and prohibition planks, differed hardly at all from the one adopted in Chicago about a week later.[59]

As might be expected, the Wilsonians responsible for the first draft of the 1932 platform turned out a moderate document. Even after it was revised at the convention in response to farm, labor, and antiprohibition demands, a leading business magazine praised it as "comparatively conservative" and even the *Commercial and Financial Chronicle* could find little to criticize.[60] It is indicative of the ideology which prevailed among Democratic leaders in the depression year of 1932 that they embraced a platform written by a man who declared, as Palmer did: "It is a platform which Wilson would approve in nearly every particular. If that be true it is good enough for me, and it seems to me it ought to be good enough for all liberals." [61]

During and after the campaign Palmer reminded Roosevelt that the Democratic platform was his "solemn pledge" to the American people and that voters would expect him to carry it out if elected. Early in the New Deal, Palmer congratulated the President on his success in basing his administration on the party platform. Over the next few years, however, Palmer gradually became uneasy and then outraged as Roosevelt's policies increasingly diverged from his "solemn pledge." After visiting the White House, where he saw the 1932 platform with its planks endorsing economy in government and a balanced budget prominently displayed beneath the glass top of the

President's desk, Palmer wondered to his wife whether Roosevelt had gone blind.[62]

Palmer suffered his final heart attack on May 11, 1936. To most Americans who remembered him, he died a somewhat unsavory figure, associated chiefly with the Red Scare and labor injunctions. To those who had served Woodrow Wilson, however, the name of A. Mitchell Palmer was linked to a period of glorious achievement. Many of the Wilsonians who returned to positions of national power with the Democratic triumph of 1932 had supported Palmer's campaign for the Presidential nomination in 1920.

From the large group of Wilsonians who were in Washington when he died came Palmer's pallbearers. Among those who served were Secretary of State Hull, Attorney-General Cummings, Secretary of Commerce Daniel C. Roper; Senate leaders Byrnes, Guffey, and Joseph T. Robinson of Arkansas; former congressmen Carlin and Sherley, and Tumulty. These men, and other still prominent Wilsonians like Glass, McAdoo, McReynolds, Baker, Brandeis, and McCormick, had lived to bridge the gap between the New Freedom and the New Deal. None of them thoroughly approved of what they considered the radical new direction in which their party was leading the nation. Their discomfort, and Palmer's, revealed, even more clearly than the last years of Wilson's administration and the campaign of 1920, the limitations of Wilsonian liberalism. The New Freedom had aimed, after all, chiefly at protecting and increasing individual economic opportunity; which is why Palmer's child labor bill, sanctioning unprecedented government intervention in the economy, was termed by Arthur Link "the most momentous measure of the progressive era." Palmer's disenchantment with the New Deal offered a final bit of evidence that he was, in most respects, typical of the leaders of the Wilson administration, men who had represented well what now seems the intellectual narrowness, the class and racial bias, as well as the reform aspirations of middle-class America.

Palmer's career illustrates much more than the shortcomings of the Wilsonians, however; his story has implications which reach into the heart of American history. Entering the Cabinet with high political ambitions and a well-earned reputation as "progressive and fearless," Palmer found himself standing in the breach when Americans panicked with fear that the Russian Revolution was being exported here. Although he shared the widespread hostility to radicals and immigrants, and eventually the current hysteria as well, it was only in the face of mounting opposition that he dropped—one by one—his liberal objectives. His original policies as Attorney-General included neutrality in labor disputes, release of political prisoners, rejection of assistance from private patriotic associations, and a plea that America remain a haven for oppressed peoples from all nations. Not until he was hounded with criticism from the press and public, and rebuked by a unanimous Senate resolution, did Palmer embark upon his repressive policies against labor, immigrants, and radicals. By then almost all his fellow Cabinet members had joined the public outcry against strikes and the Red Menace, and his closest advisers were warning him that the country stood in immediate danger of violent upheaval.

When Palmer finally responded to the immense pressure upon him a crucial election campaign was near, compelling him to act swiftly. Characteristically, he took insufficient precaution to protect Constitutional guarantees, especially in ordering the mass round-up of radicals; but his moves were not more drastic than most Americans demanded. Certainly a public official is obligated to heed the will of a vocal majority—even the Supreme Court has been praised for following the election returns and censured for obstructing popular policies—and an ambitious politician ignores public demands at the peril of his career. The crucial question raised by Palmer's action as Attorney-General and Alien Property Custodian is whether a leading government official has a higher duty than giving the public—or his party—what it wants.

Palmer's story, then, is a classic example of democracy's most notorious weakness. Sagacious commentators, beginning with those who drafted the American Constitution, have warned that rule by majority is both the greatest glory and the most serious hazard of our system; that our liberties are endangered most not by tyrants, but by democrats. If Palmer was one of the most dangerous men in our history, it was not because he attempted to impose his rule or his policies upon the people, but because he tried to win power by carefully attuning himself to what he felt were the strong desires of most Americans.

NOTES

I: A PENNSYLVANIA POOR BOY'S PROGRESS

1. H. W. Palmer, *Palmers in America*, XVI–XVII, 2318, 2338, 2351, 2361; Rupp, *History*, p. 152; Palmer Family Bible, Monroe County Historical Society, Stroudsburg, Pennsylvania, notations on pp. 677–80; A. M. Palmer, "A History of the Quakers in Stroudsburg, an address before the Monroe County Historical Society, July 31, 1929," copies in the Monroe County Historical Society and in the Swarthmore College Library, Swarthmore, Pennsylvania.

2. A. M. Palmer, "History of the Quakers in Stroudsburg"; H. W. Palmer, *Palmers in America*, XVI–XVIII, 2338; Rupp, *History*, p. 148.

3. Keller, *History of Monroe County*, pp. 333–34.

4. Unidentified obituary of Charles Palmer in scrapbook kept by Mrs. Charles Stroud Palmer, now deposited in the Monroe County Historical Society, cited as Mrs. C. S. Palmer scrapbook. A large portrait of Charles Palmer now hangs in the main room of the Historical Society.

5. *Ibid.;* East Stroudsburg *Morning Press,* December 11, 1916; Stroudsburg *Times,* December 29, 1904; H. W. Palmer, *Palmers in America,* XVI–XVIII, 2351.

6. East Stroudsburg *Morning Press,* December 11, 1916; Monroe *Record* (Stroudsburg), April 9, 1908; Easton *Daily Express,* May 27, 1910. The Palmer family finances became a public issue during the Monroe County primary campaigns of 1908 and 1910 when Mitchell was opposed by one of the family's creditors.

7. Stroudsburg *Sun,* May 12, 1936; Stroudsburg *Times,* December 29, 1904; interviews between the author and Gilbert B. McClintick, Harrisburg, May 19, 1959, and Hal B. Harris, Stroudsburg, June 13, 1959.

8. Frank B. Lord, "The Story of the Hon. A. Mitchell Palmer," *National Monthly,* VI, 39; *Biographical Directory of the American Congress,* p. 1647; Monroe *Record,* April 9, 1908.

9. I am indebted to the late Mrs. Hannah Clothier Hull for the opportunity to see photographs in her possession. Interview with Mrs. Hull, June 9, 1958.

10. Swarthmore *Phoenix*, XXX, 62. This article is unsigned but was written by Mrs. Hull.

11. Swarthmore *Phoenix*, XI, 110.

12. *Ibid.*, XI, 112–13.

13. *Ibid.*, XXX, 62; Lord, "The Story of the Hon. A. Mitchell Palmer," *National Monthly*, VI, 39; John M. Moore, Registrar, Swarthmore College, to the author, January 24, 1958.

14. Swarthmore *Phoenix*, IX, 175.

15. *Ibid.*, IX, 176.   16. *Ibid.*, IX, 135–36; 177; *Ibid.*, XI, 98.

17. As late as November, 1909, Wilson told the City Club of Philadelphia: "I believe that the short ballot is the key to the whole question of the restoration of government by the people." Link, *Road to the White House*, p. 125.

18. Swarthmore *Phoenix*, IX, 94.   19. *Ibid.*, XXX, 62.

20. U. S. *Ninth Census* (1872), I, 58, 252–53; U. S. *Twelfth Census* (1902), I, 344; Tower, "A Regional and Economic Geography of Pennsylvania," *Bulletin of the Geographical Society of Philadelphia*, V, 32, 42.

21. U. S. *Census Reports* (1901), I, Part I, 518.

22. U. S. *Twelfth Census* (1902), I, 593; Tower, "Regional and Economic Geography of Pennsylvania," *Bulletin of the Geographical Society of Philadelphia*, V (January, 1907), Part II, 40. Pike county had the lowest density of population per square mile in the state, and the figure for Monroe was not much higher.

23. Democratic majorities in the district hardly changed at all between 1857 and 1866 while political control in the state changed hands. *Smull's Manual for the Government of . . . Pennsylvania* (1860), pp. 300–1; *Smull's Legislative Handbook* (1870), pp. 284–85, 315, 321.

24. Scranton *Republican*, April 15, 1914, clipping in the A. Mitchell Palmer scrapbooks, Monroe County Historical Society, Stroudsburg, cited as Palmer scrapbooks. I am grateful to Dr. John C. Appel, President of the Society, and to his assistants for their help.

25. *Biographical Directory of the American Congress*, p. 1873; Lord, "The Story of the Hon. A. Mitchell Palmer," *National Monthly*, VI, 39; Stroudsburg *Times*, August 28, 1902; Easton *Argus*, May 9, 1910.

26. Unidentified clippings in scrapbooks in the possession of Palmer's daughter, Mrs. David Lichtenburg, Swarthmore, Pennsyl-

vania, cited as Lichtenburg scrapbooks. These scrapbooks were kept by the first Mrs. A. Mitchell Palmer. Stroudsburg *Times,* May 25, 1899; February 13, 1902; Easton *Daily Express,* April 9, 1908; *St. John's Herald,* October 1, 1914, p. 12; clippings in Palmer scrapbooks.

27. Stroudsburg *Jeffersonian,* May 29, 1902; unidentified clippings, Lichtenburg scrapbooks; interview with Frank Stackhouse, President of the First Stroudsburg National Bank, June 12, 1959; Keller, *History,* p. 389.

28. Unidentified clippings, Lichtenburg scrapbooks; Keller, *History,* pp. 193; Monroe *Record,* March 5, 1908.

29. New York *American,* January 5, 1922; *National Monthly,* V, clippings in Palmer scrapbooks; unidentified obituary of Mrs. A. Mitchell Palmer, in scrapbook kept by Mrs. Laura F. Carmer and presented to the Monroe County Historical Society, cited as Carmer scrapbook.

30. *Biographical Directory of the American Congress,* p. 1888; Stroudsburg *Times,* August 28, 1902. Interview with Hal. H. Harris. Harris, one of the younger members of the Shull faction in 1908, later became a leader of the group and served as Mayor of Stroudsburg for 20 years.

31. Stroudsburg *Times,* August 28, September 25, November 6, 1902; September 29, October 27, November 3, November 10, 1904; *Biographical Directory of the American Congress,* p. 892.

32. Interview with Hal H. Harris; Easton *Daily Express,* May 13, 27, 1910.

33. Easton *Daily Argus,* March 4, 26, 1908; Monroe *Record,* March 5, 1908.

34. Interview with Hal H. Harris; Monroe *Record,* March 5, 12, 1908; Easton *Daily Argus,* May 9, 1910.

35. Easton *Daily Argus,* March 4, 16, 26, 1908; May 9, 1910; Easton *Daily Express,* April 3, 1908.

36. *Ibid.,* April 3, 4, 5, 1908; Easton *Daily Argus,* April 3, 4, 9, 1908.

37. Interview with Jacob M. Hill (now chairman of the School Board of East Stroudsburg, Pennsylvania), East Stroudsburg, July 9, 1956. In 1913, Palmer obtained an appointment for Eckert as Postmaster in East Stroudsburg.

38. Interviews with Jacob M. Hill, Gilbert B. McClintock, Frank Stackhouse, and Hal H. Harris.

39. Monroe *Record,* April 9, 1908; Easton *Daily Argus,* June 1, 1910.

40. Easton *Daily Express,* April 14, 1908; Monroe *Record,* April 16, August 6, 1908.

41. Monroe *Record,* September 24, October 1, November 5, 1908; Easton *Daily Express,* October 28, 29, 1908.

II: THE WORKINGMAN'S FRIEND

1. Watson, *Memoirs,* p. 27.

2. *Congressional Record,* 61 Cong., 1 Sess. (August 5, 1909), pp. 5092, 5093.

3. For Palmer's speech, see *ibid.* (March 31, 1909), pp. 697–700.

4. Hechler, *Insurgency,* p. 98; Philadelphia *Record,* April 1, 2, July 14, 1909.

5. *Congressional Record,* 61 Cong., 1 Sess. (July 20, 1909), pp. 4556–58.

6. *Ibid.,* p. 4556.   7. *Ibid.,* p. 4564.

8. The resolution was passed by voice vote. Representative Joseph A. Tawney of Minnesota, chairman of the Appropriations Committee, later said there were only 5 nays. *Congressional Record,* 61 Cong., 3 Sess. (February 28, 1911), p. 3691.

9. *Ibid.* (March 4, 1911), pp. 3692, 4330–31.

10. *Ibid.,* pp. 4554–55.

11. *Ibid.* (Feburary 28, 1911), p. 3745; unidentified clippings, Lichtenburg scrapbooks. Mrs. Palmer's maiden name was Roberta Bartlett Dixon.

12. *Congressional Record,* 63 Cong., 1 Sess. (April 25, 1913), p. 438; (April 30, 1913), p. 854.

13. *Ibid.,* 61 Cong., 2 Sess. (March 22, 1910), pp. 3552–55. The chairman of the House Committee on Public Lands was Representative Frank W. Mondell of Wyoming, an opponent of most conservation measures.

14. Easton *Daily Express,* March 22, 1910.

15. Monroe *Democrat,* April 20, 1910.

16. *Congressional Record,* 66 Cong., 1 Sess. (September 2, 1919), p. 4609.

17. Monroe *Democrat,* February 9, 1910; Easton *Daily Argus,* May 9, 21, 30, 1910. In a Memorial Day speech in Easton, Palmer complained that the country's annual bill for veterans' pensions totaled only $150,000,000. It was necessary to "increase this miserable pittance," he declared (*ibid.,* May 31, 1910).

18. *Congressional Record,* 61 Cong., 2 Sess. (January 25, 1910), Appendix, p. 9.

19. Monroe *Democrat*, May 25, 1910; Easton *Daily Argus*, April 1, May 24, 1910.

20. Easton *Daily Argus*, April 1, May 24, 1910.

21. Easton *Daily Argus*, April 6, 7, May 9, 24, 1910; *Easton Daily Express*, April 7, 1910; Monroe *Democrat*, May 25, 1910. Palmer asserted that during the campaign he met Schwab in the Bellevue-Stratford Hotel in Philadelphia and that Schwab complained angrily about the congressman's actions. Palmer said he replied that he had not been sent to Washington to represent the steel company (*Argus*, May 24, 1910).

22. Easton *Daily Argus*, May 4, 9, 1910; *Congressional Record*, 62 Cong., 2 Sess. (January 26, 1912), p. 343.

23. Easton *Daily Express*, April 25, 30, May 13, 1910.

24. Easton *Daily Argus*, May 9, 19; Easton *Daily Express*, May 9, 19, 24, 1910.

25. Stroudsburg *Times*, November 3, 1904.

26. Easton *Daily Argus*, May 9, 1910.

27. Monroe *Democrat*, February 2; Easton *Daily Argus*, May 30, 1910.

28. Easton *Daily Argus*, May 24, 30, June 1; Easton *Daily Express*, May 24, 1910.

29. Easton *Daily Argus*, April 1, May 18; Philadelphia *Record*, May 18, 1910.

30. Easton *Daily Argus*, May 19, 1910.

31. Easton *Daily Argus*, May 16, 1910.

32. Easton *Daily Argus*, May 24; Easton *Daily Express*, May 24; Monroe *Democrat*, May 25, 1910.

33. Monroe *Democrat*, June 8; Easton *Daily Express*, June 6; Stroudsburg *Times*, June 10, 1910.

34. Monroe *Democrat*, November 16, 1910; Harrisburg *Patriot*, February 22, 1911.

III: THE PRACTICAL REFORMER

1. New York *Times*, March 12, 1911.

2. McDonald, "The Democratic Party in Philadelphia; A Study in Political Pathology," *National Municipal Review*, XIV, 295–96; A Pennsylvania Manufacturer, "Wanted in Pennsylvania—A Man," *Outlook*, LXXX, 370.

3. Guffey, *Seventy Years*, p. 18. Guffey's uncle, Col. James Guffey, head of the state party until Palmer took over, had his nephew made Superintendent of City Deliveries in the Pittsburgh Post Office

in 1894, when Joe was only twenty-four but already a member of the Allegheny County Democratic committee. Joe served his uncle until 1912, when he became one of Palmer's most trusted assistants. He managed Palmer's 1920 campaign for the Presidency, and succeeded Palmer as Pennsylvania's national committeeman. Guffey served as United States Senator from 1935 to 1947.

4. Rathgeber, *Democratic Party in Pennsylvania*, pp. 345–62. Guffey was perhaps the largest independent oil producer in the world.

5. Jere S. Black to Warren Worth Bailey, June 21, 1912, in the Warren Worth Bailey papers, Princeton University Library, cited as Bailey papers; Sprigle, "Lord Guffey of Pennsylvania," *American Mercury*, XXXIX, 276–77.

6. Wister, "The Keystone Crime," *Everybody's Magazine*, XVII, 442–45; F. Howland, "A Costly Triumph," *Outlook*, LXXXV, 193–210; LXXXII, 484–87; "Pittsburgh: A City Ashamed," in Steffens, *Shame of the Cities*, pp. 118–19, 125–27; *Dictionary of American Biography*, VIII, 60.

7. Bailey to Palmer, March 7, 1914, Bailey papers; Philadelphia *Press*, March 22 and 24, April 22 and 23, 1908.

8. New York *World*, June 25, 1912.

9. Mowry, *The California Progressives*, pp. 130–33; Link, "The Wilson Movement in Texas, 1910–1912," *Southwestern Historical Quarterly*, XLVIII, 170–74, 184; Noble, *New Jersey Progressivism*, pp. 146–53.

10. Link, *The New Freedom*, pp. 158–73.

11. "Memorandum of an Interview with Roland S. Morris at Philadelphia, March 7, 8, 1926," in the R. S. Baker papers, Library of Congress; Bailey to Palmer, March 7, 1914, Bailey papers; Philadelphia *Press*, April 22, 1908. Black, son of former Lieutenant Governor Chauncey F. Black, and grandson of Buchanan's Attorney General and Secretary of State Jeremiah S. Black, was president of the Bryan League. Bailey was secretary and chief organizer.

12. Easton *Daily Express*, April 6, 7, 1910. The *Express* reported on April 7: "The conference was attended by many men not hitherto identified with the State Democratic organization, prominent among them being Jere S. Black, of York; Warren Worth Bailey, of Johnstown; and Francis Fisher Kane, of Philadelphia." One of the most valuable sources of information about the reorganization of the Democratic Party is a series of three articles by Charles G. Miller, who knew many of the principal participants, in the Harrisburg

Evening News, December 21, 22, 23, 1939. Citations of these dates refer to the Miller articles. The meeting in April, 1910, is mentioned on December 21, 1939.

13. For examples of the Guffey–Hall group's attempts to woo Wilson, see M. S. Murray to Wilson, September 5, 1904, and A. G. Dewalt to Wilson, September 8, 1910, in the William B. Wilson papers at the Historical Society of Pennsylvania, cited as W. B. Wilson papers.

14. Harrisburg *Evening News,* December 21, 1939; Easton *Daily Argus,* April 7, 1910; Monroe *Democrat* (Stroudsburg), April 3, 1910. McCormick was an extremely wealthy reformer, straightforward and completely honest. He had been football captain and class president at Yale, and neither drank nor smoked. In 1902, at the age of thirty, he was elected mayor of Harrisburg, and in 1916 was appointed chairman of the Democratic national committee. Although Palmer tried to give him an equal share of the credit, McCormick was not the kind of schemer who could organize a campaign such as the one which reorganized the Democratic Party in Pennsylvania. Blakeslee was one of Palmer's lieutenants.

15. Easton *Daily Argus,* April 4, 19, 1910; Stroudsburg *Times,* April 22, 1910; Harrisburg *Evening News,* December 21, 1939.

16. *The American Review of Reviews,* XLII, 144; Easton *Daily Express,* April 14, 1910; Harrisburg *Evening News,* December 21, 1939.

17. Pittsburgh *Leader,* June 15, 1910, quoted in the New York *Times,* June 16, 1910; Harrisburg *Evening News,* December 21, 1939. Two weeks after the gubernatorial election, Boies Penrose nominated Munson for appointment as judge of the newly created Commerce Court. So strong were Democratic protests to Taft that the nomination was not made. Easton *Daily Express,* November 24, 1910; Monroe *Democrat,* November 31, 1910.

18. Pittsburgh *Dispatch,* May 5, 1914; clippings in the papers of Gifford Pinchot at the Library of Congress, cited as Pinchot papers. Scranton *Truth,* June 22, 1910, quoted in Monroe *Democrat,* June 22, 1910.

19. *Congressional Record,* 61 Cong., 1 Sess., 697–700; App., 9; Easton *Daily Express,* May 24, June 6, 1910; Easton *Daily Argus,* May 16, 24, 1910.

20. Philadelphia *Record,* May 16, 17, 1914. The *Record* printed the correspondence between Hall and Palmer concerning the contribution on May 16. The Guffey organization had carried on a long feud with Howard Mutchler, political boss of Northampton County,

whose hold on the district Palmer was trying to break. See Rath-geber, *Democratic Party in Pennsylvania,* p. 317.

21. Berry and Munson were the only two proven vote-getters in the state party.

22. *American Review of Reviews,* XLII, 144.

23. Stroudsburg *Times,* April 22, 1910. Harrisburg *Evening News,* December 21, 1939; Harrisburg *Patriot,* February 22, 1911.

24. If Berry had won, the new governor and not Palmer would have had control of the reform movement, and probably of the Democratic Party as well. *Smull's Legislative Handbook,* pp. 553, 582. Berry's fine showing is even more impressive when allowance is made for the Republican machine's undoubted ability to fix elections. Tener won a plurality of 21,000 votes in South Philadelphia where election returns were "made to order" by the Vare brothers. Davenport, *Power and Glory,* p. 139; Vare, *My Forty Years in Politics,* pp. 115–17; A Pennsylvania Manufacturer, "Wanted in Pennsylvania—A Man," *Outlook,* LXXX, 374; New York *Times,* March 12, 1911.

25. Monroe *Democrat,* November 16, 1910.

26. Pittsburgh *Gazette-Times,* April 13, 1914.

27. New York *Times,* March 12, 1911; Harrisburg *Evening News,* December 22, 1939; Pittsburgh *Gazette-Times,* April 13, 1911.

28. New York *Times,* March 12, 1911; Harrisburg *Evening News,* December 22, 1939; Pittsburgh *Gazette-Times,* April 13, 1914. Warren Worth Bailey took some of the credit for the success of this movement to force the old guard's hand. He sent daily copies of his Johnstown *Democrat,* which was rabidly in favor of reorganization, to "every Democrat and every independent newspaper in Pennsylvania and on occasion [to] every man who had been prominently identified with the Bryan Democratic League in 1908." Bailey to Palmer, March 7, 1914, Bailey papers.

29. Harrisburg *Patriot,* February 22, 1911.

30. *Ibid.,* March 2, 1911.

31. *Ibid.,* March 3, 1911; Northampton *Democrat* (Easton), March 3, 1911; Philadelphia *Press,* March 3, 1911.

32. Philadelphia *Press,* March 3, 1911.

33. Philadelphia *Record,* March 3, 1911; Harrisburg *Patriot,* March 3, 1911; Northampton *Democrat,* March 3, 1911.

34. Philadelphia *Press,* March 3, 1911.

35. Harrisburg *Evening News,* December 22, 1939; Philadelphia *Record,* March 3, 1911.

36. Harrisburg *Patriot,* March 15, 1911; Northampton *Democrat,* March 17, 1911.

37. The two men had studied law in the same office and had campaigned for each other in previous primary elections. Easton *Daily Argus*, May 19, 1910; Stroudsburg *Times*, September 29, October 27, 1904; Easton *Daily Express*, April 6, 1908.

38. *Alien Property Custodian Report, 1919*, p. 256. See also U. S. Senate Committee on the Judiciary, *Charges of Illegal Practices of the Department of Justice, Hearings*, p. 526.

39. Rathgeber, *Democratic Party in Pennsylvania*, p. 84.

40. Berry to Bailey, March 29, 1911, Bailey papers; Philadelphia *Record*, June 13, 1911.

41. Easton *Argus*, July 3, 1911.

42. Stroudsburg *Times*, July 14, 1911.

43. Harrisburg *Patriot*, July 20, 1911; Harrisburg *Evening News*, December 22, 1939.

44. *Proceedings of the Democratic National Convention, 1912*, p. 439; New York *Times*, January 9, 1912; interview with Homer Cummings, Washington, D. C., July 20, 1955; Wilson to Palmer, January 16, 1912, Wilson papers.

45. Philadelphia *Record*, April 24, 1912.

46. Philadelphia *Inquirer*, May 6, 1912.

47. Gordon had been the brains behind the last Democratic state administration. See Rathgeber, *Democratic Party in Pennsylvania*, pp. 95, 99, 260.

48. Philadelphia *Public Ledger*, April 23, 1912.

49. Palmer's effectiveness in this role was recognized by House Democratic leaders, who made him their caucus chairman in 1913. New York *Times*, March 6, 1913.

50. Harrisburg *Patriot*, May 7, 1912; Philadelphia, *Inquirer*, May 9, 1912, clipping in Palmer scrapbooks.

51. Harrisburg *Patriot*, May 7, 1912.

52. Philadelphia *Inquirer*, May 9, 1912, clipping in Palmer scrapbooks; Harrisburg *Patriot*, May 8, 1912. Palmer sent a lengthy report on the convention to Woodrow Wilson. Palmer to Wilson, May 11, 1912, Wilson papers.

53. Philadelphia *Inquirer*, May 8, 1912, clipping in Palmer scrapbooks.

54. Entry for January 8, 1913, in the diary of Edward M. House, House papers, Yale University, cited as House diary.

55. Pittsburgh *Dispatch*, June 3, 1911.

56. *Congressional Record*, 62 Cong., 2 Sess. (February 29, 1912), p. 2615.

57. *Nation*, XCII, 235.

58. Quotations are from Robinson, *Thomas B. Reed*, pp. 155, 222.

59. Croly, "Democratic Factions and Insurgent Republicans," *North American*, CXCI, 631; *Nation*, XCI, (1910), 462.

60. Bone, "Democrats in Congress Making Good," *American Review of Reviews*, XLIV, 209–10.

61. Johnstown *Democrat*, April 4, 1911, clipping in Palmer scrapbooks. The subcommittee, appointed by Underwood, consisted of Palmer as chairman, Cordell Hull of Tennessee, and Claude Kitchin of North Carolina.

62. Philadelphia *Record*, April 10, 1911.

63. New York *World*, April 3, 1911; *Congressional Record*, 62 Cong., 1 Sess. (May 9, 1911), pp. 1148, 1155.

64. *Ibid*. (July 31, 1911), pp. 3398–3404.

65. Philadelphia *Record*, December 17, 1911; *Congressional Record*, 62 Cong., 2 Sess. (December 16, 1911), pp. 436–41.

66. *Ibid*., 62 Cong., 1 Sess. (August 22, 1911), p. 4397.

67. Underwood declared that he sent everyone who approached him on matters of committee room assignments to Palmer. *Ibid*. (April 10, 1911), p. 141.

68. *Ibid*.

69. *Ibid*., 63 Cong., 1 Sess. (June 3, 1913), p. 1877.

70. Philadelphia *Record*, January 23, 1912.

71. *Congressional Record*, 62 Cong., 2 Sess. (January 26, 1912), pp. 338–52.

72. *Ibid*. (January 27, 1912), p. 1417. Congressman James Lloyd of Missouri found Schwab's opinion of Palmer unchanged a year later. "In conversation with Mr. Schwab last night" Lloyd told the House, "he made the statement that the worst enemy of the Bethlehem Steel Company in the United States was their Representative in Congress, Mr. Palmer"; *ibid*., 63 Cong., 1 Sess. (April 25, 1913), p. 440.

73. *Ibid*., 62 Cong., 2 Sess. (January 26, 1912), p. 1343.

74. *Ibid*.   75. Philadelphia *Record*, January 27, 1912.

76. New York *Times*, March 1, 1912.

77. Philadelphia *Record*, April 9; Philadelphia *Public Ledger*, May 9, 1911. Bryan attempted unsuccessfully to get Speaker Clark to intervene on behalf of free wool. See Bryan to Clark, May 30, 1912, Bryan papers. The Democratic tariff bills passed the Senate with the aid of insurgent Republican votes, but were vetoed by President Taft.

78. *Congressional Record*, 62 Cong., 2 Sess. (May 29, 1912), p. 7390.

79. Bone, "Democrats in Congress Making Good," *American Review of Reviews*, XLIV, 209–10.

80. Easton *Daily Argus*, November 1, 1912.

IV: MAKING WILSON PRESIDENT

1. "Memorandum of Interview with Roland Morris," R. S. Baker papers.

2. Guffey, *Seventy Years*, p. 12.

3. Wilson to Morris, June 16, 1910, in the papers of Roland Morris, Library of Congress, Washington, cited as Morris papers.

4. Guffey, *Seventy Years*, p. 15; "Memorandum of an Interview with Roland Morris," R. S. Baker papers.

5. Link, *Road to the White House*, pp. 119, 123, 125.

6. McCormick to R. S. Baker, November 21, 1927, R. S. Baker papers.

7. Harrisburg *Patriot*, February 22, 1911; Link, *Road to the White House*, p. 331; McCormick to R. S. Baker, November 21, 1927, R. S. Baker papers.

8. Bailey to Wilson, March 28, 1911, Wilson papers; Wilson to Bailey, March 29, 1911, Bailey papers.

9. Stroudsburg *Times*, July 14, 1911.

10. *Ibid.*, Philadelphia *North American*, June 11, 1911.

11. Harrisburg *Patriot*, July 20, 1911; Harrisburg *Evening News*, December 22, 1939.

12. Palmer to Wilson, July 20; Wilson to Palmer, July 20, 1911, Wilson papers.

13. New York *Times*, April 10, 1912.

14. *Ibid.*, April 12, 1912. Clark carried primaries in Massachu setts, April 30; California, May 14; and Iowa, May 16, as well as contests in other, smaller states. McAdoo, *Crowded Years*, p. 129.

15. Wilson to Palmer, April 11, 1912, Wilson papers; Link, *Road to the White House*, p. 413.

16. Guffey, *Seventy Years*, p. 37; Palmer to Wilson, May 11, 1912, Wilson papers.

17. Philadelphia *Record*, May 7, 1912; W. B. Wilson to R. S. Baker, June 4, 1925, R. S. Baker papers.

18. Palmer to Wilson, May 11, 1912, Wilson papers; Philadelphia *Record*, Harrisburg *Patriot*, May 8, 1912.

19. Palmer to Wilson, May 11, 1912, Wilson papers.

20. St. Paul *Pioneer Press*, May 16, 1912, clipping in Palmer scrapbooks.

21. Wilson to Palmer, June 4, 5, 1912, Wilson papers.

22. Palmer to McCormick, cited in McCormick to R. S. Baker, September 17, 1928, R. S. Baker papers; R. S. Baker, "Memorandum of a Conversation with Burleson," March 17–19, 1927, R. S. Baker papers.

23. New York *World,* June 22; Philadelphia *Record,* May 6, 1912.

24. Wilson to Palmer, May 12, 1912, Wilson papers; Wilson to Morris, May 13, 1912, Morris papers. In March, 1912, Wayne Mac-Veagh and Charles Francis Adams tried to convince Morris that Wilson could not be nominated and that the Pennsylvania delegation should support Clark. R. S. Baker, "Memorandum of Conversation with Morris," R. S. Baker papers.

25. New York *World,* Philadelphia *Record,* June 25, 1912.

26. *Congressional Record,* 62 Cong., 2 Sess. (August 5, 1912), App., pp. 468–69.

27. Philadelphia *Record,* June 30, 1912; *Proceedings, Democratic National Convention, 1912,* pp. 196–215.

28. *Ibid.,* pp. 219–21.

29. *Ibid.,* pp. 221–22; Link, "The Baltimore Convention of 1912," *American Historical Review,* L, 702; McCormick to R. S. Baker, September 17, 1928, R. S. Baker papers.

30. New York *World,* June 30, 1912.

31. Lyons, *William F. McCombs,* p. 94.

32. Link, "The Baltimore Convention of 1912," *American Historical Review,* L, 104.

33. McCombs, *Making Wilson President,* p. 157.

34. Link, *Road to the White House,* pp. 454–55.

35. R. S. Baker, "Memorandum of Conversation with Vance McCormick," Baker papers; Ellis, "The Presidency Spurned," *Harper's Weekly,* LIX, 426; Guffey, *Seventy Years,* p. 41.

36. New York *Times,* July 1, 1912.

37. New York *World,* Philadelphia *Record,* July 1, 1912.

38. R. S. Baker, "Memorandum of a Conversation with Burleson," R. S. Baker papers; Ellis, "The Presidency Spurned," *Harper's Weekly,* LIX, 426; McAdoo, *Crowded Years,* p. 156; Guffey, *Seventy Years,* pp. 41–42. The political bosses probably projected a Palmer-Underwood ticket, as Hobson had suggested in May. Murphy and his friends were preparing a stampede to Underwood when Wilson's managers suddenly broke the deadlock. John Quinn to Augustus John, July 8, 1912, in papers of John Quinn, New York Public Library, cited as Quinn papers.

39. McAdoo, *Crowded Years,* p. 156; Lyons, *McCombs,* p. 101.

40. Daniels, *Wilson Era,* p. 61.

41. On this committee see Link, *Road to the White House,* p. 481, and R. S. Baker, *Woodrow Wilson,* III, 371.

42. R. McArdle (Burleson's secretary) to W. B. Wilson, August 31, 1912; Palmer to W. B. Wilson, September 2, 20, 1912; Lee Crandall to W. B. Wilson, November 8, 1912, W. B. Wilson Papers. Palmer managed to squeeze $15,000 from the national committee for the Pennsylvania campaign; Philadelphia *Inquirer*, April 26, 1914, clipping in Palmer scrapbooks.

43. Cox to Palmer, August 12, 1912; Palmer to Wilson, August 17, 1912; Wilson to Palmer, August 19, 1912, Wilson papers; Link, *Road to the White House*, p. 507.

44. Daniels, *Wilson Era*, p. 70; Philadelphia *Record*, July 25, 1912.

45. New York *Times*, September 24, 1912. 46. *Ibid.*

47. Wilson to Palmer, October 23, 25, 1912; Kane to Wilson, October 14, 1912, Wilson papers; Link, *Road to the White House*, pp. 518–19, 521.

48. Philadelphia *Record*, July 18, 19, 1912.

49. Philadelphia *Record*, July 14, 1912.

50. Easton *Daily Argus*, October 18, November 1, 1912. The name Washington was used for the new party in Pennsylvania, because before the party was formed the state Republicans had prudently registered every possible name which might include the words progressive or Roosevelt.

51. Easton *Daily Free Press*, November 2, 1912, clipping in Palmer scrapbooks.

52. New York *Times*, September 24, 1912.

53. *Smull's Legislative Handbook*, 1914, p. 604.

54. *Ibid.*, p. 587. 55. Link, *The New Freedom*, pp. 6–7.

56. *Ibid.*, p. 5. Link believes that McCombs' report of this conversation is "essentially accurate," although perhaps exaggerated.

57. House diary, January 5, 1913.

58. Link, *The New Freedom*, pp. 5–21; Baker, "Memorandum of Conversation with Roland Morris," Baker papers. Morris described, more graphically than anyone else, the separation Wilson attempted to achieve between his personal feelings and his important political appointments. Wilson was formal and reserved when State Chairman Morris approached him on political matters; but he treated Morris like the old, personal friend he was when the two men had lunch after their political conferences.

59. Link, *The New Freedom*, pp. 5, 6; Philadelphia *Record*, February 4, 1913.

60. Wilson to Burleson, January 2; Burleson to Wilson, January 4; Papers of Albert S. Burleson, cited as Burleson papers.

61. House diary, January 5, 1913.

62. *Ibid.*, January 6, 1913; New York *Times*, January 7, 1913.

63. Link, *The New Freedom,* p. 6.

64. House diary, January 6, 1913.

65. McCombs, *Making Wilson President,* p. 163.

66. House diary, January 6, 1913.

67. New York *Times,* January 7, 1913.

68. House diary, December 18, 1912; Link, *New Freedom,* pp. 11–13.

69. House diary, January 6, 1913. Most of the important Cabinet selections were decided upon during conversations between House and Wilson. Palmer's shifting fortunes in this period can be followed in House's diary.

70. *Ibid.,* January 24, 1913.   71. *Ibid.,* January 8, 1913.

72. *Ibid.,* January 17, 1913. Wilson's changing plans for Palmer were reported, with fair accuracy, in the New York *Evening Post,* February 3; New York *World,* February 17; Philadelphia *Record,* February 4, 16, 25, 26.

73. House diary, January 24, 1913.

74. *Ibid.,* January 26, February 14, 1913. Bryan preferred former Governor Joseph M. Folk of Missouri for the post.

75. *Ibid.,* February 15, 1913.

76. Philadelphia *Public Ledger,* February 16, 1913.

77. House diary, February 16, 1913, and memoranda on Palmer's career prepared by McReynolds, House papers.

78. House diary, February 16, 1913.

79. Link, *The New Freedom,* p. 13; McAdoo, *Crowded Years,* pp. 183–84.

80. Kerney, *Political Education of Wilson,* p. 300; Daniels, *Wilson Era,* p. 117.

81. Palmer to Wilson, February 23, 1913, Wilson papers. Before his final refusal to enter Wilson's cabinet, Palmer suggested to Burleson that he would be willing to take the Treasury secretaryship, if McAdoo would shift to the War Department. Wilson would not agree to this. House diary, February 23, 1913.

82. Daniels, *Wilson Era,* p. 117.

83. Wilson to Palmer, February 25, 1913, Wilson papers.

84. House diary, February 22, 1913.

85. Interview with Mrs. Hannah Clothier Hull.

v: THE CONGRESS OF ACHIEVEMENT

1. Croly, "Democratic Factions and Insurgent Republicans," *North American,* CXCI, 631.

2. *Nation,* CI, 299. The *American Review of Reviews* declared in October, 1913: "The Democratic party . . . has surprised both its

friends and its enemies by the firmness with which it has faced its pledges and kept its word"; *ibid.,* XLVIII, 390.

3. Hofstadter, *The Age of Reform,* p. 166.

4. *World Almanac and Encyclopedia,* pp. 506–8; New York *Evening Post,* April 5, 1913. There were 103 new Democratic members in the Sixty-third House, the great majority of them northerners.

5. Bryan to Bailey, December 15, 1902; Keating to Bailey, March 11, 1913, and Daniel Kiefer to Bailey, June 12, 1917, Bailey papers; *Congressional Record,* 63 Cong., 2 Sess. (June 1, 1914), p. 9556.

6. *Literary Digest,* XLVIII, 1423.

7. New York *Times,* January 4, 1913. New York *World,* January 4, 1913. Both papers named Warren Worth Bailey as the center of the plot. Also, Welliver, "Leaders of the New Congress," *Munsey's,* XLVII, 720, 723. For evidence of southern opposition to the legislative objectives of northern progressives, see Abrams, "Woodrow Wilson and the Southern Congressmen, 1913–1916," *Journal of Southern History,* XX, 417–37.

8. New York *Times,* January 4, 1913.

9. Goeke to Wilson, August 8, 1913, Wilson papers.

10. New York *Times,* January 10, 1913; Link, *New Freedom,* pp. 157–60.

11. New York *World,* February 26, 1913.

12. New York *Times,* March 6, 1913.   13. *Ibid.*   14. *Ibid.*

15. See, for example, Link, *New Freedom,* pp. 177–78, and Hofstadter, *Age of Reform,* p. 172.

16. Rogers, "The Democratic Party," *Yale Review,* II, 35, 47; *Historical Statistics of the United States. Supplement to the Statistical Abstract of the United States,* p. 231.

17. House diary, February 23, 1913.

18. House Committee on Ways and Means, *Hearings on Schedule C—Metals,* pp. 965–68.

19. *Ibid., Hearings on Schedule A—Chemicals, oils and paints,* pp. 35–36.

20. *Ibid.,* p. 433.   21. *Ibid.,* p. 307.   22. *Ibid.,* p. 776.

23. *Ibid., Hearings on Schedule C,* p. 1101. Schwab's words were echoed by officers of other Pennsylvania steel corporations. W. H. Donner, President of Cambria Steel Company, for example, warned the Committee of an invasion of foreign steel which "would mean . . . idleness for thousands of American workmen. . . ." Cambria employed 19,000; *ibid.,* p. 1024.

24. Taussig, *Tariff History,* pp. 440–41.

25. Link, *New Freedom,* pp. 179–80; Philadelphia *Press,* April 2, 3, 4, 5, 1913.

26. New York *Times*, April 12, 13, 17, 1913; New York *World*, April 17, 1913; Philadelphia *Press*, April 17, 1913.

27. Link, *New Freedom*, pp. 180–81.

28. *Congressional Record*, 63 Cong., 1 Sess. (May 6, 1913), p. 1250.

29. *Ibid.* (April 25, 1913), p. 434.

30. Thomas J. Pence to Burleson, June 12, 1913, in the papers of Albert S. Burleson, cited as Burleson papers; Henry F. Hollis to Wilson, August 13, 1913; Wilson to Palmer, August 15, 1913, Wilson papers.

31. Palmer to R. S. Baker, January 22, 1929, R. S. Baker papers.

32. Wilson to Palmer, and enclosure, February 5, 1913, Wilson papers.

33. Palmer to Wilson, February 7, 1913, Wilson papers. There were reports early in 1913 that Bryan would refuse to serve in Wilson's Cabinet unless the President-elect disclaimed any intention of running for a second term (New York *World*, January 6, February 21, 1913). Bryan, however, had already declared privately that he did not believe that the new law should apply to Wilson or Theodore Roosevelt. Bryan to Smith, February 6, 1913, Bryan papers.

34. Palmer to R. S. Baker, January 22, 1929, R. S. Baker papers; Clayton to Palmer, July 17, 1915; Clayton to Palmer, July 17, 1915, Wilson papers; New York *Times*, October 16, 1914.

35. Daniels, *Wilson Era*, p. 102; Link, *New Freedom*, pp. 22–23.

36. Palmer to Tumulty, June 30, 1913; Clayton to Palmer, July 17, 1915; Palmer to Wilson, July 30, 1915; Wilson to Palmer, August 2, 1915, Wilson papers. See Chap. 7.

37. House diary, January 24, 1913; New York *Times*, January 27, 1914; Link, *New Freedom*, pp. 304–11; Leuchtenburg, "Progressivism and Imperialism," *Mississippi Valley Historical Review*, XXXIX, 493–94.

38. New York *Times*, February 20, 26, 1914.

39. New York *Times*, March 27, 1914; R. S. Baker, *Wilson*, IV, 414.

40. R. S. Baker memorandum of interview with Burleson, R. S. Baker papers; Thomas R. Marshall to Tumulty, April 9, 1915, Wilson papers; R. S. Baker, *Wilson*, IV, 414.

41. New York *Times*, March 28, 1914.

42. *Congressional Record*, 63 Cong., 2 Sess. (March 27, 1914), p. 5616.

43. *Ibid.*, 5628; New York *Times*, March 28, 1914.

44. *Congressional Record*, 63 Cong., 2 Sess. (March 31, 1914), pp. 6099–89. Palmer's stand on the exemption repeal was said to have lost him a good many Democratic votes in 1914. Philadelphia *Pub-*

lic Ledger, April 6, 1914; Philadelphia *Press,* March 31, 1914. Pinchot campaigned for a return to exemption. "What Gifford Pinchot Stands For," campaign pamphlet, 1914, in Pinchot papers.

45. Commager, ed., *Documents of American History,* pp. 262–64.

46. Link, *New Freedom,* pp. 469–70.

47. Philadelphia *Press,* February 3, 1914; Link, *New Freedom,* p. 258; R. S. Baker, *Wilson,* IV, 226.

48. New York *Times,* February 4, 1914.

49. *Congressional Record,* 63 Cong., 2 Sess. (April 6, 1913), p. 6313; New York *Times,* April 7, 1914.

50. New York *American,* January 5, 1922, obituary of Mrs. Palmer.

51. Philadelphia *Record,* October 11, 1914; Philadelphia *Public Ledger,* October 11, 1914.

52. Swarthmore *Phoenix,* XI, 110.

53. *Congressional Record,* 63 Cong., 3 Sess. (January 12, 1915), pp. 1407–81.

54. *Ibid.* (January 12, 1915), Appendix, pp. 149–51.

55. *Ibid.,* pp. 1483–84. Palmer voted in favor of the resolution.

56. Link, *New Freedom,* p. 256; for discussion of the bill, *Congressional Record,* 63 Cong., 3 Sess. (February 15, 1915), pp. 3827–28. Violators of the law would have been liable to a year in jail or a fine of $1,000, or both.

57. Philadelphia *Record,* February 13, 1913.

58. McKelway, "Another Emancipation Proclamation," *American Review of Reviews,* LXV, 425, Lovejoy, "Federal Government and Child Labor," *Child Labor Bulletin,* II, 19; Owen R. Lovejoy to author, May 12, 17, 1956.

59. Lindsay, "National Child Labor Standards," *Child Labor Bulletin,* III, 24–28; Link, *New Freedom,* pp. 255–56.

60. Fuller, *Child Labor,* pp. 236–38; Lindsay, "National Child Labor Standards," *Child Labor Bulletin,* III, 26.

61. A. J. McKelway, "The National Child Labor Bill," undated manuscript in the files of the National Child Labor Committee, New York City; Lovejoy to the author, May 12, 17, 1956.

62. House Committee on Labor, *Hearings on HR 12292, A Bill to Prevent Interstate Commerce in the Products of Child Labor and for Other Purposes,* February 27 and March 9, 1914; *Congressional Record,* 63 Cong., 3 Sess. (February 15, 1915), p. 3834.

63. *Ibid.,* pp. 3827–36. Labor Secretary Wilson assured the Chairman of the House Committee on Labor that Palmer's bill was "the most practical method which has yet been presented for reaching

the Child Labor Problem." Wilson to Daniel J. Lewis, July 3, 1914, Department of Labor Records.

64. McKelway, "Another Emancipation Proclamation," *American Review of Reviews*, LXL, 425; Link, *New Freedom*, p. 257.

65. McKelway to Felix Adler, January 29, 1914, in the papers of A. J. McKelway, Library of Congress, cited as McKelway papers; McKelway to Wilson, February 6, 1914, Wilson papers; Link, *New Freedom*, pp. 256–57.

66. McKelway, "Another Emancipation Proclamation," *American Review of Reviews*, LXV, 425; Link, *Progresisve Era*, pp. 226–67; *Congressional Record*, 64 Cong., 1 Sess. (August 8, 1916), p. 12313.

VI: THE "SIEGE OF PENROSE"

1. Bryce, *The American Commonwealth*, I, 540; Steffens, *Shame of the Cities*, pp. 101, 134. Among the most revealing articles about political corruption in Pennsylvania, are Alfred H. Lewis, "Penrose—Pernicious and Petty Politicians," *Hearst's*, XXIV, 352; Marcosson, "The Fall of the House Quay," *World's Work*, XI, 7119–24; Hearst, "More Standard Oil Letters," *Hearst's*, XXII, 4–21; and articles referred to in Chap. 3.

2. Steffens, *Shame of the Cities*, p. 148.

3. Tarbell, *Tariff in Our Times*, p. 362.

4. For the development of protectionist sentiment in Pennsylvania, see Eisilin, *Rise of Pennsylvania Protectionism*.

5. Berglund and Wright, *Tariff on Iron and Steel*, pp. 120–29.

6. *Ibid.*, p. 123; Taussig, *Tariff History*, pp. 129–30; House Committee on Ways and Means, *Hearings on Schedule B*, p. 809; *ibid.*, *Hearings on Schedule C*, pp. 976–83, 1320, 1747–50, 1951–56, 2045–46.

7. Philadelphia *Press*, January 22, February 4, 1914.

8. Bowden, *Boies Penrose*, p. 187; Howland, "A Costly Triumph," *Outlook*, LXXXV, 193–210.

9. Monroe *Democrat*, April 20, 1910.   10. See Chap. 3.

11. For an opinion of the effectiveness of Palmer's regime by an expert in such matters, see Guffey, *Seventy Years*, p. 40.

12. Burleson to Tumulty, July 20, 1914, Wilson papers.

13. For Palmer's part in obtaining these and other major appointments, see Seymour, *House*, I, 129; McAdoo to Wilson, April 8, 1913; Dwyer to Wilson, April 20, 1913; and Palmer to Wilson, January 30, 1914, all in Wilson papers; Palmer to Bailey, July 10, 1913, Bailey papers. Secretary of Labor William B. Wilson, another

reorganizer leader, would probably have been appointed no matter who was in power in Pennsylvania.

14. Hugo W. Noren to Wilson, July 20, 1914, Wilson papers; J. A. Osborne to Bailey, July 4, 1914, Bailey papers; Sprigle, "Lord Guffey," *American Mercury*, XXXIX (November, 1936), p. 279.

15. Palmer to Tumulty, August 13, 1915, with enclosed Guffey to Palmer, August 9, 1915, Wilson papers.

16. Philadelphia *North American*, April 1, 1914; Pittsburgh *Gazette-Times*, April 1, 1914, Palmer scrapbooks.

17. John Dwyer to Tumulty, May 6, 1913, April 22, 1914; Noren to Tumulty, September 24, 1913; John Sullivan to Tumulty, December 9, 1914, Wilson papers.

18. Wilson to Palmer, May 7, 1913; Palmer to Wilson, May 12, 1913; Wilson to Palmer, May 14, 1913, Wilson papers.

19. Dwyer to Wilson, September 27, 1913, with enclosed clippings from Philadelphia *Inquirer*, September 27, 1913, and Philadelphia *Public Ledger*, September 27, 1913, Wilson papers.

20. Philadelphia *North American*, May 29, 1914, clipping in Palmer scrapbooks. The *North American* was the state's leading Progressive Party journal.

21. Michael J. Gibbons to Wilson, January 10, 1914, W. B. Wilson papers.

22. Philadelphia *Inquirer*, July 13, 1913, Palmer scrapbooks.

23. Philadelphia *Record*, July 23, 1913; Philadelphia *Public Ledger*, July 23, 1913; Philadelphia *Dispatch*, July 27, 1913, Palmer scrapbooks.

24. Bailey to Palmer, March 7, 1914, Bailey papers.

25. Philadelphia *Inquirer*, August 9, 1914, Palmer scrapbooks.

26. Philadelphia *Press*, April 12, 1914.

27. Pittsburgh *Dispatch* and Pittsburgh *Gazette-Times*, May 29, 1914, clippings in Palmer scrapbooks. Among the other bones of contention were the posts of Surveyor of the Port of Philadelphia and head of the subtreasury in Philadelphia.

28. Philadelphia *Public Ledger*, August 8, 9, 1914.

29. New York *Times*, February 5, 1914; Hugh Kerwin to L. B. Siebert, February 12, 1914, W. B. Wilson papers.

30. Gompers to Woodrow Wilson, January 28, 1914; Gompers to W. B. Wilson, January 29, 1914; W. B. Wilson to Gompers, February 1, 1914; Gompers to W. B. Wilson, February 12, 1914, with undated enclosure from Woodrow Wilson to Gompers, all in W. B. Wilson papers.

31. New York *Times*, February 5, 1914; Kerwin to Siebert, February 12, 1914, W. B. Wilson papers.

32. New York *Times*, May 8; Washington *Post*, July 27; Philadelphia *Public Ledger*, November 8, 1914.

33. Philadelphia *Press*, February 4, 6, 1914; Pittsburgh *Gazette-Times*, April 13, 1914, clippings in Pinchot papers and Palmer scrapbooks.

34. Philadelphia *Press*, February 5, 1914. McCormick's brother was the largest financial contributor to Palmer's primary campaign, Philadelphia *Public Ledger*, May 6, 1914.

35. Philadelphia *Inquirer*, April 26, 1914; Philadelphia *North American*, May 13, 1914; Philadelphia *Public Ledger*, April 28, 1914; Philadelphia *Record*, May 16, 1914. The *Record* published Palmer's letter in full, as well as Hall's reply.

36. Philadelphia *Record*, May 16, 17, 1914; Pittsburgh *Gazette-Times*, May 15, 1914.

37. Philadelphia *Press*, February 18–20, 22, 26, 1914; Philadelphia *Record*, February 22, 1914.

38. *Ibid.*, February 22, 1914; Philadelphia *Press*, February 17, 19, 20, May 17, 1914.

39. Philadelphia *Press*, February 22, 1914.

40. *Ibid.*, February 7, 1914.

41. The most prominent prospect was Charles B. Staples, of Stroudsburg, the judge whose renomination Palmer had opposed. William J. Brennen, who had taken over the broken remnants of Colonel James Guffey's organization in Pittsburgh, was so disgusted at the reluctance of party members to run against Palmer that he announced, "If no one else will run, I will." Philadelphia *Press*, February 26, 1914.

42. *Ibid.*, April 7, 1914.

43. Philadelphia *North American*, April 3, 1914, clipping in Palmer scrapbooks; Philadelphia *Record*, April 3, 1914.

44. Philadelphia *Press*, March 16, 1914.

45. Liquor interests fought McCormick's candidacy so fiercely in 1914 that two years later, when Colonel House asked him whether he was available for the national chairmanship of the Democratic national committee, McCormick answered that he could not accept, because he feared that the liquor men would respond by opposing Wilson's reelection. See House to Wilson, May 28, 1916, Wilson papers.

46. L. B. Siebert to Hugh Kerwin, February 18, 1914; Kerwin to Siebert, February 12, 1914; W. B. Wilson to Palmer, February 14, 1914; Palmer to W. B. Wilson, February 20, 1914, all in W. B. Wilson papers.

47. Palmer to W. B. Wilson, April 27, 1914, with enclosed J. T.

McGuiness to McCormick, April 25, 1914; W. B. Wilson to James Purcell, April 30, 1914, W. B. Wilson papers.

48. Philadelphia *Public Ledger,* April 17, 1914; Philadelphia *Press,* May 2, 1914.

49. Philadelphia *Public Ledger,* May 12, 1914; Philadelphia *Inquirer,* May 12, 1914, and Scranton *News,* May 14, 1914, Palmer scrapbooks. Palmer announced early in the campaign that Bryan might come to Pennsylvania to speak for the Palmer-McCormick ticket. Ryan immediately protested, and John Dwyer warned that if Wilson allowed the Secretary of State to campaign people would say the administration opposed Ryan because of his race and creed. Philadelphia *Press,* February 17, 18, 1914; Theodore Wright to Woodrow Wilson, May 17, 1914; with enclosure, Wilson papers.

50. Palmer to Wilson, May 20, 1914, Wilson papers; Philadelphia *Press,* May 21, 1914.

51. Kenneth M. Pray, "The Siege of Penrose," *Harper's Weekly,* LIX, 375.

52. New York *Times,* October 20, 1914; Philadelphia *Public Ledger,* October 20, 25, 1915.

53. Philadelphia *Public Ledger,* October 11, November 1, 1914.

54. T. R. Shipp, "Prospects of Pennsylvania Campaign," December, 1913, seventeen-page manuscript in Pinchot papers.

55. Philadelphia *Public Ledger,* December 3, 1913. See debate between Palmer and Moore, *Congressional Record,* 63 Cong., 2 Sess. (December 4, 1913), p. 211.

56. Philadelphia *Press,* January 30, 1914.

57. Philadelphia *Public Ledger,* October 21, 1914; Palmer was so bold as to state on September 30, "Senator Penrose is saying that the tariff is the chief issue, and is raising the cry of calamity under a Democratic administration. But I have been going up and down the hills and dales of Pennsylvania as well as he and nowhere are there signs of a slackening of the State's great industries." Philadelphia *Public Ledger,* October 1, 1914.

58. A few days after the election, the *Public Ledger* reported that manufacturing plants, mostly steel mills in the Pittsburgh area, which employed over 20,000 men were expected to reopen within ten days and to resume full or partial operations. Philadelphia *Public Ledger,* November 6, 1914.

59. *Commercial and Financial Chronicle,* XCIX, 1119.

60. Philadelphia *Press,* March 28, 1914.

61. Quoted in *Commercial and Financial Chronicle,* XCIX, 1188.

62. *Independent,* LXXVII, 38.

63. Gary is quoted in *Commercial and Financial Chronicle,* XCIX (July 4, 1914), 14–15.

64. Berglund and Wright, *Tariff on Iron and Steel,* p. 120.

65. *Commercial and Financial Chronicle,* XCIX, 237. Berglund and Wright found: "This reduction (in imports on steel ingots) had no effect in retarding production or encouraging imports." See their *Tariff on Iron and Steel,* p. 120. Taussig concluded that imports of some steel specialties increased, but that, "in the main [however], the changes in the iron and steel schedules signified little." *Tariff History,* p. 442.

66. Link, *Progressive Era,* pp. 445–46.

67. "On Guard, Progressives," *Harper's Weekly,* LIX, 377.

68. Benjamin S. Smith to Pinchot, January 16, 1915; Dewitt G. Smith to Pinchot, January 25, 1915, Pinchot papers. Many other letters to Pinchot emphasized the hostility of the Republicans-turned-Progressives to the Democrats; for example, O. K. Davis to Pinchot, April 12, 1914; W. H. Bridenbaugh to Pinchot, January 1, 1915, J. V. Stephenson to Pinchot, January 2, 1915, Pinchot papers.

69. In part, Pinchot's decision to stay in the race may have been due to a personal grudge against Palmer. See Chap. 2.

70. Philadelphia *Press,* August 13, 1914; Philadelphia *Public Ledger,* October 21, 1914.

71. Washington *Post,* October 30, 1914.

72. William Flinn carried on 'a war of nerves against Palmer. He organized letter campaigns to the Democratic candidate, especially from temperance groups, requesting his withdrawal. He also spread rumors that Palmer was about to withdraw. Pittsburgh *Dispatch,* September 19; Philadelphia *Record,* October 15, Philadelphia *North American,* October 14, 1914; clippings in Palmer scrapbooks. Philadelphia *Public Ledger,* October 15; Washington *Post,* October 16, 1914.

73. Washington *Post,* October 19, 1914.

74. Philadelphia *Record,* October 28, 1914. Pinchot adopted the same line, Philadelphia *Inquirer,* October 20, 1914, clipping in Palmer scrapbooks.

75. Philadelphia *North American,* October 10, 1914, clipping in Palmer scrapbooks. The Philadelphia *Public Ledger,* a Republican newspaper, but hostile to Penrose, reported on November 1 that recent reports from its correspondents in every county showed Penrose behind, and "Mr. Palmer's outlook seems bright." Another story in the same issue, however, stated that Roosevelt's tour was severely hurting Palmer's chances.

76. The Philadelphia *Public Ledger* estimated that the mailing

cost was $19,000. *Ledger,* October 31, 1914; McGeary, "Gifford Pinchot's 1914 Campaign," *Pennsylvania Magazine of History and Biography,* LXXXI, 317.

77. Washington *Post,* October 27, 1914.

78. *Ibid.,* October 30, 1914; Philadelphia *Public Ledger,* November 1, 1914.

79. Philadelphia *Press,* May 21; Philadelphia *Public Ledger,* October 3, 9, 1914.

80. Philadelphia *Public Ledger,* April 6, November 1; Stroudsburg *Times,* May 20; Easton *Daily Argus,* May 20, 1914. The Northampton County democratic committee voted down a motion to endorse Palmer's record, and another to approve the program of the Wilson administration. Easton *Free Press,* June 6, 1914.

81. Pittsburgh *Dispatch,* May 29; Pittsburgh *Gazette-Times,* May 29, 1914; Philadelphia *Inquirer,* May 29, 1914, Palmer scrapbooks.

82. Quoted in Bowden, *Boies Penrose,* p. 110.

83. *Ibid.,* pp. 227–30.

84. Stackpole, *Behind the Scenes,* pp. 114–15. Representative Martin B. Madden of Illinois said of Penrose—with perhaps a bit too much enthusiasm—"He made the most wonderful campaign [in 1914] that has ever been made by any man for that great office." See *Senators from Pennsylvania, Memorial Addresses,* p. 97.

85. New York *Times,* July 19, 1914; Dunlap, "Boies Penrose," unpublished master's essay, p. 173. The Republicans acknowledged spending $750,000 during the campaign, and Palmer offered to produce before an investigating committee conclusive evidence that the true amount was much higher. Democratic expenditures were declared to be $75,000, of which $33,000 was contributed by McCormick and spent on his own behalf. *Congressional Record,* 63 Cong., 3 Sess. (February 18, 1915), pp. 4022–23. Joe Guffey told the Senate in 1940 of a long conversation he had had two years before with Charles Schwab, then long retired from Bethlehem Steel. During his reminiscences, Schwab declared, according to Guffey: "I never received a telegram from the late Senator Penrose without dropping everything and coming to Washington. He never asked for less than $250,000 on each visit, and sometimes more." *Congressional Record,* 76 Cong., 3 Sess. (March 9, 1940), p. 2599.

86. Philadelphia *Press,* May 1; Philadelphia *Public Ledger,* October 1, 1914.

87. Philadelphia *Record,* October 28, 1914, clipping in Palmer scrapbooks. The Philadelphia *Inquirer* backed Penrose with the assertion that, "Mr. Pinchot can mend a sick tree, but there has never been the slightest suspicion that he could tell a tariff sched-

ule, if he should happen to see one, from a hole in the wall."
Quoted in McGeary, "Gifford Pinchot's 1914 Campaign," *Pennsylvania Magazine of History and Biography*, LXXI, 314.

88. Philadelphia *Public Ledger*, September 24, 1914.

89. Philadelphia *Public Ledger*, June 4, 1914; Palmer to Wilson, May 25, 1914, Wilson papers.

90. Philadelphia *Record*, October 9, 1914; Philadelphia *Inquirer*, October 10, 1914, clippings in Palmer scrapbooks; Washington *Post*, July 31, 1914; Link, *New Freedom*, p. 466.

91. New York *Times*, October 21, 24, 1914.

92. Easton *Daily Argus*, September 28, 1914.

93. Philadelphia *Record*, August 27; Philadelphia *Public Ledger*, October 13, 1914.

94. Pittsburgh *Leader*, October 14, 1914, Palmer scrapbooks; Philadelphia *Public Ledger*, October 15, 1914.

95. Uniontown (Pennsylvania) *Record*, October 7; Uniontown (Pennsylvania) *Standard*, October 10, 1914, Palmer scrapbooks. Washington *Post*, October 6; Philadelphia *Public Ledger*, October 21, 26, 1914.

96. Viellard (pseudonym), "A Well Disguised Reformer," *Nation*, CI, 227. Penrose was careful to leave himself free to oppose Palmer's child labor bill, workmen's compensation legislation, and other measures strongly opposed by Pennsylvania manufacturers.

97. Philadelphia *Inquirer*, October 7, 1914, Palmer scrapbooks.

98. *Ibid.*, October 13; Philadelphia *Record*, October 13; Philadelphia *Public Ledger*, October 14, 1914.

99. New York *Times*, November 4, 1914; Philadelphia *Public Ledger*, November 4, 1914.

100. Philadelphia *Public Ledger*, November 4, 1914; *Smull's Legislative Handbook for 1916*, p. 740.

101. Talcott Williams, "After Penrose, What?" *Century*, CV, 51.

VII: A POLITICIAN OUT OF OFFICE

1. New York *Times*, May 8, 1914; Washington *Post*, July 27, 1914; Philadelphia *Public Ledger*, November 8, 1914.

2. Palmer to Wilson, March 6, 1915, Wilson papers.

3. Palmer to Wilson, April 1, 1915; Tumulty to Palmer, April 2, 1915; Palmer to Tumulty, undated, written at bottom of Tumulty's letter, Wilson papers.

4. Philadelphia *Public Ledger*, October 6, 8, 26, 1914; Washington *Post*, October 6, 1914.

5. New York *Times,* January 7, February 20, 1915; Philadelphia *Public Ledger,* February 20, 21, 1915.

6. Memorandum dated March 13, 1915, probably made by Tumulty; Wilson to Palmer, April 5, 1915, Wilson papers.

7. Philadelphia *Public Ledger,* March 16, 1915.

8. *Ibid.,* March 18, 1915.

9. Dwyer to Tumulty, March 19, 1915, and enclosures, Wilson papers.

10. Palmer to Wilson, April 1, 1915, and Wilson to Palmer, April 5, June 5, 1915, Wilson papers; New York *Times,* June 6, 1915.

11. Philadelphia *Public Ledger,* February 21, March 14, 1915.

12. Palmer to Wilson, April 1; Wilson to Palmer, April 5, 1915, Wilson papers.

13. See above, pp. 80–81.

14. Palmer to Tumulty, June 30, 1914, Wilson papers. The New York *Times* reported on October 16, 1914: "Mr. Bryan, there is reason to believe, has since [the 1912 Convention] changed his mind about the necessity for this [single-term] legislation."

15. Palmer to Wilson, July 30, 1915, with enclosure from Clayton to Palmer, July 17, 1915, Wilson papers. Bryan had written at least one other similar letter. Bryan to Smith, February 6, 1913, Bryan papers.

16. Wilson to Palmer, August 2, 1915, Wilson papers; New York *Times,* February 16, 17, 1916.

17. Washington *Star,* February 15, 1920, clipping in Pinchot papers. The records of Palmer's law firm, like his other papers, have disappeared. On July 27, 1915, he appeared before Secretary of the Interior Franklin K. Lane as the chief spokesman for a large group of small and middle-sized oil companies, which had claims on Osage Indian lands. House Committee on the Judiciary, *Southern Pacific Hearings,* pp. 17–18.

18. New York *Times,* August 1, 1915.

19. *Ibid.,* July 22, 1915.

20. House to Burleson, July 25, 1915, Burleson papers.

21. House to Pence, July 31, 1915, House papers.

22. Burleson to House, August 13, 1915, Burleson papers. Eventually, the post went to Frank L. Polk of New York. Lansing had succeeded to the Secretaryship because Wilson and Bryan split over the Lusitania issue. I am indebted to John A. Garraty for pointing out that the new Secretary may have hesitated to appoint Palmer partly because his published views on the subject resembled Bryan's.

23. New York *Times,* May 9, 1915.

24. *Congressional Record,* 66 Cong., 1 Sess. (September 2, 1919), p. 4602.

25. New York *World,* August 23, 1915. Because of the war, there was a glut of cotton in the United States, and a great deal of political pressure from southern representatives for government assistance in marketing it.

26. *Ibid.*   27. *Ibid.*

28. *Ibid.,* July 2, 1912, August 24, 1915. Stanchfield was the Democratic candidate for Governor of New York in 1900 and one of Wilson's leading supporters in New York before the 1912 convention.

29. New York *Times,* August 24, 1915.

30. Senate Committee on the Judiciary, *Hearing on Nomination of A. Mitchell Palmer,* pp. 7–9, *Congressional Record,* 65 Cong., 1 Sess. (September 2, 1919), p. 4608.

31. Memorandum, F. Frazier to Burleson, August 31, 1916, Wilson papers.

32. Palmer to Wilson, August 18, 23, November 17, 1916; Wilson to Burleson, January 23, 1917; Blakeslee to Burleson, undated, probably early 1917, Wilson papers. Wilson to Burleson, undated, probably early 1917, Burleson papers.

33. Philadelphia *Public Ledger,* May 1, 17, 18, 1916; Palmer to Wilson, May 22, 1916, Wilson papers.

34. House to Wilson, May 30, 1916, Wilson papers.

35. House to Wilson, May 19, 28, 1916, Wilson papers.

36. House to Wilson, May 30, 31, June 9, 12, 13, 1916, Wilson papers.

37. House to Wilson, June 13, 1916, Wilson papers.

38. Palmer to Wilson, June 14, 1916, Wilson papers.

39. *Proceedings of the Democratic National Convention, 1916,* Appendix, pp. 290–319.

40. Philadelphia *Press,* October 6, 15; Philadelphia *Public Ledger,* October 15, 1916.

41. *Ibid.,* November 2, 1916.

42. Philadelphia *Press,* October 10; Philadelphia *Public Ledger,* September 28, October 10, 1916.

43. *Ibid.,* November 1, 1916.

44. Palmer to Tumulty, with enclosures, October 17, 1916, Wilson papers; Philadelphia *Public Ledger,* October 15, 28, November 2; Philadelphia *Press,* November 1, 3, 1916.

45. *Ibid.,* October 1, November 1, 1916.

46. New York *Times,* November 2, 1916.

47. *Ibid.*, November 11; Philadelphia *Public Ledger,* November 9, 1916.

48. For a full discussion, see Chap. 10.

VIII: ALIEN PROPERTY CUSTODIAN

1. Heaton, *Cobb,* pp. 269–70.

2. Ellis, "The 'Fighting Quaker' of the Cabinet," *American Review of Reviews,* LXI, 35.

3. Memorandum, Tumulty to Wilson, August 8, 1917, Wilson papers.

4. Washington *Post,* February 28, 1919.

5. Tumulty to McCormick, September 11, 1917; McCormick to Tumulty, September 13, 1917; Vance C. McCormick papers, Yale University Library, New Haven, cited as McCormick papers.

6. Bonham to Tumulty, October 30, 1917, Wilson papers.

7. New York *Times,* June 29, 1923.

8. A. M. Palmer, "The Great Work of the Alien Property Custodian," *American Law Review,* LIII, 45.

9. "How Seized German Millions Fight Germany," *New York Times Magazine,* January 27, 1918.

10. *Alien Property Custodian Report for 1918,* p. 10.

11. *Ibid.;* "He Balked the Hun Attempt to Grab Our Industries," *Literary Digest,* LX, 277.

12. *Alien Property Custodian Report for 1917,* p. 3.

13. *Alien Property Custodian Report for 1918,* pp. 11–12, 105.

14. New York *Times,* October 31, November 2, 7, 28, 1917.

15. Memorandum, Palmer to Ralph J. Baker, July 15, 1918. Alien Property Custodian Records.

16. Haynes, *American Chemical Industry,* III, 260. Letter from member of Palmer's staff to the author; interview of the author with member of Palmer's staff. Garvan had a pronounced tendency to exaggerate the strength of his enemies and the extent of their plots. He told one of his investigators, for example: "I know that all the brains of the German metal world are at work twenty-four hours a day to circumvent our endeavors." Garvan to Kresel, July 29, 1918, File of F. P. Garvan, Alien Property Custodian Records.

17. New York *Times,* November 28, 1917. Dreher's personal papers, like Palmer's and Garvan's, have been destroyed, according to relatives.

18. Interview of the author with Gilbert S. McClintock, May 19, 1959; Wilhelm, "If He Were President," *Independent,* CII, 64–5.

For analysis of the Custodian's legal powers see Gathings, *International Law,* pp. 74–77; and Bishop. "Judicial Construction of the Trading With the Enemy Act," *Harvard Law Review,* LXII, 126.

19. Wilson to Palmer, November 9, 1917, Wilson papers.

20. See, for example, Public Information Committee, *Official United States Bulletin,* October 9, 1918, p. 8; October 11, 1918, pp. 1, 6; October 19, 1918, pp. 2, 4; November 2, 1918, pp. 1, 5; November 5, 1918, pp. 1–2, 3; November 12, 1918, p. 24.

21. *Alien Property Custodian Report for 1918,* pp. 159–61; Palmer, "The Great Work of the Alien Property Custodian," pp. 45–49. The Custodian continued to make occasional public appeals for assistance; see "Wanted: Information about Enemy-Owned Property," *Literary Digest,* LVIII, 38–40; *Journal of Industrial and Engineering Chemistry,* X (November, 1918), 947–48.

22. This figure is based upon a comparison of the State Counsels listed in Alien Property Custodian, *Bulletin of Information,* pp. 63–65, with the lists of delegates and national committeemen in *Proceedings, Democratic National Convention, 1916,* pp. 50, 55–78; and *ibid., 1920,* pp. 43–71, 457–58.

23. Alien Property Custodian, *Bulletin of Information,* pp. 63–65.

24. *Alien Property Custodian Report for 1917–1922,* pp. 86, 87, 117, 133, 510.

25. *Alien Property Custodian Report for 1917–1922,* pp. 3–8, 15, 93, 205, 248, 258, 260, 336, 423, 434, 446, 460, 474, 581, 603, 617.

26. *Alien Property Custodian Report for 1917–1922;* for Fitzgerald's fees, see pp. 29, 57, 616; for Delehanty's, pp. 42, 60, 227, 298, 369, 438, 467, 558; Quinn's, pp. 44, 141, 227, 535, 543; Kresel's, pp. 29, 93, 581; Crocker's, pp. 30, 35, 86, 93, 117, 205, 335, 364, 366, 367, 423, 478, 557, 569, 572, 581, 595, 621, 628. The report includes a description of the work done in each case. Total fees (approximate): Quinn, $174,000; Delehanty, $137,000; Kresel, $128,000; Crocker, $100,000. For financial contributions to Palmer's 1920 presidential campaign by Crocker, Covington, Lynch, McClosky, Garvan, and others, see Senate Subcommittee on Presidential Expenses, *Hearings,* I, 138.

27. New York *Times,* January 1, October 15, November 9, December 12, 21, 31, 1916; August 17, March 9, 12, April 10, 11, 1917.

28. Knox, ed., *Who's Who in New York* (1918), p. 246; New York *Herald,* March 1, 1916; New York *Tribune,* March 1, 1916; Crocker to Garvan, December 12, 1920, Corporate Management Cases Handled by Crocker, Corporate Management Division, 1917–34, Alien Property Custodian Records.

29. Downs, ed., *Who's Who in New York* (1929), p. 978; New York *Times,* March 2, 1920; see also Chap. 7.

30. Quinn to Augustus John, July 8, 1912, Vol. II, Quinn papers. Quinn was a delegate to the 1912 Democratic national convention, and a member of the platform committee in the state conventions of 1908 and 1910.

31. Quinn was described by the New York *Times* July 29, 1924, as "one of the world's leading collectors of modern art." At one time he owned all of Joseph Conrad's original manuscripts; New York *Times,* July 29, 1924, November 14, 1923, January 6, 17, 1924. See also the brief biography of Quinn in Volume I, Quinn papers. Walsh, "John Quinn: Lawyer, Booklover, Art Amateur," *Catholic World,* CXX, 176–84; *Alien Property Custodian Report for 1912–1922,* pp. 142–54.

32. Gregory to Robert H. Vinson, May 13, 1918, in the papers of Thomas Watt Gregory, Library of Congress, cited as Gregory papers.

33. Gregory to Dr. T. U. Taylor, April 15, 1918, Gregory papers.

34. *Alien Property Custodian Report for 1918,* p. 14. Palmer told a group of New York bankers in November, 1918: "I want the bankers of this country to help me crush the strangle hold which Germany . . . has had upon many of the essential industries of this nation" (*Commercial and Financial Chronicle,* CVII, 2050).

35. See Chap. 11.

36. *Alien Property Custodian Report for 1918,* p. 15.

37. New York *Times,* June 29, 1923.

38. Quoted in Link, *New Freedom,* p. 69.

39. New York *Times,* June 29, 1923.

40. *Ibid.,* March 10, 12, 13, 1918.

41. New York *Times,* New York *World,* July 16, 1918; Senate Committee on the Judiciary, *Hearing on Nomination of A. Mitchell Palmer.*

42. "Statement of George L. Ingraham, November 12, 1920," enclosed with Frank Davis, Jr., to Thomas J. Walsh, January 13, 1927, in the papers of Thomas J. Walsh, Library of Congress, cited as Walsh papers. The Minutes of Advisory Committee Meetings, Alien Property Custodian Records, show many bids rejected for various reasons. In December, 1919, for example, the Advisory Committee rejected Garvan's request that Botany Mills, a large textile manufacturing firm, be disposed of at private sale. The Advisory Committee could be fooled, however, as it probably was in the sale of Bosch Magneto.

43. Comptroller General, "Administration of the Office of the Alien Property Custodian," copy in Alien Property Custodian Records, pp. 34, 41. Palmer informed a correspondent who was seeking APC funds for the Harriman National Bank: "Under the law we are compelled to deposit all money forthwith into the Treasury of the United States. We only use banks as depositaries for securities and other property." Palmer to H. C. Wallace, August 3, 1918, Bureau of Trusts Files, Depositary Section, Alien Property Custodian Records; *ibid.,* Palmer to S. B. Philson, May 6, 1918.

44. Comptroller General, "Administration of the Office of the Alien Property Custodian," pp. 45, 55–64, 179; "Memo from Sutherland to Castro re Joseph F. Guffey Trust Account," January 7, 1926, R.G. 131, Corporate Management Division, Alien Property Custodian Records; New York *Times,* New York *World,* April 10, 1924.

45. New York *Times,* December 29, 1922. Guffey's indictment was later quashed under suspicious circumstances.

46. *Congressional Record,* 63 Cong., 1 Sess. (April 10, 1913), p. 146; (April 29, 1913), pp. 758–60; New York *Times,* April 15, August 21, 1913; *Biographical Directory of the American Congress,* p. 1275.

47. See Raymond Benjamin, "Report of Philippine Investigation," R.G. 131, Alien Property Custodian Records, pp. 1–161; Comptroller General, "Administration of the Office of Alien Property Custodian," pp. 68–9, 96–104; New York *World,* April 17, 1924.

48. McIntyre to Harrison, March 16, 22, April 4, 18; Paredes to Harrison, May 28; Harrison to Palmer, April 6, June 2, July 13, 15; Palmer to Harrison, May 29, June 29, July 10, 1918, all in "Report of Philippine Investigation," R.G. 131, Alien Property Custodian Records.

49. *Ibid.,* Wilson to Harrison, July 22, and Harrison to Wilson, July 23, 1918, pp. 68, 71–85. Despite Palmer's pleas for speed, Harrison proceeded so slowly that Wilson was obliged to order the nullification of the sales.

50. *Ibid.,* Palmer to Harrison, September 12, 1918, p. 80; New York *World,* April 17, 1924.

51. *Ibid.,* Quinn to Harrison, July 31; Harrison to Berry, September 28; Erlenger to Denegre, September 25; Denegre to Green, October 18; Green to Denegre, November 4; Moffat to Palmer, November 7; Palmer to Moffat, November 12, 1918, pp. 71–104.

52. Justice Department accountant George W. Storck made an investigation of the Philippine sales in the early years of the Harding administration, and as a result Judge Milton O. Purdy was sent

to Manila to investigate further. Purdy acknowledged to Storck that he had been royally entertained in the Philippines. When Storck asked whether he was going to recommend prosecution, Purdy allegedly replied: "Storck, what has gone over the dam is spilled. We must be charitable. We must forget these things"; *Senate Investigation of Daugherty*. A more thorough investigation was made in 1930; but again no prosecutions resulted, perhaps because of the deaths of many of the principals and witnesses. Benjamin to Sutherland, January 14, 1930, R.G. 131, Alien Property Custodian Records.

53. Senate Committee on the Judiciary, *Hearing on Nomination of A. Mitchell Palmer*, I, 127.

54. *Alien Property Custodian Report for 1917–1922*, pp. 133–34.

55. New York *Times*, October 22, 1926; "Annual Report of the Bosch Magneto Corporation" (March 20, 1920). Murray and MacDonald were also awarded cash bonuses amounting to about 50 percent of their annual salaries shortly before the transfer was completed. *Alien Property Custodian Report for 1917–1922*, p. 134.

56. New York *Times*, December 29, 1922; *ibid.* and New York *World*, April 10, 1924; Bethlehem Motors Corporation, "Stockholders' Committee, To the Stockholders of Bethlehem Motors Corporation" (February 21, 1921).

57. Alien Property Custodian, "Prospectus of Sale, Bosch Magneto Company," Corporate Management Division, Alien Property Custodian Records; New York *Times*, October 23, 1926; Senate Committee on the Judiciary, *Hearing on the Nomination of A. Mitchell Palmer*, II, 270.

58. *Ibid.*, II, 311.

59. Comptroller General, "Administration of the Office of the Alien Property Custodian," p. 45; *Alien Property Custodian Report for 1918*, p. 111.

60. Senate Committee on the Judiciary, *Hearing on the Nomination of A. Mitchell Palmer*, I, 66.

61. *Ibid.*, I, 111; New York *Times*, December 8, 1918.

62. *Senate Investigation of Daugherty*, I, 931–32. The company earned $1,469,872 after taxes in 1920; "Annual Report, American Bosch Magneto Corporation, 1920."

63. American Bosch Magneto Corporation, *$1,800,000 American Bosch Magneto Corporation 7 per cent Serial Gold Notes*, dated January 15, 1919; New York *Times*, October 22, 1926.

64. Senate Committee on the Judiciary, *Hearing on the Nomination of A. Mitchell Palmer*, I, 128. Palmer's nomination was approved unanimously by the committee. New York *Times*, March 2, 1919.

65. Quoted in the New York *Times,* April 17, 1924. Despite this letter, Bannard and Ingraham, who investigated the sale for the Advisory Sales Committee, were led to believe that the real purchasers were a group of bankers led by Hornblower and Weeks and the Chase Securities Company. The Advisory Committee also decided that the price paid by Kern was a fair one. Ingraham to Grim, April 14, 1922; Bannard to Elihu Root, July 15, 1926, Walsh papers.

66. "Prospectus of Sale, Bosch Magneto Company," copy in Corporate Management Division, 1917–34, Alien Property Custodian Records.

67. New York *World,* April 10, 1924; New York *Times,* April 10, 1924. An additional 20,000 shares were sold to the public late in 1919 at $100 a share. The original offering was at sixty dollars a share; "Annual Report, American Bosch Magneto Corporation, 1919."

68. New York *Times,* October 2, 1926; December 6, 1927; January 26, 1930. A. R. Johnson, Jr., to the Attorney-General, October 3, 1923, File 9-17-78, Department of Justice Records, is a summary and evaluation of the evidence in the case. Kern was indicted in 1922 for his part in the alleged conspiracy, but never tried; New York *Times,* December 29, 1922.

69. Mason, *Harlan Fiske Stone,* pp. 171, 174. The newspaper quoted by Mason was the Omaha *Bee,* September 15, 1924.

70. *Journal of Industrial and Engineering Chemistry,* X, 256; Haynes, *American Chemical Industry,* III, 210, 228, 229, 312; *Alien Property Custodian Report for 1919,* p. 27.

71. *Alien Property Custodian Report for 1918,* p. 48; Haynes, *American Chemical Industry,* III, 259–60.

72. *Alien Property Custodian Report for 1918,* pp. 61–62; *for 1919,* p. 60; Haynes, *American Chemical Industry,* III, 260; New York *Times,* June 29, 1923.

73. New York *Times,* June 30, 1923.

74. Mason, *Harlan Fiske Stone,* pp. 173–74; "Legalizing Fraud," *Nation,* CXVIII, 80; New York *Times,* October 12, November 5, 1925. United States v. Chemical Foundation, Inc., 272 U. S. 1 (1926).

75. Palmer, "The Great Work of the Alien Property Custodian," pp. 51–52.

76. *Ibid.*

77. Wilson to Palmer, September 4, 1918; Palmer to Wilson, October 3, 1918, Wilson papers.

78. *Ibid.,* Wilson to Palmer, November 20, 1918, *Wilson Papers.* A month earlier, the President had informed Palmer of the At-

torney-General's opinion that "we have no legal right to retain the property." *Ibid.,* Wilson to Palmer, October 21, 1918.

79. *Ibid.,* Wilson to Palmer, November 22, 1918.

80. New York *Times,* November 14, 1916; New York *World,* January 13, 1919.

81. Blum, *Tumulty,* pp. 167–68, 187.

82. New York *World,* January 13, 1919.

83. Blum, *Tumulty,* pp. 187–88.

84. Charles B. Ames to Herbert Hoover, January 27, 1918, copy enclosed with Palmer to Tumulty, February 5, 1919, Wilson papers.

85. Wilson to Gregory, January 31, 1919, Gregory papers.

86. See Chap. 4.

87. Kerney, *Political Education of Wilson,* p. 302.

88. New York *World,* February 27, 1919.

89. New York *World,* January 15, 1919.

90. McCormick to R. S. Bright, February 6, 1919, McCormick papers.

91. Hollister to McCormick, January 16, 1919, McCormick papers.

92. Kerney, *Political Education of Wilson,* p. 303.

93. Blum, *Tumulty,* p. 188.

94. Kerney, *Political Education of Wilson,* p. 304.

95. New York *World,* February 26, 1919; interview with Homer Cummings.

96. Wilson to Gregory, February 26, 1919, Gregory papers.

97. New York *World,* February 27, 1919.

IX: THE HIGH COST OF LIVING

1. *Congressional Record,* 66 Cong. 1 Sess. (August 15, 1919), 3892. There is no comprehensive study of the war's effects on the American mind. For brief treatments see May, *The End of American Innocence,* pp. 361–67; Gabriel, *Course of American Democratic Thought,* pp. 387, 404; Curti, *Growth of American Thought,* pp. 687–705; Leuchtenburg, *Perils of Prosperity,* p. 13; Lord, *The Good Years,* pp. 338–42; Siegried, *America Comes of Age,* p. 3.

2. We also lack a full study of the postwar societal disruption and its effects. For a suggestive analysis of similar responses in various cultures see Anthony F. C. Wallace, "Revitalization Movements," *American Anthropologist,* LVIII, 264–81.

3. New York *Times,* March 1, 1920.

4. Ellis, "Fighting Quaker of the Cabinet," *American Review of Reviews,* III, 35.

5. Backman, *Wages and Prices*, p. 81.

6. United States Department of Labor, *Retail Prices, 1913 to December, 1920*, p. 4.

7. Not all Americans were equally affected, of course. For example, wages of farm and factory laborers advanced at least as fast as prices during this period. See Ahearn, *Wages of Farm and Factory Laborers*, p. 227.

8. New York *World*, July 30; Philadelphia *Public Ledger*, August 5, 1919; *Independent*, XCIX, 74–75.

9. Washington *Post*, August 1; New York *Times*, July 30, August 1, 1919. Philadelphia *Public Ledger*, July 31, 1919. Cummings reported that Americans were also disturbed about the meat packing trust and about industrial strikes, although high prices were the predominant issue. A chief complaint against the packing trust and strikes was that they acted to raise prices.

10. Washington *Post*, August 4; Philadelphia *Public Ledger*, August 5, 1919.

11. Bry, *Wages in Germany*, pp. 440–43; Soule, *Prosperity Decade*, pp. 88–95; Gordon, *Business Fluctuations*, pp. 362–67.

12. *Independent*, XCIX, 74–75; Congressional Record, 66 Cong., 1 Sess. (July 26, 1919), pp. 3200–5; New York *World*, July 31; Washington *Post*, August 1, 1919.

13. New York *World*, July 31, 1919.

14. According to newspaper reports the meeting was called on Palmer's initiative. New York *Times*, August 1; Washington *Post*, August 1, 1919.

15. Washington *Post*, August 1, 1919.

16. New York *World*, August 2, 1919.

17. *Ibid.*, August 4, 1919; *Congressional Record*, 66 Cong., 1 Sess. (July 26, 1919), pp. 3200–05; (August 1, 1919), pp. 3290–91; (August 4, 1919), pp. 3590–98.

18. New York *World*, August 5, 1919; *Congressional Record*, 66 Cong., 1 Sess. (August 6, 1919), p. 3665.

19. New York *World*, August 6, 1919; letters and circulars to and from United States Attorneys in File 181092–231, Department of Justice Records.

20. New York *Times*, Washington *Post*, August 7, 1919.

21. Washington *Post*, August 6; New York *World*, August 8, 1919. Actually, the most frantic phase of the politicians' attempt to do something about prices began about August 1. On August 2, the Philadelphia *Public Ledger* declared: "The high cost of living took complete command in Washington today."

22. New York *Times,* New York *World,* Washington *Post,* August 9, 1919.

23. House Committee on Agriculture, *Food Control Hearings,* pp. 63–82; New York *Times,* August 14, 15, 1919.

24. New York *Times,* August 15, 1919. The reenacted food section of the Lever Act was declared unconstitutional in 1921 on the grounds that Congress had not set standards for fair prices. United States v. L. Cohen Grocery Company, 255 U. S. 81 (1921).

25. *Congressional Record,* 66 Cong., 1 Sess. (August 22, 1919), p. 4183.

26. *Ibid.,* p. 4228; (August 30, 1919), p. 4589; (September 10, 1919), p. 5157–68; (September 11, 1919), p. 5225–37, 5294–5305; (October 16, 1919), p. 7014, 7016–26. Palmer's request for an additional appropriation was granted in full, New York *World,* September 12, 1919. Other departments, which proposed to fight high prices by the sale of surplus goods, control of exports, and investigations, had their requests for money cut severely by the House Committee on Appropriations.

27. G. W. Bryan to Palmer, August 8, 1919, and enclosed list of Federal Food Administrators, R. G. 60, HCL Division, Office Files, Department of Jusice Records; New York *Times,* August 11, 1919.

28. Mullendore, *United States Food Administration;* House Committee on Agriculture *Food Control Hearings,* pp. 66–7.

29. H. Figg to C. B. Ames, September 19, 1919, R. G. 60, HCL Division, Office Files, Department of Justice Records; New York *World,* August 17, 1919. "Fair" retail prices were published prominently every week by local newspapers. For example, New York *World,* September 16, 1919.

30. New York *Times,* August 16, 17, 1919.

31. *Ibid.,* August 23, 1919.

32. Figg, "Supplementary Report, Prosecutions and Seizures Under Sections 6 and 7 of the Food Control Act," October 16, 1919, R. G. 60, HCL Division, Office Files, Department of Justice Records.

33. *Ibid.*

34. Figg to Palmer, September 26, 1919, with enclosed W. F. Priebe to Figg, September 13, 1919, and F. A. Horne to Figg, September 25, 1919; R. G. 60, HCL Division, Office Files, Department of Justice Records.

35. Palmer's efforts to reduce consumer spending on nonessentials came in for a good deal of criticism from business interests and their spokesmen, *Literary Digest,* LXIV, 19.

36. Figg, "Memorandum for Judge Ames," October 16, 1919, R. G. 60, HCL Division, Office Files, Department of Justice Rec-

ords; Division of Women's Activities; HCL, "Platform;" list of eighty-one national women's organizations engaged in distributing HCL Division material; also list of state women's organizations co-operating with the HCL Division, R. G. 60, HCL Division, Office Files, Department of Justice Records.

37. New York *Times,* August 19, 1919; House Committee on Agriculture, *Food Control Hearings,* p. 63; Palmer, "How to Bring Down Prices," *Independent,* C, 167.

38. *Ibid.*

39. U. S. Attorney-General, *Annual Report, 1919,* pp. 17–18.

40. Figg to Representative J. Will Taylor, December 30, 1919, R. G. 60, HCL Division, Office Files, Department of Justice Records; House Committee on Agriculture, *Food Control Hearings,* p. 80; House Committee on the Judiciary, *Sugar Hearings,* p. 161.

41. New York *World,* December 23, 1919; House Committee on Agriculture, *Food Control Hearings,* p. 81. A Utica clothing store was fined $55,000 for profiteering, New York *Times,* June 3, 1920.

42. Figg to Representative L. C. Dyer, March 17, 1920, R. G. 60, HCL Division, Office Files, Department of Justice Records.

43. W. R. Smallwood to Figg, May 15, 1920; "Memorandum for Mr. Figg," May 18, 1920; E. C. Atwood to Figg, July 17, 1920; Figg to J. L. Bowles, April 30, 1920; and miscellaneous reports and letters, R. G. 60, HCL Division, Office Files, Department of Justice Records.

44. The best accounts of wartime sugar controls are Bernhardt, *Government Control of the Sugar Industry;* and Mullendore, *Food Administration,* Chap. 10.

45. Federal Trade Commission, *Report on Sugar Supply and Prices,* pp. 12–16, 142–48; Justice Department Circular Number 989, August 9, 1919, File 181092, Department of Justice Records.

46. New York *World,* August 14, 1919; House Committee on Agriculture, *Food Control Hearings,* p. 81. A retail profit of two cents a pound was considered "fair," no matter what the wholesale price.

47. Figg to Palmer, November 4, 1919; P. B. Brashears to Figg, April 19, 1920; Palmer to Senator F. M. Simmons, May 19, 1920; R. G. 60, HCL Division, Office Files, Department of Justice Records; "Meeting of Representatives of Sugar Refineries, April 26, 1920," minutes in R. G. 60, HCL Division, Office Files, Department of Justice Records; *Commercial and Financial Chronicle,* CIX (November 22, 1919), 1948.

48. For the details of the crisis in our sugar supply, see Federal Trade Commission, *Report on Sugar Supply and Prices;* House

Committee on the Judiciary *Sugar Hearings;* Bernhardt, *Government Control of the Sugar Industry,* Chapters 6, 7; "Meeting of Representatives of Sugar Refineries, April 26, 1920; "Figg to Palmer, December 1, 1919, R. G. 60, HCL Division, Office Files, Department of Justice Records.

49. Figg to Ames, October 16, 1919; Figg to Palmer, November 13, 1919, R. G. 60, HCL Division, Office Files; *Commercial and Financial Chronicle,* CIX (November 22, 1919), p. 1947; House Committee on the Judiciary, *Sugar Hearings,* p. 102.

50. Figg to Palmer, December 1, 1919; Palmer to C. C. Oliver, September 9, 1920; "Meeting of Representatives of Sugar Refineries, April 26, 1920"; R.G. 60, HCL Division, Office Files; *Commercial and Financial Chronicle,* CX, 36.

51. Figg to Ames, September 13, 1919; Figg to Palmer, December 1, 1919, R.G. 60, HCL Division, Office Files; *Commercial and Financial Chronicle,* CX, 36.

52. House Committee on the Judiciary, *Sugar Hearings,* pp. 6–7, 75, 152–56; Federal Trade Commission, *Report on Sugar Supplies and Prices,* pp. 111–15; Figg to Palmer, November 13, 1919, R.G. 60, HCL Division, Office, Department of Justice Records.

53. New York *Times,* Philadelphia *Public Ledger,* March 5, 1920; House Committee on the Judiciary, *Sugar Hearings,* pp. 8–9.

54. *Ibid.,* pp. 164, 169–70.

55. New York *Times,* June 3, 1920.

56. *Commercial and Financial Chronicle,* CXII, 707.

57. New York *Times,* September 21, 1919; *Independent,* XCIX, 167; *Literary Digest,* LXIV, 18–19. Palmer's optimistic statements may be explained in part by his belief, expressed to an interviewer in December, 1919, that, "if you make people believe prices are going to come down, prices will come down." Wilhelm, "If He Were President," *Independent,* CII, 46.

58. *Seventh Annual Report of the Federal Reserve Board for the Year* 1920, p. 7; New York *Times,* May 21, 1920.

59. House Committee on the Judiciary, *Sugar Hearings,* p. 59; *Commercial and Financial Chronicle,* CX, 36.

60. P. Dobrovolsky, *Corporate Income Retention, 1915–43,* pp. 110–11; Gordon, *Business Fluctuations,* p. 254.

61. Epstein, *Industrial Profits,* pp. 219–22, 248, 254, 302–3, 304–5.

62. Hoover to Palmer, September 19, 1919, R.G. 60, HCL Division, Office Files, Department of Justice Records. The *American Legion* Weekly, I, 9, suggested that the government experiment with broad price, trade, and currency controls, stating that while such federal interference in private affairs would be uncalled for under

ordinary circumstances, "dangerous diseases require drastic remedies, and high prices are emphatically a dangerous disease." For an evaluation of the government's experience with wartime controls, see Soule, *Prosperity Decade,* Chaps. 1, 2, especially pp. 28, 57–59.

X: BETWEEN CAPITAL AND LABOR

1. New York *Times,* March 11, 1920.
2. William F. Schnitzler, Secretary-Treasurer, AFL-CIO, to the author, July 1, 1958, with enclosed copy of "Legislative Record of Representative A. Mitchell Palmer of 26th District, Pennsylvania, on Measures of Interest to Labor."
3. See Chap. 7.
4. W. B. Wilson to Siebert, November 25, 1912, W. B. Wilson papers.
5. See Chaps. 5, 7; H. J. Friedman to Walsh, November 28; Walsh to Friedman, December 1; and Palmer to Walsh, December 22, 1919, Walsh papers.
6. *New Republic,* XIX, 310. The *Literary Digest,* LXIII, 12–13 published statements, from a variety of sources, reflecting the prevalent belief that the middle class was caught in a war between capital and labor.
7. Justice C. J. Wrightsman to Palmer, October 30, 1919, File 16–130–0, Department of Records. This file contains a great many similar letters from small business and professional men. Note that the letter quoted was written before Palmer began rounding up radicals.
8. See Chap. 1.
9. Easton *Daily Argus,* April 1, May 16, 19, 1910.
10. Peterson, *Strikes in the United States,* p. 21.
11. Murray, *Red Scare,* Chaps. 4, 8.
12. E. N. Nockles to W. B. Wilson, October 14, 1919, W. B. Wilson papers; New York *Times,* October 8, 15, 16, 17, 1919; Senate Committee on Education and Labor, *Steel Strike Investigation,* pp. 907–27; Murray, "Communism and the Great Steel Strike of 1919," *Mississippi Valley Historical Review,* XXXVII, 458–60.
13. Senate Committee on Education and Labor, *Steel Strike Investigation,* pp. 398–423; Murray, "Communism and the Steel Strike," 458–60.
14. Draper, *Roots of American Communism,* pp. 198–99, 311–14, 435; Saposs, *Left Wing Unionism,* pp. 49–50; Interchurch World Movement, *Report on the Steel Strike,* p. 36.

15. Senate Committee on Education and Labor, *Steel Strike Investigation,* p. 14.

16. Gambs, *Decline of the I.W.W.,* p. 133; Saposs, *Left Wing Unionism,* pp. 152–57; Perlman and Taft, *Labor in the United States,* IV, 421, 431–32; Interchurch World Movement, *Report on the Steel Strike,* p. 36; *One Big Union Monthly,* II, 13.

17. Draper, *Roots of American Communism,* pp. 188–99, 312–13; Interchurch World Movement, *Report on the Steel Strike,* p. 36.

18. New York *Times,* September 24, October 15, 16, 17, November 26, 1919; Senate Committee on Education and Labor, *Steel Strike Investigation,* p. 907.

19. For some aspects of popular hostility to organized labor in this period, Murray, *Red Scare,* pp. 122, 134, 150, 155–56, 165.

20. See Chap. 9.

21. *Congressional Record,* 66 Cong., 1 Sess. (October 17, 1919), p. 7063.

22. Blum, *Tumulty,* pp. 218–23.

23. W. B. Wilson to Woodrow Wilson, September 5, 1919. W. B. Wilson papers. Daniels, *Wilson Era,* p. 546–47, says that he and Lane agreed with Wilson's objections to the coal injunctions, although Lane was usually listed among the proponents of coercion. Baker had earlier declared himself in thorough agreement with the Secretary of Labor's viewpoint on the government's postwar policy toward workers. Felix Frankfurter to W. B. Wilson, November 9, 1918, W. B. Wilson papers. In 1919, however, Baker's public pronouncements were in favor of the government's actions, New York *World,* October 31, 1919. Lansing, W. B. Wilson, and Garfield all left relatively full accounts of the coal crisis and all indicate that Wilson received no effective support within the administration until Palmer, Tumulty, and Lansing shifted their ground. Lansing desk diaries, entries for October 22, 25, 1919; Lansing private memoranda, November 26, December 12, 1919; Garfield to Lansing, January 13, 1920, in the papers of Robert Lansing, Library of Congress, cited as Lansing papers. "Memorandum of the Secretary of Labor relative to the coal strike," manuscript in W. B. Wilson papers; W. B. Wilson to J. Duncan, April 22, 1920, W. B. Wilson papers.

24. Secretary Wilson wrote his old friend, labor leader James Duncan, about the coal strike, "I know something of the inside story of it. Lewis was the residuary legatee of a mass of demands that had been accumulating as a result of individual and partisan political efforts within the organization." W. B. Wilson to Duncan, April 22, 1920, W. B. Wilson papers. See also, *United Mine Workers Convention* (1919), III.

25. *Railway Maintenance of Way Employees Journal*, XXIX, 10; *Brotherhood of Locomotive Firemen and Enginemen's Magazine*, LXVIII, 8–9.

26. New York *Times*, October 26, 1919; Blum, *Tumulty*, p. 219.

27. Wilson, *My Memoir*, p. 289; Grayson to R. S. Baker, October 25, 1919, Papers of Ray Stannard Baker at Princeton University, cited as R. S. Baker papers, Princeton. Grayson's bulletins to the press on Wilson's conditions were deceptively optimistic. See especially, New York *World*, October 30, 31, 1919.

28. *Proceedings, 27th United Mine Workers Convention*, 1920, pp. 18, 19; New York *Times* and New York *World*, October 30, 31, 1919.

29. New York *World*, October 27, 28, 1919.

30. Gompers to Palmer, November 22, 1919, with enclosures; Palmer to Gompers, December 15, 1919; Gompers to Palmer, February 10, 1920; File 205722, Department of Justice Records; New York *World*, October 28–30, 1919; Gompers, "The Broken Pledge," *American Federationist*, XXVII, 41–50.

31. New York *World*, October 29, 1919.

32. New York *Times*, October 30, 1919; correspondence between Ames, in Indianapolis, and Palmer is in File 205194, Department of Justice Records. Other reports on the coal situation can be found *ibid.*, File 16–130–26.

33. New York *Times*, October 31, 1919; Palmer to Ames, October 30, 1919, File 205194, Department of Justice Records.

34. New York *Times*, November 1, 3, 1919.

35. *Literary Digest*, LXIII, 13; Tumulty to Palmer, November 1, 1919, in the notes of John M. Blum on the papers of Joseph P. Tumulty, Yale University, cited as Tumulty Notes. I am greatly indebted to Professor Blum for permission to examine these notes, stored in the Manuscript Division, Yale University Library. Tumulty's papers have recently been given to the Library of Congress. For many statements by political leaders see, New York *World*, October 27, 28, 1919. The *World* was usually as fair as any major newspaper in its treatment of labor disputes, but it turned bitterly against the coal strikers. An editorial on October 28 fumed: "This is no assertion of the right to strike. It is the assertion by a ridiculously small minority . . . of a right to sacrifice the welfare of the vast majority. . . . The Government that is prepared to concede any such right as that is prepared to sign its own death warrant."

36. New York *Times*, November 3, 1919; *Independent*, C, 87; For evidence of the strenuous efforts of the Justice Department to hold down coal prices, see File 181092–231, Department of Justice

Records; Speer to Palmer, December 16, 1920, File 181092–265, *ibid.*, is a report on this subject.

37. New York *Times,* New York *World,* November 8, 9, 10, 1919.

38. New York *Times,* November 10, 11, 1919.

39. *Ibid.,* November 11, 12, 1919.

40. Negotiations after the mandatory injunction was issued can best be followed in the contemporary accounts of Lansing, Garfield, and W. B. Wilson, mentioned in note 22, this chapter. See also Blum, *Tumulty,* pp. 221–23.

41. New York *Times,* November 25, 26, 1919. McAdoo also wrote the President that Palmer and Garfield were aiding the enemies of the Democratic Party, and that continued support for their position would "make the triumph of reaction, toryism, and privilege certain in 1920"; Blum, *Tumulty,* p. 221.

42. Lansing private memoranda, December 12, 1919, in Lansing papers.

43. This proposal was prepared by Palmer, Glass, and Houston as representatives of the Cabinet and probably was shown to Woodrow Wilson before Green and Lewis arrived, Lansing private memoranda, December 12, 1919, in Lansing papers.

44. New York *World,* December 20, 1919.

45. *United Mine Workers Convention,* (1919), p. 88.

46. Garfield to Lansing, January 13, 1920, Lansing papers; W. B. Wilson to Duncan, January 3, 1921, W. B. Wilson papers.

47. Garfield to Lansing, January 13, 1920; Lansing desk diaries, entry for December 9, 1919, Lansing papers; Blum, *Tumulty,* pp. 222–23.

48. New York *World,* New York *Times,* December 10, 11, 20, 1919, January 6, 1920.

49. N. Buckner to Palmer, November 26, 1919; F. L. Blackman to Palmer, November 13, 1919; L. A. Beck to Palmer, November 11, 1919; R. Chapman to Palmer, November 14, 1919; T. A. Lancaster to Palmer, November 18, 1919, File 16–130–0, Department of Justice Records.

50. Palmer to Walsh, December 22, 1919, Walsh papers.

51. The events leading up to the strike order were reviewed in the *Railway Maintenance of Way Employes Journal,* XXIX, 9–10. Wilson had turned down the railroad workers' first request for more pay after being informed by Palmer that: "Any substantial increase of wages in leading lines of industry at this time would utterly crush the general campaign which the government is waging . . . to reduce the high cost-of-living." Palmer to Wilson, August 22, 1919, Wilson papers.

52. Washington *Post,* February 11, 12, 1920; New York *Times,* New York *World,* February 11–16, 1920.

53. New York *Times,* April 3–9, 1920; New York *World,* April 7–9, 1920; "Memorandum of Conversation between Judge Ames and Mr. Mitchell," April 10, 1920, File 16–145, Department of Justice Records; Henry S. Mitchell, Special Assistant to the Attorney-General, interviewed the strike leaders as part of his investigation of the strike for Ames.

54. New York *Times,* New York *World,* April 11–19, 23, 24, 1920.

55. New York *Times,* April 14, 1920. Foster, temporarily disillusioned with organized labor, was in seclusion in New York, writing a book. Questioned about the strike, he replied: "I have nothing whatsoever to do with it in any shape or form." New York *Times,* April 16, 1920.

56. *Ibid.,* New York *World,* April 21, 1920. "Memorandum of Conversation between Judge Ames and Mr. Mitchell," April 10, 1920, File 16–145, Department of Justice Records.

57. U. S. House Committee on Rules, *Palmer on Charges by Post,* pp. 569–83.

58. New York *Times,* April 17, 1920.

59. Draper, *Roots of American Communism,* pp. 198–99; *One Big Union Monthly,* II, (May, 1920), 13. John Gambs, who has made the most thorough study of the IWW in this period, concluded that the organization had only insignificant influence on the great strikes of 1919–20, except for the Seattle general strike. See his *Decline of the IWW,* p. 133; and Perlman and Taft, *History of Labor,* pp. 452–56.

60. Many lengthy reports from railroads, most of them dated April 13, 1920, are in File 16–145, Department of Justice Records.

61. New York *World,* April 8, 10, 1920.

62. Radical Division, "Report," April 13, 1920, File 16–145, Department of Justice Records.

63. New York *Times,* April 25, 1920.

64. *Locomotive Engineers Journal,* LIV, 538.

65. Palmer, "Three Strikes and Out," p. 267.

66. Murray traces the attempt by business organizations to place the stigma of radicalism on unions in *Red Scare,* pp. 92–93, 164–65, 267–69.

67. New York *Times,* November 2, 8, 1919.

68. Palmer, "Three Strikes and Out," pp. 267–68. He repeated this theme in testimony; see House Committee on Rules, *Palmer on Charges by Post,* pp. 170–84.

69. *Department of Justice Report, 1920*, pp. 35, 44–48; *ibid., 1921*, pp. 18–19; New York *Sun*, December 6, 1919, clipping in Pinchot papers.

70. *Department of Justice Report, 1919*, pp. 53–62.

71. *Ibid.*, 1920, pp. 35–48; 1921, pp. 18–24.

72. Palmer to E. P. Brown, November 10, 1919, Palmer to Ames, November 3, 1919, File 110897, Department of Justice Records.

73. Cummings and McFarland, *Federal Justice*, p. 348.

74. Federal Trade Commission, *Report on Meat Packing Industry*, Colver to Gregory, December 2, 1918; Todd to Clyne, December 5, 1918, File 60–50–0, Department of Justice Records; Simon N. Whitney, *Antitrust Policies, American Experience in Twenty Industries*, I, 36–37.

75. "Memorandum of Conversation in the Attorney-General's Office," June 5, 1919, File 60–50–0, Department of Justice Records. Kresel received a copy of the FTC's final report in April about ten weeks before its publication. Fort to Palmer, April 9, 1919; Kresel to Palmer, April 19, 1919, *ibid.*, File 60–50–0.

76. Federal Trade Commission, *Report on Meat Packing Industry;* "The Packers at the Bar of Public Opinion," *Literary Digest*, LXIII, 21–23.

77. Washington *Post*, July 25, 1919; *Congressional Record*, 66 Cong., 1 Sess. (August 15), pp. 3886–88, 3899–3903.

78. Atwood was a leading attorney in Kansas City, Missouri, popular with labor and reform groups. New York *Times*, August 7, 1919; Ames to Colver, September 4, 1919; Atwood to Palmer, August 30, 1919, File 60–50–0, Department of Justice Records.

79. Yoder to Hardy, October 1, 1919, File 60–50–0, Department of Justice Records, U. S. House Committee on Agriculture, *Meat Packer Hearings*, Part 31, p. 2312.

80. New York *Times*, November 18, 1919.

81. New York *World*, December 18, 19, 1919; House Committee on Agriculture, *Meat Packer Hearings*, pp. 2314–15; Whitney, *Antitrust Policies*, I, 38.

82. *Commercial and Financial Chronicle*, LX, 15; New York *Times*, New York *World*, December 29, 1919.

83. Palmer to Fisher, January 14, 1920, Atwood to Scott, March 27, 1920; Scott to Garvan, March 31, 1920; Form letter to all United States Attorneys ordering them to report to Atwood, File 60–50–0, Department of Justice Records; New York *Times*, August 20, September 1, 18, 29, 1920.

84. "Memorandum to Colonel Goff from Mr. Galloway in *Re United States vs Swift and Company and Others*," April 22, 1921,

File 60–50–0, Department of Justice Records; Cummings and Mc-Farland, *Federal Justice,* p. 349; Whitney, *Antitrust Policies,* I, 38–45; Laidler, *Concentration of Control in American Industry,* pp. 205–13.

85. For Palmer's earlier conflicts with Pinchot, see Chaps. 2 and 7.

86. House Committee on the Judiciary, *Southern Pacific Hearings,* pp. 29–37; Cummings and McFarland, *Federal Justice,* pp. 402–3.

87. House Committee on the Judiciary, *Southern Pacific Hearings,* pp. 21–37; Cummings and McFarland, *Federal Justice,* pp. 403–4.

88. Biggs to Kearful, May 16, 1918; June 7, 1918; Biggs to Gregory, January 31, 1919; File 153972, Department of Justice Records; House Committee on the Judiciary, *Southern Pacific Hearings,* pp. 34, 43–44.

89. Daniels to Palmer, December 6, 1919; Palmer to Daniels, December 9, 1919, File 164672, Department of Justice Records; Daniels Diary, entry for February 14, 1920, Daniels papers. Daniels and Biggs were close friends and long-time political associates. Daniels, *Wilson Era,* p. 37.

90. Pinchot to Palmer, January 9, 1920, File 164672, Department of Justice Records.

91. Pinchot to Wilson, February 3, 1920, Wilson papers.

92. See pp. 19–20.

93. Notation by Tumulty on Pinchot to Wilson, February 3, 1920, Wilson papers.

94. Cummings and McFarland, *Federal Justice,* p. 404; clippings in Pinchot papers.

95. House Committee on the Judiciary, *Southern Pacific Hearings,* pp. 21–44. Cummings and McFarland concluded that the government had no grounds for an appeal; see *Federal Justice,* p. 404.

96. John Ise, who sympathized with Pinchot, nevertheless wrote that the value placed upon the lands by Palmer's critics was "probably a gross exaggeration"; see Ise, *The United States Oil Policy,* p. 292.

XI: THE RED SCARE

1. Washington *Post,* May 7, 1919; Sullivan, *Our Times,* VI, 169; *Nation,* CX, 510–11.

2. Murray, *Red Scare,* especially Chap. 1; Higham, *Strangers in the Land,* especially Chap. 8; Blum, "Nativism, Anti-Radicalism, and the Foreign Scare, 1917–1920," *Midwest Journal,* III, 46–53.

3. Barham to Palmer, October 27, 1919, File 202600, Department of Justice Records; unidentified correspondent to McAdoo, February 10, 1920, McAdoo papers.

4. Higham, *Strangers in the Land,* p. 227; Murray, *Red Scare,* p. 16.

5. Schlesinger, *Crisis of the Old Order,* p. 43.

6. A superb account of the postwar nativistic movement is Higham, *Strangers in the Land,* Chaps. 8, 9.

7. For a discussion see Chap. 1. The district's representative in Congress for almost thirty years has been Francis E. Walter, an archenemy of radicals and of immigration from southern and eastern Europe.

8. Swarthmore *Phoenix,* XI, 94–95. Palmer sometimes boasted of ancestors who came to this country with William Penn.

9. *Congressional Record,* 62 Cong., 2 Sess. (May 29, 1912), p. 7391. See also *ibid.,* (January 27, 1912), pp. 1343, 1349.

10. House Committee on Rules, *Palmer on Charges by Post,* p. 27.

11. Palmer, "The Case Against the Reds," *Forum,* LXVII, 175.

12. Washington *Post,* February 3, 5, 6, 1919; New York *World,* January 11, 12, 1919.

13. Claghorn, *The Immigrant's Day in Court,* pp. 336–57; "Skimming the Melting Pot," *Literary Digest,* IX, 16; "The Deportations," *Survey,* XLI, 722; New York *World,* February 11, 12, 1919.

14. Hough, *The Web,* is an authorized history of the APL. Gregory, at first, called upon the League to "carry on steadfastly" after the Armistice. Gregory to National Directors, APL, November 15, 1918, File 186751, Department of Justice Records.

15. New York *Times,* April 1, 2, 1919; Cleveland *News,* April 23, 1919, clipping in File 186751, Department of Justice Records.

16. Cox to Palmer, March 13, 1919; Palmer to Cox, March 19, 1919, File 186751, Department of Justice Records.

17. Gregory to Wilson, March 1, 1919; John Hanna, "Memorandum for the Attorney-General," September 5, 1919; Palmer to all United States Attorneys, March 10, 1919, all File 197009, Department of Justice Records; mimeographed statement on the Department's review of cases, *ibid.,* April 11, 1919, File 9–12–394. Gregory was prepared to suggest clemency for fifty-two of these prisoners when he left office.

18. New York *Times,* April 12, 1919.

19. Westenhaven to Wertz, March 8, 1919; O'Brian to Westenhaven, March 19, 1919; Westenhaven to Palmer, March 21, 1919,

R.G. 60, File 77175, Department of Justice Records. Westenhaven changed his mind in October, 1920 about two months after Palmer finally recommended clemency. Shannon, *Socialist Party,* pp. 160–61.

20. Supplemental memorandum by Bettman, March 25, 1919, R.G. 60, File 77175, Department of Justice Records. Bettman had made a similar recommendation to Gregory, *ibid.*, memorandum by Bettman, February 10, 1919, R.G. 60, File 77175. For a tribute to Bettman's record on civil liberties, see O'Brian, "Alfred Bett-man," *Journal of the American Institute of Planners,* XI, 5.

21. O'Brian to G. H. Harris, April 8, 1919, R.G. 60, File 77175, Department of Justice Records. Bettman and O'Brian's activities as defenders of civil liberties in the Justice Department and after their retirement are discussed in Chafee, *Free Speech in the United States,* pp. 67, 101, 147, 442, 470.

22. Wilson to Tumulty, March 26, 1919, R.G. 60, File 77175, Department of Justice Records; Tumulty to Wilson, April 4, 1919, Tumulty notes.

23. Palmer to Wilson, July 30, 1919; Wilson to Palmer, August 1, 1919, Wilson papers. For Wilson's more generous sentiments, Wilson to Gregory, November 20, 1918, Gregory papers; Wilson to Sayre, March 3, 1919; Wilson to Palmer, August 4, 29, 1919; and Wilson to Spargo, August 29, 1919, Wilson papers.

24. Shannon, *Socialist Party,* pp. 160–6.

25. "Minutes of a Conference between the Attorney-General and Committee Elected by the National Convention of the Social-ist Party," May 14, 1920, p. 18. File 77175, Department of Justice Records. For further evidence on this point, Higham, *Strangers in the Land,* pp. 207–9, 223–28; Hilton, "Public Opinion and Civil Liberties in Wartime, 1917–1919," *Southwestern Social Science Quarterly,* XXVIII, 208–11.

26. Johnson, "American Civil Liberties Union," unpublished doctoral dissertation, pp. 258–59.

27. D. J. Pickle to Palmer, April 10, 1919, R.G. 60, File 77175, Department of Justice Records, and other letters from the public in this file. Case histories of 197 prisoners not recommended for pardon show that almost all were radicals. Box 57, Pardon Attorney papers, Department of Justice Records.

28. Johnson, "American Civil Liberties Union," pp. 265–66.

29. New York *Times,* Washington *Post,* May 1, 1919; Murray, *Red Scare,* pp. 69–73.

30. New York *Times,* Washington *Post,* May 2, 1919; Murray, *Red Scare,* pp. 73–77, gives a good description of some of the riots.

31. New York *Times,* May 2, 1919.   32. *Ibid.,* May 4, 1919.

33. *Ibid.,* June 4; Washington *Post,* June 4, 5, 1919; Roosevelt,

Affectionately, F.D.R., p. 59; Freidel, *Roosevelt: The Ordeal,* p. 29. The *Times* interviewed Roosevelt within hours of the explosion and quoted his account of the incident.

34. Freidel, *Roosevelt: The Ordeal,* p. 29. When James failed his Groton entrance exams in June, 1920, he came up with the ingenuous alibi that "I was still upset because of the excitement . . . when the anarchists tried to blow up Attorney-General Palmer." Roosevelt, *Affectionately, F.D.R.*, p. 112.

35. Murray, *Red Scare,* pp. 77–79.

36. Senate Committee on the Judiciary, *Charges of Illegal Practices,* p. 580.

37. New York *Times,* June 4, July 17, 1919; *Department of Justice Report,* 1919, pp. 6–7, 12.

38. *Department of Justice Report,* 1919, p. 15; *ibid.,* 1920, p. 172; Whitehead, *FBI Story,* p. 46.

39. Washington *Post,* June 27, 1919.

40. *Ibid.,* July 3, 1919. Numerous clues to the culprit (or culprits') identity were reported in the daily newspapers, for example, the Washington *Post,* June 4–18, but none indicated a link between the bombings and the Communists or the German government. Late in 1920, Flynn obtained what he believed was conclusive proof that the criminals were Italian anarchists. Flynn to Daugherty, April 4, 1922, File 202600, Section 5, Department of Justice Records.

41. New York *Times,* April 25, 1919. Also see p. 88.

42. Senate Committee on the Judiciary, *Charges of Illegal Practices,* p. 455.

43. Draper, *Roots of American Communism,* p. 224.

44. Senate Committee on the Judiciary, *Charges of Illegal Practices,* p. 302.

45. Draper, *Roots of American Communism,* pp. 150–53, 161–63, 198–200, 237–41, 244–45, 294, 312–14; Murray, *Red Scare,* pp. 106–10; Saposs, *Left Wing Unionism,* pp. 49–50. For an interesting analysis of the reasons for the negative response of American workers to radical propaganda, written for an IWW periodical, see *One Big Union Monthly,* I, 27.

46. Davis, *The Russian Immigrant,* pp. 114–18; Claghorn, *The Immigrant's Day in Court,* pp. 363–73; House Committee on Rules, *Palmer on Charges by Post,* p. 166.

47. Gambs, *Decline of the IWW,* p. 133; Perlman and Taft, *History of Labor,* p. 431; Saposs, *Left Wing Unionism,* pp. 152–57.

48. Lansing, "Spread of Bolshevism," memorandum of July 26, 1919; Lansing, "Tendency toward Communistic Ideas," memorandum of September 1, 1919, Lansing papers.

49. New York *Times,* February 16, October 16, 1919.

50. *Ibid.*, February 19, 1919; Washington *Post*, February 21, 1919. As late as April, 1920, Wilson agreed with Palmer, during a Cabinet meeting, that the nationwide rail walkout had been caused by the Communists and the IWW; Daniels diary entry for April 14, 1920, Daniels papers.

51. "Address of President Wilson, September 4–September 15, 1919," 66 Cong., 1 Sess., Senate Document 120, p. 60; See also New York *World*, September 27, 1919; Scheiber, *Wilson Administration*, 55–56.

52. Washington *Post*, May 7, 1919.   53. *Ibid.*, June 18, 19, 1919.
54. New York *World*, June 19, 1919.

55. *Ibid.*, June 27, 1919. All evidence indicates that there was little communication, in mid-1919, between American Communists and the new Bolshevik regime in Russia. Nor is there reason to believe that sizable amounts of Russian money were sent here to subsidize American Communists in 1919. When the Russian Trade Delegation in Washington ran desperately short of funds, the Foreign Commissariat, which had no available foreign exchange, sent crown jewels, worth as much as $250,000. During 1919, these traveled back and forth between here and Europe, but were never used to assist the Communist cause in America. The only other large sum of money known to have been sent to the United States was approximately $20,000, given to Louis Fraina by the Comintern in December, 1919, and Fraina absconded with some of this. Draper, *Roots of American Communism*, pp. 150–53, 161–63, 237–41, 244–45, 294.

56. Washington *Post*, June 19, 1919.

57. Draper, *Roots of American Communism*, p. 167.

58. Claghorn, "Ellis Island's Gates Ajar," *Literary Digest*, LXIII, 17.

59. New York *World*, June 19, 1919; Washington *Post*, June 5, 1919.

60. New York *Times*, New York *World*, Washington *Post*, July 3–5, 1919.

61. Washington *Post*, July 20–23, 28–31; New York *Times*, July 31, August 1, 1919. In November, 1919, Palmer released evidence of radical propaganda aimed at Negroes. New York *Times*, November 23, 1919.

62. New York *World*, July 27, 1919; New York *Times*, November 10, 1919; *Literary Digest*, LXIII, 15.

63. New York *Times*, October 16, 1919.

64. For an account of the change in public opinion on this subject, see Higham, *Strangers in the Land*, Chap. 11.

65. New York *Times,* October 17, 1919.

66. Braman to Woodrow Wilson, November 11, 1919; Beck to Palmer, November 25, 1919; Starkweather to Palmer, November 15, 1919, File 202600, Department of Justice Records.

67. *Congressional Record,* 66 Cong., 1 Sess. (October 14, 1919), pp. 6865, 6869.

68. *Ibid.,* p. 7063.

69. *Ibid.,* p. 6869; Senate Committee on Education and Labor, *Steel Strike Investigation,* p. 945.

70. Senate Committee on the Judiciary, *Charges of Illegal Practices,* p. 580.

71. Palmer, "Great Work of the Alien Property Custodian," *American Law Review,* LIII, 51–52.

XII: THE PALMER RAIDS

1. Higham, *Strangers in the Land,* p. 227.

2. House Committee on Rules, *Palmer on Charges by Post,* pp. 166–68; Whitehead, *F.B.I. Story,* pp. 53–54. Judge Hazel administered the oath of office to Theodore Roosevelt in 1904, after President McKinley was assassinated in Buffalo.

3. Claghorn, *Immigrant's Day in Court,* pp. 316, 328–34, 339–41.

4. Washington *Post,* June 18, 19, 1919; New York *World,* June 19, 27, 1919; Senate Committee on the Judiciary, *Charges of Illegal Practices,* p. 403.

5. *Ibid.,* pp. 7, 409; Post, *Deportations Delirium,* pp. 56, 77–78; W. B. Wilson to Duncan, April 22, 1920, W. B. Wilson papers.

6. Davis, *Russian Immigrant,* pp. 115–6; House Committee on Immigration and Naturalization, *IWW Deportation Cases, Hearings, 1920,* p. 79.

7. Davis, *Russian Immigrant,* pp. 114–18; Claghorn, *Immigrant's Day in Court,* pp. 363–73.

8. New York *Times,* New York *World,* New York Evening *Post,* November 8, 1919. For the Justice Department's side of the story, with accompanying affidavits, see House Committee on Rules, *Palmer on Charges by Post,* pp. 100–2. For testimony about violence by the raiders, Claghorn, *Immigrant's Day in Court,* pp. 418–35; National Popular Government League, *To the American People,* pp. 16–23; Murray, *Red Scare,* pp. 196–97.

9. New York *Times,* November 8, 1919; Claghorn, *Immigrant's Day in Court,* pp. 395–96, 405; National Popular Government League, *To the American People,* pp. 12–16. Ethelbert Stewart, "Confidential Report on Hartford Connecticut to the Assistant Sec-

retary of Labor," March 20, 1920, File 167/642, Department of Labor Records.

10. Shorr to Palmer, November 13, 1919; Hoover to Creighton, December 4, 1919, Department of Justice Records.

11. For samples of press opinion, see "Shipping Lenin's Friends to Him," *Literary Digest*, LXIV, 15; Murray, *Red Scare*, pp. 198, 208–9; New York *Times*, November 16, 1919.

12. See Chaps. 9, 10.

13. New York *Times*, New York *World*, November 21, 1919.

14. Hoover to Caminetti, December 17, 1919, File 203557, Department of Justice Records.

15. Senate Committee on the Judiciary, *Charges of Illegal Practices*, pp. 60–61, 397–401. When Hoover was questioned before the Senate Judiciary Committee in January, 1921, he declared: "Now, in so far as the Department of Justice is concerned in the change of Rule 22, it had no part in it whatsoever. The rule was changed at the instance of the immigration officers" *Ibid.*, p. 649.

16. Draper, *Roots of American Communism*, pp. 179, 188–89. Jacob Spolansky, head of the Chicago office of the Bureau of Investigation, related that the final decision to round up members of the two parties was made at a meeting of Justice and Labor Department officials in November, Spolansky, a Russian immigrant who knew many Communists, says he suggested that only the party leaders be arrested, but he was overruled. See Spolansky, *Communist Trail*, p. 15.

17. Caminetti to Hoover, December 24, 1919, Hoover to Caminetti, December 24, 1919, File 205492, Department of Justice Records.

18. Caminetti to Hoover, December 24, 1919, Hoover to Caminetti, December 24, 1919, File 205492, Department of Justice Records.

19. Hoover to Caminetti, December 24, 1919, File 205492, Department of Justice Records.

20. Senate Committee on the Judiciary, *Charges of Illegal Practices*, p. 35.

21. Post, *Deportations Delirium*, pp. 77–78.

22. *Ibid.;* Senate Committee on the Judiciary, *Charges of Illegal Practices*, p. 403.

23. Post, *Deportations Delirium*, p. 78; W. B. Wilson to Palmer, December 30, 1919, W. B. Wilson papers.

24. Wilson was preoccupied at the time with the serious illnesses of his wife and mother. W. B. Wilson to Duncan, April 22, 1920, January 3, 1921, W. B. Wilson papers.

25. Post, *Deportations Delirium,* pp. 68–69.

26. Alexander, *Rights of Aliens,* pp. 34–35, 75–76, 95.

27. House Committee on Rules, *Palmer on Charges by Post,* pp. 213–15; Senate Committee on the Judiciary, *Charges of Illegal Practices,* pp. 12–14. According to Burke's instructions, all communications from agents during the raids were to be addressed to Hoover. Hoover has denied that he had any other role in the round-ups than this passive one of liaison man. Knebel, "Cop and the Man," *Look,* XIX, 33.

28. Senate Committee on the Judiciary, *Charges of Illegal Practices,* p. 19.

29. National Popular Government League, *To the American People,* pp. 37–42, 46. The Department's undercover agents, about whom much was made in subsequent investigations, seem to have been innocent of charges that they acted as agents provocateurs. House Committee on Rules, *Palmer on Charges by Post,* pp. 49–54, 213.

30. For extended descriptions of the raids, Claghorn, *Immigrant's Day in Court,* Chap. 10; Murray, *Red Scare,* Chap. 13; Chafee, *Free Speech in the United States,* pp. 204–17; National League for Popular Government, *To the American People,* pp. 3–56; Post, *Deportations Delirium,* pp. 91–147; Panunzio, *Deportation Cases of 1919–1920.* Newspaper clippings about the raids, from papers throughout the country, are collected in scrapbooks in the Papers of the American Civil Liberties Union, Princeton University, cited as ACLU papers.

31. Senate Committee on the Judiciary, *Charges of Illegal Practices,* p. 58; House Committee on Immigration and Naturalization, *Administration of Immigration Laws,* p. 7.

32. New York *Times,* January 3, 1920; Senate Committee on the Judiciary, *Charges of Illegal Practices,* pp. 470, 493, 500; *Administration of Immigration Laws,* pp. 6–7; *To the American People,* pp. 51–52; Johnson, "The Political Career of A. Mitchell Palmer," *Pennsylvania History,* XXV, 359.

33. Knebel, "Cop and the Man," *Look,* XIX, 33.

34. New York *World,* January 4, 1920; Panunzio, *Deportation Cases of 1919–1920,* p. 81; Stewart to Post, March 20, April 5, 6, 1920, W. B. Wilson papers; Chafee, *Free Speech in the United States,* pp. 207–8; Murray, *Red Scare,* pp. 213–15; Claghorn, *Immigrant's Day in Court,* pp. 448–50. The quotation is from Stewart's report of April 5, 1920, File 167–642, Department of Labor Records.

35. Stewart to W. B. Wilson, June 1, 1920, File 176–255, Department of Labor Records; Stewart to Post, April 5, 1920, W. B.

Wilson papers; Spolansky, *Communist Trail in America,* p. 16; Knebel, "Cop and the Man," *Look,* XIX, 33, quoting Hoover; Claghorn, *Immigrant's Day in Court,* pp. 449–50; Post, *Deportations Delirium.*

36. For letters about the raids to the Justice Department, see File 202600, especially letters 130–329, Department of Justice Records; "Extent of the Bolshevik Infection Here," *Literary Digest,* LXIV, 13–15; "Deporting the Communist Party," *Literary Digest,* LXIV, 18; New York *Times,* January 5, 1920.

37. Lansing desk diary, entry for January 6, 1920, Lansing papers. W. B. Wilson was absent; but the Labor Department had issued the 3,000 arrest warrants and Wilson could hardly have criticized the mass round-ups on the basis of facts known January 6.

38. For Kane's testimony about his objections, and copies of his letters, see Senate Committee on the Judiciary, *Charges of Illegal Practices,* pp. 295–352.

39. "Extent of the Bolshevik Infection Here," *Literary Digest,* XLIV, 13–15; *ibid.,* "Deporting the Communist Party," p. 18; "Deporting a Political Party," *New Republic,* XXI, 186; "Sowing the Wind to Reap the Whirlwind," *Nation,* CX, 94; White, *Forty Years,* pp. 317–18.

40. Post to W. B. Wilson, October 5, 1918, W. B. Wilson papers; House Committee on Rules, *Investigation of Post.* Post gave the Rules Committee a brief summary of his political ideas and a history of his political associations. *Ibid.,* pp. 242–45.

41. *Ibid.,* pp. 4, 150–52.   42. *Ibid.,* p. 80.

43. Post, *Deportations Delirium,* especially pp. 159–60, 177–78, 180–85, 188–89. The more recent decision on illegally taken evidence was handed down by Judge G. M. Bourquin of the Montana District Court in the case of John Jackson. It is reprinted in full in House Committee on Rules, *Investigation of Post,* pp. 145–47. For precedents, see Alexander, *Rights of Aliens,* pp. 60–76. Post suggested to Palmer that he appeal Bourquin's decision so that the matter could be settled finally by the Supreme Court, but the Attorney-General was content to let it drop. Post to Palmer, March 30, 1920, W. B. Wilson papers.

44. Post, "Report of Principal Activities of the Assistant Secretary during the absence of the Secretary," April 14, 1920, W. B. Wilson papers; Post to Caminetti, March 18, 1920; Post to Caminetti, March 22, 1920, File 167–642, Department of Labor Records; House Committee on Rules *Investigation of Post,* pp. 78–79; Post, *Deportations Delirium,* pp. 193–200. Many of Post's recommendations were based on reports from the various detention centers by

Ethelbert Stewart, whom he sent out as an investigator on March 11. Post, "To All Officers and Employees of the Bureau of Immigration and Immigration Service in the Department of Labor," March 11, 1920, File 167–642, Department of Labor Records.

45. Ex parte Chin Loy You (1915), 223 F. 833; House Committee on Rules *Investigation of Post,* pp. 73–78; Senate Committee on the Judiciary, *Charges of Illegal Practices,* p. 561; Alexander, *Rights of Aliens,* p. 75. Post said his release of aliens who were denied the opportunity for counsel was in accordance with Judge Bourquin's decision in the Jackson case; but Bourquin did not base his opinion on that factor. House Committee on Rules *Investigation of Post,* pp. 145–47. William B. Wilson, finally stiffened by his assistant's fortitude, decided on May 5, with the aid of some tortured reasoning, that unlike the Communist Party, the Communist Labor Party did not fall under the deportation statute. Ironically, leaders of the two Communist parties were still arguing about which was more devoted to the world-wide proletarian revolution and the Third International. Draper, *Roots of American Communism,* pp. 179, 187.

46. Pittsburgh *Post,* May 4, 1920, clipping in the Palmer scrapbook now in the possession of Kurt Wimer, Stroudsburg, cited as Palmer scrapbook, 1920. New York *Times,* February 29, 1920; Lansing Private Memoranda, entry for April 14, 1920, Lansing papers; Post, *Deportations Delirium,* pp. 223–28.

47. New York *Times,* January 23, 1920; Hoover to Caminetti, April 19, 22, 30, 1920, File 202600, Department of Justice Records. There are a considerable number of similar messages from Hoover to Caminetti in File 202600. Also see Files 203557, 205492, 207155.

48. House Committee on Rules *Investigation of Post,* pp. 3–4, 6.

49. Ibid., especially pp. 84–231; evidence in the Truss case is printed on pp. 84–137.

50. House Committee on Rules, *Palmer on Charges by Post,* pp. 187–89, 583–614.

51. *Ibid.,* p. 186; Murray, *Red Scare,* p. 252. The headlines quoted are from the Pittsburgh *Post,* April 29, 1920; Palmer scrapbook, 1920. Similar lines could have been taken from almost any other newspaper in the country on April 29, 30, and May 1, 1920.

52. New York *Times,* May 1, 1920; Boston *Transcript,* April 30, 1920, facsimile in Weeks, ed., *Commonwealth vs. Sacco and Vanzetti;* Murray, *Red Scare,* pp. 252–53.

53. New York *Times,* May 2, 1920; Washington *Post,* May 2, 1920; Chicago *Tribune,* May 4, 1920, clipping Palmer scrapbook, 1920.

54. Daniels, *Wilson Era,* p. 546. There is no other authority for this statement, which appears in Daniels diary as a paraphrase rather than as a quotation of Wilson's words. Daniels was extremely angry with Palmer at the time, and it is possible that he misinterpreted what the President said. Daniels diary, entries for March 25, April 14, 1920.

55. New York *World,* February 19, 1919.

56. National Popular Government League, *To the American People,* pp. 42–56; Senate Committee on the Judiciary, *Charges of Illegal Practices,* pp. 38–82, 181, 196. The New York *World* commented on June 2: "Far more weighty than any opinions expressed by the Assistant Secretary of Labor . . . were the criticisms uttered from the bench [by Anderson]."

57. De Silver to Le Sueur, April 20, 1920, ACLU papers; Senate Committee on the Judiciary, *Charges of Illegal Practices,* pp. 167, 199, 452; National Popular Government League, *To the American People,* p. 9.

58. *Ibid.,* p. 3.

59. Hughes, "Some Observations on Legal Education and Democratic Process," in two addresses delivered before the alumni of the Harvard Law School (at Cambridge, June 21, 1920), p. 24; Mason, *Stone,* pp. 112–13.

60. On the business groups, see Higham, *Strangers in the Land,* p. 232.

61. New York *Times,* February 1, 1920; Higham, *Strangers in the Land,* pp. 257–58.

62. New York *Times,* February 1, 1920; Higham, *Strangers in the Land,* p. 232.

63. House Committee on Rules, *Palmer on Charges by Post,* p. 19.

64. For evidence of Palmer's high prestige, see Philadelphia *Public Ledger,* April 3, 1920; House Committee on Rules, *Palmer on Charges by Post,* pp. 5–186, 213; House Committee on the Judiciary, *Sugar Hearings,* p. 176.

65. National League for Popular Government, *To the American People,* pp. 64–67; House Committee on Rules, *Palmer on Charges by Post,* pp. 19, 29–30, 155; Hoover to Garvan, April 5, 1920, Department of Justice Records.

66. For a psychological study of group adherence to such beliefs, despite strong contradictory evidence, see Festinger, *et al., When Prophecy Fails,* especially pp. 3–28, 216–29.

67. The quotations are from Palmer's testimony in rebuttal to Post's charges, given before the Rules Committee on June 1. House Committee on Rules, *Palmer on Charges by Post,* pp. 6, 51, 73, 156.

68. *Ibid.,* pp. 59, 76, 10–12.

69. New York *Times,* March 29, June 19, November 16, 1919; Palmer to Aswell, July 25, 1919, File 202600, Department of Justice Records.

70. Murray, *Red Scare,* pp. 231–35; New York *Times,* November 16, 1919.

71. New York *World,* January 4, 5, 1920. Newspaper opinion on the sedition acts was surveyed in, "Alien and Sedition Bills of 1920," *Literary Digest,* LXIV, 11–13.

72. "Two Infamous Measures," *Nation,* CX, 132; Claghorn, "Alien and Sedition in the New Year," *Survey,* XLIII, 423.

73. House Committee on the Judiciary, *Sedition Hearings,* p. 6; New York *World,* January 5, 1920, New York *Times,* January 23, 1920.

74. House Committee on Rules, *Rule Making in Order the Consideration of S. 3317, Hearings; Brotherhood of Locomotive Firemen and Enginemen's Magazine,* LXXIX, 7–8, 12–13; Gompers, "The Graham-Rice Sedition Bill would Manufacture Law-Breakers," *American Federationist,* XXVII, 138–39.

75. For Palmer's Testimony, see House Committee on the Judiciary, *Sedition Hearings,* pp. 6–34. For analysis of the Davey Bill, see *Congressional Record,* 66 Cong., 2 Sess. (January 23, 1920), pp. 1930–31.

76. House Committee on the Judiciary, *Sedition Hearings,* pp. 23, 173–266.

77. Palmer's subsequent awareness of his remissness is indicated by the fact that in February, 1920, he ordered Justice Department agents assigned to prohibition cases not to make arrests or seize evidence without warrants. Action taken without warrants, he pointed out, was unconstitutional. New York *Times,* February 27, 1920.

XIII: THE CAMPAIGN FOR THE PRESIDENCY—AND AFTERWARD

1. Sullivan, "Your Move Democracy," *Colliers,* LXV (1920), 9.

2. Conversation of the author with Homer Cummings; Funk to McAdoo, January 26, 1920, McAdoo papers.

3. H. C. Evans to E. T. Meredith, February 2, 1920; W. D. Boyce to McAdoo, February 4, 1920; E. T. Meredith to McAdoo, February 6, 1920, McAdoo papers; Pittsburgh *Post,* March 16, 18, clippings in Palmer scrapbook, New York *Times,* June 23, July 18; New York *World,* July 1, 1920.

4. See Chap. 8.

5. Funk to McAdoo, March 28, 1920; K. Sullivan to McAdoo, April 3, 1920, McAdoo papers.

6. Warner, "Bartering for the Presidency," *Nation*, CXV, 577–79. Spellacy's reports were turned over to former Assistant Attorney-General Bielaski by Spellacy's secretary, who had formerly worked for Bielaski. Bielaski gave or sold them to the Republican national committee, which was prepared to use them against Palmer had he been nominated in 1920. The letters were published in 1922, when Spellacy was the Democratic candidate for Senator in Connecticut.

7. Sullivan, "Your Move, Democracy," Collier's, LXV, 9.

8. New York *Times,* February 6, 1920.

9. Byrnes, *All in One Lifetime* p. 48; Atlanta *Constitution,* April 6, 1920, Palmer scrapbook, 1920.

10. Philadelphia *Public Ledger,* March 2; Washington *Post,* March 24, 1920. Pittsburgh *Post,* February, March 2, 1920, clipping in Palmer scrapbook, 1920.

11. Sullivan, "Your Move, Democracy," *Colliers,* LXV, 18.

12. Bridge to McAdoo, February 9; Brewster to McAdoo, April 19, McAdoo papers; New York *Times,* May 3, 9, June 28, 1920.

13. New York *Times,* May 19; Philadelphia *Public Ledger,* June 16, 1920.

14. Cleveland *Plain Dealer,* June 22, 1920, clipping in Palmer scrapbook, 1920.

15. New York *Times,* January 9, 1920; Atlanta *Constitution,* April 7, 1920, clipping in Palmer scrapbook, 1920; *Proceedings, Democratic National Convention, 1920,* pp. 113–18.

16. New York *Times,* March 1, 3, 5, 1920; Washington *Post,* March 5, 1920; Philadelphia *Public Ledger,* March 7, 1920.

17. Atlanta *Constitution,* April 7, 1920, clipping in Palmer scrapbook, 1920.

18. Daniels diary, entry for April 20, 1920, Daniels papers.

19. Philadelphia *Public Ledger,* June 16, 1920; Washington *Post,* June 26, 1920.

20. New York *Times,* January 11, 1920.

21. This incident is reported, in slightly different forms, in House diary entry for January 31, 1920, House papers; Daniels diary, entry for February 27, 1920, Daniels papers; Funk to Roper, February 27, 1920, McAdoo papers.

22. Tumulty, *Wilson, as I Know Him,* pp. 495–96.

23. Grayson, *Wilson,* pp. 116–17.

24. For an astute analysis of the 1920 campaign, see Bagby, "Progressivism's Debacle, the Election of 1920," unpublished doctoral dissertation.

25. Hull, *Memoirs,* I, 150; Palmer to Tumulty, September 2, 1932, Tumulty Notes.

26. *Brotherhood of Locomotive Firemen and Enginemen's Magazine,* LXVIII, 3; New York *World,* May 7, 1920. Healy referred to the current campaign for "open shop" laws, in which Palmer took no part.

27. Maurer to De Silver, November 13, 1919, ACLU papers; Philadelphia *Public Ledger,* May 12, 1920.

28. Gompers, "The Broken Pledge," *American Federationist,* XXVII, 41–50; New York *Times,* November 11, 1919; Gompers, "Labor's Protest Against a Rampant Tragedy," *American Federationist,* XXVII, 526.

29. House Committee on the Judiciary, *Sedition Hearings,* pp. 233–35.

30. New York *Times,* February 9, 1920; *American Federationist,* XXVII, 233–35; Lorwin, *AF of L,* pp. 193–94; Nathan Fine, *Labor and Farmer Parties,* pp. 383–89. The platform of the National Labor Party demanded Palmer's impeachment; New York *Times,* May 30, 31, 1920.

31. New York *Times,* June 30, 1920.

32. Funk to McAdoo, April 5, 1920, conveying the statement of E. Moore of Ohio, Cox's campaign manager, McAdoo papers; Seattle *Times,* April 1, 1920, clipping in Palmer scrapbook, 1920.

33. Cleveland *Plain Dealer,* Cincinnati *Enquirer,* Atlanta *Constitution,* April 7, 1920, Palmer scrapbook, 1920; Hannah to McAdoo, April 7, 1920, McAdoo papers.

34. Atlanta *Constitution,* April 11, 1920, clipping in Palmer scrapbook, 1920.

35. On these themes in the campaign of Palmer's Georgia supporters, see *ibid.,* March 30, 1920.

36. Woodward, *Watson,* pp. 447, 464, 468.

37. Atlanta *Constitution,* March 30, April 11, 1920, clippings in Palmer scrapbook, 1920; Grantham, *Hoke Smith,* pp. 347 49; Woodward, *Watson,* p. 469.

38. The Secretary of the Michigan Democratic State Committee acknowledged the absence of effort on behalf of Palmer in a letter to the New York *Times,* April 8, 1920.

39. Atlanta *Constitution,* April 23, 1920, clipping in Palmer scrapbook, 1920.

40. *Literary Digest,* LXV, 21. McAdoo finished far ahead of the other Democratic contenders in this poll. He was followed by Wilson, Edward, Byran, Cox, Clark, and Palmer, in that order.

41. Palmer to All United States Attorneys, June 17, 1920; Palmer to Kelly, June 22, 1920, File 181092–231, Department of Justice Records; New York *Times,* June 9, 10, 15, 18, 1920.

42. According to the AF of L, Harding's record in three Con-

gresses showed ten votes unfavorable to labor, seven favorable, one paired unfavorably. *International Steam Engineer,* XXXVII, 181.

43. Pittsburgh *Post,* June 24, 1920, clipping in Palmer scrapbook, 1920; Hale, "Another Convention—the Democratic," *Nation,* CXI, 69–70; New York *Times,* June 23, 26, 1920.

44. New York *World,* Philadelphia *Public Ledger,* June 18; Washington *Post,* June 19; New York *Times,* June 19, 20, 1920.

45. Washington *Post,* New York *Times,* June 24, 1920.

46. McLean to McAdoo, June 28; McAdoo to McLean, June 29; McAdoo to Adams, June 28; McAdoo to Mason, June 28; McAdoo to Wilson, June 29; McAdoo to Mack, June 29, 1920, McAdoo papers.

47. Cleveland *Plain Dealer,* June 22, 1920, clipping in Palmer scrapbook, 1920.

48. New York *Times,* June 30, 1920.

49. Connor, *Sidelights, Democratic National Convention,* p. 8.

50. Philadelphia *Public Ledger,* June 16; New York *Times,* New York *World,* June 26–28; San Francisco *Chronicle,* July 1–3, 1920.

51. *Proceedings, Democratic National Convention, 1920,* pp. 270–71.

52. *Ibid.,* pp. 272–396.

53. *Ibid.,* pp. 398–405; San Francisco *Chronicle,* July 6, 1920.

54. New York *Times,* October 13, 1920; Blum, *Tumulty,* p. 249.

55. Philadelphia *Record,* June 22, 1920, Palmer scrapbook, 1920; Keller, *History of Monroe County,* p. 389; conversations of the author with Frank Stackhouse and Hal H. Harris; Philadelphia *Public Ledger,* April 10, 1920.

56. New York *Times,* September 13, 1924, November 1, 1928; conversations of the author with Mrs. A. Mitchell Palmer.

57. Roosevelt to Palmer, September 5, 1924; and attached calling card, Group 16, Box 13, *papers of Franklin D. Roosevelt,* Hyde Park, New York, cited as F.D.R. papers; Palmer to Roosevelt, November 10, 1928, Box 648, Papers of the Democratic National Committee, Hyde Park, New York, cited as Democratic national committee papers.

58. Freidel, *F. D. Roosevelt: The Triumph,* p. 230.

59. Hull, *Memoirs,* I, 150–51; New York *Times,* June 21, 1932; conversations of the author with Mrs. A. Mitchell Palmer.

60. *Barron's,* XII, 4; *Commercial and Financial Chronicle,* CXXXV, 1–2.

61. Palmer to J. D. Stern, August 6, 1932, attached to Palmer to Roosevelt, August 9, 1932, Box 665, Democratic national committee papers.

62. Conversations of the author with Mrs. A. Mitchell Palmer; Palmer to Mrs. Roosevelt, July 8, 1932; Palmer to Stern, August 6, 1932, Box 655, Democratic National Committee Papers; Palmer to Roosevelt, March 30, 1933, Group 13, File 239, FDR papers. Despite his disenchantment with the New Deal, Palmer at Roosevelt's request, was preparing to write the 1936 Democratic platform when he died. This time, however, his co-workers were to be New Dealers Thomas Corcoran and Benjamin Cohen rather than Cummings, Glass and the other conservative Senators who had helped him in 1932. Scott to Cummings, June 18, 1936, Group 13, File 239, FDR papers. Guffey, *Seventy Years,* p. 42; Ickes, *First Thousand Days,* I, 563.

BIBLIOGRAPHY

MANUSCRIPT COLLECTIONS

The Papers of the Alien Property Custodian, National Archives.
The Papers of the American Civil Liberties Union, Princeton University Library.
The Papers of Warren Worth Bailey, Princeton University Library.
The Papers of Newton D. Baker, Library of Congress.
The Papers of Ray Stannard Baker, Library of Congress and Princeton University Library.
The Papers of John H. Bankhead, Alabama State Department of Archives and History.
Notes of John Blum on the Papers of Joseph Tumulty, Yale University Library.
The Papers of William Jennings Bryan, Library of Congress.
The Papers of Albert S. Burleson, Library of Congress.
The Papers of Josephus Daniels, Library of Congress.
The Papers of the Democratic National Committee, Hyde Park, New York.
The Papers of Thomas Watt Gregory, Library of Congress.
The Papers of Edward M. House, Yale University Library.
The Papers of the Department of Justice, National Archives.
The Papers of the Department of Labor, National Archives.
The Papers of Robert Lansing, Library of Congress.
The Papers of William G. McAdoo, Library of Congress.
The Papers of Vance C. McCormick, Yale University Library.
The Papers of Roland Morris, Library of Congress.
The Papers of Gifford Pinchot, Library of Congress.
The Papers of Frank L. Polk, Yale University Library.
The Papers of Louis F. Post, Library of Congress.
The Papers of John Quinn, New York Public Library.
The Papers of Franklin Delano Roosevelt, Hyde Park, New York.
The Papers of Oscar W. Underwood, Alabama State Department of Archives and History.

The Papers of Thomas J. Walsh, Library of Congress.
The Papers of William B. Wilson, Historical Society of Pennsylvania.
The Papers of Woodrow Wilson, Library of Congress and Princeton University Library.

U. S. GOVERNMENT DOCUMENTS *

Addresses of President Wilson, September 4–September 15, 1919. U. S. Senate Document No. 120. 1919.
Alien Property Custodian. *Bulletin of Information.*
—— *Prospectus of Sale, Bosch Magneto Company.* New York, 1918.
—— *Report,* 1917, 1918, 1917–22.
Attorney-General, Office of the. *Annual Report of the Department of Justice:* 1919, 1920, 1921.
Biographical Directory of the American Congress, 1774–1949. 1950.
Commerce, Department of. Bureau of the Census. *Historical Statistics of the United States.* 1949.
—— Bureau of the Census. *U. S. Census Reports:* 1872, 1882, 1901, 1902.
Federal Reserve Board. *Seventh Annual Report for the Year 1920.*
Federal Trade Commission. *Report on the Meat Packing Industry.* 1919.
House of Representatives. Committee on Agriculture. *Amendments Proposed to the Food Control Act.* Hearings, 66 Congress, 1 Session. 1919.
—— Committee on Agriculture. *Meat Packer Legislation.* Hearings, 66 Congress, 1 Session. 1920.
—— Committee on Immigration and Naturalization. *Administration of Immigration Laws.* Hearings, 66 Congress, 2 Session. 1919.
—— Committee on Immigration and Naturalization. *I.W.W. Deportation Cases.* Hearings, 66 Congress, 2 Session. 1920.
—— Committee on the Judiciary. *The Question of an Appeal in the Case United States Against the Southern Pacific Company and Others.* Hearings, 66 Congress, 2 Session. 1920.
—— Committee on the Judiciary. *Investigation of the Action of the Attorney-General Relating to the Price of Louisiana Sugar.* 66 Congress, 2 Session. 1920.
—— Committee on the Judiciary. *Sedition Hearings.* 66 Congress, 2 Session. 1920.

* Printed in Washington, D. C., Government Printing Office, unless otherwise noted.

—— Committee on Labor. *H.R. 12292, a Bill to Prevent Interstate Commerce in the Products of Child Labor and for Other Purposes.* Hearings, 63 Congress, 3 Session. 1914.

—— Committee on Rules. *Attorney-General A. Mitchell Palmer on Charges Made Against Department of Justice by Louis F. Post and Others.* Hearings, 66 Congress, 2 Session. 1920.

—— Committee on Rules. *Investigation of Administration of Louis F. Post, Assistant Secretary of Labor, in the matter of Deportation of Aliens.* Hearings, 66 Congress, 2 Session. 1920.

—— Committee on Rules. *Rule Making in Order the Consideration of S. 3317.* Hearings, 66 Congress, 2 Session. 1920.

—— Committee on Ways and Means. *Tariff Hearings.* 62 Congress, 1 Session. 1913.

Labor, Department of. Bureau of Labor Statistics. *Retail Prices, 1913 to December, 1920.* Bulletin No. 300.

Public Information Committee. *Official U. S. Bulletin.* 1918–19.

Senate. Committee on Education and Labor. *Investigation of Strike in Steel Industry.* Hearings, report, 66 Congress, 3 Session. 1921.

—— Committtee on the Judiciary. *Charges of Illegal Practices of the Department of Justice.* Hearings, 66 Congress, 3 Session. 1921.

—— Committee on the Judiciary, subcommittee. *The Nomination of Hon. A. Mitchell Palmer to be Attorney-General.* Hearings, 65 Congress, 1 Session. 1919.

—— Committee on Privileges and Elections, subcommittee. Hearings, 66 Congress, 2 Session, 1920.

—— Select Committee. *Investigation of Hon. Harry M. Daugherty.* 2 vols. 68 Congress, 1 Session. 1924.

Senators from Pennsylvania. *Memorial Addresses Delivered in the Senate and House of Representatives in Memory of Philander C. Knox, Boies Penrose and William B. Crow.* 1924.

SECONDARY SOURCES

Abrams, Richard M. "Woodrow Wilson and the Southern Congressmen, 1913–1916," *Journal of Southern History*, XX (November, 1956), 417–37.

Ahearn, Daniel J., Jr. *The Wages of Farm and Factory Laborers, 1914–1944.* Columbia University Studies in History, Economics, and Public Law, Number 518. New York, Columbia University Press, 1945.

Alexander, Norman. *Rights of Aliens Under the Federal Constitution.* Montpelier, Vt., privately printed, 1931.

"Alien and Sedition Bills of 1920," *Literary Digest,* LXIV (February 7, 1920), 11–13.

American Bosch Magneto Corporation. *$1,800,000 American Bosch Magneto Corporation 7 Per Cent Serial Gold Notes.* January 15, 1919.

Annual Report of the American Bosch Magneto Corporation, 1918, 1919, 1920.

Backman, Jules. *Wages and Prices.* Irvington-on-Hudson, N. Y., Foundation for Economic Education, 1947.

Bagby, Wesley Marvin. *Progressivism's Debacle: The Election of 1920.* Microfilmed Ph.D. dissertation, Columbia University, 1953.

Baker, Ray Stannard. *Woodrow Wilson: Life and Letters.* 8 vols. Garden City, N. Y., Doubleday, 1927, 1931, 1935, 1937, 1939.

Berglund, Abraham and Phillips Wright. *The Tariff on Iron and Steel.* Washington, D. C., Brookings Institution, 1929.

Bernhardt, Joshua. *Government Control of the Sugar Industry in the United States.* New York, Macmillan, 1920.

Bishop, Joseph W., Jr. "Judicial Construction of the Trading With the Enemy Act," *Harvard Law Review,* LXII (March, 1949), 721–59.

Bone, Scott. "Democrats in Congress Making Good," *American Review of Reviews,* XLIV (August, 1911), 209–10.

Bowden, Robert Douglas. *Boies Penrose: Symbol of an Era.* New York, Greenberg, 1937.

Bry, Gerhard. *Wages in Germany, 1871–1945.* National Bureau of Economic Research General Series, Number 86. Princeton, Princeton University Press, 1960.

Bryce, James. *The American Commonwealth.* 2 vols. New York, Macmillan, 1895.

Bryan, William J. and Mary B. Bryan. *The Memoirs of William Jennings Bryan.* Philadelphia, Winston, 1925.

Brynes, James F. *All in One Lifetime.* New York, Harper, 1948.

Claghorn, Kate Holladay. "Alien Sedition in the New Year," *Survey,* XLII (January 17, 1920), 423.

—— "Ellis Island's Gates Ajar," *Literary Digest,* LXIII (December 13, 1919), 17.

—— *The Immigrant's Day in Court.* New York, Harper, 1923.

Commager, Henry Steele, ed. *Documents of American History.* New York, Appleton, 1943.

Connor, Edwin M. *Sidelights of the Democratic National Convention.* South Bend, Wash., privately printed, 1920.

Croly, Herbert, "Democratic Factions and Insurgent Republicans." *North American,* CXCI (May, 1910), 626–35.

Curti, Merle. *The Growth of American Thought.* New York, Harper, 1951.

Daniels, Josephus. *The Wilson Era, Years of Peace: 1910–1917.* Chapel Hill, University of North Carolina Press, 1946.

Davenport, Walter. *Power and Glory: The Life of Boies Penrose.* New York, Putnam, 1931.

Davis, Jerome. *The Russian Immigrant.* New York, Macmillan, 1922.

"The Deportations," *Survey,* XLI (February 22, 1919), 722.

"Deporting the Communist Party," *Literary Digest,* LXIV (February 14, 1920), 18.

Draper, Theodore. *The Roots of American Communism.* New York, Viking, 1957.

Dunlap, Aurie Nichols. "Boies Penrose." Master's essay, Columbia University, 1951.

Eisilin, Malcolm Rogers. *The Rise of Pennsylvania Protectionism.* Philadelphia, University of Pennsylvania Press, 1932.

Ellis, William T. "The 'Fighting Quaker' of the Cabinet," *American Review of Reviews,* LXI (January, 1920), 35–8.

—— "The Presidency Spurned," *Harper's Weekly,* LIX (October 13, 1914), 426.

"Extent of the Bolshevik Infection Here," *Literary Digest,* LXIV (January 17, 1920), 13–15.

Fine, Nathan. *Labor and Farmer Parties in the United States, 1828–1928.* New York, Rand School, 1928.

Freidel, Frank. *Franklin D. Roosevelt: The Ordeal.* Boston, Little, Brown, 1948.

Fuller, Raymond G. *Child Labor and the Constitution.* New York, Crowell, 1923.

Gabriel, Ralph Henry. *The Course of American Democratic Thought.* New York, Ronald, 1956.

Gathings, James A. *International Law and American Treatment of Alien Enemy Property.* Washington, American Council on Public Affairs, 1940.

Gompers, Samuel, "Labor's Protest Against a Rampant Tragedy," *American Federationist,* XXVII (June, 1920), 526.

Gordon, Robert A. *Business Fluctuations.* New York, Harper, 1952.

Grantham, Dewey W. *Hoke Smith and the Politics of the New South.* Baton Rouge, Louisiana State University Press, 1958.

Guffey, Joseph F. *Seventy Years on the Red Fire Wagon.* Privately printed, 1952.

Hale, Robert. "Another Convention—The Democratic," *Nation,* CXI (July 17, 1920), 69–70.

Haynes, William. *American Chemical Industry*. 6 vols. New York, Van Nostrand, 1945.

"He Balked the Hun Attempt to Grab Our Industries," *Literary Digest*, LX (January 18, 1919), 227.

Hearst, William Randolph. "More Standard Oil Letters," *Hearst's*, XXII (October, 1912), 4–21.

Heaton, John L. *Cobb of "The World."* New York, Dutton, 1924.

Hechler, Kenneth W. *Insurgency: Personalities and Politics of the Taft Era*. New York, Columbia University Press, 1940.

Hilton, O. A. "Public Opinion and Civil Liberties in Wartime, 1917–1919," *Southwestern Social Science Quarterly*, XXVIII (December, 1947), 208–11.

Hofstadter, Richard. *The Age of Reform*. New York, Knopf, 1955.

Hough, Emerson. *The Web*. Chicago, Reilly and Lee, 1919.

Howland, Harold F. "A Costly Triumph," *Outlook*, LXXXV (January 26, 1907), 193–210.

Ickes, Harold. *The Secret Diary of Harold L. Ickes*. 2 vols. New York, Simon and Schuster, 1953.

Interchurch World Movement. Commission of Inquiry. *Report on the Steel Strike of 1919*. New York, Harcourt Brace, 1920.

Ise, John. *The United States Oil Policy*. New Haven, Yale University Press, 1926.

Johnson, Donald. "The Political Career of A. Mitchell Palmer," *Pennsylvania History*, XXV (October, 1958), 345–70.

Keller, Robert Brown. *History of Monroe County, Pennsylvania*. Stroudsburg, Pa., Monroe, 1927.

Kerney, James. *The Political Education of Woodrow Wilson*. New York, Century, 1926.

"Legalizing Fraud," *Nation*, CXVIII (January 23, 1924), 80.

Leuchtenburg, William E. "Progressivism and Imperialism: The Progressive Movement and American Foreign Policy, 1898–1916," *Mississippi Valley Historical Review* XXXIX (December, 1952), 483–504.

Lewis, Alfred H. "Penrose—Pernicious and Petty Politician," *Hearst's*, XXIV (September, 1913), 344–52.

Lindsay, Samuel McCune. "National Child Labor Standards," *Child Labor Bulletin*, III (May, 1914), 25–28.

Link, Arthur. *Wilson: The Road to the White House*. Princeton, Princeton University Press, 1947.

—— *Wilson: The New Freedom*. Princeton, Princeton University Press, 1956.

—— "The Baltimore Convention of 1912," *American Historical Review*, L (July, 1945), 691–713.

Lord, Frank B. "The Story of the Hon. A. Mitchell Palmer," *National Monthly*, VI (June, 1914), 27, 39.

Lord, Walter. *The Good Years from 1900 to the First World War.* New York, Harper, 1960.

Lovejoy, Owen R. "Federal Government and Child Labor," *Child Labor Bulletin*, II (February, 1914), 27, 29.

Lyons, Maurice F. *William F. McCombs: The President Maker.* Cincinnati, Bancroft, 1922.

McAdoo, William G. *Crowded Years: The Reminiscences of William G. McAdoo.* Boston, Houghton Mifflin, 1931.

McCombs, William F. *Making Woodrow Wilson President.* New York, Fairview, 1931.

MacDonald, Austin F. "The Democratic Party in Philadelphia: A Study in Political Pathology," *National Municipal Review*, XIV (May, 1925), 293–99.

McGeary, M. Nelson. "Gifford Pinchot's 1914 Campaign," *Pennsylvania Magazine of History and Biography*, LXXXI (July, 1957), 308–18.

McKelway, A. J. "Another Emancipation Proclamation," *American Review of Reviews*, LIV (October, 1916), 425.

Marcosson, Isaac F. "The Fall of the House Quay," *World's Work*, XI (January, 1906), 7119–24.

Mason, Alpheus Thomas. *Harlan Fiske Stone: Pillar of the Law.* New York, Viking, 1956.

May, Henry F. *The End of American Innocence.* New York, Knopf, 1959.

Mowry, George E. *The California Progressives.* Berkeley, University of California Press, 1951.

Mullendore, William Clinton. *History of the United States Food Administration, 1917–1919.* Palo Alto, Stanford University Press, 1941.

Murray, Robert K. *Red Scare: A Study in National Hysteria.* Minneapolis, University of Minnesota Press, 1955.

—— "Communism and the Great Steel Strike of 1919," *Mississippi Valley Historical Review*, XXXVII (December, 1951).

National Popular Government League. *To the American People: Report upon the Illegal Practices of the Department of Justice.* Washington, D. C., Government Printing Office, 1920.

Noble, Ransom E., Jr. *New Jersey Progressivism before Wilson.* Princeton, Princeton University Press, 1946.

O'Brian, John Lord. "Alfred Bettman," *Journal of the American Institute of Planners*, XI (October-December, 1945), 5.

Official Report of the Proceedings of the Democratic National Convention. Chicago, privately printed, 1912, 1916, 1920.

"On Guard, Progressives," *Harper's Weekly,* LIX (October 17, 1914).

"The Packers at the Bar of Public Opinion," *Literary Digest,* LXII (August 2, 1919), 21–23.

Palmer, A. Mitchell. "The Great Work of the Alien Property Custodian," *American Law Review,* LIII (January-February, 1919), 45–52.

——— *A History of the Quakers in Stroudsburg,* Privately printed, n.d.

Palmer, Horace Wilbur. *Palmers in America.* 18 vols. Madison, N. J., privately printed, 195?.

Panunzio, Constantine. *The Deportation Cases of 1919–1920.* New York, 1920.

A Pennsylvania Manufacturer, "Wanted in Pennsylvania—A Man!" *Outlook,* LXXX (June 10, 1905), 370–76.

Peterson, Florence. *Strikes in the United States, 1880–1936.* U. S. Department of Labor Bulletin Number 651. Washington, D. C., Government Printing Office, 1938.

Post, Louis F. *The Deportations Delirium of Nineteen-Twenty.* Chicago, Kerr, 1923.

Pray, K. M. "The Siege of Penrose," *Harper's Weekly,* LIX (October 13, 1914), 375–76.

Rathgeber, Lewis Wesley. *The Democratic Party in Pennsylvania,* microfilmed Ph.D. Dissertation, University of Pittsburgh, 1955.

Robinson, William A. *Thomas A. Reed, Parliamentarian.* New York, Dodd, Mead, 1930.

Rogers, Henry Wade. "The Democratic Party," *Yale Review,* II (October, 1912), 33–58.

Roosevelt, James and Sidney Shallett. *Affectionately, F.D.R.: A Son's Story of a Lonely Man.* New York, Harcourt, Brace, 1959.

Rupp, I. Daniel. *History of Northampton, Lehigh, Monroe, Carbon and Schuylkill Counties.* Harrisburg, G. Hill, 1845.

Saposs, David J. *Left Wing Unionism: A Study in Politics and Tactics.* New York, International, 1926.

Scheiber, Harry N. *The Wilson Administration and Civil Liberties, 1917–1921.* Cornell University Studies in American History, Literature and Folklore, Number VI. Ithaca, Cornell University Press, 1960.

Seymour, Charles, ed. *The Intimate Papers of Colonel House.* 4 vols. Boston, Houghton Mifflin, 1926, 1928.

Shannon, David A. *The Socialist Party of America: A History*. New York, Macmillan, 1955.

"Shipping Lenin's Friends to Him," *Literary Digest*, LXIV (January 3, 1920), 15.

Siegfried, André. *America Comes of Age*. New York, Harcourt Brace, 1927.

"Skimming the Melting Pot," *Literary Digest*, LX (March 1, 1919), 16.

Smull's Legislative Handbook and Manual of the State of Pennsylvania. Harrisburg, Harrisburg Publishing Company, 1860–1918.

Soule, George. *Prosperity Decade, from War to Depression: 1917–1929*. New York, Holt, Rinehart & Winston, 1947.

"Sowing the Wind to Reap the Whirlwind," *Nation*, CX (January 17, 1920), 94.

Spolansky, Jacob. *The Communist Trail in America*. New York, Macmillan, 1951.

Sprigle, Ray. "Lord Guffey of Pennsylvania," *America Mercury*, XXXIX (November, 1936), 273–84.

Stackpole, Edward J. *Behind the Scenes with a Newspaper Man*. Philadelphia, Lippincott, 1927.

Steffens, Lincoln. *The Shame of the Cities*. New York, Sagamore Press, 1957.

Sullivan, Mark. "Your Move Democracy," *Colliers*, LXV (June 19, 1920), 9, 18.

Tarbell, Ida M. *The Tariff in Our Times*. New York, Macmillan, 1912.

Taussig, Frank W. *The Tariff History of the United States*. New York, G. P. Putnam's Sons, 1931.

Tower, Walter S. "A Regional and Economic Geography of Pennsylvania," *Bulletin of the Geographical Society of Philadelphia*, V (January, 1907), 37–49.

Tumulty, Joseph. *Woodrow Wilson as I Know Him*. Garden City. New York, Garden City Publishing, 1925.

"Two Infamous Measures," *Nation*, CX (January 31, 1920), 132.

United Mine Workers. *Proceedings of Convention of the United Mine Workers*. Indianapolis, n.p., 1919. (Printed by Capitol Printing, Columbus, Ohio, 1920.)

Vare, William S. *My Forty Years in Politics*. Philadelphia, Roland Swain, 1913.

Vieillard (pseudonym), "A Well Disguised Performer," *CI* (August 19, 1915), p. 227.

Wallace, Anthony F. C. "Revitalization Movements," *American Anthropologist*, LVIII (1956), 264–81.

Walsh, James J. "John Quinn: Lawyer, Book-Lover, Art Amateur," *Catholic World*, CXX (November, 1924), 176–84.

Warner, Arthur. "Bartering for the Presidency," *Nation*, C (November 29, 1922), 577–79.

Watson, James E. *As I Knew Them; Memoirs of James E. Watson.* New York, Bobbs-Merrill, 1936.

Weeks, Robert P., ed. *Commonwealth vs. Sacco and Vanzetti.* Englewood Cliffs, N. J., Prentice-Hall, 1958.

White, William Allen. *Forty Years on Main Street.* New York, Farrar and Rinehart, 1937.

Whitehead, Don. *The F.B.I. Story.* New York, Pocket Books, 1958.

Wilhelm, Donald. "If He Were President," *Independent*, CII (April, 1920), 46–47.

Williams, Talcott. "After Penrose What?" *Century*, CV (November, 1922), 49–55.

Wilson, Edith Bolling. *My Memoir.* Indianapolis, Bobbs-Merrill, 1938.

Wimer, Kurt. "Woodrow Wilson's Plans to Enter the League of Nations Through an Executive Agreement," *Western Political Quarterly*, XI (December, 1958), 800–11.

Woodward, C. Vann. Tom Watson, Agrarian Rebel. New York, Macmillan, 1938.

INDEX

Abercrombie, John W., 218, 223–25 *passim*, 227, 231
Adams, Charles Francis, 280
Adamson, William C., 82
Adamson Act, 123, 125, 126, 259
Advertising, and Palmer's projects, 131–32, 149, 162, 163
Advisory Sales Committee (Alien Property Custodian), 139, 297, 300
AF of L, *see* American Federation of Labor
Agriculture; and tariff, 79; Secretary of, 159
Albert, Caroline, 2
Albert, Heinrich F., 119
Alexander Brown and Sons, 139
Alien Property Custodian, 38, 72, 128–50, 247, 266
Aliens, on parole, 200–1; *see also* Deportation; Immigration; Radicals
Allentown, Pa., 31, 35
American Association of Portland Cement Manufacturers, 78–79
American Bosch Magneto Company, 146–47; see also Bosch Magneto Company
American Federation of Labor, 25, 28, 186, 244, 325–26; and Palmer, 88, 171, 172, 240, 254–56 *passim*; and Gompers, 97; versus Penrose, 110; and Foster, 174–75; and public opinion, 176; and coal strike, 179–81 *passim*
Americanism, Palmer's, 250–51, 257
American Legion Weekly, 305–6
American Protective League, 199–200, 228
American Review of Reviews, quoted, 282–83

American Trans-Atlantic Shipping Line, 133
American Trust Company, 140, 141
Ames, Charles B., 179, 186
Anarchists, 209, 218–21 *passim; see also* Deportation; Radicals
Anderson, Albert B., 179
Anderson, George W., 237–38, 240
Anthony, A. W., 144
Anti-Penrose League of Pennsylvania, 101
Antitrust suits, 188–95
Appropriations: House Committee on, 21, 211; Senate Committee on, 211
Armour, 189–92 *passim*
Arrests, 185, 198, 218–44 *passim*
Asheville, N. C., 183
Aspirin, patent for sold by Alien Property Custodian, 147
Assassination plot, 203–4
Attorney-General: Palmer candidate for, 67–72, 150–54; Palmer's policies as, 266; *see also* Palmer, Alexander Mitchell
Atwood, John W., 190, 191–92

Bailey, Joe, 30
Bailey, Warren Worth, 54, 74, 96, 126; and Democratic Party in Pennsylvania, 31, 33, 40, 274, 276
Baker, Newton D., 177, 210, 250, 265, 307
Baker and Adamson Chemical Company, 78
Ballinger, Richard A., 194, 195
Ballot reform, 5–6, 54, 270
Baltimore, 10–11, 22, 34; 1912 Democratic convention in, 40–41, 58–62
Bankhead, John H., 62